Praise for

THE ESSENTIAL GINSBERG

"An intellectually impeccable selection, distilling Ginsberg as visionary mystic and *dark prophet* foretelling what people in power didn't want to hear."   —Lawrence Ferlinghetti

"Allen Ginsberg brilliantly adhered to the poet's job of looking into the darkness of his time, seeing the generative aspects of imagination, composing texts as orality and believing in the power of poetry to reawaken the world to itself. He never lost that faith and manifested it in myriad directions with as empathetic a heart as I have ever known. His humanity embraced others all over the world. His spirit matches Whitman for its profound candor, adhesiveness, and trickster transgression. When planet Earth is dust, this will be one of the books to take to Mars to remember us by."   —Anne Waldman

"In these memory orchards Allen Ginsberg flashes from the divinely practical to inspired songs and factual revelations. . . . They shine on the future."   —Michael McClure

"The career-arching overview [Ginsberg's work] deserves. . . . What distinguishes this book from other posthumous Ginsberg collections is that it also presents small samples of his songwriting, essays, interviews, letters, journal excerpts, and understated photography. . . . An essential starting point for any reader encountering the artist's still-controversial work for the very first time."   —*Library Journal* (starred review)

"A representative sampling from an iconic American poet. . . . .
A well-chosen selection of [Ginsberg's] writings . . . testimony
to an often outrageous, groundbreaking poet and tireless so-
cial activist."   —*Kirkus*

THE ESSENTIAL GINSBERG

Also by Allen Ginsberg

POETRY

Howl and Other Poems, 1956
Kaddish and Other Poems, 1961
Empty Mirror, Early Poems, 1961
Reality Sandwiches, 1963
Planet News, 1968
The Fall of America, Poems of These States, 1972
The Gates of Wrath: Rhymed Poems 1948–52, 1973
Iron Horse, 1973
First Blues, 1975
Mind Breaths, Poems 1971-76, 1978
Plutonian Ode, Poems 1977-1980, 1982
Collected Poems 1947-1980, 1984
White Shroud, Poems 1980-1985, 1986
Cosmopolitan Greetings, Poems 1986-1992, 1994
Selected Poems 1947-1995, 1996
Death & Fame: Poems 1993-1997, 1999
Collected Poems 1947-1997, 2006
Howl (animated by Eric Drooker), 2010

PROSE

The Yage Letters (with William Burroughs), 1963
Indian Journals, 1970, 1996
Gay Sunshine Interview (with Allen Young), 1974
Allen Verbatim: Lectures on Poetry, Politics, Consciousness (Edited by Gordon Ball), 1974
Chicago Trial Testimony, 1975
To Eberhart from Ginsberg, 1976
As Ever: Collected Correspondence Allen Ginsberg & Neal Cassady (with Neal Cassady) (edited by Barry Gifford), 1977
Neal Cassady, 1977
Journals Early Fifties Early Sixties (edited by Gordon Ball), 1977, 1993
Composed on the Tongue: Literary Conversations 1967-1977, 1980
Straight Hearts Delight, Love Poems and Selected Letters 1947-1980 (with Peter Orlovsky), 1980

Howl, Original Draft Facsimile, Fully Annotated (edited by Barry Miles), 1986, 1995

The Visions of the Great Rememberer (with Visions of Cody, Jack Kerouac), 1993

Journals Mid-Fifties: 1954-1958 (edited by Gordon Ball), 1994

Luminous Dreams, 1997

Deliberate Prose: Selected Essays 1952-1995 ((edited by Bill Morgan), 2000

Family Business: Selected Letters Between a Father & Son (with Louis Ginsberg) (edited by Michael Schumacher) 2000

Spontaneous Mind: Selected Interviews 1958–1996 (edited by David Carter), 2001

The Book of Martyrdom and Artifice: First Journals and Poems 1937-1952 (edited by Juanita Lieberman-Plimpton and Bill Morgan), 2006

Yage Letters Redux (with William Burroughs) (edited by Oliver Harris), 2006

The Letters of Allen Ginsberg (edited by Bill Morgan), 2008

The Selected Letters of Allen Ginsberg and Gary Snyder (with Gary Snyder) (edited by Bill Morgan), 2009

Jack Kerouac and Allen Ginsberg: The Letters (edited by Bill Morgan and David Stanford), 2010

I Greet You at the Beginning of a Great Career: The Selected Correspondence of Lawrence Ferlinghetti and Allen Ginsberg (with Lawrence Ferlinghetti) (edited by Bill Morgan), 2015

PHOTOGRAPHY

Photographs, 1991

Snapshot Poetics, 1993

VOCAL WORDS & MUSIC

Howl & Other Poems, 1959, 1998

Allen Ginsberg Reads Kaddish, 1966, 2006

First Blues: Rags, Ballads and Harmonium Songs (produced by Ann Charters), 1981

First Blues (produced by John Hammond) 1981, 2006

The Lion for Real, 1989, 1996

Hydrogen Jukebox (opera with Philip Glass), 1993

Holy Soul Jelly Roll: Poems & Songs 1949-1993, 1994

The Ballad of the Skeletons (with Paul McCartney, Philip Glass), 1996

Howl U. S. A., Kronos Quartet, Lee Hyla score, 1996

Wichita Vortex Sutra, 2004

The Allen Ginsberg Poetry Collection, 2004

THE
ESSENTIAL
GINSBERG

Allen Ginsberg

Edited by Michael Schumacher

HARPER  PERENNIAL

NEW YORK • LONDON • TORONTO • SYDNEY • NEW DELHI • AUCKLAND

HarperCollins books may be purchased for educational, business, or sales promotional use. For information, please e-mail the Special Markets Department at SPsales@harpercollins.com.

FIRST EDITION

Designed by Sunil Manchikonti

Library of Congress Cataloging-in-Publication Data

Ginsberg, Allen, 1926–1997.
[Works. Selections]
The Essential Ginsberg / Allen Ginsberg ; edited by Michael Schumacher.
pages cm
Summary: "A collection of essential poems, essays, letters, songs, and photographs which aims to introduce new readers to the scope of Allen Ginsberg's work in its prolific and profound diversity"— Provided by publisher.
ISBN 978-0-06-236228-5 (pbk.)—ISBN 978-0-06-236229-2 (ebook)
I. Schumacher, Michael, 1950– editor. II. Title.
PS3513.I74A6 2015
811'.54—dc23
2014034852

15 16 17 18 19 OV/RRD 10 9 8 7 6 5 4 3 2 1

CONTENTS

Introduction by Michael Schumacher   xi

I. POEMS

II. SONGS

III. ESSAYS

IV. JOURNALS

---

* previously unpublished

INTRODUCTION

Allen Ginsberg, one of the most influential poets of the twentieth century, was such a familiar face in newspapers and magazines and on television that he was internationally famous to millions who had never read any of his poetry. He spent much of his life as an advocate for human rights, freedom of expression, gay liberation, and other causes; he was one of the early, vocal opponents of the Vietnam war. He was a teacher, Buddhist, essayist, songwriter, photographer. One of the core members of the Beat Generation, he slipped easily into a position of leadership among war protesters, college students, Flower Power hippies, and political radicals. "It occurs to me that I am America," he wrote, semihumorously, in one of his early poems, but he wound up being much more than that. Poet/editor J. D. McClutchy summed up Ginsberg's influence in one simple statement published in the *New York Times* following Ginsberg's death in 1997: "His work is finally a history of our era's psyche, with all its contradictory urges."

Given the man Ginsberg became, it's hard to believe that, at one time, people feared for his psychological well being—even for his survival. Louis Ginsberg, Allen's father, worried that he might be following the path of his mother, Naomi Ginsberg, a bright but troubled schoolteacher who spent much of her adult life institutionalized for mental disorders. William Carlos Williams, Allen's early mentor and sponsor, expressed his concern when, in his introduction to *Howl and Other Poems*, he wrote: "I never thought he'd live to grow up and write a book of poems. His ability to survive, travel, and go on writing astonishes me. That he has gone on developing his art is no less amazing to me."

How did Allen Ginsberg's life develop from his difficult youthful days to a point where he would be honored for his intellectual and artistic mind? This book, aside from assembling selections of Ginsberg's most memorable poetry, prose, music, and photographs, will attempt to answer this question. Ginsberg described his work as "a graph of my mind." He spent a lifetime trying to expand his own consciousness, employing everything from drugs to meditation to provide different inducements to that expansion. He believed that his writings, music, and photography might be "useful" (as he liked to put it) to readers, whether that usefulness came from art in the strictest sense, from the way his work pinpointed precise moments in history, or from assuring others that they were not alone, that their thoughts and longings were part of a universal consciousness greater than any individual's.

Here, in a single volume, you will find a sampling of the range and topography of Ginsberg's mental landscapes. There are the long, rhythmic lines found in Whitman, one of Ginsberg's most significant influences; the prophetic voice of William Blake, whom Ginsberg had heard in a series of auditory "visions" in Harlem in 1948; the "bop prosody" of Jack Kerouac, novelist and poet and enduring Ginsberg friend. There are dream notations, travel journals, autobiographical fragments, chatty letters to friends, details of his expulsions from Cuba and Czechoslovakia in 1965, photographs of the important people in his life—even the testimony he gave to a U.S. Senate subcommittee. He writes in great depth about the creation of "Howl" (1955) and "Kaddish" (1959), two masterworks, and speaks of how his meditation practices informed and added texture to his work. From the prose poem, "The Bricklayer's Lunch Hour," to the rhymed lyrics of "Starry Rhymes," one of Ginsberg's final poems, the reader is introduced to one of the most compelling minds that the American literary world has ever encountered.

"Kaddish," Ginsberg's moving elegy to his mother, goes beyond providing the details of Ginsberg's difficult youth and his family's dealing with Naomi Ginsberg's mental illness. The poem, like "Howl," offers a powerful backstory to Ginsberg's lifelong empathy for the disenfranchised, the embattled pilgrims, the souls wandering in uncharted space—the "beat." Ginsberg's empathy is evident in "Portrait of Huncke," a fragment of a large 1949 journal entry, in which a naïve young Allen Ginsberg takes pity on a homeless street hustler and invites him into his home, only to be dragged into his schemes and ultimately a run-in with the law. His 1979 letter to Diana Trilling, essayist and wife of one of his most trusted college professors, Lionel Trilling, is an account of an incident that led to Ginsberg's being expelled from Columbia University. Then there are accounts (in his letter to John Clellon Holmes and in his *Paris Review* interview) of his 1948 Blake "visions," which alarmed his family and some of his friends, and caused them to wonder if he was losing his mind. These "visions" started Ginsberg on a fifteen-year quest to discover and expand the unexplored regions of his mind.

And this was all before he celebrated his twenty-third birthday.

For all the difficulties in his late-teens and twenties, Ginsberg never abandoned his extremely self-disciplined writing of poetry. The early work, derivative of poets he studied in high school and college, evolved rapidly after he met Jack Kerouac, William S. Burroughs, Neal Cassady, and others—all of whom served as mentors in his intellectual and creative development. "The Bricklayer's Lunch Hour" (1947) and "The Trembling of the Veil" (1948), two poems fashioned from journal entries, pleased William Carlos Williams when the older poet saw them, and with Williams's encouragement, Ginsberg shed the skin of his youth. He grew at an astonishing rate, especially in the mid-1950s, after he moved to the West Coast, met Peter Orlovsky, became involved in what became known as the San Francisco Poetry Renaissance, and wrote such classics as "Howl," "A Supermarket in California," "America," and others that were included in *Howl and Other Poems*, his first published collection of poems. Ginsberg's lengthy explanatory letter to Richard Eberhart on the writing of "Howl" proves, if there was any doubt, that Ginsberg's work was the result of a convergence of acquired knowledge, a continuous process of self-discovery, experience, and creative courage.

The Beat Generation phenomenon, coupled with the attention Ginsberg garnered from "Howl" and its successful defense in a celebrated obscenity trial, changed Ginsberg's life. He enjoyed celebrity status, his poetry was in constant demand, and the press sought his opinions on just about every imaginable topic. Ginsberg basked in the limelight, and he used the interview and occasional essay to expound on a wide spectrum of subjects, from literature to politics. He grew up listening to his parents bicker over politics and had nurtured an interest in political and social issues dating back to his teenaged years, when he and his older brother, Eugene, wrote letters to the editors of area newspapers, including the *New York Times*. Fame became Ginsberg's soapbox, and from the 1960s he was not shy about expressing his views on censorship, psychedelic drugs, gay liberation, international politics, Vietnam, and the suppression of individual freedoms. Poems such as "Wichita Vortex Sutra" and "Plutonian Ode" smoulder with Ginsberg's passionate feelings about the war in Vietnam and the proliferation of nuclear power. A calmer, yet still firm and reasoned, approach can be found in his senate subcommittee testimony on LSD or his statement on censorship. His accounts of his 1965 misadventures in Cuba and Czechoslovakia, found here in a previously unpublished journal entry and in his letter to Nicanor Parra, are exceptional supplements to "Kral Majales," Ginsberg's poem on his election as King of May and subsequent expulsion from Czechoslovakia.

Ginsberg believed that one of the keys to effective writing (and self-awareness) was to "notice what you notice," and his travel writings, in general, found him in this state of mind, whether he was sending William S. Burroughs a letter about his trip to South America in search of the hallucinogenic drug, ayahuasca, or offering, in "Wales Visitation," one of his most beautiful poems, his observations of the minute particulars of the natural wonders of the Welsh countryside. His massive, previously unpublished letter to Jack Kerouac about his extended journey to India is a strong contrast to a journal entry written during the same 1962-1963 stay. Ginsberg's travels rewarded him with a profound, mature worldview that added depth to all of his writing.

Jack Kerouac had been encouraging Ginsberg to study Buddhism as far back as the early 1950s, a study that Ginsberg, with all of his other preoccupations, undertook only sporadically. But his exposure to Eastern religions while he was in India and the Far East nudged him more in that direction. He chanted mantras as part of his poetry readings and began a rudimentary, undisciplined meditation practice. His 1971 meeting of Chögyum Trungpa Rinpoche, a controversial but influential Buddhist teacher, helped him focus—and, to a large extent, focus was what he needed. In "The Change," his long poem inspired by his meditations as he watched bodies being cremated at the burning ghats in India, Ginsberg had written about the need to return to his own body and mind, rather than search for answers elsewhere; the thought might have given him peace of mind, but it wasn't all that different from ideas expressed much more simply in his 1954 poem "Song," written shortly after his return from an extensive visit to Mexico.

Trungpa preached a form of meditation that required the following of one's thoughts as they emerged through the exhaling of one's own breath. One meditated by sitting in a relaxed position, eyes fixed on a nearby point. As Ginsberg illustrates in "Mind Breaths," thoughts formed and expanded not unlike the way they had when he was experimenting with mind-expanding drugs. Trungpa encouraged his students to have faith in where their thoughts would take them. On one occasion, when Ginsberg insisted that he could not improvise poetry onstage, Trungpa scoffed, "Why depend upon a piece of paper? Don't you trust your own mind?"

This was an idea Kerouac had been advocating from the beginning of their friendship. Kerouac's practice of spontaneous composition appealed to Ginsberg, who had succeeded with it in a number of poems, most notably "Sunflower Sutra," a gem with virtually no revision from its handwritten original draft. "First thought, best thought," Ginsberg asserted, though he found it difficult to practice. The impulse to revise was too great. It was the thought, he insisted, that had to remain pure and unaltered.

Allen Ginsberg never published an autobiography or memoirs. His body of work, he felt, would suffice. He wrote much of it (particularly the letters and journals) with little thought of its ever being published, and to his credit he never held back after he attained international fame and his journals and letters were published. He continued to record his most private thoughts until he died.

This book, then, acts as a mosaic of Ginsberg's life story and massive body of published and unpublished work, an introduction to readers unfamiliar with his poetry, prose, and photography. The contents represent only a small fraction of Ginsberg's published output. One hopes that, after sampling the offerings in this book, curious or adventurous readers will delve deeper into Ginsberg's work, and that they have a call to discovery—of a man, his times, and a personal odyssey that changed the face of poetry and dared others to step outside the containment of the ordinary.

—MICHAEL SCHUMACHER

PART ONE

Poems

The Bricklayer's Lunch Hour

Two bricklayers are setting the walls
of a cellar in a new dug out patch
of dirt behind an old house of wood
with brown gables grown over with ivy
on a shady street in Denver. It is noon
and one of them wanders off. The young
subordinate bricklayer sits idly for
a few minutes after eating a sandwich
and throwing away the paper bag. He
has on dungarees and is bare above
the waist; he has yellow hair and wears
a smudged but still bright red cap
on his head. He sits idly on top
of the wall on a ladder that is leaned
up between his spread thighs, his head
bent down, gazing uninterestedly at
the paper bag on the grass. He draws
his hand across his breast, and then
slowly rubs his knuckles across the
side of his chin, and rocks to and fro
on the wall. A small cat walks to him
along the top of the wall. He picks
it up, takes off his cap, and puts it
over the kitten's body for a moment.
Meanwhile it is darkening as if to rain
and the wind on top of the trees in the
street comes through almost harshly.

Denver, Summer 1947

3

The Trembling of the Veil

Today out the window
the trees semed like live
organisms on the moon.

Each bough extended upward
covered at the north end
with leaves, like a green

hairy protuberance. I saw
the scarlet-and-pink shoot-tips
of budding leaves wave

delicately in the sunlight,
blown by the breeze,
all the arms of the trees
bending and straining downward

at once when the wind
pushed them.

Paterson, August 1948

The Shrouded Stranger

Bare skin is my wrinkled sack
When hot Apollo humps my back
When Jack Frost grabs me in these rags
I wrap my legs with burlap bags

My flesh is cinder my face is snow
I walk the railroad to and fro
When the city streets are black and dead
The railroad embankment is my bed

I sup my soup from old tin cans
And take my sweets from little hands
In Tiger Alley near the jail
I steal away from the garbage pail

In darkest night where none can see
Down in the bowels of the factory
I sneak barefoot upon stone
Come and hear the old man groan

I hide and wait like a naked child
Under the bridge my heart goes wild
I scream at a fire on the river bank
I give my body to an old gas tank

I dream that I have burning hair
Boiled arms that claw the air
The torso of an iron king
And on my back a broken wing

Who'll go out whoring into the night
On the eyeless road in the skinny moonlight
Maid or dowd or athlete proud
May wanton with me in the shroud

Who'll come lie down in the dark with me
Belly to belly and knee to knee
Who'll look into my hooded eye
Who'll lie down under my darkened thigh?

New York, 1949-1951

The Green Automobile

If I had a Green Automobile
      I'd go find my old companion
      in his house on the Western ocean.
          Ha! Ha! Ha! Ha! Ha!

I'd honk my horn at his manly gate,
      inside his wife and three
      children sprawl naked
          on the living room floor.

He'd come running out
      to my car full of heroic beer
      and jump screaming at the wheel
          for he is the greater driver.

We'd pilgrimage to the highest mount
      of our earlier Rocky Mountain visions
      laughing in each other's arms,
          delight surpassing the highest Rockies,

and after old agony, drunk with new years,
      bounding toward the snowy horizon
      blasting the dashboard with original bop
          hot rod on the mountain

we'd batter up the cloudy highway
      where angels of anxiety
      careen through the trees
          and scream out of the engine.

We'd burn all night on the jackpine peak
      seen from Denver in the summer dark,
      forestlike unnatural radiance
          illuminating the mountaintop:

childhood youthtime age & eternity
      would open like sweet trees
      in the nights of another spring
          and dumbfound us with love,

for we can see together
                 the beauty of souls
                 hidden like diamonds
                          in the clock of the world,

like Chinese magicians can
                 confound the immortals
                 with our intellectuality
                          hidden in the mist,

in the Green Automobile
                 which I have invented
                 imagined and visioned
                          on the roads of the world

more real than the engine
                 on a track in the desert
                 purer than Greyhound and
                          swifter than physical jetplane.

Denver! Denver! we'll return
                 roaring across the City & County Building lawn
                 which catches the pure emerald flame
                          streaming in the wake of our auto.

This time we'll buy up the city!
                 I cashed a great check in my skull bank
                 to found a miraculous college of the body
                          up on the bus terminal roof.

But first we'll drive the stations of downtown,
                 poolhall flophouse jazzjoint jail
                 whorehouse down Folsom
                          to the darkest alleys of Larimer

paying respects to Denver's father
                 lost on the railroad tracks,
                 stupor of wine and silence
                          hallowing the slum of his decades,

salute him and his saintly suitcase
                 of dark muscatel, drink

and smash the sweet bottles
              on Diesels in allegiance.

Then we go driving drunk on boulevards
              where armies march and still parade
              staggering under the invisible
                     banner of Reality—

hurtling through the street
              in the auto of our fate
              we share an archangelic cigarette
                     and tell each other's fortunes:

fames of supernatural illumination,
              bleak rainy gaps of time,
              great art learned in desolation
                     and we beat apart after six decades . . .

and on an asphalt crossroad,
              deal with each other in princely
              gentleness once more, recalling
                     famous dead talks of other cities.

The windshield's full of tears,
              rain wets our naked breasts,
              we kneel together in the shade
                     amid the traffic of night in paradise

and now renew the solitary vow
              we made each other take
              in Texas, once:
                     I can't inscribe here. . . .
                     •   •   •   •   •
                     •   •   •   •   •

How many Saturday nights will be
              made drunken by this legend?
              How will young Denver come to mourn
                     her forgotten sexual angel?

How many boys will strike the black piano
              in imitation of the excess of a native saint?

Or girls fall wanton under his spectre in the high
            schools of melancholy night?

While all the time in Eternity
            in the wan light of this poem's radio
            we'll sit behind forgotten shades
                        hearkening the lost jazz of all Saturdays.

Neal, we'll be real heroes now
            in a war between our cocks and time:
            let's be the angels of the world's desire
                        and take the world to bed with us before we die.

Sleeping alone, or with companion,
            girl or fairy sheep or dream,
            I'll fail of lacklove, you, satiety:
                        all men fall, our fathers fell before,

but resurrecting that lost flesh
            is but a moment's work of mind:
            an ageless monument to love
                        in the imagination:

memorial built out of our own bodies
            consumed by the invisible poem—
            We'll shudder in Denver and endure
                        though blood and wrinkles blind our eyes.

So this Green Automobile:
            I give you in flight
            a present, a present
                        from my imagination.

We will go riding
            over the Rockies,
            we'll go on riding
                        all night long until dawn,

then back to your railroad, the SP
            your house and your children
            and broken leg destiny
                        you'll ride down the plains

in the morning: and back
to my visions, my office
and eastern apartment
I'll return to New York.

New York, May 22–25, 1953

Song

The weight of the world
       is love.
Under the burden
       of solitude,
under the burden
       of dissatisfaction

       the weight,
the weight we carry
       is love.

Who can deny?
       In dreams
it touches
       the body,
in thought
       constructs
a miracle,
       in imagination
anguishes
       till born
in human—

looks out of the heart
       burning with purity—
for the burden of life
       is love,

but we carry the weight
       wearily,
and so must rest
in the arms of love
       at last,
must rest in the arms
       of love.

No rest
       without love,
no sleep
       without dreams

of love—
      be mad or chill
obsessed with angels
      or machines,
the final wish
      is love
—cannot be bitter,
      cannot deny,
cannot withhold
      if denied:

the weight is too heavy

      —must give
for no return
      as thought
is given
      in solitude
in all the excellence
      of its excess.

The warm bodies
      shine together
in the darkness,
      the hand moves
to the center
      of the flesh,
the skin trembles
      in happiness
and the soul comes
      joyful to the eye—

yes, yes,
      that's what
I wanted,
      I always wanted,
I always wanted,
      to return
to the body
      where I was born.

San Jose, 1954

On Burroughs' Work

The method must be purest meat
    and no symbolic dressing,
actual visions & actual prisons
    as seen then and now.

Prisons and visions presented
    with rare descriptions
corresponding exactly to those
    of Alcatraz and Rose.

A naked lunch is natural to us,
    we eat reality sandwiches.
But allegories are so much lettuce.
    Don't hide the madness.

San Jose, 1954

Howl

For Carl Solomon

I

I saw the best minds of my generation destroyed by madness, starving
    hysterical naked,

dragging themselves through the negro streets at dawn looking for an
    angry fix,

angelheaded hipsters burning for the ancient heavenly connection to
    the starry dynamo in the machinery of night,

who poverty and tatters and hollow-eyed and high sat up smoking in
    the supernatural darkness of cold-water flats floating across the
    tops of cities contemplating jazz,

who bared their brains to Heaven under the El and saw Mohammedan
    angels staggering on tenement roofs illuminated,

who passed through universities with radiant cool eyes hallucinating
    Arkansas and Blake-light tragedy among the scholars of war,

who were expelled from the academies for crazy & publishing obscene
    odes on the windows of the skull,

who cowered in unshaven rooms in underwear, burning their money
    in wastebaskets and listening to the Terror through the wall,

who got busted in their pubic beards returning through Laredo with a
    belt of marijuana for New York,

who ate fire in paint hotels or drank turpentine in Paradise Alley,
    death, or purgatoried their torsos night after night

with dreams, with drugs, with waking nightmares, alcohol and cock
    and endless balls,

incomparable blind streets of shuddering cloud and lightning in the
    mind leaping toward poles of Canada & Paterson, illuminating
    all the motionless world of Time between,

Peyote solidities of halls, backyard green tree cemetery dawns, wine
    drunkenness over the rooftops, storefront boroughs of tea-
    head joyride neon blinking traffic light, sun and moon and
    tree vibrations in the roaring winter dusks of Brooklyn, ashcan
    rantings and kind king light of mind,

who chained themselves to subways for the endless ride from Battery
    to holy Bronx on benzedrine until the noise of wheels and
    children brought them down shuddering mouth-wracked and
    battered bleak of brain all drained of brilliance in the drear
    light of Zoo,

who sank all night in submarine light of Bickford's floated out and sat
through the stale beer afternoon in desolate Fugazzi's, listen-
ing to the crack of doom on the hydrogen jukebox,
who talked continuously seventy hours from park to pad to bar to Bel-
levue to museum to the Brooklyn Bridge,
a lost battalion of platonic conversationalists jumping down the stoops
off fire escapes off windowsills off Empire State out of the
moon,
yacketayakking screaming vomiting whispering facts and memories
and anecdotes and eyeball kicks and shocks of hospitals and
jails and wars,
whole intellects disgorged in total recall for seven days and nights with
brilliant eyes, meat for the Synagogue cast on the pavement,
who vanished into nowhere Zen New Jersey leaving a trail of ambigu-
ous picture postcards of Atlantic City Hall,
suffering Eastern sweats and Tangerian bone-grindings and migraines
of China under junk-withdrawal in Newark's bleak furnished
room,
who wandered around and around at midnight in the railroad yard
wondering where to go, and went, leaving no broken hearts,
who lit cigarettes in boxcars boxcars boxcars racketing through snow
toward lonesome farms in grandfather night,
who studied Plotinus Poe St. John of the Cross telepathy and bop kab-
balah because the cosmos instinctively vibrated at their feet in
Kansas,
who loned in through the streets of Idaho seeking visionary indian
angels who were visionary indian angels,
who thought they were only mad when Baltimore gleamed in super-
natural ecstasy,
who jumped in limousines with the Chinaman of Oklahoma on the
impulse of winter midnight streetlight smalltown rain,
who lounged hungry and lonesome through Houston seeking jazz or
sex or soup, and followed the brilliant Spaniard to converse
about America and Eternity, a hopeless task, and so took ship
to Africa,
who disappeared into the volcanoes of Mexico leaving behind nothing
but the shadow of dungarees and the lava and ash of poetry
scattered in fireplace Chicago,
who reappeared on the West Coast investigating the FBI in beards and
shorts with big pacifist eyes sexy in their dark skin passing out
incomprehensible leaflets,

who burned cigarette holes in their arms protesting the narcotic
tobacco haze of Capitalism,

who distributed Supercommunist pamphlets in Union Square weep-
ing and undressing while the sirens of Los Alamos wailed
them down, and wailed down Wall, and the Staten Island ferry
also wailed,

who broke down crying in white gymnasiums naked and trembling
before the machinery of other skeletons,

who bit detectives in the neck and shrieked with delight in policecars
for committing no crime but their own wild cooking pederasty
and intoxication,

who howled on their knees in the subway and were dragged off the
roof waving genitals and manuscripts,

who let themselves be fucked in the ass by saintly motorcyclists, and
screamed with joy,

who blew and were blown by those human seraphim, the sailors,
caresses of Atlantic and Caribbean love,

who balled in the morning in the evenings in rosegardens and the grass
of public parks and cemeteries scattering their semen freely to
whomever come who may,

who hiccuped endlessly trying to giggle but wound up with a sob
behind a partition in a Turkish Bath when the blond & naked
angel came to pierce them with a sword,

who lost their loveboys to the three old shrews of fate the one eyed
shrew of the heterosexual dollar the one eyed shrew that winks
out of the womb and the one eyed shrew that does nothing but
sit on her ass and snip the intellectual golden threads of the
craftsman's loom,

who copulated ecstatic and insatiate with a bottle of beer a sweet-
heart a package of cigarettes a candle and fell off the bed, and
continued along the floor and down the hall and ended faint-
ing on the wall with a vision of ultimate cunt and come elud-
ing the last gyzym of consciousness,

who sweetened the snatches of a million girls trembling in the sunset,
and were red eyed in the morning but prepared to sweeten the
snatch of the sunrise, flashing buttocks under barns and naked
in the lake,

who went out whoring through Colorado in myriad stolen night-cars,
N.C., secret hero of these poems, cocksman and Adonis of
Denver—joy to the memory of his innumerable lays of girls
in empty lots & diner backyards, moviehouses' rickety rows,
on mountaintops in caves or with gaunt waitresses in famil-

iar roadside lonely petticoat upliftings & especially secret gas-
station solipsisms of johns, & hometown alleys too,

who faded out in vast sordid movies, were shifted in dreams, woke on
a sudden Manhattan, and picked themselves up out of base-
ments hung-over with heartless Tokay and horrors of Third
Avenue iron dreams & stumbled to unemployment offices,

who walked all night with their shoes full of blood on the snowbank
docks waiting for a door in the East River to open to a room
full of steamheat and opium,

who created great suicidal dramas on the apartment cliff-banks of the
Hudson under the wartime blue floodlight of the moon & their
heads shall be crowned with laurel in oblivion,

who ate the lamb stew of the imagination or digested the crab at the
muddy bottom of the rivers of Bowery,

who wept at the romance of the streets with their pushcarts full of
onions and bad music,

who sat in boxes breathing in the darkness under the bridge, and rose
up to build harpsichords in their lofts,

who coughed on the sixth floor of Harlem crowned with flame under
the tubercular sky surrounded by orange crates of theology,

who scribbled all night rocking and rolling over lofty incantations
which in the yellow morning were stanzas of gibberish,

who cooked rotten animals lung heart feet tail borsht & tortillas
dreaming of the pure vegetable kingdom,

who plunged themselves under meat trucks looking for an egg,

who threw their watches off the roof to cast their ballot for Eternity
outside of Time, & alarm clocks fell on their heads every day
for the next decade,

who cut their wrists three times successively unsuccessfully, gave up
and were forced to open antique stores where they thought
they were growing old and cried,

who were burned alive in their innocent flannel suits on Madison Ave-
nue amid blasts of leaden verse & the tanked-up clatter of the
iron regiments of fashion & the nitroglycerine shrieks of the
fairies of advertising & the mustard gas of sinister intelligent
editors, or were run down by the drunken taxicabs of Absolute
Reality,

who jumped off the Brooklyn Bridge this actually happened and
walked away unknown and forgotten into the ghostly daze of
Chinatown soup alleyways & firetrucks, not even one free beer,

who sang out of their windows in despair, fell out of the subway win-
dow, jumped in the filthy Passaic, leaped on negroes, cried

all over the street, danced on broken wineglasses barefoot
smashed phonograph records of nostalgic European 1930s
German jazz finished the whiskey and threw up groaning into
the bloody toilet, moans in their ears and the blast of colossal
steamwhistles,

who barreled down the highways of the past journeying to each oth-
er's hotrod-Golgotha jail-solitude watch or Birmingham jazz
incarnation,

who drove crosscountry seventytwo hours to find out if I had a vision
or you had a vision or he had a vision to find out Eternity,

who journeyed to Denver, who died in Denver, who came back to
Denver & waited in vain, who watched over Denver & brooded
& loned in Denver and finally went away to find out the Time,
& now Denver is lonesome for her heroes,

who fell on their knees in hopeless cathedrals praying for each other's
salvation and light and breasts, until the soul illuminated its
hair for a second,

who crashed through their minds in jail waiting for impossible crimi-
nals with golden heads and the charm of reality in their hearts
who sang sweet blues to Alcatraz,

who retired to Mexico to cultivate a habit, or Rocky Mount to tender
Buddha or Tangiers to boys or Southern Pacific to the black
locomotive or Harvard to Narcissus to Woodlawn to the daisy-
chain or grave,

who demanded sanity trials accusing the radio of hypnotism & were
left with their insanity & their hands & a hung jury,

who threw potato salad at CCNY lecturers on Dadaism and subse-
quently presented themselves on the granite steps of the mad-
house with shaven heads and harlequin speech of suicide,
demanding instantaneous lobotomy,

and who were given instead the concrete void of insulin Metrazol
electricity hydrotherapy psychotherapy occupational therapy
pingpong & amnesia,

who in humorless protest overturned only one symbolic pingpong
table, resting briefly in catatonia,

returning years later truly bald except for a wig of blood, and tears
and fingers, to the visible madman doom of the wards of the
madtowns of the East,

Pilgrim State's Rockland's and Greystone's foetid halls, bickering with
the echoes of the soul, rocking and rolling in the midnight
solitude-bench dolmen-realms of love, dream of life a night-
mare, bodies turned to stone as heavy as the moon,

with mother finally ******, and the last fantastic book flung out of the
tenement window, and the last door closed at 4 A.M. and the
last telephone slammed at the wall in reply and the last fur-
nished room emptied down to the last piece of mental fur-
niture, a yellow paper rose twisted on a wire hanger in the
closet, and even that imaginary, nothing but a hopeful little bit
of hallucination—

ah, Carl, while you are not safe I am not safe, and now you're really in
the total animal soup of time—

and who therefore ran through the icy streets obsessed with a sudden
flash of the alchemy of the use of the ellipsis catalog a variable
measure and the vibrating plane,

who dreamt and made incarnate gaps in Time & Space through images
juxtaposed, and trapped the archangel of the soul between 2
visual images and joined the elemental verbs and set the noun
and dash of consciousness together jumping with sensation of
Pater Omnipotens Aeterna Deus Father Omnipotent Aeterna
Deus

to recreate the syntax and measure of poor human prose and stand
before you speechless and intelligent and shaking with shame,
rejected yet confessing out the soul to conform to the rhythm
of thought in his naked and endless head,

the madman bum and angel beat in Time, unknown, yet putting
down here what might be left to say in time come after death,

and rose reincarnate in the ghostly clothes of jazz in the goldhorn
shadow of the band and blew the suffering of America's naked
mind for love into an eli eli lamma lamma sabacthani saxo-
phone cry that shivered the cities down to the last radio

with the absolute heart of the poem of life butchered out of their own
bodies good to eat a thousand years.

II
What sphinx of cement and aluminum bashed open their skulls and
ate up their brains and imagination?

Moloch! Solitude! Filth! Ugliness! Ashcans and unobtainable dol-
lars! Children screaming under the stairways! Boys sobbing in
armies! Old men weeping in the parks!

Moloch! Moloch! Nightmare of Moloch! Moloch the loveless! Mental
Moloch! Moloch the heavy judger of men!

Moloch the incomprehensible prison! Moloch the crossbone soul-
less jailhouse and Congress of sorrows! Moloch whose build-
ings are judgment! Moloch the vast stone of war! Moloch the

stunned governments!

Moloch whose mind is pure machinery! Moloch whose blood is running money! Moloch whose fingers are ten armies! Moloch whose breast is a cannibal dynamo! Moloch whose ear is a smoking tomb!

Moloch whose eyes are a thousand blind windows! Moloch whose skyscrapers stand in the long streets like endless Jehovahs! Moloch whose factories dream and croak in the fog! Moloch whose smokestacks and antennae crown the cities!

Moloch whose love is endless oil and stone! Moloch whose soul is electricity and banks! Moloch whose poverty is the specter of genius! Moloch whose fate is a cloud of sexless hydrogen! Moloch whose name is the Mind!

Moloch in whom I sit lonely! Moloch in whom I dream Angels! Crazy in Moloch! Cocksucker in Moloch! Lacklove and manless in Moloch!

Moloch who entered my soul early! Moloch in whom I am a consciousness without a body! Moloch who frightened me out of my natural ecstasy! Moloch whom I abandon! Wake up in Moloch! Light streaming out of the sky!

Moloch! Moloch! Robot apartments! invisible suburbs! skeleton treasuries! blind capitals! demonic industries! spectral nations! invincible madhouses! granite cocks! monstrous bombs!

They broke their backs lifting Moloch to Heaven! Pavements, trees, radios, tons! lifting the city to Heaven which exists and is everywhere about us!

Visions! omens! hallucinations! miracles! ecstasies! gone down the American river!

Dreams! adorations! illuminations! religions! the whole boatload of sensitive bullshit!

Breakthroughs! over the river! flips and crucifixions! gone down the flood! Highs! Epiphanies! Despairs! Ten years' animal screams and suicides! Minds! New loves! Mad generation! down on the rocks of Time!

Real holy laughter in the river! They saw it all! the wild eyes! the holy yells! They bade farewell! They jumped off the roof! to solitude! waving! carrying flowers! Down to the river! into the street!

III
Carl Solomon! I'm with you in Rockland
       where you're madder than I am
I'm with you in Rockland
       where you must feel very strange
I'm with you in Rockland
       where you imitate the shade of my mother
I'm with you in Rockland
       where you've murdered your twelve secretaries
I'm with you in Rockland
       where you laugh at this invisible humor
I'm with you in Rockland
       where we are great writers on the same dreadful typewriter
I'm with you in Rockland
       where your condition has become serious and is reported on
       the radio
I'm with you in Rockland
       where the faculties of the skull no longer admit the worms of
       the senses
I'm with you in Rockland
       where you drink the tea of the breasts of the spinsters of Utica
I'm with you in Rockland
       where you pun on the bodies of your nurses the harpies of the
       Bronx
I'm with you in Rockland
       where you scream in the straightjacket that you're losing the
       game of the actual pingpong of the abyss
I'm with you in Rockland
       where you bang on the catatonic piano the soul is innocent and
       immortal it should never die ungodly in an armed madhouse
I'm with you in Rockland
       where fifty more shocks will never return your soul to its body
       again from its pilgrimage to a cross in the void
I'm with you in Rockland
       where you accuse your doctors of insanity and plot the Hebrew
       socialist revolution against the fascist national Golgotha
I'm with you in Rockland
       where you will split the heavens of Long Island and resurrect
       your living human Jesus from the superhuman tomb
I'm with you in Rockland
       where there are twentyfive thousand mad comrades all
       together singing the final stanzas of the Internationale

I'm with you in Rockland
> where we hug and kiss the United States under our bedsheets
> the United States that coughs all night and won't let us sleep

I'm with you in Rockland
> where we wake up electrified out of the coma by our own souls' airplanes roaring over the roof they've come to drop angelic bombs the hospital illuminates itself   imaginary walls collapse   O skinny legions run outside   O starry-spangled shock of mercy the eternal war is here   O victory forget your underwear we're free

I'm with you in Rockland
> in my dreams you walk dripping from a sea-journey on the highway across America in tears to the door of my cottage in the Western night

San Francisco, 1955-1956

Footnote to Howl

Holy! Holy! Holy! Holy! Holy! Holy! Holy! Holy! Holy! Holy! Holy!
    Holy! Holy! Holy! Holy!

The world is holy! The soul is holy! The skin is holy! The nose is holy!
    The tongue and cock and hand and asshole holy!

Everything is holy! everybody's holy! everywhere is holy! everyday is
    in eternity! Everyman's an angel!

The bum's as holy as the seraphim! the madman is holy as you my soul
    are holy!

The typewriter is holy the poem is holy the voice is holy the hearers
    are holy the ecstasy is holy!

Holy Peter holy Allen holy Solomon holy Lucien holy Kerouac holy
    Huncke holy Burroughs holy Cassady holy the unknown bug-
    gered and suffering beggars holy the hideous human angels!

Holy my mother in the insane asylum! Holy the cocks of the grandfa-
    thers of Kansas!

Holy the groaning saxophone! Holy the bop apocalypse! Holy the
    jazzbands marijuana hipsters peace peyote pipes & drums!

Holy the solitudes of skyscrapers and pavements! Holy the cafeterias
    filled with the millions! Holy the mysterious rivers of tears
    under the streets!

Holy the lone juggernaut! Holy the vast lamb of the middleclass! Holy
    the crazy shepherds of rebellions! Who digs Los Angeles IS
    Los Angeles!

Holy New York Holy San Francisco Holy Peoria & Seattle Holy Paris
    Holy Tangiers Holy Moscow Holy Istanbul!

Holy time in eternity holy eternity in time holy the clocks in space
    holy the fourth dimension holy the fifth International holy the
    Angel in Moloch!

Holy the sea holy the desert holy the railroad holy the locomotive holy
    the visions holy the hallucinations holy the miracles holy the
    eyeball holy the abyss!

Holy forgiveness! mercy! charity! faith! Holy! Ours! bodies! suffering!
    magnanimity!

Holy the supernatural extra brilliant intelligent kindness of the soul!

Berkeley, 1955

A Supermarket in California

What thoughts I have of you tonight, Walt Whitman, for I walked down the sidestreets under the trees with a headache self-conscious looking at the full moon.

In my hungry fatigue, and shopping for images, I went into the neon fruit supermarket, dreaming of your enumerations!

What peaches and what penumbras! Whole families shopping at night! Aisles full of husbands! Wives in the avocados, babies in the tomatoes!—and you, García Lorca, what were you doing down by the watermelons?

I saw you, Walt Whitman, childless, lonely old grubber, poking among the meats in the refrigerator and eyeing the grocery boys.

I heard you asking questions of each: Who killed the pork chops? What price bananas? Are you my Angel?

I wandered in and out of the brilliant stacks of cans following you, and followed in my imagination by the store detective.

We strode down the open corridors together in our solitary fancy tasting artichokes, possessing every frozen delicacy, and never passing the cashier.

Where are we going, Walt Whitman? The doors close in an hour. Which way does your beard point tonight?

(I touch your book and dream of our odyssey in the supermarket and feel absurd.)

Will we walk all night through solitary streets? The trees add shade to shade, lights out in the houses, we'll both be lonely.

Will we stroll dreaming of the lost America of love past blue automobiles in driveways, home to our silent cottage?

Ah, dear father, graybeard, lonely old courage-teacher, what America did you have when Charon quit poling his ferry and you got out on a smoking bank and stood watching the boat disappear on the black waters of Lethe?

Berkeley, 1955

Sunflower Sutra

I walked on the banks of the tincan banana dock and sat down under the huge shade of a Southern Pacific locomotive to look at the sunset over the box house hills and cry.

Jack Kerouac sat beside me on a busted rusty iron pole, companion, we thought the same thoughts of the soul, bleak and blue and sad-eyed, surrounded by the gnarled steel roots of trees of machinery.

The oily water on the river mirrored the red sky, sun sank on top of final Frisco peaks, no fish in that stream, no hermit in those mounts, just ourselves rheumy-eyed and hung-over like old bums on the riverbank, tired and wily.

Look at the Sunflower, he said, there was a dead gray shadow against the sky, big as a man, sitting dry on top of a pile of ancient sawdust—

—I rushed up enchanted—it was my first sunflower, memories of Blake—my visions—Harlem

and Hells of the Eastern rivers, bridges clanking Joes Greasy Sandwiches, dead baby carriages, black treadless tires forgotten and unretreaded, the poem of the riverbank, condoms & pots, steel knives, nothing stainless, only the dank muck and the razor-sharp artifacts passing into the past—

and the gray Sunflower poised against the sunset, crackly bleak and dusty with the smut and smog and smoke of olden locomotives in its eye—

corolla of bleary spikes pushed down and broken like a battered crown, seeds fallen out of its face, soon-to-be-toothless mouth of sunny air, sunrays obliterated on its hairy head like a dried wire spiderweb,

leaves stuck out like arms out of the stem, gestures from the sawdust root, broke pieces of plaster fallen out of the black twigs, a dead fly in its ear,

Unholy battered old thing you were, my sunflower O my soul, I loved you then!

The grime was no man's grime but death and human locomotives,

all that dress of dust, that veil of darkened railroad skin, that smog of cheek, that eyelid of black mis'ry, that sooty hand or phallus or protuberance of artificial worse-than-dirt—industrial—modern—all that civilization spotting your crazy golden crown—

and those blear thoughts of death and dusty loveless eyes and ends and withered roots below, in the home-pile of sand and sawdust, rubber dollar bills, skin of machinery, the guts and innards of the weeping coughing car, the empty lonely tincans with their rusty tongues alack, what more could I name, the smoked ashes of some cock cigar, the cunts of wheelbarrows and the milky breasts of cars, wornout asses out of chairs & sphincters of dynamos—all these

entangled in your mummied roots—and you there standing before me in the sunset, all your glory in your form!

A perfect beauty of a sunflower! a perfect excellent lovely sunflower existence! a sweet natural eye to the new hip moon, woke up alive and excited grasping in the sunset shadow sunrise golden monthly breeze!

How many flies buzzed round you innocent of your grime, while you cursed the heavens of the railroad and your flower soul?

Poor dead flower? when did you forget you were a flower? when did you look at your skin and decide you were an impotent dirty old locomotive? the ghost of a locomotive? the specter and shade of a once powerful mad American locomotive?

You were never no locomotive, Sunflower, you were a sunflower!

And you Locomotive, you are a locomotive, forget me not!

So I grabbed up the skeleton thick sunflower and stuck it at my side like a scepter,

and deliver my sermon to my soul, and Jack's soul too, and anyone who'll listen,

—We're not our skin of grime, we're not our dread bleak dusty imageless locomotives, we're all golden sunflowers inside, blessed by our own seed & hairy naked accomplishment-bodies growing into mad black formal sunflowers in the sunset, spied on by our own eyes under the shadow of the mad locomotive riverbank sunset Frisco hilly tincan evening sitdown vision.

Berkeley 1955

America

America I've given you all and now I'm nothing.
America two dollars and twentyseven cents January 17, 1956.
I can't stand my own mind.
America when will we end the human war?
Go fuck yourself with your atom bomb.
I don't feel good don't bother me.
I won't write my poem till I'm in my right mind.
America when will you be angelic?
When will you take off your clothes?
When will you look at yourself through the grave?
When will you be worthy of your million Trotskyites?
America why are your libraries full of tears?
America when will you send your eggs to India?
I'm sick of your insane demands.
When can I go into the supermarket and buy what I need with my
    good looks?
America after all it is you and I who are perfect not the next world.
Your machinery is too much for me.
You made me want to be a saint.
There must be some other way to settle this argument.
Burroughs is in Tangiers I don't think he'll come back it's sinister.
Are you being sinister or is this some form of practical joke?
I'm trying to come to the point.
I refuse to give up my obsession.
America stop pushing I know what I'm doing.
America the plum blossoms are falling.
I haven't read the newspapers for months, everyday somebody goes on
    trial for murder.
America I feel sentimental about the Wobblies.
America I used to be a communist when I was a kid I'm not sorry.
I smoke marijuana every chance I get.
I sit in my house for days on end and stare at the roses in the closet.
When I go to Chinatown I get drunk and never get laid.
My mind is made up there's going to be trouble.
You should have seen me reading Marx.
My psychoanalyst thinks I'm perfectly right.
I won't say the Lord's Prayer.
I have mystical visions and cosmic vibrations.
America I still haven't told you what you did to Uncle Max after he
    came over from Russia.

I'm addressing you.
Are you going to let your emotional life be run by Time Magazine?
I'm obsessed by Time Magazine.
I read it every week.
Its cover stares at me every time I slink past the corner candystore.
I read it in the basement of the Berkeley Public Library.
It's always telling me about responsibility. Businessmen are serious.
       Movie producers are serious. Everybody's serious but me.
It occurs to me that I am America.
I am talking to myself again.

Asia is rising against me.
I haven't got a chinaman's chance.
I'd better consider my national resources.
My national resources consist of two joints of marijuana millions of
       genitals an unpublishable private literature that jetplanes 1400
       miles an hour and twenty-five-thousand mental institutions.
I say nothing about my prisons nor the millions of underprivileged
       who live in my flowerpots under the light of five hundred suns.
I have abolished the whorehouses of France, Tangiers is the next to go.
My ambition is to be President despite the fact that I'm a Catholic.

America how can I write a holy litany in your silly mood?
I will continue like Henry Ford my strophes are as individual as his
       automobiles more so they're all different sexes.
America I will sell you strophes $2500 apiece $500 down on your old
       strophe
America free Tom Mooney
America save the Spanish Loyalists
America Sacco & Vanzetti must not die
America I am the Scottsboro boys.
America when I was seven momma took me to Communist Cell meet-
       ings they sold us garbanzos a handful per ticket a ticket costs
       a nickel and the speeches were free everybody was angelic and
       sentimental about the workers it was all so sincere you have
       no idea what a good thing the party was in 1835 Scott Near-
       ing was a grand old man a real mensch Mother Bloor the Silk-
       strikers' Ewig-Weibliche made me cry I once saw the Yiddish
       orator Isreal Amter plain. Everybody must have been a spy.
America you don't really want to go to war.
America it's them bad Russians.
Them Russians them Russians and them Chinamen. And them Russians.

The Russia wants to eat us alive. The Russia's power mad. She wants
   to take our cars from out our garages.
Her wants to grab Chicago. Her needs a Red *Reader's Digest.* Her
   wants our auto plants in Siberia. Him big bureaucracy running
   our fillingstations.
That no good. Ugh. Him make Indians learn read. Him need big black
   niggers. Hah. Her make us all work sixteen hours a day. Help.
America this is quite serious.
America this is the impression I get from looking in the television set.
America is this correct?
I'd better get right down to the job.
It's true I don't want to join the Army or turn lathes in precision parts
   factories, I'm nearsighted and psychopathic anyway.
America I'm putting my queer shoulder to the wheel.

Berkeley, January 17, 1956

Kaddish

For Naomi Ginsberg, 1894–1956

I

Strange now to think of you, gone without corsets & eyes, while I
    walk on the sunny pavement of Greenwich Village.
downtown Manhattan, clear winter noon, and I've been up all night,
    talking, talking, reading the Kaddish aloud, listening to Ray
    Charles blues shout blind on the phonograph
the rhythm the rhythm—and your memory in my head three years
    after—And read Adonais' last triumphant stanzas aloud—
    wept, realizing how we suffer—
And how Death is that remedy all singers dream of, sing, remember,
    prophesy as in the Hebrew Anthem, or the Buddhist Book
    of Answers—and my own imagination of a withered leaf—at
    dawn—
Dreaming back thru life, Your time—and mine accelerating toward
    Apocalypse,
the final moment—the flower burning in the Day—and what comes
    after,
looking back on the mind itself that saw an American city
a flash away, and the great dream of Me or China, or you and a phan-
    tom Russia, or a crumpled bed that never existed—
like a poem in the dark—escaped back to Oblivion—
No more to say, and nothing to weep for but the Beings in the Dream,
    trapped in its disappearance,
sighing, screaming with it, buying and selling pieces of phantom, wor-
    shipping each other,
worshipping the God included in it all—longing or inevitability?—
    while it lasts, a Vision—anything more?
It leaps about me, as I go out and walk the street, look back over my
    shoulder, Seventh Avenue, the battlements of window office
    buildings shouldering each other high, under a cloud, tall as
    the sky an instant—and the sky above—an old blue place.
or down the Avenue to the south, to—as I walk toward the Lower East
    Side—where you walked 50 years ago, little girl—from Russia,
    eating the first poisonous tomatoes of America—frightened on
    the dock—
then struggling in the crowds of Orchard Street toward what?—
    toward Newark—

toward candy store, first home-made sodas of the century, hand-
    churned ice cream in backroom on musty brownfloor boards—
Toward education marriage nervous breakdown, operation, teaching
    school, and learning to be mad, in a dream—what is this life?
Toward the Key in the window—and the great Key lays its head of
    light on top of Manhattan, and over the floor, and lays down
    on the sidewalk—in a single vast beam, moving, as I walk down
    First toward the Yiddish Theater—and the place of poverty
you knew, and I know, but without caring now—Strange to have
    moved thru Paterson, and the West, and Europe and here
    again,
with the cries of Spaniards now in the doorstoops doors and dark boys
    on the street, fire escapes old as you
—Tho you're not old now, that's left here with me—
Myself, anyhow, maybe as old as the universe—and I guess that dies
    with us—enough to cancel all that comes—What came is gone
    forever every time—
That's good! That leaves it open for no regret—no fear radiators, lack-
    love, torture even toothache in the end—
Though while it comes it is a lion that eats the soul—and the lamb,
    the soul, in us, alas, offering itself in sacrifice to change's fierce
    hunger—hair and teeth—and the roar of bonepain, skull bare,
    break rib, rot-skin, braintricked Implacability.
Ai! ai! we do worse! We are in a fix! And you're out, Death let you
    out, Death had the Mercy, you're done with your century,
    done with God, done with the path thru it—Done with your-
    self at last—Pure—Back to the Babe dark before your Father,
    before us all—before the world—
There, rest. No more suffering for you. I know where you've gone, it's
    good.
No more flowers in the summer fields of New York, no joy now, no
    more fear of Louis,
and no more of his sweetness and glasses, his high school decades,
    debts, loves, frightened telephone calls, conception beds, rela-
    tives, hands—
No more of sister Elanor,—she gone before you—we kept it secret—
    you killed her—or she killed herself to bear with you—an
    arthritic heart—But Death's killed you both—No matter—
Nor your memory of your mother, 1915 tears in silent movies weeks
    and weeks—forgetting, aggrieve watching Marie Dressler
    address humanity, Chaplin dance in youth,

or Boris Godunov, Chaliapin's at the Met, halling his voice of a weep-
ing Czar—by standing room with Elanor & Max—watching also
the Capitalists take seats in Orchestra, white furs, diamonds,
with the YPSL's hitch-hiking thru Pennsylvania, in black baggy gym
skirts pants, photograph of 4 girls holding each other round
the waste, and laughing eye, too coy, virginal solitude of 1920
all girls grown old, or dead, now, and that long hair in the grave—
lucky to have husbands later—
You made it—I came too—Eugene my brother before (still grieving
now and will gream on to his last stiff hand, as he goes thru his
cancer—or kill —later perhaps—soon he will think—)
And it's the last moment I remember, which I see them all, thru
myself, now—tho not you
I didn't foresee what you felt—what more hideous gape of bad mouth
came first—to you—and were you prepared?
To go where? In that Dark—that—in that God? a radiance? A Lord in
the Void? Like an eye in the black cloud in a dream? Adonoi at
last, with you?
Beyond my remembrance! Incapable to guess! Not merely the yel-
low skull in the grave, or a box of worm dust, and a stained
ribbon—Deaths-head with Halo? can you believe it?
Is it only the sun that shines once for the mind, only the flash of exis-
tence, than none ever was?
Nothing beyond what we have—what you had—that so pitiful—yet
Triumph,
to have been here, and changed, like a tree, broken, or flower—fed
to the ground—but mad, with its petals, colored, thinking
Great Universe, shaken, cut in the head, leaf stript, hid in an
egg crate hospital, cloth wrapped, sore—freaked in the moon
brain, Naughtless.
No flower like that flower, which knew itself in the garden, and fought
the knife—lost
Cut down by an idiot Snowman's icy—even in the Spring—strange
ghost thought—some Death—Sharp icicle in his hand—
crowned with old roses—a dog for his eyes—cock of a
sweatshop—heart of electric irons.
All the accumulations of life, that wear us out—clocks, bodies, con-
sciousness, shoes, breasts—begotten sons—your Communism—
'Paranoia' into hospitals.
You once kicked Elanor in the leg, she died of heart failure later. You
of stroke. Asleep? within a year, the two of you, sisters in
death. Is Elanor happy?

Max grieves alive in an office on Lower Broadway, lone large mustache over midnight Accountings, not sure. His life passes—as he sees—and what does he doubt now? Still dream of making money, or that might have made money, hired nurse, had children, found even your Immortality, Naomi?

I'll see him soon. Now I've got to cut through—to talk to you—as I didn't when you had a mouth.

Forever. And we're bound for that, Forever—like Emily Dickinson's horses—headed to the End.

They know the way—These Steeds—run faster than we think—it's our own life they cross—and take with them.

Magnificent, mourned no more, marred of heart, mind behind, married dreamed, mortal changed—Ass and face done with murder.

In the world, given, flower maddened, made no Utopia, shut under pine, almed in Earth, balmed in Lone, Jehovah, accept.

Nameless, One Faced, Forever beyond me, beginningless, endless, Father in death. Tho I am not there for this Prophecy, I am unmarried, I'm hymnless, I'm Heavenless, headless in blisshood I would still adore

Thee, Heaven, after Death, only One blessed in Nothingness, not light or darkness, Dayless Eternity—

Take this, this Psalm, from me, burst from my hand in a day, some of my Time, now given to Nothing—to praise Thee—But Death

This is the end, the redemption from Wilderness, way for the Wonderer, House sought for All, black handkerchief washed clean by weeping—page beyond Psalm—Last change of mine and Naomi—to God's perfect Darkness—Death, stay thy phantoms!

II

Over and over—refrain—of the Hospitals—still haven't written your history—leave it abstract—a few images

run thru the mind—like the saxophone chorus of houses and years—remembrance of electrical shocks.

By long nites as a child in Paterson apartment, watching over your nervousness—you were fat—your next move—

By that afternoon I stayed home from school to take care of you—once and for all—when I vowed forever that once man disagreed with my opinion of the cosmos, I was lost—

By my later burden—vow to illuminate mankind—this is release of particulars—(mad as you)—(sanity a trick of agreement)—

But you stared out the window on the Broadway Church corner, and spied a mystical assassin from Newark,

So phoned the Doctor—'OK go way for a rest'—so I put on my coat and walked you downstreet—On the way a grammarschool boy screamed, unaccountably—'Where you goin Lady to Death'? I shuddered—

and you covered your nose with motheaten fur collar, gas mask against poison sneaked into downtown atmosphere, sprayed by Grandma—

And was the driver of the cheesebox Public Service bus a member of the gang? You shuddered at his face, I could hardly get you on—to New York, very Times Square, to grab another Greyhound—

where we hung around 2 hours fighting invisible bugs and jewish sickness—breeze poisoned by Roosevelt—

out to get you—and me tagging along, hoping it would end in a quiet room in a Victorian house by a lake.

Ride 3 hours thru tunnels past all American industry, Bayonne preparing for World War II, tanks, gas fields, soda factories, diners, locomotive roundhouse fortress—into piney woods New Jersey Indians—calm towns—long roads thru sandy tree fields—

Bridges by deerless creeks, old wampum loading the streambed—down there a tomahawk or Pocahontas bone—and a million old ladies voting for Roosevelt in brown small houses, roads off the Madness highway—

perhaps a hawk in a tree, or a hermit looking for an owl-filled branch—

All the time arguing—afraid of strangers in the forward double seat, snoring regardless—what busride they snore on now?

'Allen, you don't understand—it's—ever since those 3 big sticks up my back—they did something to me in Hospital, they poisoned me, they want to see me dead—3 big sticks, 3 big sticks—

'The Bitch! Old Grandma! Last week I saw her, dressed in pants like an old man, with a sack on her back, climbing up the brick side of the apartment

'On the fire escape, with poison germs, to throw on me—at night—maybe Louis is helping her—he's under her power—

'I'm your mother, take me to Lakewood' (near where Graf Zeppelin had crashed before, all Hitler in Explosion) 'where I can hide.'

We got there—Dr. Whatzis rest home—she hid behind a closet—demanded a blood transfusion.

We were kicked out—tramping with Valise to unknown shady lawn houses—dusk, pine trees after dark—long dead street filled with crickets and poison ivy—

I shut her up by now—big house REST HOME ROOMS—gave the landlady her money for the week—carried up the iron valise—sat on bed waiting to escape—

Neat room in attic with friendly bedcover—lace curtains—spinning wheel rug—Stained wallpaper old as Naomi. We were home.

I left on the next bus to New York—laid my head back in the last seat, depressed—the worst yet to come?—abandoning her, rode in torpor—I was only 12.

Would she hide in her room and come out cheerful for breakfast? Or lock her door and stare thru the window for sidestreet spies? Listen at keyholes for Hitlerian invisible gas? Dream in a chair—or mock me, by—in front of a mirror, alone?

12 riding the bus at nite thru New Jersey, have left Naomi to Parcae in Lakewood's haunted house—left to my own fate bus—sunk in a seat—all violins broken—my heart sore in my ribs—mind was empty—Would she were safe in her coffin—

Or back at Normal School in Newark, studying up on America in a black skirt—winter on the street without lunch—a penny a pickle—home at night to take care of Elanor in the bedroom—

First nervous breakdown was 1919—she stayed home from school and lay in a dark room for three weeks—something bad—never said what—every noise hurt—dreams of the creaks of Wall Street—

Before the gray Depression—went upstate New York—recovered—Lou took photo of her sitting crossleg on the grass—her long hair wound with flowers—smiling—playing lullabies on mandolin—poison ivy smoke in left-wing summer camps and me in infancy saw trees—

or back teaching school, laughing with idiots, the backward classes—her Russian specialty—morons with dreamy lips, great eyes, thin feet & sicky fingers, swaybacked, rachitic—

great heads pendulous over Alice in Wonderland, a blackboard full of C A T.

Naomi reading patiently, story out of a Communist fairy book—Tale of the Sudden Sweetness of the Dictator—Forgiveness of Warlocks—Armies Kissing—

Deathsheads Around the Green Table—The King & the Workers—Paterson Press printed them up in the '30s till she went mad, or they folded, both.

O Paterson! I got home late that nite. Louis was worried. How could I be so—didn't I think? I shouldn't have left her. Mad in Lakewood. Call the Doctor. Phone the home in the pines. Too late.

Went to bed exhausted, wanting to leave the world (probably that year newly in love with R——my high school mind hero, jewish boy who came a doctor later—then silent neat kid—

I later laying down life for him, moved to Manhattan—followed him to college—Prayed on ferry to help mankind if admitted—vowed, the day I journeyed to Entrance Exam—

by being honest revolutionary labor lawyer—would train for that—inspired by Sacco Vanzetti, Norman Thomas, Debs, Altgeld, Sandburg, Poe—Little Blue Books. I wanted to be President, or Senator.

ignorant woe—later dreams of kneeling by R's shocked knees declaring my love of 1941—What sweetness he'd have shown me, tho, that I'd wished him & despaired—first love—a crush—

Later a mortal avalanche, whole mountains of homosexuality, Matterhorns of cock, Grand Canyons of asshole—weight on my melancholy head—

meanwhile I walked on Broadway imagining Infinity like a rubber ball without space beyond—what's outside?—coming home to Graham Avenue still melancholy passing the lone green hedges across the street, dreaming after the movies—)

The telephone rang at 2 A.M.—Emergency—she'd gone mad— Naomi hiding under the bed screaming bugs of Mussolini—Help! Louis! Buba! Fascists! Death!—the landlady frightened—old fag attendant screaming back at her—

Terror, that woke the neighbors—old ladies on the second floor recovering from menopause—all those rags between thighs, clean sheets, sorry over lost babies—husbands ashen—children sneering at Yale, or putting oil in hair at CCNY—or trembling in Montclair State Teachers College like Eugene—

Her big leg crouched to her breast, hand outstretched Keep Away, wool dress on her thighs, fur coat dragged under the bed—she barricaded herself under bedspring with suitcases.

Louis in pajamas listening to phone, frightened—do now?— Who could know?—my fault, delivering her to solitude?—sitting in the dark room on the sofa, trembling, to figure out—

He took the morning train to Lakewood, Naomi still under bed— thought he brought poison Cops—Naomi screaming—Louis what happened to your heart then? Have you been killed by Naomi's ecstasy?

Dragged her out, around the corner, a cab, forced her in with valise, but the driver left them off at drugstore. Bus stop, two hours' wait.

I lay in bed nervous in the 4-room apartment, the big bed in living room, next to Louis' desk—shaking—he came home that nite, late, told me what happened.

Naomi at the prescription counter defending herself from the enemy—racks of children's books, douche bags, aspirins, pots, blood—'Don't come near me—murderers! Keep away! Promise not to kill me!'

Louis in horror at the soda fountain—with Lakewood girlscouts—Coke addicts—nurses—busmen hung on schedule— Police from country precinct, dumbed—and a priest dreaming of pigs on an ancient cliff?

Smelling the air—Louis pointing to emptiness?—Customers vomiting their Cokes—or staring—Louis humiliated—Naomi triumphant —The Announcement of the Plot. Bus arrives, the drivers won't have them on trip to New York.

Phonecalls to Dr. Whatzis, 'She needs a rest,' The mental hospital—State Greystone Doctors—'Bring her here, Mr. Ginsberg.'

Naomi, Naomi—sweating, bulge-eyed, fat, the dress unbuttoned at one side—hair over brow, her stocking hanging evilly on her legs— screaming for a blood transfusion—one righteous hand upraised—a shoe in it—barefoot in the Pharmacy—

The enemies approach—what poisons? Tape recorders? FBI? Zhdanov hiding behind the counter? Trotsky mixing rat bacteria in the back of the store? Uncle Sam in Newark, plotting deathly perfumes in the Negro district? Uncle Ephraim, drunk with murder in the politician's bar, scheming of Hague? Aunt Rose passing water thru the needles of the Spanish Civil War?

till the hired $35 ambulance came from Red Bank——Grabbed her arms—strapped her on the stretcher—moaning, poisoned by imaginaries, vomiting chemicals thru Jersey, begging mercy from Essex County to Morristown—

And back to Greystone where she lay three years—that was the last breakthrough, delivered her to Madhouse again—

On what wards—I walked there later, oft—old catatonic ladies, gray as cloud or ash or walls—sit crooning over floorspace—Chairs— and the wrinkled hags acreep, accusing—begging my 13-year-old mercy—

'Take me home'—I went alone sometimes looking for the lost Naomi, taking Shock—and I'd say, 'No, you're crazy Mama,—Trust the Drs.'—

And Eugene, my brother, her elder son, away studying Law in a furnished room in Newark—

came Paterson-ward next day—and he sat on the broken-down

couch in the living room—'We had to send her back to Greystone'—

—his face perplexed, so young, then eyes with tears—then crept weeping all over his face—'What for?' wail vibrating in his cheekbones, eyes closed up, high voice—Eugene's face of pain.

Him faraway, escaped to an Elevator in the Newark Library, his bottle daily milk on windowsill of $5 week furn room downtown at trolley tracks—

He worked 8 hrs. a day for $20/wk—thru Law School years—stayed by himself innocent near negro whorehouses.

Unlaid, poor virgin—writing poems about Ideals and politics letters to the editor Pat Eve News—(we both wrote, denouncing Senator Borah and Isolationists—and felt mysterious toward Paterson City Hall—

I sneaked inside it once—local Moloch tower with phallus spire & cap o' ornament, strange gothic Poetry that stood on Market Street—replica Lyons' Hotel de Ville—

wings, balcony & scrollwork portals, gateway to the giant city clock, secret map room full of Hawthorne—dark Debs in the Board of Tax—Rembrandt smoking in the gloom—

Silent polished desks in the great committee room—Aldermen? Bd of Finance? Mosca the hairdresser aplot—Crapp the gangster issuing orders from the john—The madmen struggling over Zone, Fire, Cops & Backroom Metaphysics—we're all dead—outside by the bus stop Eugene stared thru childhood—

where the Evangelist preached madly for 3 decades, hard-haired, cracked & true to his mean Bible—chalked Prepare to Meet Thy God on civic pave—

or God is Love on the railroad overpass concrete—he raved like I would rave, the lone Evangelist—Death on City Hall—)

But Gene, young,—been Montclair Teachers College 4 years—taught half year & quit to go ahead in life—afraid of Discipline Problems—dark sex Italian students, raw girls getting laid, no English, sonnets disregarded—and he did not know much—just that he lost—

so broke his life in two and paid for Law—read huge blue books and rode the ancient elevator 13 miles away in Newark & studied up hard for the future

just found the Scream of Naomi on his failure doorstep, for the final time, Naomi gone, us lonely—home—him sitting there—

Then have some chicken soup, Eugene. The Man of Evangel wails in front of City Hall. And this year Lou has poetic loves of suburb middle age—in secret—music from his 1937 book—Sincere—he longs for beauty—

No love since Naomi screamed—since 1923?—now lost in Grey-stone ward—new shock for her—Electricity, following the 40 Insulin.

And Metrazol had made her fat.

So that a few years later she came home again—we'd much advanced and planned—I waited for that day—my Mother again to cook &—play the piano—sing at mandolin—Lung Stew, & Stenka Razin, & the communist line on the war with Finland—and Louis in debt—suspected to be poisoned money—mysterious capitalisms

—& walked down the long front hall & looked at the furniture. She never remembered it all. Some amnesia. Examined the doilies—and the dining room set was sold—

the Mahogany table—20 years love—gone to the junk man—we still had the piano—and the book of Poe—and the Mandolin, tho needed some string, dusty—

She went to the backroom to lie down in bed and ruminate, or nap, hide—I went in with her, not leave her by herself—lay in bed next to her—shades pulled, dusky, late afternoon—Louis in front room at desk, waiting—perhaps boiling chicken for supper—

'Don't be afraid of me because I'm just coming back home from the mental hospital—I'm your mother—'

Poor love, lost—a fear—I lay there—Said, 'I love you Naomi,'—stiff, next to her arm. I would have cried, was this the comfortless lone union?—Nervous, and she got up soon.

Was she ever satisfied? And—by herself sat on the new couch by the front windows, uneasy—cheek leaning on her hand—narrowing eye—at what fate that day—

Picking her tooth with her nail, lips formed an O, suspicion—thought's old worn vagina—absent sideglance of eye—some evil debt written in the wall, unpaid—& the aged breasts of Newark come near—

May have heard radio gossip thru the wires in her head, con-trolled by 3 big sticks left in her back by gangsters in amnesia, thru the hospital—caused pain between her shoulders—

Into her head—Roosevelt should know her case, she told me—Afraid to kill her, now, that the government knew their names—traced back to Hitler—wanted to leave Louis' house forever.

One night, sudden attack—her noise in the bathroom—like croaking up her soul—convulsions and red vomit coming out of her mouth—diarrhea water exploding from her behind—on all fours in front of the toilet—urine running between her legs—left retching on the tile floor smeared with her black feces—unfainted—

At forty, varicosed, nude, fat, doomed, hiding outside the apartment door near the elevator calling Police, yelling for her girlfriend Rose to help—

Once locked herself in with razor or iodine—could hear her cough in tears at sink—Lou broke through glass green-painted door, we pulled her out to the bedroom.

Then quiet for months that winter—walks, alone, nearby on Broadway, read Daily Worker—Broke her arm, fell on icy street—

Began to scheme escape from cosmic financial murder plots— later she ran away to the Bronx to her sister Elanor. And there's another saga of late Naomi in New York.

Or thru Elanor or the Workmen's Circle, where she worked, addressing envelopes, she made out—went shopping for Campbell's tomato soup—saved money Louis mailed her—

Later she found a boyfriend, and he was a doctor—Dr. Isaac worked for National Maritime Union—now Italian bald and pudgy old doll—who was himself an orphan—but they kicked him out— Old cruelties—

Sloppier, sat around on bed or chair, in corset dreaming to herself—'I'm hot—I'm getting fat—I used to have such a beautiful figure before I went to the hospital—You should have seen me in Woodbine—' This in a furnished room around the NMU hall, 1943.

Looking at naked baby pictures in the magazine—baby powder advertisements, strained lamb carrots—'I will think nothing but beautiful thoughts.'

Revolving her head round and round on her neck at window light in summertime, in hypnotize, in doven-dream recall—

'I touch his cheek, I touch his cheek, he touches my lips with his hand, I think beautiful thoughts, the baby has a beautiful hand.'—

Or a No-shake of her body, disgust—some thought of Buchenwald—some insulin passes thru her head—a grimace nerve shudder at Involuntary (as shudder when I piss)—bad chemical in her cortex—'No don't think of that. He's a rat.'

Naomi: 'And when we die we become an onion, a cabbage, a carrot, or a squash, a vegetable.' I come downtown from Columbia and agree. She reads the Bible, thinks beautiful thoughts all day.

'Yesterday I saw God. What did he look like? Well, in the afternoon I climbed up a ladder—he has a cheap cabin in the country, like Monroe, N.Y. the chicken farms in the wood. He was a lonely old man with a white beard.

'I cooked supper for him. I made him a nice supper—lentil soup, vegetables, bread & butter—miltz—he sat down at the table and ate, he was sad.

'I told him, Look at all those fightings and killings down there, What's the matter? Why don't you put a stop to it?

'I try, he said—That's all he could do, he looked tired. He's a bachelor so long, and he likes lentil soup.'

Serving me meanwhile, a plate of cold fish—chopped raw cabbage dript with tapwater—smelly tomatoes—week-old health food—grated beets & carrots with leaky juice, warm—more and more disconsolate food—I can't eat it for nausea sometimes—the Charity of her hands stinking with Manhattan, madness, desire to please me, cold under cooked fish—pale red near the bones. Her smells—and oft naked in the room, so that I stare ahead, or turn a book ignoring her.

One time I thought she was trying to make me come lay her— flirting to herself at sink—lay back on huge bed that filled most of the room, dress up round her hips, big slash of hair, scars of operations, pancreas, belly wounds, abortions, appendix, stitching of incisions pulling down in the fat like hideous thick zippers—ragged long lips between her legs—What, even, smell of asshole? I was cold—later revolted a little, not much—seemed perhaps a good idea to try—know the Monster of the Beginning Womb—Perhaps—that way. Would she care? She needs a lover.

Yisborach, v'yistabach, v'yispoar, v'yisroman, v'yisnaseh, v'yishador, v'yishalleh, v'yishallol, sh'meh d'kudsho, b'rich hu.

And Louis reestablishing himself in Paterson grimy apartment in negro district—living in dark rooms—but found himself a girl he later married, falling in love again—tho sere & shy—hurt with 20 years Naomi's mad idealism.

Once I came home, after longtime in N.Y., he's lonely—sitting in the bedroom, he at desk chair turned round to face me—weeps, tears in red eyes under his glasses—

That we'd left him—Gene gone strangely into army—she out on her own in N.Y., almost childish in her furnished room. So Louis walked downtown to postoffice to get mail, taught in highschool— stayed at poetry desk, forlorn—ate grief at Bickford's all these years— are gone.

Eugene got out of the Army, came home changed and lone—cut off his nose in jewish operation—for years stopped girls on Broadway for cups of coffee to get laid—Went to NYU, serious there, to finish

Law.—

And Gene lived with her, ate naked fishcakes, cheap, while she got crazier—He got thin, or felt helpless, Naomi striking 1920 poses at the moon, half-naked in the next bed.

bit his nails and studied—was the weird nurse-son—Next year he moved to a room near Columbia—though she wanted to live with her children—

'Listen to your mother's plea, I beg you'—Louis still sending her checks—I was in bughouse that year 8 months—my own visions unmentioned in this here Lament—

But then went half mad—Hitler in her room, she saw his mustache in the sink—afraid of Dr. Isaac now, suspecting that he was in on the Newark plot—went up to Bronx to live near Elanor's Rheumatic Heart—

And Uncle Max never got up before noon, tho Naomi at 6 A.M. was listening to the radio for spies—or searching the windowsill,

for in the empty lot downstairs, an old man creeps with his bag stuffing packages of garbage in his hanging black overcoat.

Max's sister Edie works—17 years bookkeeper at Gimbels—lived downstairs in apartment house, divorced—so Edie took in Naomi on Rochambeau Ave—

Woodlawn Cemetery across the street, vast dale of graves where Poe once—Last stop on Bronx subway—lots of communists in that area.

Who enrolled for painting classes at night in Bronx Adult High School—walked alone under Van Cortlandt Elevated line to class—paints Naomiisms—

Humans sitting on the grass in some Camp No-Worry summers yore—saints with droopy faces and long-ill-fitting pants, from hospital—

Brides in front of Lower East Side with short grooms—lost El trains running over the Babylonian apartment rooftops in the Bronx—

Sad paintings—but she expressed herself. Her mandolin gone, all strings broke in her head, she tried. Toward Beauty? or some old life Message?

But started kicking Elanor, and Elanor had heart trouble—came upstairs and asked her about Spydom for hours,—Elanor frazzled. Max away at office, accounting for cigar stores till at night.

'I am a great woman—am truly a beautiful soul—and because of that they (Hitler, Grandma, Hearst, the Capitalists, Franco, Daily News, the '20s, Mussolini, the living dead) want to shut me up—

Buba's the head of a spider network—'

Kicking the girls, Edie & Elanor—Woke Edie at midnite to tell her she was a spy and Elanor a rat. Edie worked all day and couldn't take it—She was organizing the union.—And Elanor began dying, upstairs in bed.

The relatives call me up, she's getting worse—I was the only one left —Went on the subway with Eugene to see her, ate stale fish—

'My sister whispers in the radio—Louis must be in the apartment—his mother tells him what to say—LIARS!—I cooked for my two children—I played the mandolin—'

Last night the nightingale woke me / Last night when all was still / it sang in the golden moonlight / from on the wintry hill. She did.

I pushed her against the door and shouted 'DON'T KICK ELANOR!'—she stared at me—Contempt—die—disbelief her sons are so naive, so dumb—'Elanor is the worst spy! She's taking orders!'

'—No wires in the room!'—I'm yelling at her—last ditch, Eugene listening on the bed—what can he do to escape that fatal Mama—'You've been away from Louis years already—Grandma's too old to walk—'

We're all alive at once then—even me & Gene & Naomi in one mythological Cousinesque room—screaming at each other in the Forever—I in Columbia jacket, she half undressed.

I banging against her head which saw Radios, Sticks, Hitlers—the gamut of Hallucinations—for real—her own universe—no road that goes elsewhere—to my own—No America, not even a world—

That you go as all men, as Van Gogh, as mad Hannah, all the same—to the last doom—Thunder, Spirits, Lightning!

I've seen your grave! O strange Naomi! My own—cracked grave! Shema Y'Israel—I am Svul Avrum—you—in death?

Your last night in the darkness of the Bronx—I phonecalled—thru hospital to secret police

that came, when you and I were alone, shrieking at Elanor in my ear—who breathed hard in her own bed, got thin—

Nor will forget, the doorknock, at your fright of spies,—Law advancing, on my honor—Eternity entering the room—you running to the bathroom undressed, hiding in protest from the last heroic fate—

staring at my eyes, betrayed—the final cops of madness rescuing me—from your foot against the broken heart of Elanor,

your voice at Edie weary of Gimbels coming home to broken radio—and Louis needing a poor divorce, he wants to get married soon—Eugene dreaming, hiding at 125 St., suing negroes for money on crud furniture, defending black girls—

Protests from the bathroom—Said you were sane—dressing in a cotton robe, your shoes, then new, your purse and newspaper clippings—no—your honesty—

as you vainly made your lips more real with lipstick, looking in the mirror to see if the Insanity was Me or a carful of police.

or Grandma spying at 78—Your vision—Her climbing over the walls of the cemetery with political kidnapper's bag—or what you saw on the walls of the Bronx, in pink nightgown at midnight, staring out the window on the empty lot—

Ah Rochambeau Ave.—Playground of Phantoms—last apartment in the Bronx for spies—last home for Elanor or Naomi, here these communist sisters lost their revolution—

'All right—put on your coat Mrs.—let's go—We have the wagon downstairs—you want to come with her to the station?'

The ride then—held Naomi's hand, and held her head to my breast, I'm taller—kissed her and said I did it for the best—Elanor sick—and Max with heart condition—Needs—

To me—'Why did you do this?'—'Yes Mrs., your son will have to leave you in an hour'—The Ambulance

came in a few hours—drove off at 4 A.M. to some Bellevue in the night downtown—gone to the hospital forever. I saw her led away—she waved, tears in her eyes.

Two years, after a trip to Mexico—bleak in the flat plain near Brentwood, scrub brush and grass around the unused RR train track to the crazyhouse—

new brick 20 story central building—lost on the vast lawns of mad-town on Long Island—huge cities of the moon.

Asylum spreads out giant wings above the path to a minute black hole—the door—entrance thru crotch—

I went in—smelt funny—the halls again—up elevator—to a glass door on a Women's Ward—to Naomi—Two nurses buxom white—They led her out, Naomi stared—and I gaspt—She'd had a stroke—

Too thin, shrunk on her bones—age come to Naomi—now broken into white hair—loose dress on her skeleton—face sunk, old! withered—cheek of crone—

One hand stiff—heaviness of forties & menopause reduced by one heart stroke, lame now—wrinkles—a scar on her head, the lobotomy—ruin, the hand dipping downwards to death—

* * *

O Russian faced, woman on the grass, your long black hair is crowned with flowers, the mandolin is on your knees—

Communist beauty, sit here married in the summer among daisies, promised happiness at hand—

holy mother, now you smile on your love, your world is born anew, children run naked in the field spotted with dandelions,

they eat in the plum tree grove at the end of the meadow and find a cabin where a white-haired negro teaches the mystery of his rainbarrel—

blessed daughter come to America, I long to hear your voice again, remembering your mother's music, in the Song of the Natural Front—

O glorious muse that bore me from the womb, gave suck first mystic life & taught me talk and music, from whose pained head I first took Vision—

Tortured and beaten in the skull—What mad hallucinations of the damned that drive me out of my own skull to seek Eternity till I find Peace for Thee, O Poetry—and for all humankind call on the Origin

Death which is the mother of the universe!—Now wear your nakedness forever, white flowers in your hair, your marriage sealed behind the sky—no revolution might destroy that maidenhood—

O beautiful Garbo of my Karma—all photographs from 1920 in Camp Nicht-Gedeiget here unchanged—with all the teachers from Newark—Nor Elanor be gone, nor Max await his specter—nor Louis retire from this High School—

Back! You! Naomi! Skull on you! Gaunt immortality and revolution come—small broken woman—the ashen indoor eyes of hospitals, ward grayness on skin—

'Are you a spy?' I sat at the sour table, eyes filling with tears— 'Who are you? Did Louis send you?—The wires—'

in her hair, as she beat on her head—'I'm not a bad girl—don't murder me!—I hear the ceiling—I raised two children—'

Two years since I'd been there—I started to cry—She stared— nurse broke up the meeting a moment—I went into the bathroom to hide, against the toilet white walls

'The Horror' I weeping—to see her again—'The Horror'—as if she were dead thru funeral rot in—'The Horror!'

I came back she yelled more—they led her away—'You're not Allen—' I watched her face—but she passed by me, not looking—

Opened the door to the ward,—she went thru without a glance

back, quiet suddenly—I stared out—she looked old—the verge of the grave—'All the Horror!'

Another year, I left N.Y.—on West Coast in Berkeley cottage dreamed of her soul—that, thru life, in what form it stood in that body, ashen or manic, gone beyond joy—

near its death—with eyes—was my own love in its form, the Naomi, my mother on earth still—sent her long letter—& wrote hymns to the mad—Work of the merciful Lord of Poetry.

that causes the broken grass to be green, or the rock to break in grass—or the Sun to be constant to earth—Sun of all sunflowers and days on bright iron bridges—what shines on old hospitals—as on my yard—

Returning from San Francisco one night, Orlovsky in my room— Whalen in his peaceful chair—a telegram from Gene, Naomi dead—

Outside I bent my head to the ground under the bushes near the garage—knew she was better—

at last—not left to look on Earth alone—2 years of solitude—no one, at age nearing 60—old woman of skulls—once long-tressed Naomi of Bible—

or Ruth who wept in America—Rebecca aged in Newark— David remembering his Harp, now lawyer at Yale

or Svul Avrum—Israel Abraham—myself—to sing in the wilderness toward God—O Elohim!—so to the end—2 days after her death I got her letter—

Strange Prophecies anew! She wrote—'The key is in the window, the key is in the sunlight at the window—I have the key—Get married Allen don't take drugs—the key is in the bars, in the sunlight in the window.

Love,

your mother'

which is Naomi—

Hymmnn

In the world which He has created according to his will Blessed
    Praised
Magnified Lauded Exalted the Name of the Holy One Blessed is He!
In the house in Newark Blessed is He! In the madhouse Blessed is He!
    In the house of Death Blessed is He!
Blessed be He in homosexuality! Blessed be He in Paranoia! Blessed
    be He in the city! Blessed be He in the Book!

Blessed be He who dwells in the shadow! Blessed be He! Blessed be
     He!
Blessed be you Naomi in tears! Blessed be you Naomi in fears! Blessed
     Blessed Blessed in sickness!
Blessed be you Naomi in Hospitals! Blessed be you Naomi in solitude!
     Blest be your triumph! Blest be your bars! Blest be your last
     years' loneliness!
Blest be your failure! Blest be your stroke! Blest be the close of your eye!
     Blest be the gaunt of your cheek! Blest be your withered thighs!
Blessed be Thee Naomi in Death! Blessed be Death! Blessed be Death!
Blessed be He Who leads all sorrow to Heaven! Blessed be He in the
     end!
Blessed be He who builds Heaven in Darkness! Blessed Blessed Blessed
     be He! Blessed be He! Blessed be Death on us All!

III

Only to have not forgotten the beginning in which she drank cheap
     sodas in the morgues of Newark,
only to have seen her weeping on gray tables in long wards of her uni-
     verse
only to have known the weird ideas of Hitler at the door, the wires in
     her head, the three big sticks
rammed down her back, the voices in the ceiling shrieking out her
     ugly early lays for 30 years,
only to have seen the time-jumps, memory lapse, the crash of wars,
     the roar and silence of a vast electric shock,
only to have seen her painting crude pictures of Elevateds running
     over the rooftops of the Bronx
her brothers dead in Riverside or Russia, her lone in Long Island writ-
     ing a last letter—and her image in the sunlight at the window
'The key is in the sunlight at the window in the bars the key is in the
     sunlight,'
only to have come to that dark night on iron bed by stroke when the
     sun gone down on Long Island
and the vast Atlantic roars outside the great call of Being to its own
to come back out of the Nightmare—divided creation—with her head
     lain on a pillow of the hospital to die
—in one last glimpse—all Earth one everlasting Light in the familiar
     blackout—no tears for this vision—
But that the key should be left behind—at the window—the key in
     the sunlight—to the living—that can take
that slice of light in hand—and turn the door—and look back see

Creation glistening backwards to the same grave, size of universe,
size of the tick of the hospital's clock on the archway over the white
        door—

IV
O mother
what have I left out
O mother
what have I forgotten
O mother
farewell
with a long black shoe
farewell
with Communist Party and a broken stocking
farewell
with six dark hairs on the wen of your breast
farewell
with your old dress and a long black beard around the vagina
farewell
with your sagging belly
with your fear of Hitler
with your mouth of bad short stories
with your fingers of rotten mandolins
with your arms of fat Paterson porches
with your belly of strikes and smokestacks
with your chin of Trotsky and the Spanish War
with your voice singing for the decaying overbroken workers
with your nose of bad lay with your nose of the smell of the pickles of
        Newark
with your eyes
with your eyes of Russia
with your eyes of no money
with your eyes of false China
with your eyes of Aunt Elanor in an oxygen tent
with your eyes of starving India
with your eyes pissing in the park
with your eyes of America taking a fall
with your eyes of your failure at the piano
with your eyes of your relatives in California
with your eyes of Ma Rainey dying in an aumbulance
with your eyes of Czechoslovakia attacked by robots
with your eyes going to painting class at night in the Bronx

with your eyes of the killer Grandma you see on the horizon from the
    Fire-Escape
with your eyes running naked out of the apartment screaming into
    the hall
with your eyes being led away by policemen to an ambulance
with your eyes strapped down on the operating table
with your eyes with the pancreas removed
with your eyes of appendix operation
with your eyes of abortion
with your eyes of ovaries removed
with your eyes of shock
with your eyes of lobotomy
with your eyes of divorce
with your eyes of stroke
with your eyes alone
with your eyes
with your eyes
with your Death full of Flowers

V

Caw caw caw crows shriek in the white sun over grave stones in Long
    Island
Lord Lord Lord Naomi underneath this grass my halflife and my own
    as hers
caw caw my eye be buried in the same Ground where I stand in Angel
Lord Lord great Eye that stares on All and moves in a black cloud
caw caw strange cry of Beings flung up into sky over the waving trees
Lord Lord O Grinder of giant Beyonds my voice in a boundless field
    in Sheol
Caw caw the call of Time rent out of foot and wing an instant in the
    universe
Lord Lord an echo in the sky the wind through ragged leaves the roar
    of memory
caw caw all years my birth a dream caw caw New York the bus the
    broken shoe the vast highschool caw caw all Visions of the Lord
Lord Lord Lord caw caw caw Lord Lord Lord caw caw caw Lord

Paris, December 1957-New York, 1959

Message

Since we had changed
rogered spun worked
wept and pissed together
I wake up in the morning
with a dream in my eyes
but you are gone in NY
remembering me Good
I love you I love you
& your brothers are crazy
I accept their drunk cases
It's too long that I have been alone
It's too long that I've sat up in bed
without anyone to touch on the knee, man
or woman I don't care what anymore, I
want love I was born for I want you with me now
Ocean liners boiling over the Atlantic
Delicate steelwork of unfinished skyscrapers
Back end of the dirigible roaring over Lakehurst
Six women dancing together on a red stage naked
The leaves are green on all the trees in Paris now
I will be home in two months and look you in the eyes

Paris, May 1958

To Aunt Rose

Aunt Rose—now—might I see you
with your thin face and buck tooth smile and pain
              of rheumatism—and a long black heavy shoe
                     for your bony left leg
       limping down the long hall in Newark on the running carpet
                     past the black grand piano
                            in the day room
                                   where the parties were
                     and I sang Spanish loyalist songs
                            in a high squeaky voice
                                   (hysterical) the committee listening
                     while you limped around the room
                            collected the money—
Aunt Honey, Uncle Sam, a stranger with a cloth arm
              in his pocket
                     and huge young bald head
                            of Abraham Lincoln Brigade

—your long sad face
              your tears of sexual frustration
                     (what smothered sobs and bony hips
                            under the pillows of Osborne Terrace)
       —the time I stood on the toilet seat naked
              and you powdered my thighs with calamine
                     against the poison ivy—my tender
                            and shamed first black curled hairs
       what were you thinking in secret heart then
                     knowing me a man already—
       and I an ignorant girl of family silence on the thin pedestal
              of my legs in the bathroom—Museum of Newark.

                     Aunt Rose
       Hitler is dead, Hitler is in Eternity; Hitler is with
                     Tamburlane and Emily Brontë

Though I see you walking still, a ghost on Osborne Terrace
              down the long dark hall to the front door
       limping a little with a pinched smile
              in what must have been a silken
                     flower dress

51

welcoming my father, the Poet, on his visit to Newark
　　　—see you arriving in the living room
　　　　dancing on your crippled leg
　　　　and clapping hands his book
　　　　had been accepted by Liveright

Hitler is dead and Liveright's gone out of business
The Attic of the Past and *Everlasting Minute* are out of print
　　　　Uncle Harry sold his last silk stocking
　　　Claire quit interpretive dancing school
　　　Buba sits a wrinkled monument in Old
　　　　Ladies Home blinking at new babies

last time I saw you was the hospital
　　　pale skull protruding under ashen skin
　　　　blue veined unconscious girl
　　　　in an oxygen tent
　　　the war in Spain has ended long ago
　　　　Aunt Rose

Paris, June 1958

The Change: *Kyoto–Tokyo Express*

I
Black Magicians
Come home: the pink meat image
    black yellow image with
    ten fingers and two eyes
is gigantic already: the black
    curly pubic hair, the
    blind hollow stomach,
the silent soft open vagina
    rare womb of new birth
cock lone and happy to be home
                again
touched by hands by mouths,
    by hairy lips—

Close the portals of the festival?

Open the portals to what Is,
The mattress covered with sheets,
    soft pillows of skin,
long soft hair and delicate
    palms along the buttocks
    timidly touching,
waiting for a sign, a throb
    softness of balls, rough
    nipples alone in the dark
    met by a weird finger;
Tears allright, and laughter
    allright
I am that I am—

             Closed off from this
The schemes begin, roulette,
    brainwaves, bony dice,
    Stroboscope motorcycles
    Stereoscopic Scaly
        Serpents winding thru
           cloud spaces of
               what is not—

"... convoluted, lunging upon
a pismire, a conflagration, a—"

II
Shit! Intestines boiling in sand fire
        creep yellow brain cold sweat
        earth unbalanced vomit thru
        tears, snot ganglia buzzing
        the Electric Snake rising hypnotic
        shuffling metal-eyed coils
        whirling rings within wheels
        from asshole up the spine
        Acid in the throat the chest
        a knot trembling Swallow back
        the black furry ball of the great
        Fear

Oh!

The serpent in my bed pitiful
        crawling unwanted babes of
        snake covered with veins and pores
        breathing heavy frightened love
        metallic Bethlehem out the window
        the lost, the lost hungry
        ghosts here alive trapped
        in carpet rooms   How can I
        be sent to Hell
        with my skin and blood

Oh I remember myself so

Gasping, staring at dawn over
        lower Manhattan   the bridges
        covered with rust, the slime
        in my mouth & ass, sucking
        his cock like a baby crying Fuck
        me in my asshole   Make love
        to this rotten slave   Give me the
        power to whip & eat your heart
        I own your belly & your eyes
        I speak thru your screaming

mouth Black Mantra Fuck you
Fuck me Mother Brother Friend
old white haired creep shuddering in
the toilet slum bath floorboards—

Oh how wounded, how wounded, I
murder the beautiful chinese women

It will come on the railroad, beneath
the wheels, in drunken hate screaming
thru the skinny machine gun, it will
come out of the mouth of the pilot
the dry lipped diplomat, the hairy
teacher will come out of me
again shitting the meat out of
my ears on my cancer deathbed

Oh crying man crying woman
crying guerrilla shopkeeper
crying dysentery boneface on
the urinal street of the Self

Oh Negro beaten in the eye in my
home, oh black magicians
in white skin robes boiling the
stomachs of your children that
you do not die but shudder in
Serpent & worm shape forever
Powerful minds & superhuman
Roar of volcano & rocket in
Your bowels—

Hail to your fierce desire, your
Godly pride, my Heaven's gate
will not be closed until
we enter all—

All human shapes, all
trembling donkeys & apes, all
lovers turned to ghost
all achers on trains &
taxicab bodies sped away

from date with desire, old movies,
all who were refused—

All which was rejected, the
    leper-sexed hungry of
    nazi conventions, hollow
    cheeked arab marxists of Acco
    Crusaders dying of starvation
    in the Holy Land—

Seeking the Great Spirit of the
    Universe in Terrible Godly
    form, O suffering Jews
    burned in the hopeless fire
    O thin Bengali sadhus adoring
    Kali mother hung with
    nightmare skulls O Myself
    under her pounding
    feet!

Yes I am that worm soul under
    the heel of the daemon horses
    I am that man trembling to die
    in vomit & trance in bamboo
    eternities belly ripped by
    red hands of courteous
    chinamen kids—Come sweetly
    now back to my Self as I was—

Allen Ginsberg says this: I am
    a mass of sores and worms
    & baldness & belly & smell
    I am false Name the prey
    of Yamantaka Devourer of
    Strange dreams, the prey of
    radiation & Police Hells of Law

I am that I am I am the
    man & the Adam of hair in
    my loins   This is my spirit and
    physical shape I inhabit

this Universe Oh weeping
against what is my
own nature for now

Who would deny his own shape's
loveliness in his
dream moment of bed
Who sees his desire to be
horrible instead of Him

Who is, who cringes, perishes,
is reborn a red Screaming
baby? Who cringes before
that meaty shape in
Fear?

In this dream I am the Dreamer
and the Dreamed   I am
that I am Ah but I have
always known

oooh for the hate I have spent
in denying my image & cursing
the breasts of illusion—
Screaming at murderers, trembling
between their legs in fear of the
steel pistols of my mortality—

Come, sweet lonely Spirit, back
to your bodies, come great God
back to your only image, come
to your many eyes & breasts,
come thru thought and
motion up all your
arms the great gesture of
Peace & acceptance Abhaya
Mudra Mudra of fearlessness
Mudra of Elephant Calmed &
war-fear ended forever!

The war, the war on Man, the

war on woman, the ghost
assembled armies vanish in
their realms

Chinese American Bardo Thodols
all the seventy hundred hells from
Orleans to Algeria tremble
with tender soldiers weeping

In Russia the young poets rise
to kiss the soul of the revolution
in Vietnam the body is burned
to show the truth of only the
body in Kremlin & White House
the schemers draw back
weeping from their schemes—

In my train seat I renounce
my power, so that I do
live I will die

Over for now the Vomit, cut
up & pincers in the skull,
fear of bones, grasp
against man woman & babe.

Let the dragon of Death
come forth from his
picture in the whirling
white clouds' darkness

And suck dream brains &
claim these lambs for his
meat, and let him feed
and be other than I

Till my turn comes and I
enter that maw and change
to a blind rock covered
with misty ferns that

I am not all now

but a universe of skin and breath
     & changing thought and
     burning hand & softened
     heart in the old bed of
     my skin   From this single
     birth reborn that I am
     to be so—

My own Identity now nameless
     neither man nor dragon or
     God

but the dreaming Me full
     of physical rays' tender
     red moons in my belly &
     Stars in my eyes circling

And the Sun the Sun the
     Sun my visible father
     making my body visible
     thru my eyes!

Tokyo, July 18, 1963

Kral Majales

And the Communists have nothing to offer but fat cheeks and eye-
glasses and lying policemen
and the Capitalists proffer Napalm and money in green suitcases to
the Naked,
and the Communists create heavy industry but the heart is also heavy
and the beautiful engineers are all dead, the secret technicians con-
spire for their own glamour
in the Future, in the Future, but now drink vodka and lament the
Security Forces,
and the Capitalists drink gin and whiskey on airplanes but let Indian
brown millions starve
and when Communist and Capitalist assholes tangle the Just man is
arrested or robbed or had his head cut off,
but not like Kabir, and the cigarette cough of the Just man above the
clouds
in the bright sunshine is a salute to the health of the blue sky.
For I was arrested thrice in Prague, once for singing drunk on Narodni
street,
once knocked down on the midnight pavement by a mustached agent
who screamed out BOUZERANT,
once for losing my notebooks of unusual sex politics dream opinions,
and I was sent from Havana by plane by detectives in green uniform,
and I was sent from Prague by plane by detectives in Czechoslovakian
business suits,
Cardplayers out of Cézanne, the two strange dolls that entered Joseph
K's room at morn
also entered mine, and ate at my table, and examined my scribbles,
and followed me night and morn from the houses of lovers to the cafés
of Centrum—
And I am the King of May, which is the power of sexual youth,
and I am the King of May, which is industry in eloquence and action
in amour,
and I am the King of May, which is long hair of Adam and the Beard
of my own body
and I am the King of May, which is Kral Majales in the Czechoslova-
kian tongue,
and I am the King of May, which is old Human poesy, and 100,000
people chose my name,
and I am the King of May, and in a few minutes I will land at London
Airport,

and I am the King of May, naturally, for I am of Slavic parentage and
     a Buddhist Jew
who worships the Sacred Heart of Christ the blue body of Krishna the
     straight back of Ram
the beads of Chango the Nigerian singing Shiva Shiva in a manner
     which I have invented
and the King of May is a middleeuropean honor, mine in the XX
     century
despite space ships and the Time Machine, because I heard the voice
     of Blake in a vision,
and repeat that voice. And I am King of May that sleeps with teenag-
     ers laughing.
And I am the King of May, that I may be expelled from my Kingdom
     with Honor, as of old,
To show the difference between Caesar's Kingdom and the Kingdom
     of the May of Man—
And I am the King of May, tho' paranoid, for the Kingdom of May is
     too beautiful to last for more than a month—
and I am the King of May because I touched my finger to my forehead
     saluting
a luminous heavy girl trembling hands who said "one moment Mr.
     Ginsberg"
before a fat young Plainclothesman stepped between our bodies—I
     was going to England—
and I am the King of May, returning to see Bunhill Fields and walk on
     Hampstead Heath,
and I am the King of May, in a giant jetplane touching Albion's airfield
     trembling in fear
as the plane roars to a landing on the gray concrete, shakes & expels
     air,
and rolls slowly to a stop under the clouds with part of blue heaven
     still visible.
And *tho'* I am the King of May, the Marxists have beat me upon the
     street, kept me up all night in Police Station, followed me thru
     Springtime Prague, detained me in secret and deported me
     from our kingdom by airplane.
Thus I have written this poem on a jet seat in mid Heaven.

May 7, 1965

61

Who Be Kind To

Be kind to your self, it is only one
    and perishable
of many on the planet, thou art that
one that wishes a soft finger tracing the
    line of feeling from nipple to pubes—
one that wishes a tongue to kiss your armpit,
    a lip to kiss your cheek inside your
    whiteness thigh—
Be kind to yourself Harry, because unkindness
    comes when the body explodes
napalm cancer and the deathbed in Vietnam
is a strange place to dream of   trees
    leaning over and angry American faces
grinning with sleepwalk terror over your
    last eye—
Be kind to yourself, because the bliss of your own
    kindness will flood the police tomorrow,
because the cow weeps in the field and the
    mouse weeps in the cat hole—
Be kind to this place, which is your present
    habitation, with derrick and radar tower
    and flower in the ancient brook—
Be kind to your neighbor who weeps
    solid tears on the television sofa,
he has no other home, and hears nothing
    but the hard voice of telephones
Click, buzz, switch channel and the inspired
    melodrama disappears
and he's left alone for the night, he disappears
    in bed—
Be kind to your disappearing mother and
    father gazing out the terrace window
    as milk truck and hearse turn the corner
Be kind to the politician weeping in the galleries
    of Whitehall, Kremlin, White House
    Louvre and Phoenix City
aged, large nosed, angry, nervously dialing
    the bald voice box connected to
electrodes underground converging thru
    wires vaster than a kitten's eye can see

on the mushroom shaped fear-lobe under
    the ear of Sleeping Dr. Einstein
crawling with worms, crawling with worms, crawling
    with worms the hour has come—
Sick, dissatisfied, unloved, the bulky
    foreheads of Captain Premier President
    Sir Comrade Fear!
Be kind to the fearful one at your side
    Who's remembering the Lamentations
    of the bible
the prophecies of the Crucified Adam   Son
    of all the porters and char men of
                Bell   gravia—
Be kind to your self who weeps under
    the Moscow moon and hide your bliss hairs
    under raincoat and suede Levi's—
For this is the joy to be born, the kindness
    received thru strange eyeglasses on
    a bus thru Kensington,
the finger touch of the Londoner on your thumb,
    that borrows light from your cigarette,
the morning smile at Newcastle Central
    station, when longhair Tom blond husband
    greets the bearded stranger of telephones—
the boom bom that bounces in the joyful
    bowels as the Liverpool Minstrels of
    CavernSink
raise up their joyful voices and guitars
    in electric Afric hurrah
    for Jerusalem—
The saints come marching in, Twist &
    Shout, and Gates of Eden are named
    in Albion again
Hope sings a black psalm from Nigeria,
    and a white psalm echoes in Detroit
    and reechoes amplified from Nottingham to Prague
and a Chinese psalm will be heard, if we all
    live out our lives for the next 6 decades—
Be kind to the Chinese psalm in the red transistor
    in your breast—
Be kind to the Monk in the 5 Spot who plays
    lone chord-bangs on his vast piano

lost in space on a bench and hearing himself
    in the nightclub universe—
Be kind to the heroes that have lost their
    names in the newspaper
and hear only their own supplication for
    the peaceful kiss of sex in the giant
    auditoriums of the planet,
nameless voices crying for kindness in the orchestra,
screaming in anguish that bliss come true
    and sparrows sing another hundred years
    to white haired babes
and poets be fools of their own desire—O Anacreon
    and angelic Shelley!
Guide these new-nippled generations on space
    ships to Mars' next universe
The prayer is to man and girl, the only
    gods, the only lords of Kingdoms of
    Feeling, Christs of their own
    living ribs—
Bicycle chain and machine gun, fear sneer
    & smell cold logic of the Dream Bomb
have come to Saigon, Johannesburg,
    Dominica City, Phnom Penh, Pentagon
    Paris and Lhasa—
Be kind to the universe of Self that
    trembles and shudders and thrills
    in XX Century,
that opens its eyes and belly and breast
    chained with flesh to feel
    the myriad flowers of bliss
    that I Am to Thee—
A dream! a Dream! I don't want to be alone!
    I want to know that I am loved!
I want the orgy of our flesh, orgy
    of all eyes happy, orgy of the soul
    kissing and blessing its mortal-grown
    body,
orgy of tenderness beneath the neck, orgy of
    kindness to thigh and vagina
Desire given with meat hand
    and cock, desire taken with

mouth and ass, desire returned
    to the last sigh!
Tonite let's all make love in London
    as if it were 2001 the years
    of thrilling god—
And be kind to the poor soul that cries in
    a crack of the pavement because he
    has no body—
Prayers to the ghosts and demons, the
    lackloves of Capitals & Congresses
    who make sadistic noises
    on the radio—
Statue destroyers & tank captains, unhappy
    murderers in Mekong & Stanleyville,
That a new kind of man has come to his bliss
    to end the cold war he has borne
    against his own kind flesh
    since the days of the snake.

June 8, 1965

Wichita Vortex Sutra

I
Turn Right Next Corner
>*The Biggest Little Town in Kansas*
>>*Macpherson*
Red sun setting flat plains west streaked
>with gauzy veils, chimney mist spread
>around christmas-tree-bulbed refineries—aluminum
>>white tanks squat beneath
>winking signal towers' bright plane-lights,
>>>orange gas flares
>beneath pillows of smoke, flames in machinery—
>>transparent towers at dusk

In advance of the Cold Wave
>*Snow is spreading eastward to*
>>>*the Great Lakes*
>News Broadcast & old clarinets
>Watertower dome Lighted on the flat plain
>>car radio speeding acrost railroad tracks—

Kansas! Kansas! Shuddering at last!
>PERSON appearing in Kansas!
angry telephone calls to the University
Police dumbfounded leaning on
>their radiocar hoods
While Poets chant to Allah in the roadhouse Showboat!
Blue eyed children dance and hold thy Hand O aged Walt
>who came from Lawrence to Topeka to envision
>>Iron interlaced upon the city plain—
Telegraph wires strung from city to city O Melville!
>>Television brightening *thy rills of Kansas lone*
I come,
>lone man from the void, riding a bus
>hypnotized by red tail lights on the straight
>>>space road ahead—
>& the Methodist minister with cracked eyes
>>>leaning over the table
>>quoting Kierkegaard "death of God"
>>>a million dollars
>in the bank   owns all West Wichita

come to Nothing!
Prajnaparamita Sutra over coffee—Vortex
of telephone radio aircraft assembly framc ammunition
petroleum nightclub Newspaper streets illuminated by Bright
EMPTINESS—

Thy sins are forgiven, Wichita!
Thy lonesomeness annulled, O Kansas dear!
as the western Twang prophesied
thru banjo, when lone cowboy walked the railroad track
past an empty station toward the sun
sinking giant-bulbed orange down the box canyon—
Music strung over his back
and empty handed   singing on this planet earth
I'm a lonely Dog, O Mother!
Come, Nebraska, sing & dance with me—
Come lovers of Lincoln and Omaha,
hear my soft voice at last
As Babes need the chemical touch of flesh in pink infancy
lest they die Idiot returning to Inhuman—
Nothing—
So, tender lipt adolescent girl, pale youth,
give me back my soft kiss
Hold me in your innocent arms,
accept my tears as yours to harvest
equal   in nature to the Wheat
that made your bodies' muscular bones
broad shouldered, boy bicept—
from leaning on cows & drinking Milk
in Midwest Solitude—
No more fear of tenderness, much delight in weeping, ecstasy
in singing, laughter rises that confounds
staring Idiot mayors
and stony politicians eyeing
Thy breast,
O Man of America, be born!
Truth breaks through!
How big is the prick of the President?
How big is Cardinal Vietnam?
How little the prince of the FBI, unmarried all these years!
How big are all the Public Figures?
What kind of flesh hangs, hidden behind their Images?

                                        Approaching Salina,
Prehistoric excavation, *Apache Uprising*
                                in the drive-in theater
          Shelling Bombing Range   mapped in the distance,
          Crime Prevention Show, sponsor Wrigley's Spearmint
          Dinosaur Sinclair advertisement, glowing green—
South 9th Street lined with poplar & elm branch
                    spread over evening's tiny headlights—
          Salina Highschool's brick darkens Gothic
                    over a night-lit door—
          What wreaths of naked bodies, thighs and faces,
                    small hairy bun'd vaginas,
                    silver cocks, armpits and breasts
               moistened by tears
                          for 20 years, for 40 years?
Peking Radio surveyed by Luden's Coughdrops
               Attacks on the Russians & Japanese,
Big Dipper leaning above the Nebraska border,
                    handle down to the blackened plains,
          telephone-pole ghosts crossed
                              by roadside, dim headlights—
          dark night, & giant T-bone steaks,
               and in *The Village Voice*
          New Frontier Productions present
               Camp Comedy: *Fairies I Have Met.*
Blue highway lamps strung along the horizon east at Hebron
               Homestead National Monument near Beatrice—

Language, language
          black Earth-circle in the rear window,
                    no cars for miles along highway
               beacon lights on oceanic plain
          language, language
                    over Big Blue River
               chanting *La illaha el (lill) Allah hu*
               revolving my head to my heart like my mother
                    chin abreast at Allah
                    Eyes closed, blackness
vaster than midnight prairies,
                    Nebraskas of solitary Allah,
                    Joy, I am I

the lone One singing to myself
                        God come true—
              Thrills of fear.
              nearer than the vein in my neck—?
What if I opened my soul to sing to my absolute self
    Singing as the car crash chomped thru blood & muscle
                              tendon skull?
    What if I sang, and loosed the chords of fear brow?
          What exquisite noise wd
                        shiver my car companions?
          I am the Universe tonite
                    riding in all my Power riding
chauffeured thru my self by a long haired saint with eyeglasses
What if I sang till Students knew I was free
      of Vietnam, trousers, free of my own meat,
      free to die in my thoughtful shivering Throne?
          freer than Nebraska, freer than America—
          May I disappear
              in magic Joy-smoke! Pouf! reddish Vapor,
Faustus vanishes weeping & laughing
      under stars on Highway 77 between Beatrice & Lincoln—
      "Better not to move but let things be" Reverend Preacher?
                  We've all already disappeared!

Space highway open, entering Lincoln's ear
        ground to a stop Tracks Warning
                    Pioneer Boulevard—
        William Jennings Bryan sang
        Thou shalt not crucify mankind upon a cross of Gold!
                        O Baby Doe! Gold's
        Department Store hulks o'er 10th Street now
        —an unregenerate old fop who didn't want to be a monkey
        now's the Highest Perfect Wisdom dust
            and Lindsay's cry
            survives compassionate in the Highschool Anthology—
a giant dormitory brilliant on the evening plain
                        drifts with his memories—
There's a nice white door over there
                for me O dear!   on Zero Street.

                                February 15, 1966

69

II
Face the Nation
Thru Hickman's rolling earth hills
                   icy winter
                              gray sky   bare trees lining the road
        South to Wichita
                 you're in the Pepsi Generation   Signum enroute
Aiken Republican on the radio   60,000
        Northvietnamese troops now infiltrated but over 250,000
        South Vietnamese   armed men
                                   our Enemy—
                              Not Hanoi our enemy
                              Not China our enemy
                                The Viet Cong!
                         McNamara made a "bad guess"
"Bad Guess?" chorused the Reporters.
        Yes, no more than a Bad Guess, in 1962
                         "8000 American Troops handle the
                              Situation"
                              Bad Guess

        in 1954, 80% of the
              Vietnamese people would've voted for Ho Chi Minh
              wrote Ike   years later   *Mandate for Change*
                         A bad guess in the Pentagon
And the Hawks were guessing all along
                         Bomb China's 200,000,000
                   cried Stennis from Mississippi
                   I guess it was 3 weeks ago
        Holmes Alexander in Albuquerque Journal
              Provincial newsman
                    said I guess we better begin to do that Now,
              his typewriter clacking in his aged office
              on a side street   under Sandia Mountain?
                   Half the world away from China
Johnson got some bad advice   Republican Aiken sang
to the Newsmen over the radio
              The General guessed they'd stop infiltrating the South
                   if they bombed the North—
                         So I guess they bombed!
        Pale Indochinese boys came thronging thru the jungle
                   in increased numbers
                   to the scene of TERROR!

While the triangle-roofed Farmer's Grain Elevator
        sat quietly by the side of the road
                along the railroad track
American Eagle beating its wings over Asia
        million dollar helicopters
        a billion dollars worth of Marines
                who loved *Aunt Betty*
                Drawn from the shores and farms shaking
        from the high schools to the landing barge
        blowing the air thru their cheeks with fear
                in *Life* on Television
Put it this way on the radio
Put it this way in television language
                        Use the words
                                language, language:
                                        "A bad guess"

Put it this way in headlines
        Omaha World Herald—*Rusk Says Toughness
                        Essential For Peace*
Put it this way
        Lincoln Nebraska morning Star—
                        Vietnam War Brings Prosperity
Put it *this* way
        Declared McNamara   speaking language
                Asserted Maxwell Taylor
                General, Consultant to White House
        Viet Cong losses leveling up three five zero zero per month
                Front page testimony February '66
        Here in Nebraska same as Kansas same known in Saigon
                in Peking, in Moscow, same known
                by the youths of Liverpool three five zero zero
                the latest quotation in the human meat market—
                        Father I cannot tell a lie!

A black horse bends its head to the stubble
        beside the silver stream winding thru the woods
        by an antique red barn on the outskirts of Beatrice—
                        Quietness, quietness
                over this countryside
                        except for unmistakable signals on radio
                        followed by the honkytonk tinkle
                                of a city piano

to calm the nerves of taxpaying housewives of a Sunday morn.
                              Has anyone looked in the eyes of the dead?
U.S. Army recruiting service sign *Careers With A Future*
              Is anyone living to look for future forgiveness?
Water hoses frozen on the street, the
              Crowd gathered to see a strange happening garage—
                  Red flames on Sunday morning
                              in a quiet town!
Has anyone looked in the eyes of the wounded?
          Have we seen but paper faces, Life Magazine?
          Are screaming faces made of dots,
                  electric dots on Television—
                  fuzzy decibels registering
                  the mammal voiced howl
from the outskirts of Saigon to console model picture tubes
          in Beatrice, in Hutchinson, in El Dorado
                  in historic Abilene
                  O inconsolable!

              Stop, and eat more flesh.
"We will negotiate anywhere anytime"
                  said the giant President
      Kansas City Times 2/14/66: "Word reached U.S. authorities that
Thailand's leaders feared that in Honolulu Johnson might have tried
to persuade South Vietnam's rulers to ease their stand against negoti-
ating with the Viet Cong.
      American officials said these fears were groundless and Hum-
phrey was telling the Thais so."
                              AP dispatch
                  The last week's paper is Amnesia.

Three five zero zero is numerals
Headline language poetry, nine decades after Democratic Vistas
          and the Prophecy of the Good Gray Poet
          Our nation "of the fabled damned"
                              or else . . .
      Language, language
Ezra Pound the Chinese Written Character for truth
      defined as man standing by his word
          Word picture: forked creature
                              Man
          standing by a box, birds flying out

representing mouth speech
Ham Steak please waitress, in the warm café.
Different from a bad guess.
The war is language,
language abused
for Advertisement,
language used
like magic for power on the planet:
Black Magic language,
formulas for reality—
Communism is a 9 letter word
used by inferior magicians with
the wrong alchemical formula for transforming earth into gold
—funky warlocks operating on guesswork,
handmedown mandrake terminology
that never worked in 1956
for gray-domed Dulles,
brooding over at State,
that never worked for Ike who knelt to take
the magic wafer in his mouth
from Dulles' hand
inside the church in Washington:
Communion of bum magicians
congress of failures from Kansas & Missouri
working with the wrong equations
Sorcerer's Apprentices who lost control
of the simplest broomstick in the world:
Language
O longhaired magician come home take care of your dumb helper
before the radiation deluge floods your livingroom,
your magic errandboy's
just made a bad guess again
that's lasted a whole decade.

N B C B S U P A P I N S L I F E
Time Mutual presents
World's Largest Camp Comedy:
Magic In Vietnam—
reality turned inside out
changing its sex in the Mass Media
for 30 days, TV den and bedroom farce
Flashing pictures Senate Foreign Relations Committee room

Generals faces flashing on and off screen
                                mouthing language
State Secretary speaking nothing but language
McNamara declining to speak public language
        The President talking language,
                Senators reinterpreting language
        General Taylor *Limited Objectives*
                        Owls from Pennsylvania
                Clark's Face *Open Ended*
                        Dove's *Apocalypse*
                        Morse's hairy ears
        Stennis orating in Mississippi
                half billion chinamen crowding into the
                                polling booth,
        Clean shaven Gen. Gavin's image
                                imagining *Enclaves*
                Tactical Bombing the magic formula for
                a silver haired Symington:
Ancient Chinese apothegm:
                        Old in vain.
        Hawks swooping thru the newspapers
                talons visible
        wings outspread in the giant updraft of hot air
                        loosing their dry screech in the skies
                                over the Capitol
Napalm and black clouds emerging in newsprint
        Flesh soft as a Kansas girl's
                ripped open by metal explosion—
        three five zero zero   on the other side of the planet
                caught in barbed wire, fire ball
                bullet shock, bayonet electricity
        bomb blast terrific in skull & belly, shrapneled throbbing meat
While this American nation argues war:
                conflicting language, language
                        proliferating in airwaves
        filling the farmhouse ear, filling
                the City Manager's head in his oaken office
                the professor's head in his bed at midnight
                the pupil's head at the movies
                        blond haired, his heart throbbing with desire
                        for the girlish image bodied on the screen:
                        or smoking cigarettes

and watching Captain Kangaroo
that fabled damned of nations
prophecy come true—
Though the highway's straight,
dipping downward through low hills,
rising narrow on the far horizon
black cows browse in caked fields
ponds in the hollows lie frozen,
quietness.
Is this the land that started war on China?
This be the soil that thought Cold War for decades?
Are these nervous naked trees & farmhouses
the vortex
of oriental anxiety molecules
that've imagined   American Foreign Policy
and magick'd up paranoia in Peking
and curtains of living blood
surrounding far Saigon?
Are these the towns where the language emerged
from the mouths here
that makes a Hell of riots in Dominica
sustains the aging tyranny of Chiang in silent Taipeh city
Paid for the lost French war in Algeria
overthrew the Guatemalan polis in '54
maintaining United Fruit's banana greed
another thirteen years
for the secret prestige of the Dulles family lawfirm?

Here's Marysville—
a black railroad engine in the children's park,
at rest—
and the Track Crossing
with Cotton Belt flatcars
carrying autos west from Dallas
Delaware & Hudson gondolas filled with power stuff—
a line of boxcars far east as the eye can see
carrying battle goods to cross the Rockies
into the hands of rich longshoremen loading
ships on the Pacific—
Oakland Army Terminal lights
blue illumined all night now—
Crash of couplings and the great American train

moves on carrying its cushioned load of metal doom
Union Pacific linked together with your Hoosier Line
followed by passive Wabash
rolling behind
all Erie carrying cargo in the rear,
Central Georgia's rust colored truck proclaiming
The Right Way, concluding
the awesome poem writ by the train
across northern Kansas,
land which gave right of way
to the massing of metal meant for explosion
in Indochina—
Passing thru Waterville,
Electronic machinery in the bus humming prophecy—
paper signs blowing in cold wind,
mid-Sunday afternoon's silence in town
under frost-gray sky
that covers the horizon—
That the rest of earth is unseen,
an outer universe invisible,
Unknown except thru
language
airprint
magic images
or prophecy of the secret
heart the same
in Waterville as Saigon one human form:
When a woman's heart bursts in Waterville
a woman screams equal in Hanoi—
On to Wichita to prophesy! O frightful Bard!
into the heart of the Vortex
where anxiety rings
the University with millionaire pressure,
lonely crank telephone voices sighing in dread,
and students waken trembling in their beds
with dreams of a new truth warm as meat,
little girls suspecting their elders of murder
committed by remote control machinery,
boys with sexual bellies aroused
chilled in the heart by the mailman
with a letter from an aging white haired General
Director of selection for service in Deathwar

all this black language
                writ by machine!
                O hopeless Fathers and Teachers
          in Hué   do you know
                          the same woe too?

I'm an old man now, and a lonesome man in Kansas
          but not afraid
                to speak my lonesomeness in a car,
                because not only my lonesomeness
                      it's Ours, all over America,
                                  O tender fellows—
                      & spoken lonesomeness is Prophecy
                in the moon 100 years ago or in
                          the middle of Kansas now.
          It's not the vast plains mute our mouths
                          that fill at midnite with ecstatic language
                      when our trembling bodies hold each other
                          breast to breast on a mattress—
                Not the empty sky that hides
                              the feeling from our faces
                nor our skirts and trousers that conceal
                      the bodylove emanating in a glow of beloved skin,
                          white smooth abdomen down to the hair
                                      between our legs,
          It's not a God that bore us that forbid
                our Being, like a sunny rose
                          all red with naked joy
                between our eyes & bellies, yes
All we do is for this frightened thing
                we call Love, want and lack—
          fear that we aren't the one whose body could be
                beloved of all the brides of Kansas City,
                kissed all over by every boy of Wichita—
          O but how many in their solitude weep aloud like me—
                On the bridge over Republican River
                      almost in tears to know
                              how to speak the right language—
                on the frosty broad road
                          uphill between highway embankments
                I search for the language
                          that is also yours—

almost all our language has been taxed by war.
Radio antennae high tension
     wires ranging from Junction City across the plains—
highway cloverleaf sunk in a vast meadow
        lanes curving past Abilene
          to Denver filled with old
              heroes of love—
      to Wichita where McClure's mind
        burst into animal beauty
        drunk, getting laid in a car
           in a neon misted street
          15 years ago—
to Independence where the old man's still alive
who loosed the bomb that's slaved all human consciousness
     and made the body universe a place of fear—
Now, speeding along the empty plain,
    no giant demon machine
      visible on the horizon
but tiny human trees and wooden houses at the sky's edge
   I claim my birthright!
     reborn forever as long as Man
        in Kansas or other universe—Joy
   reborn after the vast sadness of War Gods!
A lone man talking to myself, no house in the brown vastness to hear,
   imaging the throng of Selves
     that make this nation one body of Prophecy
        languaged by Declaration as Pursuit of
        Happiness!
I call all Powers of imagination
   to my side in this auto to make Prophecy,
           all Lords
   of human kingdoms to come
Shambu Bharti Baba naked covered with ash
    Khaki Baba fat-bellied mad with the dogs
Dehorahava Baba who moans Oh how wounded, How wounded
   Sitaram Onkar Das Thakur who commands
      give up your desire
Satyananda who raises two thumbs in tranquillity
   Kali Pada Guha Roy whose yoga drops before the void
     Shivananda who touches the breast and says OM
Srimata Krishnaji of Brindaban who says take for your guru

William Blake the invisible father of English visions
Sri Ramakrishna master of ecstasy eyes
　　　half closed who only cries for his mother
Chaitanya arms upraised singing & dancing his own praise
　　　merciful Chango judging our bodies
　　　　　Durga-Ma covered with blood
　　　　　　　destroyer of battlefield illusions
　　　　　million-faced Tathagata gone past suffering
Preserver Harekrishna returning in the age of pain
Sacred Heart my Christ acceptable
　　　　　Allah the Compassionate One
　　　　　　　　Jaweh Righteous One
　　　　　all Knowledge-Princes of Earth-man, all
ancient Seraphim of heavenly Desire, Devas, yogis
　　　　　& holymen I chant to—
　　　　　　　　Come to my lone presence
　　　　　　　　　　into this Vortex named Kansas,
I lift my voice aloud,
　　　make Mantra of American language now,
　　　　　　I here declare the end of the War!
　　　　　　　　Ancient days' Illusion!—
　　　and pronounce words beginning my own millennium.
Let the States tremble,
　　　let the Nation weep,
　　　　　let Congress legislate its own delight
　　　　　　　let the President execute his own desire—
this Act done by my own voice,
　　　　　　nameless Mystery—
published to my own senses,
　　　　　　blissfully received by my own form
approved with pleasure by my sensations
　　manifestation of my very thought
　　accomplished in my own imagination
　　　　　all realms within my consciousness fulfilled
60 miles from Wichita
　　　　　near El Dorado,
　　　　　The Golden One,
in chill earthly mist
　　houseless brown farmland plains rolling heavenward
　　　　　　　　　in every direction
one midwinter afternoon Sunday called the day of the Lord—

Pure Spring Water gathered in one tower
                    where Florence is
                              set on a hill,
                    stop for tea & gas

Cars passing their messages along country crossroads
              to populaces cement-networked on flatness,
                                   giant white mist on earth
         and a Wichita Eagle-Beacon headlines
         "Kennedy Urges Cong Get Chair in Negotiations"
The War is gone,
         Language emerging on the motel news stand,
                                   the right magic
              Formula, the language known
     in the back of the mind before, now in black print
                                   daily consciousness
Eagle News Services Saigon—
         Headline Surrounded Vietcong Charge Into Fire Fight
              the suffering not yet ended
                              for others
              The last spasms of the dragon of pain
                         shoot thru the muscles
                    a crackling around the eyeballs
                    of a sensitive yellow boy by a muddy wall
Continued from page one   area
              after the Marines killed 256 Vietcong captured 31
              ten day operation Harvest Moon last December
                                   Language language
         U.S. Military Spokesmen
                         Language language
                                   Cong death toll
         has soared to 100 in First Air Cavalry
         Division's Sector of
                         Language language
                    Operation White Wing near Bong Son
Some of the
         Language language
                    Communist
                                   Language language soldiers
charged so desperately
              they were struck with six or seven bullets before they fell
         Language Language M 60 Machine Guns

Language language in La Drang Valley
the terrain is rougher infested with leeches and scorpions
The war was over several hours ago!
Oh at last again the radio opens
blue Invitations!
Angelic Dylan singing across the nation
"When all your children start to resent you
Won't you come see me, Queen Jane?"
His youthful voice making glad
the brown endless meadows
His tenderness penetrating aether,
soft prayer on the airwaves,
Language language, and sweet music too
even unto thee,
hairy flatness!
even unto thee
despairing Burns!

Future speeding on swift wheels
straight to the heart of Wichita!
Now radio voices cry population hunger world
of unhappy people
waiting for Man to be born
O man in America!
you certainly smell good
the radio says
passing mysterious families of winking towers
grouped round a quonset-hut on a hillock—
feed storage or military fear factory here?
Sensitive City, Ooh! Hamburger & Skelley's Gas
lights feed man and machine,
Kansas Electric Substation aluminum robot
signals thru thin antennae towers
above the empty football field
at Sunday dusk
to a solitary derrick that pumps oil from the unconscious
working night & day
& factory gas-flares edge a huge golf course
where tired businessmen can come and play—
Cloverleaf, Merging Traffic East Wichita turnoff
McConnell Airforce Base
nourishing the city—

Lights rising in the suburbs
Supermarket Texaco brilliance starred
                    over streetlamp vertebrae on Kellogg,
              green jeweled traffic lights
                 confronting the windshield,
Centertown ganglion entered!
                    Crowds of autos moving with their lightshine,
                 signbulbs winking in the driver's eyeball—
      The human nest collected, neon lit,
                              and sunburst signed
                 for business as usual, except on the Lord's Day—
Redeemer Lutheran's three crosses lit on the lawn
                          reminder of our sins
and Titsworth offers insurance on Hydraulic
by De Voors Guard's Mortuary for outmoded bodies
                       of the human vehicle
             which no Titsworth of insurance will customize for resale—
So home, traveler, past the newspaper language factory
          under Union Station railroad bridge on Douglas
       to the center of the Vortex, calmly returned
            to Hotel Eaton—
Carry Nation began the war on Vietnam here
                    with an angry smashing ax
                          attacking Wine—
       Here fifty years ago, by her violence
began a vortex of hatred that defoliated the Mekong Delta—
       Proud Wichita! vain Wichita
             cast the first stone!—
                    That murdered my mother
              who died of the communist anticommunist psychosis
                    in the madhouse one decade long ago
complaining about wires of masscommunication in her head
                 and phantom political voices in the air
                       besmirching her girlish character.
       Many another has suffered death and madness
                    in the Vortex from Hydraulic
                          to the end of 17th—enough!
The war is over now—
       Except for the souls
                 held prisoner in Niggertown
still pining for love of your tender white bodies O children of Wichita!

February 14, 1966

City Midnight Junk Strains

for Frank O'Hara

Switch on lights yellow as the sun
                        in the bedroom . . .
The gaudy poet dead   Frank O'Hara's bones
                  under the cemetery grass
An emptiness at 8 P.M. in the Cedar Bar
        Throngs of drunken
                guys talking about paint
    & lofts, and Pennsylvania youth.
              Kline attacked by his heart
& chattering Frank
            stopped forever—
    Faithful drunken adorers, mourn.
             The busfare's a nickel more
past his old apartment 9th Street by the park.
Delicate Peter loved his praise,
        I wait for the things he says
                    about me—
    Did he think me an Angel
        as angel I am still talking into earth's microphone willy nilly
    –to come back as words ghostly hued
                   by early death
      but written so bodied
             mature in another decade.
Chatty prophet
        of yr own loves, personal
        memory feeling fellow
      Poet of building-glass
I see you walking you said with your tie
        flopped over your shoulder   in the wind down 5th Ave
          under the handsome breasted workmen
            on their scaffolds ascending Time
              & washing the windows of Life
–off to a date with martinis & a blond
         beloved poet far from home
         –with thee and Thy sacred Metropolis
      in the enormous bliss   of a long afternoon
      where death is the shadow
             cast by Rockefeller Center

                    over your intimate street.
Who were you, black suited, hurrying to meet,
        Unsatisfied one?
                        Unmistakable,
                            Darling date
For the charming solitary   young poet with a big cock
                    who could fuck you all night long
                        till you never came,
        trying your torture on his   obliging fond body
        eager to satisfy god's whim that made you
                Innocent,   as you are.
I tried   your boys and found them ready
        sweet and amiable
            collected gentlemen
                with large sofa apartments
        lonesome to please   for pure language;
and you mixed with money
                because you knew enough language to be rich
                    if you wanted your walls to be empty—
Deep philosophical terms dear Edwin Denby serious as Herbert Read
        with silvery hair   announcing your dead gift
to the grave crowd   whose historic op art   frission was
the new sculpture your big blue wounded body made in the Universe
        when you went away   to Fire Island for the weekend
    tipsy with a family of decade-olden friends

Peter stares out the window   at robbers
            the Lower East Side   distracted in Amphetamine
I stare into my head   & look for your / broken roman nose
        your wet mouth-smell of martinis
                & a big artistic tipsy kiss.
    40's only half a life   to have filled
                with so many fine parties and evenings'
                interesting drinks together with one
                    faded friend or new
                    understanding social cat . . .
I want to be there in your garden party in the clouds
                all of us naked
strumming our harps and reading each other   new poetry
    in the boring celestial
                Friendship Committee Museum.
You're in a bad mood?

Take an Aspirin.
         In the Dumps?
                  I'm falling asleep
                           safe in your thoughtful arms.
Someone uncontrolled by History would have to own Heaven,
                                    on earth as it is.
I hope you satisfied your childhood love
      Your puberty fantasy   your sailor punishment on your knees
                                 your mouth-suck
Elegant insistency
            on the honking self-prophetic Personal
            as Curator of funny emotions to the mob,
Trembling One, whenever possible. I see New York thru your eyes
      and hear of one funeral a year nowadays—
                        from Billie Holiday's time
         appreciated more and more
a common ear
                  for our deep gossip.

July 29, 1966

Wales Visitation

White fog lifting & falling on mountain-brow
    Trees moving in rivers of wind
                The clouds arise
  as on a wave, gigantic eddy lifting mist
    above teeming ferns exquisitely swayed
                along a green crag
    glimpsed thru mullioned glass in valley raine—

Bardic, O Self, Visitacione, tell naught
  but what seen by one man in a vale in Albion,
    of the folk, whose physical sciences end in Ecology,
        the wisdom of earthly relations,
    of mouths & eyes interknit ten centuries visible
      orchards of mind language manifest human,
  of the satanic thistle that raises its horned symmetry
  flowering above sister grass-daisies' pink tiny
        bloomlets angelic as lightbulbs—

Remember 160 miles from London's symmetrical thorned tower
    & network of TV pictures flashing bearded your Self
  the lambs on the tree-nooked hillside this day bleating
  heard in Blake's old ear, & the silent thought of Wordsworth in eld
                Stillness
  clouds passing through skeleton arches of Tintern Abbey—
    Bard Nameless as the Vast, babble to Vastness!

All the Valley quivered, one extended motion, wind
        undulating on mossy hills
  a giant wash that sank white fog delicately down red runnels
        on the mountainside
  whose leaf-branch tendrils moved asway
      in granitic undertow down—
and lifted the floating Nebulous upward, and lifted the arms of the trees
    and lifted the grasses an instant in balance
      and lifted the lambs to hold still
  and lifted the green of the hill, in one solemn wave

A solid mass of Heaven, mist-infused, ebbs thru the vale,
  a wavelet of Immensity, lapping gigantic through Llanthony Valley,
the length of all England, valley upon valley under Heaven's ocean

tonned with cloud-hang,
—Heaven balanced on a grassblade.
Roar of the mountain wind slow, sigh of the body,
One Being on the mountainside stirring gently
Exquisite scales trembling everywhere in balance,
one motion thru the cloudy sky-floor shifting on the million feet of
daisies,
one Majesty the motion that stirred wet grass quivering
to the farthest tendril of white fog poured down
through shivering flowers on the mountain's head—

No imperfection in the budded mountain,
Valleys breathe, heaven and earth move together,
daisies push inches of yellow air, vegetables tremble,
grass shimmers green
sheep speckle the mountainside, revolving their jaws with empty eyes,
horses dance in the warm rain,
tree-lined canals network live farmland,
blueberries fringe stone walls on hawthorn'd hills,
pheasants croak on meadows haired with fern —

Out, out on the hillside, into the ocean sound, into delicate gusts of wet
air,
Fall on the ground, O great Wetness, O Mother, No harm on your body!
Stare close, no imperfection in the grass,
each flower Buddha-eye, repeating the story,
myriad-formed—
Kneel before the foxglove raising green buds, mauve bells drooped
doubled down the stem trembling antennae,
& look in the eyes of the branded lambs that stare
breathing stockstill under dripping hawthorn—
I lay down mixing my beard with the wet hair of the mountainside,
smelling the brown vagina-moist ground, harmless,
tasting the violet thistle-hair, sweetness—
One being so balanced, so vast, that its softest breath
moves every floweret in the stillness on the valley floor,
trembles lamb-hair hung gossamer rain-beaded in the grass,
lifts trees on their roots, birds in the great draught
hiding their strength in the rain, bearing same weight,

Groan thru breast and neck, a great Oh! to earth heart
Calling our Presence together

The great secret is no secret
            Senses fit the winds,
                Visible is visible,
rain-mist curtains wave through the bearded vale,
            gray atoms wet the wind's kabbala
Crosslegged on a rock in dusk rain,
            rubber booted in soft grass, mind moveless,
        breath trembles in white daisies by the roadside,
                Heaven breath and my own symmetric
Airs wavering thru antlered green fern
drawn in my navel, same breath as breathes thru Capel-Y-Ffn,
            Sounds of Aleph and Aum
                    through forests of gristle,
        my skull and Lord Hereford's Knob equal,
                        All Albion one.

What did I notice? Particulars! The
            vision of the great One is myriad—
        smoke curls upward from ashtray,
            house fire burned low,
The night, still wet & moody black heaven
                    starless
            upward in motion with wet wind.

July 29, 1967 (LSD)—August 3, 1967 (London)

Please Master

Please master can I touch your cheek
please master can I kneel at your feet
please master can I loosen your blue pants
please master can I gaze at your golden haired belly
please master can I gently take down your shorts
please master can I have your thighs bare to my eyes
please master can I take off my clothes below your chair
please master can I kiss your ankles and soul
please master can I touch lips to your hard muscle hairless thigh
please master can I lay my ear pressed to your stomach
please master can I wrap my arms around your white ass
please master can I lick your groin curled with blonde soft fur
please master can I touch my tongue to your rosy asshole
please master may I pass my face to your balls,
please master, please look into my eyes,
please master order me down on the floor,
please master tell me to lick your thick shaft
please master put your rough hands on my bald hairy skull
please master press my mouth to your prick-heart
please master press my face into your belly, pull me slowly strong
        thumbed
till your dumb hardness fills my throat to the base
till I swallow & taste your delicate flesh-hot prick barrel veined Please
Master push my shoulders away and stare in my eye, & make me bend
        over the table
please master grab my thighs and lift my ass to your waist
please master your hand's rough stroke on my neck your palm down
        my backside
please master push me up, my feel on chairs, till my hole feels the
        breath of your spit and your thumb stroke
please master make me say Please Master Fuck me now Please
Master grease my balls and hairmouth with sweet vaselines
please master stroke your shaft with white creams
please master touch your cock head to my wrinkled self-hole
please master push it in gently, your elbows enwrapped round my
        breast
your arms passing down to my belly, my penis you touch w/ your
        fingers
please master shove it in me a little, a little, a little,
please master sink your droor thing down my behind

& please master make me wiggle my rear to eat up the prick trunk
till my asshalfs cuddle your thighs, my back bent over,
till I'm alone sticking out, your sword stuck throbbing in me
please master pull out and slowly roll into the bottom
please master lunge it again, and withdraw to the tip
please please master fuck me again with your self, please fuck me
       Please
Master drive down till it hurts me the softness the
Softness please master make love to my ass, give body to center, &
       fuck me for good like a girl,
tenderly clasp me please master I take me to thee,
& drive in my belly your selfsame sweet heat-rood
you fingered in solitude Denver or Brooklyn or fucked in a maiden in
       Paris carlots
please master drive me thy vehicle, body of love dops, sweat fuck
body of tenderness, Give me your dog fuck faster
please master make me go moan on the table
Go moan O please master do fuck me like that
in your rhythm thrill-plunge & pull-back bounce & push down
till I loosen my asshole a dog on the table yelping with terror delight
       to be loved
Please master call me a dog, an ass beast, a wet asshole,
& fuck me more violent, my eyes hid with your palms round my skull
& plunge down in a brutal hard lash thru soft drip-fish
& throb thru five seconds to spurt out your semen heat
over & over, bamming it in while I cry out your name I do love you
please Master.

May 1968

On Neal's Ashes

Delicate eyes that blinked blue Rockies all ash
nipples, Ribs I touched w/my thumb are ash
mouth my tongue touched once or twice all ash
bony cheeks soft on my belly are cinder, ash
earlobes & eyelids, youthful cock tip, curly pubis
breast warmth, man palm, high school thigh,
baseball bicept arm, asshole anneal'd to silken skin
     all ashes, all ashes again.

August 1968

Memory Gardens

covered with yellow leaves
     in morning rain

—Quel Deluge
          he threw up his hands
               & wrote the Universe dont exist
                    & died to prove it.

Full Moon over Ozone Park
          Airport Bus rushing thru dusk to
                         Manhattan,
Jack the Wizard in his
                    grave at Lowell
for the first nite—
That Jack thru whose eyes I
          saw
     smog glory light
          gold over Mannahatta's spires
     will never see these
          chimneys smoking
anymore over statues of Mary
          in the graveyard

Black misted canyons
          rising over the bleak
                    river
Bright doll-like ads
          for Esso Bread—
Replicas multiplying beards
          Farewell to the Cross—
Eternal fixity, the big headed
          wax painted Buddha doll
               pale resting incoffined—

Empty-skulled New
          York streets
Starveling phantoms
          filling city—
Wax dolls walking park
                    Ave,

Light gleam in eye glass
Voice echoing thru Microphones
Grand Central Sailor's
        arrival 2 decades later
            feeling melancholy—
Nostalgia for Innocent World
        War II—
A million corpses running
      across 42d street
Glass buildings rising higher
          transparent
             aluminum—
artificial trees, robot sofas,
        Ignorant cars—
One Way Street to Heaven.

       *

Gray Subway Roar

A wrinkled brown faced fellow
        with swollen hands
leans to the blinking plate glass
      mirroring white poles, the heavy car
      sways on tracks uptown to Columbia—
Jack no more'll step off at Penn Station
      anonymous erranded, eat sandwich
      & drink beer near New Yorker Hotel or walk
under the shadow of Empire State.
Didn't we stare at each other length of the car
      & read headlines in faces thru Newspaper Holes?
Sexual cocked & horny bodied young, look
      at beauteous Rimbaud & Sweet Jenny
        riding to class from Columbus Circle.
"Here the kindly dopefiend lived."

and the rednecked sheriff beat the longhaired
        boy on the ass.
—103d street Broadway, me & Hal abused for sidewalk
        begging twenty-five years ago.
Can I go back in time & lay my head on a teenage
        belly upstairs on 110th Street?

or step off the iron car with Jack
        at the blue-tiled Columbia sign?
at last the old brown station where I had
a holy vision's been rebuilt, clean ceramic
over the scum & spit & come of quarter century.

                    *

Flying to Maine in a trail of black smoke
Kerouac's obituary conserves *Time*'s
                Front Paragraphs—
Empire State in Heaven Sun Set Red,
            White mist in old October
over the billion trees of Bronx—
                There's too much to see—
Jack saw sun set red over Hudson horizon
            Two three decades back
thirtynine fortynine fiftynine
                sixtynine
John Holmes pursed his lips,
                    wept tears.
Smoke plumed up from oceanside chimneys
            plane roars toward Montauk
                stretched in red sunset—
Northport, in the trees, Jack drank
        rot gut & made haiku of birds
            tweetling on his porch rail at dawn—
Fell down and saw Death's golden lite
        in Florida garden a decade ago.
Now taken utterly, soul upward,
            & body down in wood coffin
            & concrete slab-box.
I threw a kissed handful of damp earth
        down on the stone lid
                & sighed
    looking in Creeley's one eye,
Peter sweet holding a flower
    Gregory toothless bending his
            knuckle to Cinema machine—
and that's the end of the drabble tongued
            Poet who sounded his Kock-rup
                throughout the Northwest Passage.

Blue dusk over Saybrook, Holmes
            sits down to dine Victorian—
& *Time* has a ten-page spread on
         Homosexual Fairies!

Well, while I'm here I'll
         do the work—
and what's the Work?
        To ease the pain of living.
Everything else, drunken
          dumbshow.

October 22–29, 1969

Mind Breaths

Thus crosslegged on round pillow sat in Teton Space—
I breathed upon the aluminum microphone-stand a body's length
      away
I breathed upon the teacher's throne, the wooden chair with yellow
      pillow
I breathed further, past the sake cup half emptied by the breathing
      guru
Breathed upon the green sprigged thick-leaved plant in a flowerpot
Breathed upon the vast plateglass shining back th' assembled sitting
      Sangha in the meditation cafeteria
my breath thru nostril floated out to the moth of evening beating into
      window'd illumination
breathed outward over aspen twigs trembling September's top yellow
      leaves twilit at mountain foot
breathed over the mountain, over snowpowdered crags ringed under
      slow-breathed cloud-mass white spumes
windy across Tetons to Idaho, gray ranges under blue space swept
with delicate snow flurries, breaths Westward
mountain grass trembling in tiny winds toward Wasatch
Breezes south late autumn in Salt Lake's wooden temple streets,
white salt dust lifted swirling by the thick leaden lake, dust carried up
      over Kennecott's pit onto the massive Unit Rig,
out towards Reno's neon, dollar bills skittering downstreet along the
      curb,
up into Sierras oak leaves blown down by fall cold chills
over peaktops snowy gales beginning,
a breath of prayer down on Kitkitdizze's horngreen leaves close to
      ground,
over Gary's tile roof, over temple pillar, tents and manzanita arbors in
      Sierra pine foothills—
a breath falls over Sacramento Valley, roar of wind down the sixlane
      freeway across Bay Bridge
uproar of papers floating over Montgomery Street, pigeons flutter
      down before sunset from Washington Park's white churchstee-
      ple—
Golden Gate waters whitecapped scudding out to Pacific spreads
over Hawaii a balmy wind thru Hotel palmtrees, a moist warmth
      swept over the airbase, a dank breeze in Guam's rotten Cus-
      toms shed,
clear winds breathe on Fiji's palm & coral shores, by wooden hotels

in Suva town flags flutter, taxis whoosh by Friday night's
    black promenaders under the rock & roll discotheque window
    upstairs beating with English neon—
on a breeze into Sydney, and across hillside grass where mushrooms
    lie low on Cow-Flops in Queensland, down Adelaide's alleys
    a flutter of music from Brian Moore's Dobro carried in the
    wind—
up thru Darwin Land, out Gove Peninsula green ocean breeze, clack
    of Yerkalla village song sticks by the trembling wave
Yea and a wind over mercurial waters of Japan North East, a hollow
    wooden gong echoes in Kyoto's temple hall below the grave-
    yard's wavy grass
A foghorn blowing in the China Sea, torrential rains over Saigon, bomb-
    ers float over Cambodia, visioned tiny from stone Avelokitesve-
    ra's many-faced towers Angkor Wat in windy night,
a puff of opium out of a mouth yellowed in Bangkok, a puff of hashish
    flowing thick out of a bearded saddhu's nostrils & eyes in Nim-
    tallah Burning Ghat,
wood smoke flowing in wind across Hooghly Bridge, incense wafted
    under the Bo Tree in Bodh Gaya, in Benares woodpiles burn at
    Manikarnika returning incensed souls to Shiva,
wind dallies in the amorous leaves of Brindaban, still air on the vast
    mosque floor above Old Delhi's alleyways,
wind blowing over Kausani town's stone wall, Himalayan peaktops
    ranged hundreds of miles along snowy horizon, prayer flags
    flutter over Almora's wood brown housetops,
trade winds carry dhows thru Indian Ocean to Mombasa or down to
    Dar 'Salaam's riverside sail port, palms sway & sailors wrapped
    in cotton sleep on log decks—
Soft breezes up thru Red Sea to Eilat's dry hotels, paper leaflets scat-
    ter by the Wailing Wall, drifting into the Sepulchre
Mediterranean zephyrs leaving Tel Aviv, over Crete, Lassithi Plains'
    windmills still turn the centuries near Zeus' birth cave
Piraeus wave-lashed, Venice lagoon's waters blown up over the floor
    of San Marco, Piazza flooded and mud on the marble porch,
    gondolas bobbing up & down choppy waters at the Zattere,
chill September fluttering thru Milan's Arcade, cold bones & over-
    coats flapping in St. Peter's Square,
down Appian Way silence by gravesites, stelae stolid on a lonely grass
    path, the breath of an old man laboring up road—
Across Scylla & Charybdis, Sicilian tobacco smoke wafted across the
    boat deck,

into Marseilles coalstacks black fumes float into clouds, steamer's
    white drift-spume down wind all the way to Tangier,
a breath of red-tinged Autumn in Provence, boats slow on the Seine,
    the lady wraps her cloak tight round her bodice on toppa Eiffel
    Tower's iron head—
across the Channel rough black-green waves, in London's Piccadilly
    beercans roll on concrete neath Eros' silver breast, the Sunday
    Times lifts and settles on wet fountain steps—
over Iona Isle blue day and balmy Inner Hebrides breeze, fog drifts
    across Atlantic,
Labrador white frozen blowing cold, down New York's canyons
    manila paper bags scurry toward Wall from Lower East side—
a breath over my Father's head in his apartment on Park Avenue Pat-
    erson,
a cold September breeze down from East Hill, Cherry Valley's maples
    tremble red,
out thru Chicago Windy City the vast breath of Consciousness dis-
    solves, smokestacks and autos drift expensive fumes ribboned
    across railroad tracks,
Westward, a single breath blows across the plains, Nebraska's fields
    harvested & stubble bending delicate in evening airs
up Rockies, from Denver's Cherry Creekbed another zephyr risen,
across Pike's Peak an icy blast at sunset, Wind River peaktops flowing
    toward the Tetons,
a breath returns vast gliding grass flats cow-dotted into Jackson Hole,
    into a corner of the plains,
up the asphalt road and mud parking lot, a breeze of restless Septem-
    ber, up wood stairways in the wind
into the cafeteria at Teton Village under the red tram lift
a calm breath, a silent breath, a slow breath breathes outward from
    the nostrils.

September 28, 1973

Ego Confession

I want to be known as the most brilliant man in America
Introduced to Gyalwa Karmapa heir of the Whispered Transmission
      Crazy Wisdom Practice Lineage
as the secret young wise man who visited him and winked anony-
      mously decade ago in Gangtok
Prepared the way for Dharma in America without mentioning
      Dharma—scribbled laughter
Who saw Blake and abandoned God
To whom the Messianic Fink sent messages darkest hour sleeping on
      steel sheets "somewhere in the Federal Prison system" Weath-
      ermen got no Moscow Gold
who went backstage to Cecil Taylor serious chat chord structure &
      Time in a nightclub
who fucked a rose-lipped rock star in a tiny bedroom slum watched
      by a statue of Vajrasattva—
and overthrew the CIA with a silent thought—
Old Bohemians many years hence in Viennese beergardens'll recall
his many young lovers with astonishing faces and iron breasts
gnostic apparatus and magical observation of rainbow-lit spiderwebs
extraordinary cooking, lung stew & Spaghetti a la Vongole and recipe
      for salad dressing 3 parts oil one part vinegar much garlic and
      honey a spoonful
his extraordinary ego, at service of Dharma and completely empty
unafraid of its own self's spectre
parroting gossip of gurus and geniuses famous for their reticence—
Who sang a blues made rock stars weep and moved an old black gui-
      tarist to laughter in Memphis—
I want to be the spectacle of Poesy triumphant over trickery of the
      world
Omniscient breathing its own breath thru War tear gas spy hallucina-
      tion
whose common sense astonished gaga Gurus and rich Artistes—
who called the Justice department & threaten'd to Blow the Whistle
Stopt Wars, turned back petrochemical Industries' Captains to grieve
      & groan in bed
Chopped wood, built forest houses & established farms
distributed monies to poor poets & nourished imaginative genius of
      the land
Sat silent in jazz roar writing poetry with an ink pen—
wasn't afraid of God or Death after his 48th year—

let his brains turn to water under Laughing Gas his gold molar pulled
        by futuristic dentists
Seaman knew ocean's surface a year
carpenter late learned bevel and mattock
son, conversed with elder Pound & treated his father gently
—All empty all for show, all for the sake of Poesy
to set surpassing example of sanity as measure for late generations
Exemplify Muse Power to the young avert future suicide
accepting his own lie & the gaps between lies with equal good humor
Solitary in worlds full of insects & singing birds all solitary
—who had no subject but himself in many disguises
some outside his own body including empty air-filled space forests &
        cities—
Even climbed mountains to create his mountain, with ice ax & cram-
        pons & ropes, over Glaciers—

San Francisco, October 1974

Don't Grow Old

I

Old Poet, Poetry's final subject glimmers months ahead
Tender mornings, Paterson roofs snowcovered
Vast
Sky over City Hall tower, Eastside Park's grass terraces & tennis courts
        beside Passaic River
Parts of ourselves gone, sister Rose's apartments, brown corridor'd
        high schools—
Too tired to go out for a walk, too tired to end the War
Too tired to save body
too tired to be heroic
The real close at hand as the stomach
liver pancreas rib
Coughing up gastric saliva
Marriages vanished in a cough
Hard to get up from the easy chair
Hands white   feet speckled   a blue toe   stomach big   breasts
        hanging thin
hair white on the chest
too tired to take off shoes and black sox

Paterson, January 12, 1976

II

He'll see no more Times Square
honkytonk movie marquees, bus stations at midnight
Nor the orange sun ball
rising thru treetops east toward New York's skyline
His velvet armchair facing the window will be empty
He won't see the moon over house roofs
or sky over Paterson's streets.

New York, February 26, 1976

III

Wasted arms, feeble knees
        80 years old, hair thin and white
                cheek bonier than I'd remembered—
head bowed on his neck, eyes opened
        now and then, he listened—
        I read my father Wordsworth's *Intimations of Immortality*
"*. . . trailing clouds of glory do we come*
        from God, who is our home . . ."
                "That's beautiful," he said, "but it's not true."

"When I was a boy, we had a house
        on Boyd Street, Newark—the backyard
                was a big empty lot full of bushes and tall grass,
        I always wondered what was behind those trees.
When I grew older, I walked around the block,
        and found out what was back there—
                it was a glue factory."

May 18, 1976

IV

Will that happen to me?
Of course, it'll happen to thee.

Will my arms wither away?
Yes yr arm hair will turn gray.

Will my knees grow weak & collapse?
Your knees will need crutches perhaps.

Will my chest get thin?
Your breasts will be hanging skin.

Where will go—my teeth?
You'll keep the ones beneath.

What'll happen to my bones?
They'll get mixed up with stones.

June 1976

Father Death Blues

Copyright © 1978 by Poetry Music Inc., Allen Ginsberg

Hey Father Death, I'm flying home
Hey poor man, you're all alone
Hey old daddy, I know where I'm going

Father Death, Don't cry any more
Mama's there, underneath the floor
Brother Death, please mind the store

Old Aunty Death   Don't hide your bones
Old Uncle Death   I hear your groans
O Sister Death   how sweet your moans

O Children Deaths go breathe your breaths
Sobbing breasts'll ease your Deaths
Pain is gone, tears take the rest

Genius Death   your art is done
Lover Death your body's gone
Father Death   I'm coming home

Guru Death your words are true
Teacher Death I do thank you
For inspiring me to sing this Blues

Buddha Death, I wake with you
Dharma Death, your mind is new
Sangha Death, we'll work it through

Suffering is what was born
Ignorance made me forlorn
Tearful truths I cannot scorn

Father Breath once more farewell
Birth you gave was no thing ill
My heart is still, as time will tell.

July 8, 1976 (Over Lake Michigan)

VI
Near the Scrap Yard my Father'll be Buried
Near Newark Airport my father'll be
Under a Winston Cigarette sign buried
On Exit 14 Turnpike NJ South
Through the tollgate Service Road 1 my father buried
Past Merchants Refrigerating concrete on the cattailed marshes
past the Budweiser Anheuser-Busch brick brewery
in B'Nai Israel Cemetery behind a green painted iron fence
where there used to be a paint factory and farms
where Pennick makes chemicals now
under the Penn Central power Station

transformers & wires, at the borderline
between Elizabeth and Newark, next to Aunt Rose
Gaidemack, near Uncle Harry Meltzer
one grave over from Abe's wife Anna my father'll be buried.

July 9, 1976

VII
What's to be done about Death?
Nothing, nothing
Stop going to school No. 6 Paterson, N.J., in 1937?
Freeze time tonight, with a headache, at quarter to 2 A.M.?
Not go to Father's funeral tomorrow morn?
Not go back to Naropa   teach Buddhist poetics all summer?
Not be buried in the cemetery near Newark Airport some day?

Paterson, July 11, 1976

Plutonian Ode

I

1 What new element before us unborn in nature? Is there a new thing
    under the Sun?
  At last inquisitive Whitman a modern epic, detonative, Scientific
    theme
  First penned unmindful by Doctor Seaborg with poisonous hand,
    named for Death's planet through the sea beyond Uranus
  whose chthonic ore fathers this magma-teared Lord of Hades, Sire of
    avenging Furies, billionaire Hell-King worshipped once
5 with black sheep throats cut, priest's face averted from underground
    mysteries in a single temple at Eleusis,
  Spring-green Persephone nuptialed to his inevitable Shade, Demeter
    mother of asphodel weeping dew,
  her daughter stored in salty caverns under white snow, black hail, gray
    winter rain or Polar ice, immemorable seasons before
  Fish flew in Heaven, before a Ram died by the starry bush, before the
    Bull stamped sky and earth
  or Twins inscribed their memories in cuneiform clay or Crab'd flood
10 washed memory from the skull, or Lion sniffed the lilac breeze in
    Eden—
  Before the Great Year began turning its twelve signs, ere constella-
    tions wheeled for twenty-four thousand sunny years
  slowly round their axis in Sagittarius, one hundred sixty-seven thou-
    sand times returning to this night

  Radioactive Nemesis were you there at the beginning black Dumb
    tongueless unsmelling blast of Disillusion?
  I manifest your Baptismal Word after four billion years
15 I guess your birthday in Earthling Night, I salute your dreadful pres-
    ence lasting majestic as the Gods,
  Sabaot, Jehova, Astapheus, Adonaeus, Elohim, Iao, Ialdabaoth, Aeon
    from Aeon born ignorant in an Abyss of Light,
  Sophia's reflections glittering thoughtful galaxies, whirlpools of star-
    spume silver-thin as hairs of Einstein!
  Father Whitman I celebrate a matter that renders Self oblivion!
  Grand Subject that annihilates inky hands & pages' prayers, old ora-
    tors' inspired Immortalities,
20 I begin your chant, openmouthed exhaling into spacious sky over
    silent mills at Hanford, Savannah River, Rocky Flats, Pantex,
    Burlington, Albuquerque

I yell thru Washington, South Carolina, Colorado, Texas, Iowa, New
    Mexico,
where nuclear reactors create a new Thing under the Sun, where Rock-
    well war-plants fabricate this death stuff trigger in nitrogen
    baths,
Hanger-Silas Mason assembles the terrified weapon secret by ten
    thousands, & where Manzano Mountain boasts to store
its dreadful decay through two hundred forty millennia while our
    Galaxy spirals around its nebulous core
25 I enter your secret places with my mind, I speak with your presence, I
    roar your Lion Roar with mortal mouth.
One microgram inspired to one lung, ten pounds of heavy metal dust
    adrift slow motion over gray Alps
the breadth of the planet, how long before your radiance speeds blight
    and death to sentient beings?
Enter my body or not I carol my spirit inside you, Unapproachable
    Weight,
O heavy heavy Element awakened I vocalize your consciousness to six
    worlds
30 I chant your absolute Vanity. Yeah monster of Anger birthed in fear O
    most
Ignorant matter ever created unnatural to Earth! Delusion of metal
    empires!
Destroyer of lying Scientists! Devourer of covetous Generals, Inciner-
    ator of Armies & Melter of Wars!
Judgment of judgments, Divine Wind over vengeful nations, Molester
    of Presidents, Death-Scandal of Capital politics! Ah civiliza-
    tions stupidly industrious!
Canker-Hex on multitudes learned or illiterate! Manufactured Spec-
    tre of human reason! O solidified imago of practitioners in
    Black Arts
35 I dare your Reality, I challenge your very being! I publish your cause
    and effect!
I turn the Wheel of Mind on your three hundred tons! Your name
    enters mankind's ear! I embody your ultimate powers!
My oratory advances on your vaunted Mystery! This breath dispels
    your braggart fears! I sing your form at last
behind your concrete & iron walls inside your fortress of rubber &
    translucent silicon shields in filtered cabinets and baths of
    lathe oil,
My voice resounds through robot glove boxes & ingot cans and echoes
    in electric vaults inert of atmosphere,

40 I enter with spirit out loud into your fuel rod drums underground on
    soundless thrones and beds of lead
  O density! This weightless anthem trumpets transcendent through
    hidden chambers and breaks through iron doors into the Infer-
    nal Room!
Over your dreadful vibration this measured harmony floats audible,
    these jubilant tones are honey and milk and wine-sweet water
Poured on the stone block floor, these syllables are barely groats I scat-
    ter on the Reactor's core,
I call your name with hollow vowels, I psalm your Fate close by, my
    breath near deathless ever at your side
45 to Spell your destiny, I set this verse prophetic on your mausoleum
    walls to seal you up Eternally with Diamond Truth! O doomed
    Plutonium.

II

The Bard surveys Plutonian history from midnight lit with Mercury
    Vapor streetlamps till in dawn's early light
he contemplates a tranquil politic spaced out between Nations'
    thought-forms proliferating bureaucratic
& horrific arm'd, Satanic industries projected sudden with Five Hun-
    dred Billion Dollar Strength
around the world same time this text is set in Boulder, Colorado
    before front range of Rocky Mountains
50 twelve miles north of Rocky Flats Nuclear Facility in United States on
    North America, Western Hemisphere
of planet Earth six months and fourteen days around our Solar Sys-
    tem in a Spiral Galaxy
the local year after Dominion of the last God nineteen hundred sev-
    enty eight
Completed as yellow hazed dawn clouds brighten East, Denver city
    white below
Blue sky transparent rising empty deep & spacious to a morning star
    high over the balcony
55 above some autos sat with wheels to curb downhill from Flatiron's
    jagged pine ridge,
sunlit mountain meadows sloped to rust-red sandstone cliffs above
    brick townhouse roofs
as sparrows waked whistling through Marine Street's summer green
    leafed trees.

III

This ode to you O Poets and Orators to come, you father Whit-
man as I join your side, you Congress and American
people,

you present meditators, spiritual friends & teachers, you O Master
of the Diamond Arts,

60 Take this wheel of syllables in hand, these vowels and consonants
to breath's end

take this inhalation of black poison to your heart, breathe out this
blessing from your breast on our creation

forests cities oceans deserts rocky flats and mountains in the Ten
Directions pacify with this exhalation,

enrich this Plutonian Ode to explode its empty thunder through
earthen thought-worlds

Magnetize this howl with heartless compassion, destroy this
mountain of Plutonium with ordinary mind and body
speech,

65 thus empower this Mind-guard spirit gone out, gone out, gone
beyond, gone beyond me, Wake space, so Ah!

July 14, 1978

White Shroud

I am summoned from my bed
To the Great City of the Dead
Where I have no house or home
But in dreams may sometime roam
Looking for my ancient room
A feeling in my heart of doom,
Where Grandmother aged lies
In her couch of later days
And my mother saner than I
Laughs and cries She's still alive.

I found myself again in the Great Eastern Metropolis,
wandering under Elevated Transport's iron struts—
many-windowed apartments walled the crowded Bronx road-way
under old theater roofs, masses of poor women shopping
in black shawls past candy store news stands, children skipped beside
grandfathers bent tottering on their canes. I'd descended
to this same street from blackened subways Sundays long ago,
tea and lox with my aunt and dentist cousin when I was ten.
The living pacifist David Dellinger walked at my right side,
he'd driven from Vermont to visit Catholic Worker
Tivoli Farm, we rode up North Manhattan in his car,
relieved the U.S. wars were over in the newspaper,
Television's frenzied dance of dots & shadows calmed—Now
older than our shouts and banners, we explored brick avenues
we lived in to find new residences, rent loft offices
or roomy apartments, retire our eyes & ears & thoughts.
Surprised, I passed the open Chamber where my Russian Jewish
Grandmother lay in her bed and sighed eating a little Chicken
soup or borscht, potato latkes, crumbs on her blankets, talking
Yiddish, complaining solitude abandoned in Old Folks House.
I realized I could find a place to sleep in the neighborhood, what
relief, the family together again, first time in decades!—
Now vigorous Middle aged I climbed hillside streets in West Bronx
looking for my own hot-water furnished flat to settle in,
close to visit my grandmother, read Sunday newspapers
in vast glassy Cafeterias, smoke over pencils & paper,
poetry desk, happy with books father'd left in the attic,
peaceful encyclopedia and a radio in the kitchen.
An old black janitor swept the gutter, street dogs sniffed red hydrants,

nurses pushed baby carriages past silent house fronts.
Anxious I be settled with money in my own place before
nightfall, I wandered tenement embankments overlooking
the pillared subway trestles by the bridge crossing Bronx River.
How like Paris or Budapest suburbs, far from Centrum
Left Bank junky doorstep tragedy intellectual fights
in restaurant bars, where a spry old lady carried her
Century Universal View camera to record Works
Progress Administration newspaper metropolis
double-decker buses in September sun near Broadway El,
skyscraper roofs upreared ten thousand office windows shining
electric-lit above tiny taxis street lamp'd in Mid-town
avenues' late-afternoon darkness the day before Christmas,
Herald Square crowds thronged past traffic lights July noon to lunch
Shop under Macy's department store awnings for dry goods
pause with satchels at Frankfurter counters wearing stylish straw
hats of the decade, mankind thriving in their solitudes in shoes.
But I'd strayed too long amused in the picture cavalcade,
Where was I living? I remembered looking for a house
& eating in apartment kitchens, bookshelf decades ago, Aunt
Rose's illness, an appendix operation, teeth braces,
one afternoon fitting eyeglasses first time, combing wet hair
back on my skull, young awkward looking in the high school mirror
photograph. The Dead look for a home, but here I was still alive.
    I walked past a niche between buildings with tin canopy
shelter from cold rain warmed by hot exhaust from subway gratings,
beneath which engines throbbed with pleasant quiet drone.
A shopping-bag lady lived in the side alley on a mattress,
her wooden bed above the pavement, many blankets and sheets,
Pots, pans, and plates beside her, fan, electric stove by the wall.
She looked desolate, white haired, but strong enough to cook and stare.
Passersby ignored her buildingside hovel many years,
a few businessmen stopped to speak, or give her bread or yogurt.
Sometimes she disappeared into state hospital back wards,
but now'd returned to her homely alleyway, sharp eyed, old
Cranky hair, half paralyzed, complaining angry as I passed.
I was horrified a little, who'd take care of such a woman,
familiar, half-neglected on her street except she'd weathered
many snows stubborn alone in her motheaten rabbit-fur hat.
She had tooth troubles, teeth too old, ground down like horse molars—
she opened her mouth to display her gorge—how can she live
with that, how eat I thought, mushroom-like gray-white horseshoe of

incisors she chomped with, hard flat flowers ranged around her gums.
Then I recognized she was my mother, Naomi, habiting
this old city-edge corner, older than I knew her before
her life diappeared. What are you doing here? I asked, amazed
she recognized me still, astounded to see her sitting up
on her own, chin raised to greet me mocking "I'm living alone,
you all abandoned me, I'm a great woman, I came here
by myself, I wanted to live, now I'm too old to take care
of myself, I don't care, what are you doing here?" I
was looking for a house, I thought, she has one, in poor
Bronx, needs someone to help her shop and cook, needs her children
     now,
I'm her younger son, walked past her alleyway by accident,
but here she is survived, sleeping at night awake on that
wooden platform. Has she an extra room? I noticed her cave
adjoined an apartment door, unpainted basement storeroom
facing her shelter in the building side. I could live here,
worst comes to worst, best place I'll find, near my mother in
our mortal life. My years of haunting continental city streets,
apartment dreams, old rooms I used to live in, still paid rent for,
key didn't work, locks changed, immigrant families occupied
my familiar hallway lodgings—I'd wandered downhill homeless
avenues, money lost, or'd come back to the flat—But couldn't
recognize my house in London, Paris, Bronx, by Columbia
library, downtown 8th Avenue near Chelsea Subway—
Those years unsettled—were over now, here I could live
forever, here have a home, with Naomi, at long last,
at long long last, my search was ended in this pleasant way,
time to care for her before death, long way to go yet,
lots of trouble her cantankerous habits, shameful blankets
near the street, tooth pots, dirty pans, half paralyzed irritable,
she needed my middle aged strength and worldly money knowledge,
housekeeping art. I can cook and write books for a living,
she'll not have to beg her medicine food, a new set of teeth
for company, won't yell at the world, I can afford a telephone,
after twenty-five years we could call up Aunt Edie in California,
I'll have a place to stay. "Best of all," I told Naomi
"Now don't get mad, you realize your old enemy Grandma's
still alive! She lives a couple blocks down hill, I just saw her,
like you!" My breast rejoiced, all my troubles over, she was
content, too old to care or yell her grudge, only complaining
her bad teeth. What long-sought peace!

Then glad of life I woke
in Boulder before dawn, my second story bedroom windows
Bluff Street facing East over town rooftops, I returned
from the Land of the Dead to living Poesy, and wrote
this tale of long lost joy, to have seen my mother again!
And when the ink ran out of my pen, and rosy violet
illumined city treetop skies above the Flatiron Front Range,
I went downstairs to the shady living room, where Peter Orlovsky
sat with long hair lit by television glow to watch
the sunrise weather news, I kissed him & filled my pen and wept.

October 5, 1983, 6:35 A.M.

Cosmopolitan Greetings

To Struga Festival Golden Wreath Laureates
& International Bards, 1986

Stand up against governments, against God.

Stay irresponsible.

Say only what we know & imagine.

Absolutes are coercion.

Change is absolute.

Ordinary mind includes eternal perceptions.

Observe what's vivid.

Notice what you notice.

Catch yourself thinking.

Vividness is self-selecting.

If we don't show anyone, we're free to write anything.

Remember the future.

Advise only yourself.

Don't drink yourself to death.

Two molecules clanking against each other require an observer to
become scientific data.

The measuring instrument determines the appearance of the phe-
nomenal world after Einstein.

The universe is subjective.

Walt Whitman celebrated Person.

We are observer, measuring instrument, eye, subject, Person.

Universe is Person.

Inside skull vast as outside skull.

Mind is outer space.

"Each on his bed spoke to himself alone, making no sound."

"First thought, best thought."

Mind is shapely, Art is shapely.

Maximum information, minimum number of syllables.

Syntax condensed, sound is solid.

Intense fragments of spoken idiom, best.

Consonants around vowels make sense.

Savor vowels, appreciate consonants.

Subject is known by what she sees.

Others can measure their vision by what we see.

Candor ends paranoia.

Kral Majales
June 25, 1986
Boulder, Colorado

Return of Kral Majales

This silver anniversary much hair's gone from my head and I am the
    King of May
And tho I am King of May my howls & proclamations present are
    banned by FCC on America's electric airwaves 6 A.M. to mid-
    night
So King of May I return through Heaven flying to reclaim my paper
    crown
And I am King of May with high blood pressure, diabetes, gout, Bell's
    palsy, kidneystones & calm eyeglasses
And wear the foolish crown of no ignorance no wisdom anymore no
    fear no hope in capitalist striped tie & Communist dungarees
No laughing matter the loss of the planet next hundred years
And I am the King of May returned with a diamond big as the uni-
    verse an empty mind
And I am the King of May lacklove bouzerant in Springtime with a
    feeble practice of meditation
And I am King of May Distinguished Brooklyn English Professor singing
All gone all gone all overgone all gone sky-high now old mind so Ah!

April 25, 1990

After Lalon

I
It's true I got caught in
                    the world
When I was young Blake
          tipped me off
Other teachers followed:
Better prepare for Death
Don't get entangled with
              possessions
That was when I was young,
          I was warned
Now I'm a Senior Citizen
and stuck with a million
              books
a million thoughts a million
              dollars a million
                          loves
How'll I ever leave my body?
Allen Ginsberg says, I'm
          really up shits creek

II
I sat at the foot of a
              Lover
    and he told me everything
Fuck off, 23 skidoo,
          watch your ass,
          watch your step
excercise, meditate, think
          of your temper—
Now I'm an old man and
          I won't live another
20 years maybe not another
              20 weeks,
maybe the next second I'll
          be carried off to
                    rebirth
          the worm farm, maybe it's
          already happened—
How should I know, says

Allen Ginsberg
Maybe I've been dreaming
        all along—

III
It's 2 A.M. and I got to
        get up early
and taxi 20 miles to satisfy
        my ambition—
How'd I get into this fix,
this workaholic show-
        biz meditation market?
If I had a soul I sold it
        for pretty words
If I had a body I used
        it up spurting my essence
If I had a mind it got
        covered with Love—
If I had a spirit I forgot
        when I was breathing
If I had speech it was
        all a boast
If I had desire it went
        out my anus
If I had ambitions to
        be liberated
how'd I get into this
        wrinkled person?
With pretty words, Love essences,
        breathing boasts, anal
        longings, famous crimes?
What a mess I am, Allen Ginsberg.

IV
Sleepless I stay up &
        think about my Death
—certainly it's nearer
        than when I was ten
                years old
and wonderd how big the
        universe was—
If I dont get some rest I'll die faster

If I sleep I'll lose my
                chance for salvation—
asleep or awake, Allen
        Ginsberg's in bed
                in the middle of the night.

V
        4 A.M.
Then they came for me,
        I hid in the toilet stall
They broke down the toilet door
        It fell in on an innocent boy
Ach the wooden door fell
        in on an innocent kid!
I stood on the bowl & listened,
        I hid my shadow,
they shackled the other and
        dragged him away
in my place—How long can
        I get away with this?
Pretty soon they'll discover
        I'm not there
They'll come for me again, where
        can I hide my body?
Am I myself or some one else
        or nobody at all?
Then what's this heavy flesh this
        weak heart leaky kidney?
Who's been doing time
        for 65 years
in this corpse? Who else went
        into ecstasy beside me?
Now it's all over soon,
        what good was all that come?
Will it come true? Will
        it really come true?

VI
I had my chance and lost it,
many chances & didn't
        take them seriously enuf.
Oh yes I was impressed, almost

went mad with fear
I'd lose the immortal chance,
    One lost it.
Allen Ginsberg warns you
    don't follow my path
    to extinction.

March 31, 1992

The Charnel Ground

... rugged and raw situations, and having accepted them as
part of your home ground, then some spark of sympathy or
compassion could take place. You are not in a hurry to leave
such a place immediately. You would like to face the facts,
realities of that particular world. ...

CHÖGYAM TRUNGPA, RINPOCHE

Upstairs Jenny crashed her car & became a living corpse, Jake sold
    grass, the white-bearded potbelly leprechaun silent climbed
    their staircase
Ex-janitor John from Poland averted his eyes, cheeks flushed with
    vodka, wine who knew what
as he left his groundfloor flat, refusing to speak to the inhabitant of
    Apt. 24
who'd put his boyfriend in Bellevue, calling police, while the artistic
    Buddhist composer
on sixth floor lay spaced out feet swollen with water, dying slowly of
    AIDS over a year—
The Chinese teacher cleaned & cooked in Apt. 23 for the homosexual
    poet who pined for his gymnast
thighs & buttocks— Downstairs th' old hippie flower girl fell drunk
    over the banister, smashed her jaw—
her son despite moderate fame cheated of rocknroll money, twenty
    thousand people in stadiums
cheering his tattooed skinhead murderous Hare Krishna vegetarian
    drum lyrics—
Mary born in the building rested on her cane, heavy-legged with heart
    failure on the second landing, no more able
to vacation in Caracas & Dublin— The Russian landlady's husband
    from concentration camp disappeared again—nobody men-
    tioned he'd died—
tenants took over her building for hot water, she couldn't add rent &
    pay taxes, wore a long coat hot days
alone & thin on the street carrying groceries to her crooked apartment
    silent—
One poet highschool teacher fell dead mysterious heart dysrhythmia,
    konked over
in his mother's Brooklyn apartment, his first baby girl a year old, wife
    stoical a few days—
their growling noisy little dog had to go, the baby cried—

Meanwhile the upstairs apartment meth head shot cocaine & yowled
    up and down
East 12th Street, kicked out of Christine's Eatery till police cornered
    him, 'top a hot iron steamhole
near Stuyvesant Town Avenue A telephone booth calling his deaf
    mother—sirens speed the way to Bellevue—
past whispering grass crack salesman jittering in circles on East 10th
    Street's
southwest corner where art yuppies come out of the overpriced Jap-
    anese Sushi Bar—& they poured salt into potato soup heart
    failure vats at KK's Polish restaurant
—Garbage piled up, nonbiodegradable plastic bags emptied by dia-
    betic sidewalk homeless
looking for returnable bottles recycled dolls radios half-eaten
    hamburgers—thrown-away Danish—
On 13th Street the notary public sat in his dingy storefront, driver's
    lessons & tax returns prepared on old metal desks—
Sunnysides crisped in butter, fries & sugary donuts passed over the
    luncheonette counter next door—
The Hispanic lady yelled at the rude African-American behind the
    Post Office window
"I waited all week my welfare check you sent me notice I was here
    yesterday
I want to see the supervisor bitch dont insult me refusing to look in—"
Closed eyes of Puerto Rican wino lips cracked skin red stretched out
on the pavement, naphtha backdoor open for the Korean family dry
    cleaners at the 14th Street corner—
Con Ed workmen drilled all year to bust electric pipes 6 feet deep in
    brown dirt
so cars bottlenecked wait minutes to pass the M14 bus stopped mid-
    road, heavy dressed senior citizens step down in red rubble
with Reduced Fare Program cards got from grey city Aging Depart-
    ment offices downtown up the second flight by elevators don't
    work—
News comes on the radio, they bomb Baghdad and the Garden of
    Eden again?
A million starve in Sudan, mountains of eats stacked on docks, local
    gangs & U.N.'s trembling bureaucrat officers sweat near the
    equator arguing over
wheat piles shoved by bulldozers—Swedish doctors ran out of
    medicine—The Pakistan taxi driver
says Salmon Rushdie must die, insulting the Prophet in fictions—

"No that wasn't my opinion, just a character talking like in a poem no
    judgment"—
"Not till the sun rejects you do I," so give you a quarter by the Catho-
    lic church 14th St. you stand half drunk
waving a plastic glass, flush-faced, live with your mother a wounded
    look on your lips, eyes squinting,
receding lower jaw sometimes you dry out in Bellevue, most days
    cadging dollars for sweet wine
by the corner where Plump Blindman shifts from foot to foot showing
    his white cane, rattling coins in a white paper cup some weeks
where girding the subway entrance construction sawhorses painted
    orange
guard steps underground—And across the street the NYCE bank
    machine cubicle door sign reads
Not in Operation as taxis bump on potholes asphalt mounded at the
    crossroad when red lights change green
& I'm on my way uptown to get a CAT scan liver biopsy visit the car-
    diologist,
account for high blood pressure, kidneystones, diabetes, misty eyes &
    dysesthesia—
feeling lack in feet soles, inside ankles, small of back, phallus head,
    anus—
Old age sickness death again come round in the wink of an eye—
High school youth the inside skin of my thighs was silken smooth tho
    nobody touched me there back then—
Across town the velvet poets takes Darvon N, Valium nightly, sleeps
    all day kicking methadone
between brick walls sixth floor in a room cluttered with collages &
    gold dot paper scraps covered
With words: "The whole point seems to be the idea of giving away the
    giver."

                                                        August 19, 1992

Death & Fame

When I die
I don't care what happens to my body
throw ashes in the air, scatter 'em in East River
bury an urn in Elizabeth New Jersey, B'nai Israel Cemetery
But I want a big funeral
St. Patrick's Cathedral, St. Mark's Church, the largest synagogue in
    Manhattan
First, there's family, brother, nephews, spry aged Edith stepmother
    96, Aunt Honey from old Newark,
Doctor Joel, cousin Mindy, brother Gene one eyed one ear'd, sister-
    in-law blonde Connie, five nephews, stepbrothers & sisters
    their grandchildren,
companion Peter Orlovsky, caretakers Rosenthal & Hale, Bill Morgan—
Next, teacher Trungpa Vajracharya's ghost mind, Gelek Rinpoche
    there, Sakyong Mipham, Dalai Lama alert, chance visiting
    America, Satchitananda Swami,
Shivananda Dehorahava Baba, Karmapa XVI, Dudjom Rinpoche,
    Katagiri & Suzuki Roshi's phantoms
Baker, Whalen, Daido Loori, Qwong, Frail White-haired Kapleau
    Roshis, Lama Tarchin—
Then, most important, lovers over half-century
Dozens, a hundred, more, older fellows bald & rich
young boys met naked recently in bed, crowds surprised to see each
    other, innumerable, intimate, exchanging memories
"He taught me to meditate, now I'm an old veteran of the thousand
    day retreat—"
"I played music on subway platforms, I'm straight but loved him he
    loved me"
"I felt more love from him at 19 than ever from anyone"
"We'd lie under covers gossip, read my poetry, hug & kiss belly to
    belly arms round each other"
"I'd always get into his bed with underwear on & by morning my skiv-
    vies would be on the floor"
"Japanese, always wanted take it up my bum with a master"
"We'd talk all night about Kerouac & Cassady sit Buddhalike then
    sleep in his captain's bed."
"He seemed to need so much affection, a shame not to make him
    happy"
"I was lonely never in bed nude with anyone before, he was so gentle
    my stomach

shuddered when he traced his finger along my abdomen nipple to
        hips—"
"All I did was lay back eyes closed, he'd bring me to come with mouth
        & fingers along my waist"
"He gave great head"
So there be gossip from loves of 1946, ghost of Neal Cassady commin-
        gling with flesh and youthful blood of 1997
and surprise—"You too? But I thought you were straight!"
"I am but Ginsberg an exception, for some reason he pleased me,"
"I forgot whether I was straight gay queer or funny, was myself, tender
        and affectionate to be kissed on the top of my head,
my forehead throat heart & solar plexus, mid-belly, on my prick, tick-
        led with his tongue my behind"
"I loved the way he'd recite 'But at my back always hear/ time's
        winged chariot hurrying near,' heads together, eye to eye, on
        a pillow—"
Among lovers one handsome youth straggling the rear
"I studied his poetry class, 17 year-old kid, ran some errands to his
        walk-up flat,
seduced me didn't want to, made me come, went home, never saw
        him again never wanted to . . . "
"He couldn't get it up but loved me," "A clean old man," "He made
        sure I came first"
This the crowd most surprised proud at ceremonial place of honor—
Then poets & musicians—college boys' grunge bands—age-old rock
        star Beatles, faithful guitar accompanists, gay classical conduc-
        tors, unknown high Jazz music composers, funky trumpeters,
        bowed bass & french horn black geniuses, folksinger fiddlers
        with dobro tambourine harmonica mandolin autoharp penny-
        whistles & kazoos
Next, artist Italian romantic realists schooled in mystic 60's India, late
        fauve Tuscan painter-poets, Classic draftsman Massachusetts
        surreal jackanapes with continental wives, poverty sketchbook
        gesso oil watercolor masters from American provinces
Then highschool teachers, lonely Irish librarians, delicate bibliophiles,
        sex liberation troops nay armies, ladies of either sex
"I met him dozens of times he never remembered my name I loved
        him anyway, true artist"
"Nervous breakdown after menopause, his poetry humor saved me
        from suicide hospitals"
"Charmant, genius with modest manners, washed sink dishes, my stu-
        dio guest a week in Budapest"

Thousands of readers, "Howl changed my life in Libertyville Illinois"
"I saw him read Montclair State Teachers College decided be a poet—"
"He turned me on, I started with garage rock sang my songs in Kansas
   City"
"Kaddish made me weep for myself & father alive in Nevada City"
"Father Death comforted me when my sister died Boston 1982"
"I read what he said in a newsmagazine, blew my mind, realized oth-
   ers like me out there"
Deaf & Dumb bards with hand signing quick brilliant gestures
Then Journalists, editors' secretaries, agents, portraitists & photogra-
   phy aficionados, rock critics, cultured laborors, cultural histo-
   rians come to witness the historic funeral
Super-fans, poetasters, aging Beatniks & Deadheads, autograph-
   hunters, distinguished paparazzi, intelligent gawkers
Everyone knew they were part of "History" except the deceased
who never knew exactly what was happening even when I was alive

February 22, 1997

Starry Rhymes

Sun rises east
Sun sets west
Nobody knows
What the sun knows best

North star north
Southern Cross south
Hold close the universe
In your mouth

Gemini high
Pleiades low
Winter sky
Begins to snow

Orion down
North Star up
Fiery leaves
Begin to drop

March 23, 1997 4:51 A.M.

PART TWO

Songs

September on Jessore Road

Rubato

Fm

Mil-lions of ba-bies watch-ing the skies

Bb

Bellies swollen, with big round eyes On

Eb

Jessore Road long bam-boo huts

Bb

No place to shit but sand channel ruts

Fm

Mil-lions of fath-ers in rain

Bb

Mil-lions of moth-ers in pain

Eb

Mil-lions of broth-ers in woe

Bb

Mil-lions of sis-ters no-where to go

Final Verse

Fm

Mil-lions of ba-bies in pain

Bb

Mil-lions of moth-ers in rain

Eb

Mil-lions of broth-ers in woe

Bb **Eb**

Mil-lions of child-ren no-where to go

September on Jessore Road

Millions of babies watching the skies
Bellies swollen, with big round eyes
On Jessore Road—long bamboo huts
Noplace to shit but sand channel ruts

Millions of fathers in rain
Millions of mothers in pain
Millions of brothers in woe
Millions of sisters nowhere to go

One Million aunts are dying for bread
One Million uncles lamenting the dead
Grandfather millions homeless and sad
Grandmother millions silently mad

Millions of daughters walk in the mud
Millions of children wash in the flood
A Million girls vomit & groan
Millions of families hopeless alone

Millions of souls Nineteenseventyone
homeless on Jessore road under gray sun
A million are dead, the millions who can
Walk toward Calcutta from East Pakistan

Taxi September along Jessore Road
Oxcart skeletons drag charcoal load
past watery fields thru rain flood ruts
Dung cakes on treetrunks, plastic-roof huts

Wet processions   Families walk
Stunted boys   big heads dont talk
Look bony skulls   & silent round eyes
Starving black angels in human disguise

Mother squats weeping & points to her sons
Standing thin legged   like elderly nuns
small bodied   hands to their mouths in prayer
Five months small food   since they settled there

on one floor mat   with a small empty pot
Father lifts up his hands at their lot
Tears come to their mother's eye
Pain makes mother Maya cry

Two children together   in palmroof shade
Stare at me   no word is said
Rice ration, lentils   one time a week
Milk powder for warweary infants meek

No vegetable money or work for the man
Rice lasts four days   eat while they can
Then children starve   three days in a row
and vomit their next food   unless they eat slow.

On Jessore road   Mother wept at my knees
Bengali tongue   cried mister Please
Identity card   torn up on the floor
Husband still waits   at the camp office door

Baby at play I was washing the flood
Now they won't give us any more food
The pieces are here in my celluloid purse
Innocent baby play   our death curse

Two policemen surrounded   by thousands of boys
Crowded waiting   their daily bread joys
Carry big whistles   & long bamboo sticks
to whack them in line   They play hungry tricks

Breaking the line   and jumping in front
Into the circle   sneaks one skinny runt
Two brothers dance forward   on the mud stage
The guards blow their whistles   & chase them in rage

Why are these infants   massed in this place
Laughing in play   & pushing for space
Why do they wait here so cheerful   & dread
Why this is the House where they give children bread

The man in the bread door   Cries & comes out
Thousands of boys & girls   Take up his shout

Is it joy? is it prayer?   "No more bread today"
Thousands of Children at once scream   "Hooray!"

Run home to tents   where elders await
Messenger children   with bread from the state
No bread more today! & no place to squat
Painful baby, sick shit he has got.

Malnutrition skulls thousands for months
Dysentery drains   bowels all at once
Nurse shows disease card   Enterostrep
Suspension is wanting   or else chlorostrep

Refugee camps   in hospital shacks
Newborn lay naked   on mothers' thin laps
Monkeysized week-old   Rheumatic babe eye
Gastroenteritis Blood Poison   thousands must die

September Jessore   Road rickshaw
50,000 souls   in one camp I saw
Rows of bamboo   huts in the flood
Open drains, & wet families waiting for food

Border trucks flooded, food cant get past,
American Angel machine   please come fast!
Where is Ambassador Bunker today?
Are his Helios machinegunning children at play?

Where are the helicopters of U.S. AID?
Smuggling dope in Bangkok's green shade.
Where is America's Air Force of Light?
Bombing North Laos all day and all night?

Where are the President's Armies of Gold?
Billionaire Navies   merciful Bold?
Bringing us medicine   food and relief?
Napalming North Vietnam   and causing more grief?

Where are our tears? Who weeps for this pain?
Where can these families go in the rain?
Jessore Road's children close their big eyes
Where will we sleep when Our Father dies?

Whom shall we pray to for rice and for care?
Who can bring bread to this shit flood foul'd lair?
Millions of children alone in the rain!
Millions of children weeping in pain!

Ring O ye tongues of the world for their woe
Ring out ye voices for Love we dont know
Ring out ye bells of electrical pain
Ring in the conscious American brain

How many children are we who are lost
Whose are these daughters we see turn to ghost?
What are our souls that we have lost care?
Ring out ye musics and weep if you dare—

Cries in the mud by the thatch'd house sand drain
Sleeps in huge pipes in the wet shit-field rain
waits by the pump well, Woe to the world!
whose children still starve   in their mothers' arms curled.

Is this what I did to myself in the past?
What shall I do Sunil Poet I asked?
Move on and leave them without any coins?
What should I care for the love of my loins?

What should we care for our cities and cars?
What shall we buy with our Food Stamps on Mars?
How many millions sit down in New York
& sup this night's table on bone & roast pork?

How many million beer cans are tossed
in Oceans of Mother? How much does She cost?
Cigar gasolines and   asphalt car dreams
Stinking the world and dimming star beams—

Finish the war in your breast   with a sigh
Come taste the tears   in your own Human eye
Pity us millions of phantoms you see
Starved in Samsara   on planet TV

How many millions of children die more
before our Good Mothers perceive the Great Lord?

How many good fathers pay tax to rebuild
Armed forces that boast   the children they've killed?

How many souls walk through Maya in pain
How many babes   in illusory rain?
How many families   hollow eyed lost?
How many grandmothers   turning to ghost?

How many loves who never get bread?
How many Aunts with holes in their head?
How many sisters skulls on the ground?
How many grandfathers   make no more sound?

How many fathers in woe
How many sons   nowhere to go?
How many daughters   nothing to eat?
How many uncles   with swollen sick feet?

Millions of babies in pain
Millions of mothers in rain
Millions of brothers in woe
Millions of children   nowhere to go

New York, November 14–16, 1971

Gospel Noble Truths

Gospel Noble Truths

Born in this world
You got to suffer
Everything changes
You got   no soul

Try to be gay
Ignorant   happy
You get the blues
You eat jellyroll

There is one Way
You take the high road
In your big Wheel
8 steps you fly

Look at the View
Right to horizon
Talk to the sky
Act like you talk

Work like the sun
Shine in your heaven
See what you done
Come down & walk

Sit   you sit down
Breathe when you breathe
Lie down   you lie down
Walk where you walk

Talk when you talk
Cry when you cry
Lie down   you lie down
Die when you die

Look when you look
Hear what you hear
Taste what you taste   here
Smell what you smell

Touch what you touch
Think what you think
Let go Let it go   Slow
Earth Heaven & Hell

Die when you die
Die when you die
Lie down   you lie down
Die when you die

New York Subway, October 17, 1975

Capitol Air

Capitol Air

I don't like the government where I live
I don't like dictatorship of the Rich
I don't like bureaucrats telling me what to eat
I don't like Police dogs sniffing round my feet

I don't like Communist Censorship of my books
I don't like Marxists complaining about my looks
I don't like Castro insulting members of my sex
Leftists insisting we got the mystic Fix

I don't like Capitalists selling me gasoline Coke
Multinationals burning Amazon trees to smoke
Big Corporation takeover media mind
I don't like the Top-bananas that're robbing Guatemala banks blind

I don't like K.G.B. Gulag concentration camps
I don't like the Maoists' Cambodian Death Dance
15 Million were killed by Stalin Secretary of Terror
He has killed our old Red Revolution for ever

I don't like Anarchists screaming Love Is Free
I don't like the C.I.A. they killed John Kennedy
Paranoiac tanks sit in Prague and Hungary
But I don't like counterrevolution paid for by the C.I.A.

Tyranny in Turkey or Korea Nineteen Eighty
I don't like Right Wing Death Squad Democracy
Police State Iran Nicaragua yesterday
Laissez-faire please Government keep your secret police offa me

I don't like Nationalist Supremacy White or Black
I don't like Narcs & Mafia marketing Smack
The General bullying Congress in his tweed vest
The President building up his Armies in the East & West

I don't like Argentine police Jail torture Truths
Government Terrorist takeover Salvador news
I don't like Zionists acting Nazi Storm Troop

Palestine Liberation cooking Israel into Moslem soup

I don't like the Crown's Official Secrets Act
You can get away with murder in the Government that's a fact
Security cops teargassing radical kids
In Switzerland or Czechoslovakia God Forbids

In America it's Attica in Russia it's Lubianka Wall
In China if you disappear you wouldn't know yourself at all
Arise Arise you citizens of the world use your lungs
Talk back to the Tyrants all they're afraid of is your tongues

Two hundred Billion dollars inflates World War
In United States every year They're asking for more
Russia's got as much in tanks and laser planes
Give or take Fifty Billion we can blow out everybody's brains

School's broke down 'cause History changes every night
Half the Free World nations are Dictatorships of the Right
The only place socialism worked was in Gdansk, Bud
The Communist world's stuck together with prisoners' blood

The Generals say they know something worth fighting for
They never say what till they start an unjust war
Iranian hostage Media Hysteria sucked
The Shah ran away with 9 Billion Iranian bucks

Kermit Roosevelt and his U.S. dollars overthrew Mossadegh
They wanted his oil then they got Ayatollah's dreck
They put in the Shah and they trained his police the Savak
All Iran was our hostage quarter-century That's right Jack

Bishop Romero wrote President Carter to stop
Sending guns to El Salvador's Junta so he got shot
Ambassador White blew the whistle on the White House lies
Reagan called him home cause he looked in the dead nuns' eyes

Half the voters didn't vote they knew it was too late
Newspaper headlines called it a big Mandate
Some people voted for Reagan eyes open wide
3 out of 4 didn't vote for him That's a Landslide

Truth may be hard to find but Falsehood's easy
Read between the lines our Imperialism is sleazy
But if you think the People's State is your Heart's Desire
Jump right back in the frying pan from the fire

The System the System in Russia & China the same
Criticize the System in Budapest lose your name
Coca Cola Pepsi Cola in Russia & China come true
Khrushchev yelled in Hollywood "We will bury You"

America and Russia want to bomb themselves Okay
Everybody dead on both sides   Everybody pray
All except the Generals in caves where they can hide
And fuck each other in the ass waiting for the next free ride

No hope Communism no hope Capitalism Yeah
Everybody's lying on both sides Nyeah nyeah nyeah
The bloody iron curtain of American Military Power
Is a mirror image of Russia's red Babel-Tower

Jesus Christ was spotless but was Crucified by the Mob
Law & Order Herod's hired soldiers did the job
Flowerpower's fine but innocence has got no Protection
The man who shot John Lennon had a Hero-worshipper's connection

The moral of this song is that the world is in a horrible place
Scientific Industry devours the human race
Police in every country armed with Tear Gas & TV
Secret Masters everywhere bureaucratize for you & me

Terrorists and police together build a lowerclass Rage
Propaganda murder manipulates the upperclass Stage
Can't tell the difference 'tween a turkey & a provocateur
If you're feeling confused the Government's in there for sure

Aware Aware wherever you are   No Fear
Trust your heart Don't ride your Paranoia dear
Breathe together with an ordinary mind
Armed with Humor Feed & Help Enlighten   Woe Mankind

Frankfurt-New York, December 15, 1980

PART THREE

Essays

Poetry, Violence, and the Trembling Lambs

or

Independence Day Manifesto

Recent history is the record of a vast conspiracy to impose one level of mechanical consciousness on mankind and exterminate all manifestations of that unique part of human sentience, identical in all men, which the individual shares with his Creator. The suppression of contemplative individuality is nearly complete.

The only immediate historical data that we can know and act on are those fed to our senses through systems of mass communication.

These media are exactly the places where the deepest and most personal sensitivities and confessions of reality are most prohibited, mocked, suppressed.

At the same time there is a crack in the mass consciousness of America—sudden emergence of insight into a vast national subconscious netherworld filled with nerve gases, universal death bombs, malevolent bureaucracies, secret police systems, drugs that open the door to God, ships leaving Earth, unknown chemical terrors, evil dreams at hand.

Because systems of mass communication can communicate only officially acceptable levels of reality, no one can know the extent of the secret unconscious life. No one in America can know what will happen. No one is in real control. America is having a nervous breakdown. Poetry is the record of individual insights into the secret soul of the individual and because all individuals are one in the eyes of their creator, into the soul of the world. The world has a soul. America is having a nervous breakdown. San Francisco is one of many places where a few individuals, poets, have had the luck and courage and fate to glimpse something new through the crack in mass consciousness; they have been exposed to some insight into their own nature, the nature of the governments, and the nature of God.

Therefore there has been great exaltation, despair, prophecy, strain, suicide, secrecy and public gaiety among the poets of the city. Those of the general populace whose individual perception is sufficiently weak to be formed by stereotypes of mass communication disapprove and deny the insight. The police and newspapers have moved in, mad movie manufacturers from Hollywood are at this moment preparing bestial stereotypes of the scene.

The poets and those who share their activities, or exhibit some sign of dress, hair, or demeanor of understanding, or hipness, are ridiculed. Those of us who have used certain benevolent drugs (marijuana) to alter our consciousness in order to gain insight are hunted down in the street by police. Peyote, an historic vision-producing agent, is prohibited on pain of arrest. Those who have used opiates and junk are threatened with permanent jail and death. To be a junky in America is like having been a Jew in Nazi Germany.

A huge sadistic police bureaucracy has risen in every state, encouraged by the central government, to persecute the illuminati, to brainwash the public with official lies about the drugs, and to terrify and destroy those addicts whose spiritual search has made them sick.

Deviants from the mass sexual stereotype, quietists, those who will not work for money, or fib and make arms for hire, or join armies in murder and threat, those who wish to loaf, think, rest in visions, act beautifully on their own, speak truthfully in public, inspired by Democracy—what is their psychic fate now in America? An America, the greater portion of whose economy is yoked to mental and mechanical preparations for war?

Literature expressing these insights has been mocked, misinterpreted, and suppressed by a horde of middlemen whose fearful allegiance to the organization of mass stereotype communication prevents them from sympathy (not only with their own inner nature but) with any manifestation of unconditioned individuality. I mean journalists, commercial publishers, book-review fellows, multitudes of professors of literature, etc., etc. Poetry is hated. Whole schools of academic criticism have risen to prove that human consciousness of unconditioned spirit is a myth. A poetic renaissance glimpsed in San Francisco has been responded to with ugliness, anger, jealousy, vitriol, sullen protestations of superiority.

And violence. By police, by customs officials, post-office employees, by trustees of great universities. By anyone whose love of power has led him to a position where he can push other people around over a difference of opinion—or vision.

The stakes are too great—an America gone mad with materialism, a police-state America, a sexless and soulless America prepared to battle the world in defense of a false image of its authority. Not the wild and beautiful America of the comrades of Walt Whitman, not the historic America of William Blake and Henry David Thoreau where the spiritual independence of each individual was an America, a universe, more huge and awesome than all the abstract bureaucracies and authoritative officialdoms of the world combined.

Only those who have entered the world of spirit know what a vast laugh there is in the illusory appearance of worldly authority. And all men at one time or other enter that Spirit, whether in life or death.

How many hypocrites are there in America? How many trembling lambs, fearful of discovery? What authority have we set up over ourselves, that we are not as we are? Who shall prohibit an art from being published to the world? What conspirators have power to determine our mode of consciousness, our sexual enjoyments, our different labors and our loves? What fiends determine our wars?

When will we discover an America that will not deny its own God? Who takes up arms, money, police, and a million hands to murder the consciousness of God? Who spits in the beautiful face of poetry which sings of the glory of God and weeps in the dust of the world?

ca. July 4, 1959

"When the Mode of the Music Changes
the Walls of the City Shake"

Trouble with conventional form (fixed line count and stanza form) is, it's too symmetrical, geometrical, numbered and pre-fixed—unlike to my own mind which has no beginning and end, nor fixed measure of thought (or speech—or writing) other than its own cornerless mystery—to transcribe the latter in a form most nearly representing its actual "occurrence" is my "method"—which requires the skill of freedom of composition—and which will lead poetry to the expression of the highest moments of the mindbody—mystical illumination—and its deepest emotion (through tears—love's all)—in the forms nearest to what it actually looks like (data of mystical imagery) and feels like (rhythm of actual speech and rhythm prompted by direct transcription of visual and other mental data)—plus not to forget the sudden genius-like imagination or fabulation of unreal and out of this world verbal constructions which express the true gaiety and excess of freedom—(and also by their nature express the first cause of the world) by means of spontaneous irrational juxtaposition of sublimely related fact, by the dentist drill singing against the piano music; or pure construction of imaginaries, hydrogen jukeboxes, in perhaps abstract images (made by putting together two things verbally concrete but disparate to begin with)—always bearing in mind, that one must verge on the unknown, write toward the truth hitherto unrecognizable of one's own sincerity, including the avoidable beauty of doom, shame and embarrassment, that very area of personal self-recognition (detailed individual is universal remember) which formal conventions, internalized, keep us from discovering in ourselves and others—For if we write with an eye to what the poem should be (has been), and do not get lost in it, we will never discover anything new about ourselves in the process of actually writing on the table, and we lose the chance to live in our works, and make habitable the new world which every man may discover in himself, if he lives—which is life itself, past present and future.

Thus the mind must be trained, i.e. let loose, freed—to deal with itself as it actually is, and not to impose on itself, or its poetic artifacts, an arbitrarily preconceived pattern (formal or subject)—and *all* patterns, unless discovered in the moment of composition—all remembered and *applied* patterns are by their very nature arbitrarily preconceived—no matter how wise and traditional—no matter what sum of inherited experience they represent—The only pattern of value or interest in poetry is the solitary, individual pattern peculiar to the poet's moment and the poem *discovered* in the mind and in the process of writing it out on the page, as notes, transcriptions,—reproduced in the fittest accurate form, at the time of composition. ("Time is the essence," says Kerouac.) It is this personal discovery which is of value to the poet and to the reader—and it is of course more, not less, communicable of actuality than a pattern chosen in advance, with matter poured into it arbitrarily to fit, which of course distorts and blurs the matter . . . Mind is shapely, art is shapely.

II

The amount of blather and built-in misunderstanding we've encountered—usually in the name of good taste, moral virtue or (at most presumptuous) civilized value—has been a revelation to me of the absolute bankruptcy of the academy in America today, or that which has set itself up as an academy for the conservation of literature. For the academy has been the enemy and Philistine host itself. For my works will be taught in the schools in 20 years, or sooner—it is already being taught for that matter—after the first screams of disgruntled mediocrity, screams which lasted 3 years before subsiding into a raped moan.

They should treat us, the poets, on whom they make their livings, more kindly while we're around to enjoy it. After all we are poets and novelists, not Martians in disguise trying to poison man's mind with anti-earth propaganda. Though to the more conformist of the lot this beat and Buddhist and mystic and poetic exploration may seem just that. And perhaps it is: "Any man who does not labor to make himself obsolete is not worth his salt."—Burroughs.

People take us too seriously and not seriously enough—nobody interested in what *we* mean—just a lot of bad journalism about beatniks parading itself as highclass criticism in what are taken by the mob to be the great journals of the intellect.

And the ignorance of the technical accomplishment and spiritual interests is disgusting. How often have I seen my own work related to Fearing and Sandburg, proletarian literature, the 1930s—by people who don't *connect* my long line with my own obvious reading: Crane's *Atlantis*, Lorca's *Poet in NY*, Biblical structures, psalms and lamentations, Shelley's high buildups, Apollinaire, Artaud, Mayakovsky, Pound, Williams and the American metrical tradition, the new tradition of measure. And Christopher Smart's *Rejoice in the Lamb*. And Melville's prose-poem *Pierre*. And finally the spirit and illumination of Rimbaud. Do I have to be stuck with Fearing (who's alright too) by phony critics whose only encounter with a long line has been anthology pieces in collections by Oscar Williams? By intellectual bastards and snobs and vulgarians and hypocrites who have never read Artaud's *Pour En Fini Avec Le Jugement de Dieu* and therefore wouldn't begin to know that this masterpiece which in 30 years will be as famous as *Anabasis* is the actual model of tone for my earlier writing? This is nothing but a raving back at the false Jews from Columbia who have lost memory of the *Shekinah* and are passing for middle class. Must I be attacked and condemned by these people, I who have heard Blake's own ancient voice recite me the "Sun-flower" a decade ago in Harlem? and who say I don't know about "poetic tradition"?

The only poetic tradition is the voice out of the burning bush. The rest is trash, and will be consumed.

If anybody wants a statement of values—it is this, that I am ready to die for poetry and for the truth that inspires poetry—and will do so in any case—as all men, whether they like it or no —. I believe in the American Church of Poetry.

And men who wish to die for anything less or are unwilling to die for anything except their own temporary skins are foolish and bemused by illusion and had better shut their mouths and break their pens until they are taught better by death—and I am sick to death of prophesying to a nation that hath no ears to hear the thunder of the wrath and joy to come—among the "fabled damned" of nations—and the money voices of ignoramuses.

We are in American poetry and prose still continuing the venerable tradition of compositional self exploration and I would say the time has not come, historically, for any effort but the first sincere attempts at discovering those natural structures of which we have been dreaming and speaking. Generalizations about these natural patterns may yet be made—time for the academies to consider this in all technical detail—the data, the poetry and prose, the classics of original form, have already been written or are about to be—there is much to learn from them and there may be generalizations possible which, for the uninitiated, the non-poets, may be reduced to "rules and instructions" (to guide attention to what is being done)—but the path to freedom of composition goes through the eternal gateless gate which if it has "form" has an indescribable one—images of which are however innumerable.

There is nothing to agree or disagree with in Kerouac's method—there is a statement of fact (1953) of the method, the conditions of experiment, which he was pursuing, what he thought about it, how he went about it. He actually did extend composition in that mode, the results are apparent, he's learned a great deal from it and so has America. As a proposed method of experiment, as a completed accomplishment, there is nothing to agree or disagree with, it is a fact—that's what he was interested in doing, that's what he did—he's only describing his interest (his passion) for the curious craftsman or critic or friend—so be it. Why get mad and say he's in "error"? There's no more error here than someone learning how to build a unicorn table by building one. He's found out (rare for a writer) *how* he really wants to write and he is writing that way, courteously explaining his way.

Most criticism is semantically confused on this point—should and shouldn't and art is and isn't—trying to tell people to do something other than that which they basically and intelligently want to do, when they are experimenting with something new to them (and actually in this case to U.S. literature).

I've had trouble with this myself, everybody telling me or implying that I shouldn't really write the way I do. What do they want, that I should write some other way I'm not interested in? Which is the very thing which doesn't interest me in their prose and poetry and makes it a long confused bore?—all arty and by inherited rule and no surprises no new invention—corresponding inevitably to their own dreary characters—because anyway most of them have no character and are big draggy minds that don't *know* and just argue from abstract shallow moral principles in the void? These people are all too abstract, when it comes down to the poetry facts of poetry,—and I have learned in the past 2 years that argument, explanation, letters, expostulation are all vain—nobody listens anyway (not only to what I say, to what I *mean*) they all have their own mental ax to grind. I've explained the prosodic structure of *Howl* as best I can, often, and I still read criticism, even favorable, that assumes that I am not interested in, have no, form—they just don't recognize any form but what they have heard about before and expect and what they want (they, most of them, being people who don't write poetry even and so have no idea what it involves and what beauty they're violating).—And it is also tiresome and annoying to hear Kerouac or myself or others "Beat" described because of our art as incoherent, we are anything but. After all.

But so far we have refused to make arbitrary abstract generalizations to satisfy a peculiar popular greed for banality. I perhaps lose some of this ground with this writing. I occasionally scream with exasperation (or giggles); this is usually an attempt to communicate with a blockhead. And Kerouac sometimes says "Wow" for joy. All this can hardly be called incoherence except by oververbal madmen who depend on longwinded defenses of their own bad prose for a livelihood.

The literary problems I wrote of above are explained at length in Dr. Suzuki's essay "Aspects of Japanese Culture" (*Evergreen Review*) and placed in their proper aesthetic context. Why should the art of spontaneity in the void be so, seem so, strange when applied in the U.S. prosepoetry context? Obviously a lack of intuitive spirit and/ or classical experience on the part of these provincial frauds who have set themselves up as conservators of tradition and attack our work.

A sort of philistine brainwashing of the public has taken place. How long the actual sense of the new poetry will take to filter down, thru the actual writing and unprejudiced sympathetic reading of it, is beyond my power to guess and at this point beyond my immediate hope. More people take their ideas from reviews, newspapers and silly scholarly magazines than they do from the actual texts.

The worst I fear, considering the shallowness of opinion, is that some of the poetry and prose may be taken too familiarly, and the ideas accepted in some dopey sociological platitudinous form—as perfectly natural ideas and perceptions which they are—and be given the same shallow treatment, this time sympathetic, as, until recently, they were given shallow unsympathy. That would be the very we of fame. The problem has been to communicate the very spark of life, and not some opinion about that spark. Most negative criticism so far has been fearful overanxious obnoxious opinionation about this spark—and most later "criticism" will equally dully concern itself with favorable opinions about that spark. And that's not art, that's not even criticism, that's just more dreary sparkless blah blah blah—enough to turn a poet's guts. A sort of cancer of the mind that assails people whose loves are eaten by their opinions, whose tongues are incapable of wild lovely thought, which is poetry.

The brainwashing will continue, though the work be found acceptable, and people will talk as emptily about the void, hipness, the drug high, tenderness, comradeship, spontaneous creativity, beat spiritual individuality and sacramentalism, as they have been talking about man's "moral destiny" (usually meaning a good job and full stomach and no guts and the necessity of heartless conformity and putting down your brother because of the inserviceability of love as against the legal discipline of tradition because of the unavailability of God's purity of vision and consequent souls angels—or anything else worthwhile). That these horrible monsters who do nothing but talk, teach, write crap and get in the way of poetry, have been accusing us, poets, of lack of "values" as they call it is enough to make me vow solemnly (for the second time) that pretty soon I'm going to stop even trying to communicate coherently to the majority of the academic, journalistic, mass media and publishing trade and leave them stew in their own juice of ridiculous messy ideas. SQUARES SHUT UP and LEARN OR GO HOME. But alas the square world will never and has never stopt bugging the hip muse.

That we have begun a revolution of literature in America, again, without meaning to, merely by the actual practice of poetry—this would be inevitable. No doubt we knew what we were doing.

Written: 1961

Author's Note: At this time my own poetry, Kerouac's prose and poetry, and Burroughs' work were subject to amazing attack—not openly critical denunciation by younger friends and older writers who might have been expected to show interested sympathy (Hollander, Podhoretz, Kazin, Hentoff, Rexroth, Simpson and Spender stick in memory, aside from *Time* and *Life* mags)—but also legal attack. Various censorships of Corso Kerouac Burroughs and myself and our works in *Chicago Review* and *Big Table*, as well as *Howl* and *Naked Lunch* trials, and New Directions' fear of publishing complete text of Kerouac's *Visions of Cody.*

I felt at the time the poetics would be triumphant, the texts permanent, my complaints exemplary—to set example to future generations what depression and inertia and hostility we had to plough thru instruct, cajole, admonish, plead with for possession of America's heart. Why? So as to leave a record of combat against native fascist militarization of U.S. soul. It seemed to me that the poetic critics, in so disowning the new open poetics and the freedom of mind, desire, imagination, were setting the mental stage for repression of political liberty in the long run—a political liberty that could only be defended by undaunted, free, bold humorous imagination, open field mentality, open field poetics, open field democracy. The closed forms of the older poetry, it seemed to me, were ostrich-head-in-sand-like. It seemed to me the breakthroughs of new poetry were social breakthroughs, that is, political in the long run.

I thought and still think that the bulwark of libertarian-anarchist-sexualized individual poems and prose created from that era to this day—under so much middle-class critical attack—were the mental bombs that would still explode in new kid generations even if censorship and authoritarian (moral majority) fundamentalist militarily-hierarchical "New Order" neoconservative fascistoid creep Reaganomics-type philistinism ever took over the nation. Which it nearly has. Thus the title—Poetics and Politics, out of Plato out of Pythagoras—continuation of gnostic—secret and politically suppressed—liberty of consciousness and art—old bohemian—tradition—thru the existence of exquisite paperbacks too many in print to be burned. The clock could never be turned back.

Prose Contribution to Cuban Revolution

I have been sitting in lovely club-bar across the street where Greek boys congregate, they are friendly and they make love between men like in Plato, the whole classic love scene preserved intact with no faggotry involved, a huge relief to find it's really true and good as an ideal, but for real. Though I find myself now shy and so except for a few not so satisfactory flings with boys I dug for cock but not really in love with, have not been very promiscuous or don't get too deep involved, but dig watching the scene and being in presence of men who are open, that is, where my feelings are not *queer* but something out of old human love story.

This will have to be long junk letter so might as well relax and get to the point that's bothering me, you maybe right now, jump in, what to do about politics, Cuba, human history, what I should do, what you are doing. I didn't know I was your monster that much, meaning in your respect and conscience, though that's what I've tried to be for a lot of people, that's the image I had of myself as poet-prophet friend on side of love and the Wild Good. That's the karma I wanted, to be saint. That's what I told Van Doren anyway and dreamed of myself; although wanting to get into heaven without paying ugly prices as of yore. Prophesy without death as a consequence, giggle into paradise, that was the dream Peter and I had together; that was the ideal mellow feeling I had respecting Kerouac and other heroes for me, Neal, Bill, including Huncke; and anybody that dug that scene with us. Already it's an exclusive club; and my measure at the time was the sense of personal genius and acceptance of all strangeness in people as their nobility; staying *out* of conflict and politics, staying with sort of Dostoyevskian-Shakespearean *know*, ken, of things as mortal, tearful, transient, sacred—not to join one side or other for an idea, however serious, realizing the relativity and limitation of all judgements and discriminations, relying on the angel of wide consciousness in us to always sympathize or empathize with anybody, even Hitler, because that's natural as in Whitman it's natural to be everybody at once, as it is in Dostoyevsky to understand the weirdness of everybody, even if it seems to conflict or lead to conflicts; wanting to stay sympathetic, even to Trilling, as to thieves or suicides or murderers. All this in the free atmosphere of US and appropriate to it, where we are not directly faced with threat of starve or extermination; except private deaths suicides faced and touched and for me shied away from. Now Bill and Jack were my monsters in that, that is they were the broad funny minds in which I recognized this sense of life, thru whose eyes I saw; Jack always telling me I was a "hairy loss," chiding my attempts to be vain, control moralities thru my mind, seeing in me vanities of wanting to Howl on stages and be hero, be famous, or be a leader or intellectual, be superior thru mind-intelligence, criticize, get involved in politics, which in his-my eyes is always vanity trying to have power and impress other people which finally leads to beg decisions and executions and unkindnesses and loss of the mortal empathy, i.e. if you take sides you make others enemies and can't see them any more; and you become like them, a limited identity. Well all this very simpatico and true in its way, except I did have this desire to be labor leader people's hero, that is, with my Jewish left wing atheist Russian background I even made a vow (not ever to be broken) on the ferryboat when I went to take entrance exam at Columbia, vow forever that if I succeeded in the scholarship test and got a chance I would never betray the ideal—to help the masses in their misery. At the time I was very political and just recovering from Spanish Civil War which obsessed me in Jersey age 11 or 13. First upset of this idealism I had, entering to study law as per plan of becoming pure Debs, was being mocked and shamed at my idea structure of the time by Lu. C. [Lucien Carr] in workman's cafeteria on 125 Street, where as a trembling Columbia intellectual, hardly "one of the roughs" I found I was actually so self-conscious and mental I was scared of the workmen in the cafeteria—that having to do with my complete inexperience of life and also sensitive homosexual virginity and general naiveté—scared that is, in sense of feeling strange, an outsider, superior-inferior, I couldn't have a conversation with any of the soup eaters—I was obviously too gauche to fit in any way, and yet I had this image of myself as a *leader* of these imaginary masses. So then my direction turned to getting experience, working on ships and as welder and kicked out of school and hanging around lumpen and Times Square scene and dishwashing and mopping up cafeterias and all that till some rough external edges were smoothed out and I could at least fade into the landscape of the common world, so that by 20 I took pride in this wholly or part imaginary accomplishment of, though being a Columbia genteel type, at least being able to get along with non-intellectuals and poor people and knowing the argot of jazz and Times Square and varying my social experience more than is usually, or was, varied in most law students—not realizing partly that most people were not as crazy as myself and didn't make it all a big problem like I did, not being homosexual virgins like myself. Meanwhile developing with Jack a sense of poesy as mellow as could be, reading Rimbaud, and with Burroughs, a sense of Spenglerian history and respect for the "irrational" or unconscious properties of the soul and disrespect for all law. Something broader than formalistic anarchism, that is, that you can make a law as good as you want and it can be, but that still doesn't cover what you will feel when someone's trapped in your law. So a distrust of mental decisions, generalizations, sociology, a hip sense; plus then experience with love and with drugs actually causing telepathic and what were to my "mystic" experiences, i.e. feelings outside of anything I ever felt before. Meanwhile for a sense of the rightness of life I trusted people most, that is friendship and the recognition of the light in people's eyes and from then on I pursued and idealized friendship and especially in poesy which was the manifestation of this light of friendship secret in all man, open in some few.

Then as I've said but never fully described nor in context of development, came a time when college days were o'er and I had to depend on myself, and Jack and Bill went their ways in the world—though I felt bound to them by sacramental mellow lifelong-to-be ties—and the one idealistic love affair I had with Neal came to end because it was impractical and he was married and not really the same thing I was after—which was lifelong sex-soul union—he was willing but not to the extreme all out homo desire I had—anyway I realized I was alone and not ever to be loved as I wanted to be loved—though I'd had with him some great pathos love-bed scenes which surpassed in tenderness anything I'd ever be handed on earth—so that the loss was even more utterly felt, as a kind of permanent doom of my desires as I knew them since childhood—I want somebody to love me, want somebody to carry me Hoagy tenderness—and at that point living alone eating vegetables, taking care of Huncke who was too beat to live elsewhere—I opened my book of Blake (as I've said before, it's like the Ancient Mariner repeating his obsessional futile tale to every guest he can lay his hand on) and had a classical hallucinatory-mystical experience, i.e. heard his voice commanding and prophesying to me from eternity, felt my soul open completely wide all its doors and windows and the cosmos flowed thru me, and *experienced* a state of altered apparently total consciousness so fantastic and science-fictional I even got scared later, at having stumbled on a secret door in the universe all alone. Meanwhile immediately made vow No. 2 that henceforth, no matter what happened in later decades, always to be faithful to that Absolute Eternal X I had thru destiny seen face to face— several times that week. As per usual it made my social behavior frantic, but I saw I was in danger of being considered mad—and possibly (what horror) was mad—so I kept cool enough to continue somewhat normal life. However the crash came within the visions themselves, as, one time, when I summoned the Great Spirit, this Great Spirit did appear but with a sense of doom and death so universal, vast and living that it felt to me as if the universe itself had come alive and was a hostile entity in which I was trapped and by which I would be eaten consciously alive.

So these are the deepest sense experiences I have had, and the only things I can know. I can't get around them any way yet, and they are in some form or other my own destiny, any move I make I always meet that depth in new guise. At the same time afraid of meeting eternity face to face, lie tempted and fearful, like hound of heaven or moth to flame. Later somewhat similar experiences though weaker, and approximations of almost equal intensity with peyote, mescaline, ayahuasca, lysergic acid, hashish concentrates, and psylocybin mushrooms and stroboscopic lights; also at intervals of tranquillity or changes of life and personal crises, all open out to the same vastnesses of consciousness in which all I know and plan is annihilated by awareness of hidden being-ness.

For that reason then, all loves, poetries and politics and intellectual life and literary scenes and all travels or stay-home years, are by me pursued as much spontaneously, without plan, without restrictive regulation of rules and rights and wrongs and final judgments, without fixed ideas—as much as possible; and I do get into ruts that lead to habit that thin my consciousness, being actually always careful to keep myself together and pursue poesy and have a forwarding address.

However various basic rules have evolved, as far as my instincts and feelings, which is that all creation and poesy as transmission of the message of eternity is sacred and must be free of any rational restrictiveness; because consciousness has no limitations. And this led to experiments with new kinds of writings and literary renaissances and new energies and compositional techniques—most of which I got from Kerouac who all along let himself go to ball with his spontaneous art, to tell the secrets of his memory. And I expected that, given this widening of belief and tolerance and empathy, some touch of natural basic consciousness would emanate from poesy and my activities and serve to remind others outside me of human original wide nature, and thus affecting their consciousness little though it be, serve the general uplift of man and the purpose of vow No. 1, to aid the masses in their suffering. But if that end were approached directly, I always felt it would become a surface idea and get tangled in limited sometimes mistaken frontbrain judgments, such as Kerouac warns about when he laments my being what seems to him involved in politics; and that way he makes sense.

Another basic generalization that emerged was to finally trust my natural love feelings and that led to now almost decade alliance with Peter whom I thought a saint of lovely tolerance and joy—for me, strange tender ambulance driver, is what I wrote Jack announcing his presence in our company; Jack later pronounced him to be the guard at gate of heaven, "but he's so goofy he lets everybody in."

And so, on poesy and Peter and all described before, I began to get a fixed identity and creational life, with sort of basic sentiments and some ideas, which, as far as public "pronouncements" I kept to just urging freedom, of meter and technique in poesy, to follow the shape of the mind, and laws (narcotic) to follow thru to wider consciousness, and love, to follow natural desire.

However, taking drugs, and in solitude, I still was faced with omnivorous oblivion, chills of isolation and sterility not having met the woman half of the universe and progenied new babes, natural dissatisfactions with the incompleteness of the comes we could have together being men, and it made me vomit to realize the whole identity now built around me, poetry, Peter, me, visions, consciousness, all my life, were destined by dissolution of time (a la Buddha) to be separated from me and I would later if not willingly sooner be faced with having it all taken away with my corpse.

In fact in Peru with witch doctors taking ayahuasca one night I came face to face with what appeared to be the Image of Death come to warn me again as 12 years before in Harlem, that all this me-ness of mine was mere idea vanity and hollow and fleeting as the mosquitoes I was killing in the tropic night. In fact, though I'd made a principle of non-identity, I was scared to have my identity taken away, scared to die—clinging to the self-doomed (transient by nature) pleasures of dependable love, sex, income, cigarettes, poesy, fame, face and cock—clinging, frightened, to *stay in* this identity, this body, vomiting as it was—and seeing its doom as a living monster *outside* of me that would someday EAT ME ALIVE.

Thus faced with human limitation I turned back from eternity again and wanted to stay the Allen I was and am.

At this point frightened, seeing my basic saint-desire might be death and madness, I wrote Burroughs long letter from Peru asking for advice—Burroughs who had kicked junk habit and thus in very real way kicked his own identity habit, as can be seen in *Naked Lunch* hints.

His answer, go right ahead, into space, outside of Logos, outside of time, outside of concepts of eternity and god and faith and love I'd built up as an identity—Cancel all your messages, said he, and I also cancel mine.

Then thinking of wandering East with Peter and Gregory we looked into Bill in Tangier this year, and I met *someone I didn't know*; who rejected me, as far as Allen and Bill were concerned and all previous relationships they built up. And if I don't know Bill I sure don't know myself, because he was my rock of tolerance and friendship and true art. And what was he doing with his art? He was cutting it up with a razor as if it weren't no sacred texts at all, just as he was cutting up all known human feelings between us, and cutting up the newspapers, and cutting up Cuba and Russia and America and making collages; he was cutting up his own consciousness and escaping as far as I can tell outside of anything I could recognize as his previous identity. And that somewhat changed my identity since that had been something built I had thought and permanently shared with him. And Peter and I suddenly broke thru the automation love-faith habit we were junked-up and comfortable in, and looked in each others eyes—and nobody was there but a couple robots talking words and fucking. So he left for Istanbul and I stayed in Tangier and vomited off the roof.

Now the serious technical point that Burroughs was making by his cut-ups, which I resisted and resented since it threatened everything I depend on—I could stand the loss of Peter but not the loss of hope and love; and could maybe even stand the loss of them, whatever they are, if poesy were left, for me to go on being something I wanted, sacred poet however desolate; but poesy itself became a block to further awareness. For further awareness lay in dropping every fixed concept of self, identity, role, ideal, habit and pleasure. It meant dropping language itself, *words*, as medium of consciousness. It meant literally altering consciousness outside of what was already the fixed habit of language-inner-thought-monologue-abstraction-mental-image-symbol-mathematical abstraction. It meant exercising unknown and unused areas of the physical brain. Electronics, science fiction, drugs, stroboscopes, breathing exercises, exercises in thinking in music, colors, no thinks, entering and believing hallucinations, altering the neurologically fixated habit pattern reality. But that's what I thought poetry was doing all along! but the poetry I'd been practicing depended on living inside the structure of language, depended on words as the medium of consciousness and therefore the medium of conscious being.

Since then I've been wandering in doldrums, still keeping habit up with literature but uncertain if there is enough Me left to continue as some kind of Ginsberg. I can't write, except journals and dreams down; as the next step if any for poetry, I can't imagine— Perhaps we've reached point in human or unhuman evolution where art of words is oldhat dinosaur futile, and must be left behind. I also stopped reading newspapers two months ago. Also the paranoid fear that I'm degenerate robot under the mind-control of the mad spectre of Burroughs. Except that it finally seems (after dreams of killing him) that he has only taken the steps, or begun to take, steps toward actual practice of expanded consciousness that were in the cards for me anyhoo, since the first days of mind break-up with Blake, and of which I was repeatedly reminded in drug trances.

A side effect of loss of dependence on words is the final break-up of my previously monotheistic memory-conception of one holy eternity, one God. Because all that conceptualization depends on the railroad track of language. And actual experience of consciousness is not nameable as One. I suppose this is all in sophisticated form in Wittgenstein.

Meanwhile I am carrying for the last few months a dose of mushroom pills which I have been too fearful to take. Waiting for a day to look into that, or *be* that, THING, again. And operating still on language, thus this letter.

What to do about Cuba? Can the world reality (as we know it through consciousness controlled by the cortex part of the brain) be improved? Or, with expanded population and increasing need for social organization and control and centralization and standardization and socialization and removal of hidden power controllers (capitalism), will we in the long run doom man to life within a fixed and universal monopoly on reality (on materialist level) by a unison of cortex-controlled consciousness that will regulate our being's evolution? Will it not direct that evolution toward stasis of preservation of its own reality, its idea of reality, its own identity, its Logos? But this is not the problem of socialism, this is the problem of Man. Can any good society be founded, as all have been before and failed, on the basis of old-style human consciousness? Can a vast human-teeming world "democratically" regulate itself at all in future with the kind of communications mechanism this present known and used consciousness has available? How escape rigidification and stasis of consciousness when man's mind is only words and these words and their images are flashed on every brain continuously by the interconnected networks of radio television newspapers wire services speeches decrees laws telephone books manuscripts? How escape centralized control of reality of the masses by the few who want and can take power, when this network is now so interconnected, and the decision over the network? Democracy as previously sentimentally conceived now perhaps impossible (as proved in U.S.) since a vast feed-back mechanism, mass media, inescapably orients every individual, especially on subliminal levels. Same problem for Russia, China, Cuba.

I have no notion of future state or government possible for man, I don't know if continuance of machine civilization is even possible or desirable. Perhaps science may have to dismantle itself (or kill the race)—this is parallel to individual intellectual experience of cycles of reasoning leading back to non-intellectual "natural" life. However I assume (for no good reason yet) the latest cycle of human evolution is irreversible except by atomic apocalypse, so I suppose science is here to stay in one form or other, and civilizations too. I think the possible direction of development, then, to solve problems created by vast population and centralized network control, is toward increasing the efficiency and area of brain use, i.e. widening the area of consciousness in all directions feasible. For example, telepathy might annihilate mass media power centers of control. In any case the old sense of identity of human consciousness, the sense of separate identity, self and its limited language, may alter. Individuals may have to step into hitherto unrecognizable areas of awareness, which means, for practical purposes, unrecognizable or undiscovered areas of BEING.

The change may be so far out as to be unimaginable to present day two-dimensional poet's consciousness. I may have to (willingly) give up say being me, being Poet A.G., (or unwillingly depending on how fixed my cravings for security and the old life are). The social changes I can't even guess. It may be that we find the material reality we take for granted was literally an illusion all along. We may not *have* bodies. Nothing can be assumed, everything is UNKNOWN.

Space exploration is secondary and only triumphant in limited areas of consciousness; whereas an evolution or scientific exploration of consciousness itself (the brain and nervous system) is the inevitable route for man to take.

I see no reason why no government on earth is really alive in this evolutionary direction. All governments including the Cuban are still operating within the rules of identity forced on them by already outmoded means of consciousness. I say outmoded since it has brought all governments to edge of world destruction. No government, not even the most Marxian revolutionary and well-intended like Cuba presumably, is guiltless in the general world mess, no one can afford to be righteous any more. Righteous and right and wrong are still fakes of the old suicidal identity.

Now the Cuban Revolutionary government as far as I can tell is basically occupied by immediate practical problems and proud of that, heroic resistances, drama, uplift, reading and teaching language, and totally unoccupied as yet with psychic exploration in terms which I described above. When I talked with Franqui of *Revolucion* in NY he parroted the U. S. Imperialist line against marijuana and added, "It should be easier for a poet to understand a revolution than for a revolution to understand poetry." Poetry here meaning my contention that poet had right to use marijuana. He gave me all sorts of rationalistic arguments against social use of marijuana—though he added liberally that he himself was not personally opposed to it. And also I see that there has been no evidence of real technical revolution in poesy or language in recent Cuban poetry—it still is old hat mechanistic syntax and techniques. So that it is obvious that any, meaning ANY, mediocre bureaucratic attempt to censor language, diction or direction of psychic exploration is the same old mistake made in all the idiot academies of Russia and America. Arguments about immediate practical necessities are as far as I can tell from afar strictly the same old con of uninspired people who don't know what the writing problem is, and don't have any idea of the consciousness problems I'm talking about.

Re censorship of language. I wrote an article for *Show Business Illustrated* on the Cannes film festival which they accepted and paid 450 for, using the word shit (describing use of it in "The Connection"); now they want to chicken out on the single use of Shit in one sentence. I wrote back no, same day I got your letter, thus pledging myself to repay them 450 dollars I've already spent—over one little Shit. Censorship of language is direct censorship of consciousness; and if I don't fit in I can't change the shape of my mind. No. No revolution can succeed if it continues the puritanical censorship of consciousness imposed on the world by Russia and America. Succeed in what? Succeed in liberating the masses from domination by secret monopolists of communication.

I'm NOT down on the Cubans or anti their revolution, it's just that it's important to make clear *in advance, in front*, what I feel about life. Big statements saying Viva Fidel are/ would be/ meaningless and just two-dimensional politics.

Publish as much of this letter as interests you, as prose contribution to Cuban Revolution.

Oct. 16, 1961

How *Kaddish* Happened

First writing on *Kaddish* was in Paris '58, several pages of part IV which set forth a new variation on the litany form used earlier in *Howl*—a graduated lengthening of the response lines, so that the *Howl* litany looks like a big pyramid on the page. *Kaddish* IV looks like three little pyramids sitting one on top of another, plus an upside-down pyramid mirror—reflected at the bottom of the series. Considered as breath, it means the vocal reader has to build up the feeling-utterance three times to climax, and then, as coda, diminish the utterance to shorter and shorter sob. The first mess of composition had all these elements, I later cut it down to look neat and exact. (Further extension of this form, litany, can be found in poem 4 years later, "The Change".)

Sometime a year later in New York I sat up all night with a friend who played me Ray Charles' genius classics—I'd been in Europe two winters and not heard attentively before—also we chippied a little M and some then new-to-me meta-amphetamine—friend showed me his old bar-mitzvah book of Hebrew ritual and read me central Kaddish passages—I walked out in early blue dawn on to 7th Avenue and across town to my Lower East Side apartment— New York before sunrise has its own celebrated hallucinatory unreality. In the country getting up with the cows and birds hath Blakean charm, in the megalopolis the same nature's hour is a science-fiction hell vision, even if you're a milkman. Phantom factories, unpopulated streets out of Poe, familiar nightclubs bookstores groceries dead.

I got home and sat at desk with desire to write—a kind of visionary urge that's catalyzed by all the strange chemicals of the city— but had no idea what Prophecy was at hand—poetry I figured. I began quite literally assembling recollection data taken from the last hours—"Strange now to think of you gone without corsets and eyes while I walk etc." I wrote on several pages till I'd reached a climax, covering fragmentary recollections of key scenes with my mother ending with a death-prayer imitating the rhythms of the Hebrew Kaddish—"Magnificent, Mourned no more, etc."

But then I realized that I hadn't gone back and told the whole secret family-self tale—my own one-and-only eternal child-youth memories which no one else could know—in all its eccentric detail. I realized that it would seem odd to others, but *family* odd, that is to say, familiar—everybody has crazy cousins and aunts and brothers.

So I started over again into narrative—"This is release of particulars"—and went back chronologically sketching in broken paragraphs all the first recollections that rose in my heart—details I'd thought of once, twice often before—embarrassing scenes I'd half amnesiaized—hackle-raising scenes of the long black beard around the vagina—images that were central of scars on my mother's plump belly—all archetypes.

Possibly subjective archetypes, but archetype is archetype, and properly articulated subjective archetype is universal.

I sat at same desk from six AM Saturday to ten PM Sunday night writing on without moving my mind from theme except for trips to the bathroom, cups of coffee and boiled egg handed into my room by Peter Orlovsky (Peter the nurse watching over his beloved madman) and a few Dexedrine tablets to renew impulse. After the twentieth hour attention wandered, the writing became more diffuse, dissociations more difficult to cohere, the unworldly messianic spurts more awkward, but I persevered till completing the chronological task. I got the last detail recorded including my mother's death-telegram. I could go back later and clean it up.

I didn't look at the handwritten pages for a week—slept several days—and when I re-read the mass I was defeated, it seemed impossible to clean up and revise, the continuous impulse was there messy as it was, it was a patient scholar's task to figure how it could be more shapely.

Standing on a streetcorner one dusk another variation of the litany form came to me—alternation of Lord Lord and Caw Caw ending with a line of pure Lord Lord Lord Caw Caw Caw—pure emotive sound—and I went home and filled in that form with associational data. The last three lines are among the best in the poem—the *most* dissociated, on the surface, but, given all the detail of the poem, quite coherent—I mean it's a very great jump from the broken shoe to the last highschool caw caw—and in that gap's the whole Maya-Dream-Suchness of existence glimpsed.

It took me a year—trip to South America half that time—to have the patience to type poem up so I could read it. I delayed depressed with the mess, not sure it was a poem. Much less interesting to anyone else. Defeat like that is good for poetry—you go so far out you don't know what you're doing, you lose touch with what's been done before by anyone, you wind up creating a new poetry-universe. "Make it new," saith Pound, "Invention," said William Carlos Williams. That's the "Tradition"—a complete fuck-up so you're on your own.

The poem was typed, I had to cut down and stitch together the last sections of narrative—didn't have to change the expression, but did have to fit it together where it lapsed into abstract bathos or got mixed in time or changed track too often. It was retyped by Elise Cowen, a girl I'd known for years and had fitful lovers' relations with. When she gave me the copy she said, "You still haven't finished with your mother." Elise herself had been reading the Bible and heard voices saying her own mind was controlled by outside agent-machinery and several years later she died by jumping off her family apartment or roof.

By 1963 looking back on woman and on the poem for new City Lights edition I tried to make Amen: in the midst of the broken consciousness of mid twentieth century suffering anguish of separation from my own body and its natural infinity of feeling its own self one with all self, I instinctively seeking to reconstitute that blissful union which I experienced so rarely I took it to be supernatural and gave it holy name thus made it hymn laments of longing and litanies of triumphancy of self over the mind-illusion mechano-universe of un-feeling time in which I saw my self my own mother and my very nation trapped desolate our worlds of consciousness homeless and at war except for the original trembling of bliss in breast and belly of every body that nakedness rejected in suits of fear that familiar defenseless living hurt self which is myself same as all others abandoned scared to own our unchanging desire for each other. These poems almost un-conscious to confess the beatific human fact, the language intuitively chosen as in trance and dream, the rhythms rising thru breath from belly to breast, the hymn completed in tears, the movement of the physical poetry demanding and receiving decades of life while chanting Kaddish the names of Death in many mind-worlds the self seeking the key to life found at last in our self.

I've read this huge poem aloud only three times in front of an audience—I used to read the proem and last sections in the early '60s, and a recording of that time is on Fantasy Record 7006: the *Big Table* Chicago reading. The first reading of the complete text was for the *Catholic Worker* when they opened a new salvation center near the Bowery in 1960. I didn't read the whole poem aloud (except once to Kerouac in my kitchen) in public again till occasion of the recording at Brandeis University Nov. 24, 1964. I had read at Harvard several times the previous week, we'd had trouble with the administration there—kicked out of Lowell house after a poesy reading in fact—Orlovsky reading his sex experiments after our chanting Buddhist prayers had been too confusing to the Academy—the audience at the Jewish University was sympathetic and encouraging—I'd drunk a little wine—as can be heard by slowed down pace of the reading and occasionally slurred language—so for self-dramatic historic reasons I decided to open up my soul and read *Kaddish* complete. I've done it only once since then a year later in Morden Tower, Newcastle, England for a small group of longhaired kids in the presence of the greatest living British poet Basil Bunting. I was afraid that reading it over and over, except where there was spiritual reason, would put the scene into the realm of performance, an act, rather than a spontaneous poetic event, happening, in time.

March 20, 1966

Statement of Allen Ginsberg, Poet,
New York City Hearings Before a
Special Subcommittee of the
Committee on the Judiciary—U.S. Senate

I am here because I want to tell you about my own experience, and am worried that without sufficient understanding and sympathy for personal experience laws will be passed that are so rigid that they will cause more harm than the new LSD that they try to regulate. But with some sympathy, and if possible, kindness and understanding, it might be possible for all of us to get together and work out the riddle of LSD as it is approaching our society.

I hope that whatever prejudgment you may have of me or my bearded image you can suspend so that we can talk together as fellow beings in the same room of now, trying to come to some harmony and peacefulness between us. I am a little frightened to present myself, the fear of your rejection of me, the fear of not being tranquil enough to reassure you that we can talk together, make sense, and perhaps even like each other—enough to want not to offend, or speak in a way which is abrupt or hard to understand.

I am 40 years old now, a poet, this year with the status of Guggenheim Foundation fellow. I graduated from Columbia College, curiously enough, and had a practical career in market research before I went to writing full time. When I was 22 I had a crucial experience—what is called a visionary experience, or "esthetic" experience—without drugs—that deepened my life. William James' classic American book *Varieties of Religious Experience* describes similar happenings to people's consciousness. What happened to me amazed me—the whole universe seemed to wake up alive and full of intelligence and feeling. It was like a definite break in ordinary consciousness, lasted intermittently a week; then disappeared and left me vowing one thing—never to forget what I'd seen.

Now maybe that doesn't seem important, surely it's "subjective." But remember we are not machines, impersonal "objective" figures. We are subject, person, most of all we are feeling—we are alive, and this aliveness that we all know in ourselves is just that feeling of individual, unique, sensitive person. And this nation was made to be an association of such persons, and our democracy was framed to be a social structure where maximum development of individual person was to be encouraged.

I am taking the word from our prophet, Walt Whitman. This is the tradition of the Founding Fathers, this is the true myth of America, this is the prophecy of our most loved thinkers—Thoreau, Emerson, and Whitman. That each man is a great universe in himself; this is the great value of America that we call freedom.

Now in the twentieth century we have entered into a sort of science fiction space age: massive overpopulation on the planet, the possibility of planetary war and death, as in Buck Rogers, like a Biblical apocalypse, a network of electronic intercommunication which reaches and conditions our thoughts and feelings to each other, spaceships which leave earth, loss of our natural green surroundings in concrete cities filled with smoke, accelerating technology homogenizing our characters and experience. All this is inevitable, especially since presumably we have come to value material extensions of ourselves, and don't want to give those up.

We all know and complain about the drawbacks; a feeling of being caught in a bureaucratic machine which is not built to serve some of our deepest personal feelings. A machine which closes down on our senses, reduces our language and thoughts to uniformity, reduces our sources of inspiration and fact to fewer and fewer channels—as TV does—and monopolizes our attention with secondhand imagery—packaged news, and we are having it packaged now, and entertainment hours a day—and doesn't really satisfy our deeper needs for communication with each other—healthy personal adventure in environment where we have living contact with each other in the flesh, the human universe we are built to enjoy and grow in.

Maybe you already know about experiments with infant children's absolute need for contact with living bodies. If babies are totally isolated from human touch, warmth, contact, caressing, physical love, various studies have shown that they turn idiot or die. They have no life to turn to, react to, relate to. Human contact is built into our nature as a material need as strong as food, it is not an esthetic desire, it is not a fancy idea, it is an absolute fact of our existence, we can't survive without it. And this gives us an idea of what we all need, even all of us in this room grown up. We can't treat each other only as objects, categories of citizens, role players, big names, small names, objects of research or legislation—we can't treat each other as things lacking feeling, lacking sympathy. Our humanity would atrophy, cripple and die—want to die. Because life without feeling is just more "thing," more inhuman universe. There is certainly one thing we can all agree on, we all want to feel good, we don't want to feel bad basically.

What I am trying to do is articulate the common body of feeling that we all have together in this room, and I hope you will not reject my feelings of wanting mutual friendliness and communication here now—scared as my feelings are to make themselves known to you.

I had just begun to explain a vision that I once had, and immediately feared your dismissal of the idea of someone coming up in Congress and saying, "I had a vision 20 years ago," something so personal and nonobjective I want to explain why that very personal thing has a place here now.

The LSD experience is also a personal experience that can be listened to with sympathy. Then we can make up our mind how to act on it, how far it feels all right to go along with it, how far it feels bad to go along. Please follow my presentation as long as it feels all right to you.

After having had a sort of vision, as I called it, I later took some peyote, the Indian cactus, in my house in Paterson, in the presence of my family. They didn't know the changed state of mind I was in—I watched them with new eyes—a family argument became extraordinarily sad, it seemed that they were as lost, or isolated, as I was, from the depth of my strangeness, watching them. I found that speaking to them tenderly pleased them, and drew us closer. Most of the day I spent in the backyard watching the cherry tree in bloom, and writing down my observations of the blue sky as seen through changed eyes—that day the openness of the sky seemed oddly like what it was—a giant place in which I was on a planet. So this is an area of consciousness that psychedelic drugs bring to awareness.

Now, this kind of feeling is natural to us, but because of stereotypes of habit and business and overactivity and political anxiety we have been conditioned to put these feelings off. How deeply these feelings had been buried in me is measured by the fact that the first vision I had, and the peyote vision, felt so strange and familiar as if from another lifetime, that I thought they were eternal—like the myths of all religions, like the graceful appearance of divine presence, as if a god suddenly made himself in my old weekly New York universe. So that I used the word "vision" when it might be better to say I had come back to myself.

Where did I come back from? A world of thoughts, mental fantasies, schemes, words in my head, political or artistic concepts—mostly a world where language itself, or thoughts about reality, replaced my looking out on the actual place I was in, and the people there with me, with all our feelings together. A world where, for instance, you can look at death on television and not feel much or see much, only a familiar image like a movie.

I took peyote a few times again. It is nauseating and difficult for me to hold it down, and there is always a thrill of fear at returning to a larger, more detailed world than the normal mind—a world where I became conscious of being a brain and intestines and mysterious sensations called Allen Ginsberg, a lonely heart also, a world at war with itself, with unresolved conflict and fear leading to massacre between nations and neighboring races, a world which has police states, and my own nation engaged in war as well.

In 1955 I wrote a poem describing this, a text which is now taught in many universities—a central part of the poem called "Howl" was written while I was in a state of consciousness altered, or enlarged, if you will accept that, by peyote. I have the poem here and will leave it with the committee if it wishes.

The second part of the poem "Howl" was written under the influence of peyote in San Francisco.

In succeeding years I experimented with mescaline, not often, once in a while, once every few years. In 1959 I took LSD twice under controlled experimental circumstances at Stanford University. I wrote a single poem on each drug, while still high, trying to articulate the insights that appeared. I tried to keep track and make public communicable record of those moments—and continued in South America where I had the opportunity of living for a month and working with a *curandero*, that is an herb doctor, who used a psychedelic vine ayahuasca, the Latin name is *banisteriopsis caapi*, in weekly meetings with members of his community.

Use of this drug has been common for centuries all over the Amazon area, and appropriate traditions for institutionalizing the experience and integrating it into community life have been worked out so that there is minimum anxiety and little incidence of stress breakdown caused by sudden changes of feelings of the self. This is possible in some cultures, with the psychedelic "mind-manifesting," drugs. Peaceful tribes, savage tribes, the headhunters, use it as well as the Chauma, a calm, peaceful, group.

One effect I experienced in Peru I would like to explain, for what it is worth in your consideration. From childhood I had been mainly shut off from relationships with women—possibly due to the fact that my own mother, was, from my early childhood on, in a state of great suffering, frightening to me, and had finally died in a mental hospital.

In a trance state I experienced in the *curandero's* hut a very poignant memory of my mother's self, and how much I had lost in my distance from her, and my distance from other later friendly girls—for I had denied most of my feeling to them, out of old fear. And this tearful knowledge that had come up while my mind was opened through the native vine's effect did make some change— toward greater trust and closeness with all women thereafter. The human universe became more complete for me—my own feelings more complete—and that is a value which I hope you all understand and approve.

I also had had "trips"—sensations of fear, much like the feeling in nightmares—mainly the realization that one day I was going to die, and was not ready to give myself up. Later I traveled to India and sought out respectable yogis and holy men and brought my fears to them, and was reassured by their attitude of tenderness to the living community, and their attitude toward visions—"If you see something horrible, don't cling to it; if you see something beautiful, don't cling to it." So said Dudjom Rinpoche a head of the Nyingmapa sect of Tibetan Buddhism, a celebrated group which practices intensive visionary meditation. "Your own heart is your teacher" one Swami, the famous Shivananda, advised.

I had not taken LSD for several years by now, and no longer wanted to pursue self-realization through drug means, but rather through trust in my own heart's feelings. By 1965 I felt secure enough from death anxiety and last fall went to a secluded place on the Pacific Ocean coast to see what I would feel with LSD again.

I was sympathetic to the Berkeley Vietnam Day march students, who were preparing for their demonstrations at that time, and there was great anxiety in the air. There was a great deal of hostility, too—the nation was not as understanding or sympathetic to political dissent that season as it is now. We were all confused, the Oakland police, the marchers, the nation itself—many angry marchers blamed the President for the situation we were in in southeast Asia; I did, too.

The day I took LSD was the same day that President Johnson went into the operating room for his gall bladder illness. As I walked in the forest wondering what my feelings toward him were, and what I would have to say in Berkeley next week—the awesome place I was in impressed me with its old tree and ocean cliff majesty. Many tiny jeweled violet flowers along the path of a living brook that looked like Blake's illustration for a canal in grassy Eden; hug Pacific watery shore.

I saw a friend dancing long haired before giant green waves, under cliffs of titanic nature that Wordsworth described in his poetry, and a great yellow sun veiled with mist hanging over the planet's ocean horizon.

Armies at war on the other side of the planet. Berkeley's Vietnam protesters sadly preparing manifestoes for our march toward Oakland police and Hell's Angels, and the President in the valley of the shadow—himself experiencing what fear or grief?

I realized that more vile words for me would send out negative vibrations into the atmosphere—more hatred amassed against his poor flesh and soul on trial. So I knelt on the sand surrounded by masses of green kelp washed up by a storm, and prayed for President Johnson's tranquil health. Certainly more public hostility would not help him or me or anyone come through to some less rigid and more flexible awareness of ourselves or Vietnam.

On the second Vietnam Day march that November the public image of a violent clash between students and Hell's Angels escalated in everybody's minds—like a hallucination. That is, the extremists among the marchers saw the Hell's Angels as swastika brown shirts. Hell's Angels mistook the Berkeley students for Communists, because that is what it said in some papers. The newspapers were excited and reported everybody readying for a massacre. Paranoia everywhere, some marchers thought the Oakland police would back the Angels.

Actually the majority of marchers appreciated the Hell's Angels as romantic space-age cowboys. We got together for debate at San Jose College and the majority of students there in the cafeteria actually called for violence, voted aloud their hope that marchers' blood would be spilled.

The Hell's Angels chief diplomatically vowed not to begin violence and to obey police. But this wasn't reported in the newspapers, and the violent image of the Angels had to live up to was resistance in case of violence. Two days before the march nobody knew what to expect.

At this point, Ken Kesey—a man whom you may have heard of as a major contemporary novelist—who lives near San Francisco and sympathized with both marchers and Angels, intervened. We all had a party at the Hell's Angels house. Most everybody took some LSD, and we settled down to discussing the situation and listening to Joan Baez on the phonograph, and chanting Buddhist prayers.

We were all awed by the communication possible—everybody able to drop their habitual image for the night and feel more common unity than conflict. And the evening ended with understanding that nobody really wanted violence; and there was none on the day of the march. The LSD was not the whole story—there was desire for communion and fear of endless isolation—but LSD helped break down the fear barrier.

Now I would like to address myself to the social riddles proposed by LSD. If we want to discourage use of LSD for altering our attitudes, we will have to encourage such changes in our society that nobody will need it to break through to common sympathy. And now so many people have experienced some new sense of openness, and lessening of prejudice and hostility to new experience through

LSD, that I think we may expect the new generation to push for an environment less rigid, mechanical, less dominated by cold war habits. A new kind of light has rayed through our society—despite all the anxiety it has caused—maybe these hearings are a manifestation of that slightly changed awareness. I would not have thought it possible to speak like this a year ago. That we are more open to hear each other is the new consciousness itself; reveal one's vision to a congressional committee.

So I have spoken about myself and given you my direct experience of psychedelics under different conditions; in my family house, in formal research setting, in South American Indian traditional ceremonies, in solitude at the ocean. I accept the evidence of my own sense that, with psychedelics as catalysts, I have seen the world more deeply at specific times. And that has made me more peaceable.

Now I would like to offer some data to calm the anxiety that LSD is some awful mind-bending monster threat which must be kept under lock and key. There are three main ideas I would like to clarify for the committee:

1. There has been a journalistic panic exaggeration of LSD danger.
2. There is negligible danger to healthy people in trying LSD and comparatively little danger to most mentally sick people, according to what statistics we already have.
3. Research already has verified the appearance of religious or transcendental or serious blissful experience through psychedelics, and government officials would be wise to take this factor into account and treat LSD use with proper humanity and respect.

Footnote 1. The 1966 case that imprinted fear in most people's minds was that of a 5-year-old Brooklyn girl who accidentally swallowed a sugar cube left in the icebox. First, here is a quote from a reliable, authoritative medical document saying flatly that nobody dies from LSD. Next a highly hysterical and inaccurate version of the story in the *New York Post*. Then a follow-up story 24 hours later which continued to exaggerate the terror and death fear. Last, a week later in the *New York Telegram and Sun* giving the actual facts—the little girl began to "behave normally again within hours."

The Pharmacological Basis of Therapeutics, ed. Louis S. Goodman, MA, MD, (chairman, department of pharmacology, University Utah College of Medicine) and Alfred Gilman, Ph.D., (chairman, department of pharmacology, Einstein College of Medicine, New York) Macmillan Co., New York, third edition, 1965, page 207 Toxicity of LSD: "In no man, no deaths directly attributable to the drug are known. . . . "

That is a flat statement. That was the information available to everybody including the newspaper reporters at the time that this story was reported.

The *New York Post* of April 6, 1966, Wednesday, no byline:

Girl, 5, Eats LSD And Goes "Wild"

A 5-year-old Brooklyn girl, et cetera . . . people who have swallowed LSD went berserk. Some have killed—several deaths have been reported, sometimes because of the toxic effect of the drug and sometimes because of the hallucinations that lead to suicide.

New York Post, April 7, 1966, Thursday:

LSD Girl, 5, Clinging To Life
(By Ralph Blumenfield)

Five-year-old Donna Wingenroth fought for life today after swallowing an LSD-coated sugar cube she found in the family refrigerator. The blond little Brooklyn girl was reported still in "very critical" condition 18 hours after doctors pumped her stomach and treated her for convulsions at Kings County Hospital . . . said a Kings County Hospital aid, not a doctor . . . "Right now it is at the grave or serious state . . . very critical. Silent and in an apparent coma, her face pale and drawn. Glucose was being fed intravenously into her right arm and both wrists were tied to the crib-bars with gauze so she could not thrash about."

New York World Telegram and Sun, April 14, 1966, Thursday:

LSD Girl Home, Condition Seems Normal
(By Lynn Minton)

. . . was released from Kings County Hospital in apparently normal condition . . . Donna began to behave normally again within hours after her arrival at Kings County, according to Morris Kelsky, assistant hospital administrator. Despite this she was placed on the critical list. She was kept under close observation by pediatricians and neurologists to test her reflexes and all her functions before she was released . . . Kelsky explained that cases of accidental poisoning of children are not rare at the hospital . . . Candy-flavored children's aspirin is one of the biggest dangers, said Dr. Achs . . . "We have had several deaths a year in this community from children's aspirin."

I think that these quotations speak for themselves as to how all of us were imprinted with a death fear, and through the use of an inaccurate language in dealing with a deplorable situation that the girl had had LSD accidentally and was suffering from a sense of consciousness that needed care, tenderness, reassurance, understanding, not the hysteria with which it was treated.

The key thing with LSD is that a hostile environment precipitates psychosis. A friendly environment cuts down the anxiety and cuts down the psychosis. So we have now to deal with statistics on breakdown through the use of LSD, which is crucial, because in reading earlier statements to this committee, Mr. Tannenbaum's statement, I come across language like this:

One of the most common recurrent reactions to LSD is the psychotic breakdown.

There is no evidence that all users of LSD become temporarily insane.

The reason I am quoting that is to put these generalizations in the language used here in relation to the actual statistical information that we do have so far.

One of the main causes of medical and legislative worry, (particularly in New York State where legislation was taken without any kind of hearings on the actual scientific or sociological implications of LSD or the actual facts of the situation) have been reports issued on Bellevue LSD "psychosis" via the New York County Medical Society's report of May 5, 1966, and auxiliary papers detailing a few case histories in the *New England Journal of Medicine*.

New York County Medical Society report:

> Seventy-five people in 12 months admitted to Bellevue with "acute psychoses induced by LSD." Most "recovered within a week. Five remained in mental hospitals a longer time."

I would like to comment on the presuppositions of the language used and on the statistics.

As some schools of psychiatry are aware, a "flip-out" (here termed acute psychosis) may be a basically positive experience if rightly handled. This means there is a breakthrough of new awareness, temporary social disorientation as a result, and an "up-leveled" reorientation to slightly richer awareness with more variable flexible social role-playing as a result. Some of the hospitalized may qualify for this description. I have spoken to a few of those who were in Bellevue and who did feel positive about the whole experience.

And laws witch-hunting use of LSD will have the inevitable result of increasing the number of marginal "psychoses" attributable to LSD. The social anxiety caused by illegalization will enter the environmental setting and influence LSD experimenters to greater traumatic disorientation than normal under LSD influence. The answer to marginal dangers of experimentation would be for Bellevue or some other place to serve its purpose as a temporary comfortable reassuring haven where people with LSD-consciousness anxiety could come to be protected and encouraged to healthy reintegration of their self-awareness, and not labeled "psychotic."

There are no real figures on LSD taking, it might be anywhere from 1,000 to 10,000 in 12 months in New York City according to Dr. Donald B. Louria of the New York Medical Society, probably a great deal more. Above figures average perhaps one breakdown in a thousand users; it is a speculative, uncontrolled survey by New

York County Medical Society. The incidence of semipermanent breakdown may be lower than liquor-drinking, auto-driving, and marriage, much less war-making, or any business activity where a healthy amount of stress is encountered.

Footnote 2. Here are some more authoritative statements on LSD breakdown:

Cohen, Sidney, M.D.: *The Beyond Within*. Atheneum, New York, 1964, pages 210-211 says:

> Major or prolonged psychological complications were almost never described in the group of experimental subjects who had been selected for their freedom from mental disturbances . . . When patients were given these drugs for therapeutic purposes, however, the untoward reactions were somewhat more frequent. Prolonged psychotic states occurred in 1 out of every 550 individuals. These breakdowns happened to individuals who were already emotionally ill: some had sustained schizophrenic breaks in the past.

Digest of Cohen's giant survey in R.E.O. Masters and Jean Houston book, called *Varieties of Psychedelic Experience*, Holt, New York, 1966, note 23, page 319 says:

> Cohen, S., "Lysergic Acid Diethylamide: Side Effects and Complications," *Journal of Nervous and Mental Disorders*, 130: 30, 1960. Cohen's report is based on 5,000 LSD and mescaline subjects who received the drugs 25,000 times, LSD dosages. In other words, some of them have high dosages, that are mythologically reputed to be absolutely damaging, though they are not actually. Among experimental subjects there were no suicide attempts and psychotic reactions lasting longer than 48 hours were met with in only 0.8/1000 of the cases. In patients undergoing therapy the rates were, attempted suicide, 1.2/1000, completed suicide: 0.4/1000; psychotic reaction over 48 hours: 1.8/1000.

Then we have another statement which I saw in the *New Republic* magazine, May 14, 1966, by one who I presume is authoritative.

He works for the investigational drug branch of the Food and Drug Administration, Dr. Lescek Ochota, M.D., D.S.C.:

> The suicide rate (in investigational group) has been reported as 0.1 percent, a remarkably low rate considering that LSD has been usually given to the rather severely ill patients including chronic alcoholics, neurotics, psychopaths, drug addicts, et cetera.

Even after reviewing 1,000 medical publications, surveying all of the literature and there is an immense mass of literature already accumulated, the author was unable to confirm reports that a psychosis can develop in a hitherto mentally healthy individual several months after his last LSD intake.

Questions then I propose to the committee for its thought and for research by the government: What is the suicide rate among the mentally ill who don't try LSD? What is the suicide rate of the average population? Does LSD significantly affect these rates in fact?

Or may it possibly turn out, and I have no idea, this is something I think we could begin thinking about, is it possible that the suicide rate for mentally ill people who have taken LSD is lower than the suicide rates for mentally ill people who have not taken LSD?

Is it ecstasy or is it bunk, the reports of the LSD consciousness state? It plainly shows a lack of friendly commonsense for the head of an agency charged with responsibility for licensing experiments with LSD to dismiss reports of its startling religious, or if we want to use the word peak experience, or another word, transcendental, or another word, esthetic effects as "pure bunk." I saw that in the *New York Times* yesterday, a government official whose work I respect incidentally, but who I feel has not read sufficiently the literature or spoken perhaps to people who have had experience with LSD said that he thought that reports of visionary or religious experience were pure bunk, and I believe that that was repeated before one of the congressional committees.

I repeat, I recommend that those responsible for legislation and administration consider the myriad documents that have accumulated since Havelock Ellis and William James researched in the last century.

Here follows a summary of recent surveys in the book by Masters and Houston, *Varieties of Psychedelic Experience*, which came out this year [1966]:

> Taken altogether these findings must be regarded as remarkable in the five studies just cited between 32 and 75 percent of psychedelic subjects will report religious-type experiences if the setting is supportive, that means friendly, and in a setting providing religious stimuli, from 75 to 90 percent report experiences of a religious or even mystical nature.

The studies cited were—I have listed a series of very legitimate proper studies, one done for the Rand Corp.; one done by Timothy Leary. That may be questionable scientifically if anybody continues to insist on questioning Leary's experience, which is considerable in the matter, but also there are studies that were printed in the *Journal of Nervous and Mental Disease*, and a paper delivered at a meeting of the American Psychiatric Association in St. Louis. I have got these listed for your reference.

Exhibit No. 76
Suggested Aspects of Creative Research on LSD

Informal conversations with two dozen MD's who had done clinical experimental and exploratory work with LSD and other psychedelic chemicals have articulated the following suggestions for formal research. Some were characterized as logical research needs, others as likely areas for study according to classical traditions of normal intelligent scientific curiosity. The language here used to characterize these possible aspects of creative research is informal, the points made are not fixed points but suggestions for consideration.

(1) A giant voluntary study of all persons who have taken LSD, with no shadow of punitive anxiety attached to the research: scientific inquiry into the statistics, subjective reports of the experience, post-experience intelligence and psychological testings to be compared with pre-experience school testing data commonly available,

comparative evaluations of statistics on "bad" trips and "good" trips, inquiry into the quality of the trip matched with circumstantial environment, detailed surveys of indifferent or "good" trips matching already heavily emphasized analyses of "bad" trips, etc. It is generally claimed that non-medical (and medical) usefulness of LSD is neither "proved" or "unproved"; statistics and data should therefore be gathered from the massive numbers of people who have experimented with LSD in the last decades.

(2) Enlarged systematic research on efficacy of LSD with dying patients.

(3) Enlarged systematic research on efficacy of LSD against alcoholism.

(4) Research on LSD effects on psychosomatic ills.

(5) Research on LSD influence on problems of obesity.

(6) Research on usefulness of LSD to break up depression states.

(7) Research on usefulness of LSD with autistic children.

(8) Research on usefulness of LSD against opiate addiction and other psychochemical addictions.

(9) Massive research on efficacy of LSD use with neurotics in psychotherapeutic situations (which research on the part of individual MD's is now effectively forbidden).

(10) Research on efficacy or non-efficacy of LSD use with neurotics in non-psychotherapeutic situations.

(11) Research into classification of personality types, mental illnesses and other human characteristics in terms of LSD drug reactions.

(12) Research on LSD influence on problems of homosexuality in psychotherapeutic circumstances.

(13) Research on usefulness of LSD experience in preventing psychic crises leading to hospitalization. (i.e. how many who *had* been in hospitals took LSD and then did *not* go back to hospitals?)

(14) Depth evaluation of recorded LSD breakdown statistics by case to determine—

(a) Was total experience positive and creative or negative and destructive in actual context? and by hindsight?

(b) To what extent was hospitalization during or after LSD stress the "elegant" acting out of prior wish for psychotherapeutic help? (The word "elegant" here used was suggested by the head of a hospital in Long Island.)

(15) Research on statistics of "breakdown" where LSD is taken freely and legally compared to circumstances where its use is illegal: i.e. research on the imagery, sensations, and psychic effects caused by illegalization of LSD.

(16) Massive research on social conditions, tradition, ritual, terminology, effects, medical data, etc. of American Indians in their use of psychedelic cactus peyote; and projections of possibilities for adapting Indian traditional forms to other American subcultures. In other words, research into safe forms of social-institutional use of psychedelics.

(17) Research into chemistry, metabolic changes and subjective phenomenology of LSD experience as compared with experience of weightlessness, sensory deprivation, space-travel, dance, chanting, yoga, religious ritual practice, drowning visions, progressive relaxation, hypnosis, starvation states, Amerindian vision-questing, sleeplessness, and stroboscope stimulation of alpha-rhythms, etc.

(18) Research into the practicality or non-practicality, value or valueless-ness, of such Utopian LSD communities (aside from Amerindian) already come into being as available models for study: Neo-American Church, Ken Kesey's Merry Pranksters Community, Dr. T. Leary's Millbrook Research Center, and the mutual help communities already evolved informally in Midwest campuses, etc.

(19) Depth research and evaluation of commonly observed LSD effect of "impairment of socially learned behavior." Is this due to changed *motive*, and is this change of motive creatively valid or not? Are we, in effect, in regulating LSD actually regulating value judgments? What are the consequences (as far as social scientists and psychotherapists can determine) of authoritative regulation of value-judgments?

(20) Comparative study and correlation of language and attitudes used by various social groups according to their roles

in reacting to LSD experience directly and indirectly: Legislators, police, psychoanalysts with experimental experience, psychoanalysts without experimental experience, anthropologists, artists, newsmen, theologians, Marxists (re Dr. Jiri Roubichek's language in Prague, "LSD inhibits conditioned reactions"), college administrators, FDA chiefs, Indians, culture morphologists, musicians, painters, cinéasts. Correlation would be useful in determining whether terminology used by different groups coincided in any respect, and in what respects differ, from categorization of the event under survey, namely the effect of LSD.

(21) Straight research and gathering of data in how to handle LSD panic, stress or crisis reaction: "We need research to know what to do when people come in sick, doctors need to be able to work with it to get experience—otherwise it's hush hush like VD and public and professional ignorance spreads." Unquote a lady doctor, head of a mid-town Manhattan hospital research section.

Thank you for listening to my paper, which has been very long.

Testimony given: June 14, 1966

Public Solitude

I am speaking from this pulpit conscious of history, of my role as poet, of the addresses and essays in public consciousness by my transcendental predecessors in this city, with all the awesome prophecies about these states pronounced by Thoreau and Emerson, and elsewhere the more naked Whitman: prophecies that have now come true.

> "—I say of all this tremendous and dominant play of solely materialistic bearings upon current life in the United States, with the results already seen, accumulating, and reaching far into the future, that they must either be confronted and met by at least an equally subtle force-infusion for purposes of spiritualization, for the pure conscience, for genuine esthetics, and for absolute and primal manliness and womanliness—or else our modern civilization, with all its improvements, is in vain, and we are on the road to a destiny, a status, equivalent, in its real world, to that of the fabled damned."
>
> —Democratic Vistas

Because our governors and politicos have failed to perceive the obvious I wish to make some political suggestions to this community; make them as poet, and claim powers of prophecy as did the good grey bards before me in this country, because one who looks in his heart and speaks frankly can claim to prophecy. And what is prophecy? I can not propose right and wrong, or objective future event such as purple balloons on Jupiter in 1984: but I can have the confidence to trust my own fantasy and express my own private thought. All have this gift of prophecy, who dare assume it though?

The present condition of life for American person is one of deathly public solitude. We've built a technological Tower of Babel around ourselves, and are literally (as in Gemini) reaching into heaven to escape the planet. Now giant overpopulation depends on a vast metallic superstructure to feed and transport all the bodies here together. The stupendous machinery surrounding us conditions our "thoughts feelings and apparent sensory impressions," and reinforces our mental slavery to the material universe we've invested in.

Yet according to Chuang Tzu 2,500 years ago, "The understanding of the men of ancient times went a long way. How far did it go? To the point where some of them believed that things have never existed—so far, to the end, where nothing can be added . . . Words like these will be labeled the Supreme Swindle. Yet, after ten thousand generations, a great sage may appear who will know their meaning, and it will still be as though he appeared with astonishing speed." Yeats appearing in Ireland in this century declared:

"This preposterous pig of a world, its farrow that so solid seem
Must vanish on an instant, did the mind but change its theme."

How can we Americans make our minds change theme? For unless the theme changes—encrustation of the planet with machinery, inorganic metal smog violent outrage and mass murder will take place. We witness these horrors already.

Abruptly then, I will make a first proposal: on one level symbolic, but to be taken as literally as possible, it may shock some and delight others—that everybody who hears my voice, directly or indirectly, try the chemical LSD at least once; every man woman and child American in good health over the age of 14—that, if necessary, we have a mass emotional nervous breakdown in these States once and for all; that we see bankers laughing in their revolving doors with strange staring eyes. May everybody in America turn on, whatever the transient law—because individual soul development (as once declared by a poet in jail in this city) is our law transcending the illusions of the political state. Soul also transcends LSD, may I add, to reassure those like myself who would fear a chemical dictatorship. I propose, then, that everybody including the President and his and our vast hordes of generals, executives, judges and legislators of these States go to nature, find a kindly teacher or Indian peyote chief or guru guide, and assay their consciousness with LSD.

Then, I prophecy, we will all have seen some ray of glory or vastness beyond our conditioned social selves, beyond our government, beyond America even, that will unite us into a peaceable community.

The LSD I am proposing is literal. I hope it will be understood as not the solution, but a typical, and spiritually revolutionary catalyst, where many varieties of spiritual revolution are necessary to transcend specifically the political COLD WAR we are all involved in.

Anger and control of anger is our problem. Already we have enough insight into politics to be aware of one very simple thing: that we can judge all politics and all public speech and ideology by perceiving the measure of anger manifested therein. All present political parties propose violence to resolve our confusions, as in Vietnam. We might look for a third party, specifically named a Peace Party—referring to individual subjective peaceableness (such as we have not seen in our populace or our leaders) as well as consequent public peaceableness; a party founded on psychology not ideology. We obviously need to feed China and India not ignore, manipulate, or threaten to destroy them. The earth is yet to be saved from our aggression, and living organic life like unto our own nature be replaced on its surface which has been overgrown with cancerous inanimate matter, metal and asphalt. And though many mammal species have been made extinct in this century there are many we can yet save including ourselves.

Driving out of NY or into Boston at night we see the transparent apparitional glitter of buildings walling the horizon, and we know that these are transient specters. In cold daylight we believe in their finality. But it is that half-dreaming insight of normal consciousness that may provide the direction for our imagination to manifest itself in the material world.

What can the young do with themselves faced with this American version of the planet? The most sensitive and among the "best minds" do drop out. They wander over the body of the nation looking into the faces of their elders, they wear long Adamic hair and form Keristan communities in the slums, they pilgrimage to Big Sur and live naked in forests seeking natural vision and meditation, they dwell in the Lower East Side as if it were a hermetic forest. And they assemble thousands together as they have done this year in Golden Gate Park San Francisco or Tompkins Park in New York to manifest their peaceableness in demonstrations of fantasy that transcend protest against—or for—the hostilities of Vietnam. Young men and women in speckled clothes, minstrel's garb, jester's robes, carrying balloons, signs 'President Johnson we are praying for you', gathered chanting Hindu and Buddhist mantras to calm their fellow citizens who are otherwise entrapped in a planetary barroom brawl.

But there has been no recognition of this insight on the part of the fathers and teachers (Father Zossima's famous cry!) of these young. What's lacking in the great institutions of learning? The specific wisdom discipline that that young propose: search into inner space.

Children drop out of schools because there are no, or very few, gurus. Those elders concerned with this practical problem might consider that there is an easy practical solution: the establishment within centers of learning of facilities for wisdom search which the ancients proposed as the true function of education in the first place: academies of self-awareness, classes in spiritual teaching, *darshan* with holymen of disciplined mind-consciousness. One might well, in fact, employ the drop-out beatniks as instructors in this department, and thereby officially recognize and proclaim the social validity of exploration of inner space. Tibetan monks, swamis, *yogins* and *yoginis*, psychedelic guides, Amerindian peyote chiefs, even a few finished Zen Roshis and many profound poets are already present and available in our cities for such work, though at present they battle immigration bureaucracies and scholarly heads of departments of Oriental Religion.

What I am proposing as policy, for us elders, for what community we have, is self-examination as Official Politics; an Official Politics of Control of Anger. With state propaganda reversed in that direction, church and university teaching and research in that direction, and request to the government for vast sums of money equal to the outerspace program; and consequent billboards on the highways "Control Your Anger—Be Aware of Yourself."

There is a change of consciousness among the younger generations, in a direction always latent to Elder America, toward the most complete public frankness possible. As the Gloucester poet Charles Olson formulated it, "Private is public, and public is how we behave." This means revision of standards of public behavior to include indications of private manners heretofore excluded from public consciousness.

Thus, new social standards, more equivalent to private desire—as there is increased sexual illumination, new social codes may be found acceptable to rid ourselves of fear of our own nakedness, rejection of our own bodies.

Likely an enlarged family unit will emerge for many citizens; possibly, as the Zen Buddhist anarchist anthropologist Gary Snyder observed, with matrilineal descent as courtesy to those *dakinis* whose *saddhana* or holy path is the sexual liberation and teaching of *dharma* to many frightened males (including myself) at once. Children may be held in common, with the orgy an acceptable community sacrament—one that brings all people closer together. Certainly one might seduce the Birch Society to partake in naked orgy, and the police with their wives, together with LeRoi Jones the brilliantly angry poet. America's political need is orgies in the parks, on Boston Common and in the Public Gardens, with naked bacchantes* in our national forests.

I am not proposing idealistic fancies, I am acknowledging what is already happening among the young in fact and fantasy, and proposing official blessing for these breakthroughs of community spirit. Among the young we find a new breed of White Indians in California communing with illuminated desert redskins; we find our teenagers dancing Nigerian Yoruba dances and entering trance states to the electric vibration of the Beatles who have borrowed shamanism from Afric sources. We find communal religious use of *ganja*, the hemp sacred to Mahadev (Great Lord) Shiva. There's now heard the spread of mantra chanting in private and such public manifestations as peace marches, and soon we will have Mantra Rock over the airwaves. All the available traditions of U.S. Indian vision-quest, peyote ritual, mask dancing, Oriental *pranayama*, east Indian ear music are becoming available to the U.S. unconscious through the spiritual search of the young. Simultaneously there is a new Diaspora of Tibetan Lamaist initiates; texts such as the

---

* bacchante—priestess of Bacchus.

Book of the Dead and *I Ching* have found fair-cheeked and dark-browed Kansas devotees. And rumor from the West Coast this season brings the legendary Hevajra Tantra—a document central to Vajrayana Buddhism's Lightningbolt Illumination—into public light as a source book for tantric community rules. LSD structured by ancient disciplines for meditation and community regulation.

Ideas I have dwelled on are mixed: there is some prescription for public utopia thru education in inner space. There is more prescription here for the individual: as always, the old command to free ourselves from social conditioning, laws and traditional mores.

And discover the guru in our own hearts.—And set forth within the new wilderness of machine America to explore open spaces of consciousness in self and fellow selves. If there be the necessary revolution in America it will come that way. It's up to us older hairs who still have relation with some of the joy of youth to encourage this revolutionary individual search.

But how can peaceful psychological politics succeed when $50 billion a year is spent to busy participation in armed conflict? "Vietnam War Brings Prosperity"—headline *Lincoln Nebraska Star*, February 1966. Certainly the awareness itself of this condition will help some of us: as did Ike's warning against the military-industrial complex running the mind of the nation.

As a side note: there *are* specific methods for combating the mental dictatorship over "thoughts feelings and apparent sensory impressions" imposed on us by military-industrial control of language and imagery in public media. W.S. Burroughs has provided a whole armamentarium of counter-brainwash techniques: cut-up of newspapers and ads, collage of political entertainment news to reveal the secret intention of the senders, observation of TV imagery with sound off and simultaneous apperception of voices on the radio or street. These methods are effective in jolting the soft machine of the brain out of its conditioned hypnosis.

Cutting out, or dropping out, of the culture will not lead to a chaos of individuality: what it will mean, for the young, is training in meditation and art (and perhaps Neolithic lore), and responsibility of a new order, to the community of the heart, not to our heartless society wherein we have read the headline in the *Omaha World Herald*: "Rusk Says Toughness Essential For Peace."

The "oversoul" to be discovered is a pragmatic reality. We can all tell signs of an illuminated man in business of the church—one who is open-hearted, non-judging, empathetic, compassionate to the rejected and condemned. The tolerant one, the observer, the aware. And we see that these souls do influence action.

Finally, detachment comes naturally: we all know the war is camp, hate is camp, murder is camp, even love is camp, the universe is a grand camp according to Chuang Tzu and the *Prajnaparamita Sutra*. This detachment is salvation. We have an international youth society of solitary children—stilyagi, provo, beat, mufada, nadaista, energumeno, mod and rocker—all aghast at the space age horror world they are born to, not habituated to—and now questioning the nature of the universe itself *as is proper* in the space age.

There are many contradictions here, especially between proposed communal sex orgy and contemplative choiceless awareness (as the sage Krishnamurti articulated it this Fall in New York). Whitman noticed that too: "Do I contradict myself? Very well, I contradict myself." A dialogue between these contradictions is a good healthy way of life, one correcting the other. Indulgence in sexuality and sensational ecstasy may well lead to contemplative awareness of desire and cessation of desire.

> *"I know although when looks meet*
> *I tremble to the bone,*
> *The more I leave the door unlatched*
> *The sooner love is gone."*

What satisfaction is now possible for the young? Only the satisfaction of their desire—love, the body, and orgy: the satisfaction of a peaceful natural community where they can circulate and explore persons, cities, and the nature of the planet—the satisfaction of encouraged self-awareness, and the satiety and cessation of desire, anger, grasping and craving.

Respect for the old? Yea when the old are tranquil and not nervous and respect the sport of the young. Holymen do inspire respect. One conservative Vaishnavite Swami Bhaktivedanta moved into the Lower East Side this year and immediately dozens of young LSD freak-outs flocked to sing the Hare Krishna Maha mantra with him—chant for the preservation of the planet.

But a nation of elders convinced that spiritual search is immaturity, and that national war and metallic communication is maturity, cannot ask for respect from the young. For the present conduct of the elders in America is a reflection of lack of Self-respect.

I am in effect setting up moral codes and standards which include drugs, orgy, music and primitive magic as worship rituals— educational tools which are supposedly contrary to our cultural mores; and I am proposing these standards to you respectable ministers, once and for all, that you endorse publicly the private desire and knowledge of mankind in America, so to inspire the young.

It may appear from this address that I find myself increasingly alienated from the feeling-tone, ideology and conduct of the supposed majority of my fellow citizens: thus the title public solitude. But I do not feel myself alienated from all our inmost private desire, which the prophet Walt Whitman articulated in his second preface to his life work 90 years ago, still passionately expressive of our hearts in space-age America:

> Something more may be added—for, while I am about it, I would make a full confession. I also sent out "Leaves of Grass" to arouse and set flowing in man's and women's hearts, young and old, endless streams of living, pulsating love and friendship, directly from them to myself, now and ever. To this terrible, irrepressible yearning (surely more or less down underneath in most human souls)—this never-satisfied appetite for sympathy, and this boundless offering of sympathy—this universal democratic comradeship—this old, eternal, yet ever-new interchange of adhesiveness, so fitly emblematic of America—I have given in that book, undisguisedly, declaredly, the openest expression. Besides, important as they are in my purpose as "Calamus" cluster of "Leaves of Grass" (and more or less running through the book, and cropping out in "Drum-Taps") mainly resides in its political significance. In my opinion, it is by a fervent, accepted development of comradeship, the beautiful and sane affection of man for man, latent in all the young fellows, north and south, east and west,—it is by this, I say, and by what goes directly and indirectly along with it, that the United States of the future (I cannot too often repeat,) are to be most effectually welded together, intercalated, anneal'd into a living union.

Footnote to Public Solitude Essay, Boston 1966

Our life consciousness is increasingly conditioned by the massive material structure we have erected around ourselves to sustain the innumerable population born of technological meditation. A circular feedback: the more thought for these bodies, the more bodies, and the more need for thought for the care sustenance and prolongation of body life. These thoughts have led us to escape the physical limit of the planet. So we find ourselves preparing to spread our seed throughout a physical universe, and all our thought consciousness trapped in this particular universe; and conditioning to this area of consciousness continually reinforced on threat of pain starvation death by the Tower of Babel we are building.

That is one thought, that passes through our minds often. Another thought we all have entertained is that "this preposterous pragmatic pig of a world, its farrow that so solid seem, would vanish on the instant, did the mind but change its theme." We have Buddhist meditation documents to prove this experience; we also have a technological chemistry to precipitate this sensation. We have texts such as the *Tibetan Book of the Dead*, that link the two traditions of transcendentalism, ancient and modern. Ancient documents, presently unearthed or translated, reveal a certain secret about the ordinary world we inhabit. Chuang Tzu's yatter, "I'm going to try speaking some reckless words and I want you to listen to them recklessly . . . The understanding of the men of ancient times went a long way. How far did it go? To the point where some of them believed that things have never existed—" And Highest Perfect Wisdom Heart Sutra hints the same. Thus we are in the nightmarish condition of beings existing in a dream universe wherein our politics have led us to expand our claims to that dream stuff unto its physical limits. And we have a dream chemistry that like a few puffs of DMT can make the "apparent sensory impression" of Maya disappear instantly in a radiant explosion of wave vibrations that look like Einstein's platonic eyeball and just as real as the First National Bank.

Written: Nov. 12, 1966

"The Fall Of America" Wins an Award

[Editor's Note: This was Ginsberg's acceptance speech for the National Book Award in Poetry. It was delivered by Peter Orlovsky at the Alice Tulley Hall, Lincoln Center, New York on April 18, 1974.]

Poem book *Fall of America* is time capsule of personal national consciousness during American war-decay recorded 1965 to 1971. It includes one prophetic fragment, written on speakers platform of May 9, 1970 Washington D.C. Peace Protest Mobilization:

White sunshine on sweating skulls
Washington's Monument pyramided high granite clouds
over a soul mass, children screaming in their brains on quiet grass
(black man strapped hanging in blue denims from an earth cross)—
Soul brightness under blue sky
Assembled before White House filled with mustached Germans
and police buttons, army telephones, CIA Buzzers, FBI bugs
Secret Service walkie-talkies, Intercom Squawkers to Narco
Fuzz and Florida Mafia Real Estate Speculators.
One hundred thousand bodies naked before an Iron Robot
Nixon's brain Presidential cranium case spying thru binoculars
from the Paranoia Smog Factory's East Wing.

Book here honored with public prize, best proclaim further prophetic foreboding that our United States is now the fabled "damned of nations" foretold by Walt Whitman a hundred years ago. The materialist brutality we have forced on ourselves and world is irrevocably visible in dictatorships our government has established thru

South and Central America, including deliberate wreckage of Chilean democracy. From Greece to Persia we have established police states, and throughout Indochina wreaked criminal mass murder on millions, subsidized opium dealing, destroyed land itself, imposed military tyranny both openly and secretly in Cambodia, Vietnam, and Thailand.

Our quote "Defense of the free world" is an aggressive hypocrisy that has damaged the very planet's chance of survival. Now we have spent thousands of billions on offensive war in decades, and half the world is starving for food. The reckoning has come now for America. 100 billion goes to the War Department this year out of 300 billion budget. Our militarization has become so top heavy that there is no turning back from military tyranny. Police agencies have become so vast—National Security Agency alone the largest police bureaucracy in America yet its activities are almost unknown to all of us—that there is no turning back from computerized police state control of America.

Watergate is a froth on the swamp: impeachment of a living president does not remove the hundred billion power of the military nor the secret billion power of the police state apparatus. Any president who would try to curb power of the military-police would be ruined or murdered.

So I take this occasion of publicity to call out the fact: our military has practices subversion of popular will abroad and can do so here if challenged, create situations of chaos, take over the nation by military coup, and proclaim itself guardian over public order. And our vast police networks can, as they have in last decade, enforce that will on public and poet alike.

We have all contributed to this debacle with our aggression and self-righteousness, including myself. There is no longer any hope for the salvation of America proclaimed by Jack Kerouac and others of our Beat Generation, aware and howling, weeping and singing *Kaddish* for the nation decades ago, "rejected yet confessing out the soul." All we have to work from now is the vast empty quiet space of our own consciousness. AH! AH! AH!

Written: April 17, 1974

A Definition of the Beat Generation

The phrase "beat generation" rose out of a specific conversation with Jack Kerouac and John Clellon Holmes around '50-'51 when, discussing the nature of generations recollecting the glamour of the lost generation, Kerouac said, Ah, this is nothing but a beat generation. They discussed whether it was a "Found" generation, which Kerouac sometimes referred to, or "Angelic" generation, and/ or various other epithets. But, Kerouac waved away the question and said, "beat generation" not meaning to name the generation but to un-name it.

John Clellon Holmes' celebrated article in late '52 in the *New York Times* magazine section carried the headline title "This is the Beat Generation"; that caught public eye. Then Kerouac published anonymously a fragment of *On the Road* in *New American Writing*, a paperback anthology of the 50s, called "Jazz of the Beat Genera-tion", and that reinforced the curiously poetic phrase. So that's the early history of the term "Beat Generation" itself.

Herbert Huncke, author of *The Evening Sun Turned Crimson* and friend of Kerouac, Burroughs and others of that literary circle from the 40s, introduced them to what was then known as "hip lan-guage." In that context the word "beat" is a carnival "subterranean" (subcultural) term, a term much used in Times Square in the '40s. "Man, I'm beat . . . " meaning without money and without a place to stay. Could also refer to those "who walked all night with shoes full of blood on the snowbank docks waiting for a door in the East River to open to a room full of steam heat and opium" (*Howl*). Or, as in a conversation, "Would you like to go to the Bronx Zoo?" "Nah, man, I'm too *beat*, I was up all night." So, the original street usage meant exhausted, at the bottom of the world, looking up or out, sleepless, wide-eyed, perceptive, rejected by society, on your own, streetwise. Or, as it was once implied, finished, undone, completed, in the dark night of the soul or in the cloud of unknowing. "Open," as in Whitmanic sense of "openness," equivalent to humility, and so it *was* interpreted in various circles to mean emptied out, exhausted, and at the same time wide-open—perceptive and receptive to a vision.

A third meaning of the term beatific was articulated in 1959 by Kerouac, counteracting abuse of the term in media (the term being interpreted as being beaten completely, a "loser" without the aspect of humble intelligence, or "Beat" as "the beat of the drums" and "the beat goes on": varying mistakes of interpretation or etymology). Kerouac did try to indicate the correct sense of the word by pointing out the root—beat—as in beatitude, or beatific, (various interviews and lectures). In his essay, *Origins of the Beat Generation*, Kerouac defined it so. This is a definition made early within the popular culture, (circa late-fifties) though it was already a basic understanding of the subculture (circa mid-forties): he clarified his intention, 'beat' as beatific, the necessary beatness or darkness that precedes opening up to the light, egolessness, giving room for religious illumination.

A fourth meaning accumulated, that of the "beat generation literary movement." This was a group of friends who had worked together on poetry, prose and cultural conscience from the mid-forties until the term became popular nationally in the late fifties. The group consisting of Kerouac and his prototype hero of *On the Road*—Neal Cassady, William Burroughs, author of *Naked Lunch* and other books, Herbert Huncke, John Clellon Holmes, author of *Go*, *The Horn*, and other books, Allen Ginsberg, myself; we met Carl Solomon and Philip Lamantia in '48: encountered Gregory Corso in 1950, and we first saw Peter Orlovsky in 1954.

By the mid-fifties this smaller circle, through natural affinity of modes of thought or literary style or planetary perspective, was augmented in friendship and literary endeavor by a number of writers in San Francisco, including Michael McClure, Gary Snyder, Philip Whalen and a number of other powerful but lesser-known poets such as Jack Micheline, Ray Bremser, or the better-known black poet LeRoi Jones—all of whom accepted the term at one time or another, humorously or seriously, but sympathetically, and were included in a survey of beat general manners, morals, and litera-

ture by *Life* magazine in a lead article in the late 50s by one Paul
O'Neill, and by the journalist Alfred Aronowitz in a large series
on the Beat Generation in the *New York Post*. Neal Cassady, who
was interviewed in both surveys, was writing at the time: his works
were published posthumously.

By the mid-fifties a sense of some mutual trust and interest was
developed with Frank O'Hara and Kenneth Koch, as well as with
Robert Creeley and other alumni of Black Mountain. Of that lit-
erary circle, Kerouac, Whalen, Snyder, poet Lew Welch, Orlovsky
as well as Ginsberg and others were interested in meditation and
Buddhism. Relationship between Buddhism and its friends in the
"beat generation" can be found in a recent scholarly survey of the
evolution of Buddhism in America, *How the Swans Came to the
Lake*, by Rick Fields.

The fifth meaning of the phrase "Beat Generation" is the
influence of the literary and artistic activities of poets, filmmak-
ers, painters, writers and novelists who were working in concert
in anthologies, publishing houses, independent filmmaking, and
other media. Some effects of the aforementioned groups refreshed
the bohemian culture which was already a long tradition (in film
and still photography, Robert Frank and Alfred Leslie; in music,
David Amram; in painting, Larry Rivers; in poetry publishing,
Don Allen, Barney Rosset, and Lawrence Ferlinghetti) extended
to fellow artists, such as Susan Sontag and Norman Mailer, and
to the youth movement of that day, which was also growing; and
was absorbed by the mass and middle class culture of the late 50s
and early 60s. These effects can be characterized in the following
terms;

- Spiritual Liberation; Sexual "Revolution" or "Liberation,"
  i.e. Gay Liberation, Black Liberation, Women's Libera-
  tion, Grey Panther activism, etc.,
- Liberation of the Word from censorship,
- Demystification and/or decriminalization of some laws
  against marijuana and other drugs,
- The evolution of rhythm and blues into rock 'n' roll into
  high art form, as evidenced by the Beatles, Bob Dylan,
  and other popular musicians influenced in the late 1950s
  and 60s by beat generation poets' and writers' works,

- The spread of ecological consciousness, emphasized early by Gary Snyder and Michael McClure; notion of a "Fresh Planet,"
- Opposition to the military-industrial machine civilization, as emphasized in the works of Burroughs, Huncke, Ginsberg, and Kerouac,
- Attention to what Kerouac called, after Spengler, "Second Religiousness" developing within an advanced civilization,
- Return to appreciation of idiosyncrasy as against state regimentation, and
- Respect for land and indigenous peoples and creatures as proclaimed by Kerouac in his slogan from *On the Road*, "The Earth Is An Indian Thing."

The essence of the phrase "beat generation" can be found in *On the Road* in another celebrated phrase, "Everything belongs to me because I am poor."

1981

Meditation and Poetics

It's an old tradition in the West among great poets that poetry is rarely thought of as "just poetry." Real poetry practitioners are practitioners of mind awareness, or practitioners of reality, expressing their fascination with a phenomenal universe and trying to penetrate to the heart of it. Poetics isn't mere picturesque dilettantism or egotistical expressionism for craven motives grasping for sensation and flattery. Classical poetry is a "process," or experiment—a probe into the nature of reality and the nature of the mind.

That motif comes to a climax in both subject matter and method in our own century. Recent artifacts in many fields of art are examples of "process," or "work in progress," as with the preliminary title of Joyce's last work, *Finnegan's Wake*. Real poetry isn't consciously composed as "poetry," as if one only sat down to compose a poem or a novel for publication. Some people do work that way: artists whose motivations are less interesting than those of Shakespeare, Dante, Rimbaud, and Gertrude Stein, or of certain surrealist verbal alchemists—Tristan Tzara, André Breton, Antonin Artaud—or of the elders Pound and William Carlos Williams, or, specifically in our own time, of William Burroughs and Jack Kerouac. For most of "The Moderns," as with the Imagists of the twenties and thirties in our century, the motive has been purification of mind and speech. Thus we have the great verses of T.S. Eliot:

> Since our concern was speech, and speech impelled us
>> To purify the dialect of the tribe
>> And urge the mind to aftersight and foresight,
> Let me disclose the gifts reserved for age

To set a crown upon your lifetime's effort.
First, the cold friction of expiring sense
Without enchantment, offering no promise
But bitter tastelessness of shadow fruit
As body and soul begin to fall asunder.

There's a common misconception among puritanical medita-tors and puritanical businessmen, who think they've got "reality" in their hands, that high poetics and art as practiced in the twen-tieth century are practiced as silly Bohemian indulgence, rather than for the reason that one practices mindfulness in meditation or accuracy in commerce. Western fine art and other meditation practices are brother-and-sister-related activities. (Which is quite different from the notion that East is East and West is West and never the twain shall meet—an idiot slogan denying the fact East and West the brain's the same.) It's an important insight to have so that as meditation practitioners and businessmen we don't become inhibited in expressing and probing ourselves through various art means that we've inherited—from poetry to music to tea ceremony to archery to horsemanship to cinema to jazz blues to painting, even New Wave electric music.

Major works of twentieth-century art are probes of consciousness—particular experiments with recollection or mind-fulness, experiments with language and speech, experiments with forms. Modern art is an attempt to define or recognize or experi-ence perception—pure perception. I'm taking the word "probe" for poetry—poetry as a probe into one subject or another—from the poet Gregory Corso. He speaks of poetry as a probe into Marriage, Hair, Mind, Death, Army, Police, which are the titles of some of his earlier poems. He uses poetry to take an individual word and probe all its possible variants. He'll take a concept like death, for instance, and pour every archetypal thought he's ever thought or could recollect having thought about death and lay them out in poetic form—making a whole mandala of thoughts about it.

Kerouac and I, following Arthur Rimbaud and Baudelaire, our great-grandfathers among hermetic poets and philosophers, were experimenting naively with what we thought of as "new reality," or "supreme reality." Actually that was a phrase in use in 1945; we were thinking in terms of a new vision or a new consciousness, after the little passage in Rimbaud's *A Season in Hell:* "Noël sur la terre!" "When shall we go beyond the shores and the mountains, to salute the birth of new work, new wisdom, the flight of tyrants and demons, end of superstition, to adore—the first!—Christmas on earth!" In fact, the phrase "new consciousness" circulated among Beat Generation writers as our poetic motif in the early fifties. The specific intention of that decade's poetry was the exploration of consciousness, which is why we were interested in psychedelic or mind-manifesting substances—not necessarily synthetic; they might also be herbs or cacti.

Kerouac's motive for his probe was disillusionment: the heavy experience of the lives, old age, sickness and death of his father and his older brother, whose dying he experienced as he took care of them and watched them in their beds, close to their deaths. As he wrote in *Visions of Cody*, in 1951:

> I'm writing this book because we're all going to die—in the lone-
> liness of my life, my father dead, my brother dead, my mother far
> away, my sister and wife far away, nothing here but my own tragic
> hands . . . that are now left to guide and disappear their own way
> into the common dark of all our death, sleeping in me raw bed,
> alone and stupid: with just this one pride and consolation: my
> heart broke in the general despair and opened up inwards to the
> Lord, I made a supplication in this dream.

As a motive for writing a giant novel, this passage from *Visions of Cody* is a terrific stroke of awareness and *bodhisattva* heart, or out-goingness of heart. So I'm speaking about the ground of poetry and purification of motive. A few Buddhist *dharma* phrases correlate charmingly with the process of Bohemian art of the twentieth century—notions like "Take a non-totalitarian attitude," "Express yourself courageously," "Be outrageous to yourself," "Don't conform to your idea of what is expected but conform to your present spontaneous mind, your raw awareness." That's how *dharma* poets "make it new"—which was Pound's adjuration.

You need a certain deconditioning of attitude—a deconditioning of rigidity and unyieldingness—so that you can get to the heart of your own thought. That's parallel with traditional Buddhist ideas of renunciation—renunciation of hand-me-down conditioned conceptions of mind. It's the meditative practice of "letting go of thought"—neither pushing them away nor inviting them in, but, as you sit meditating, watching the procession of thought forms pass by, rising, flowering and dissolving, and disowning them, so to speak: you're not responsible any more than you're responsible for the weather, because you can't tell in advance what you're going to think next. Otherwise you'd be able to predict every thought, and that would be sad for you. There are some people whose thoughts are all predictable.

So it requires cultivation of tolerance towards one's own thoughts and impulses and ideas—the tolerance necessary for the perception of one's own mind, the kindness to the self necessary for acceptance of that process of consciousness and for acceptance of the mind's raw contents, as in Walt Whitman's "Song of Myself," so that you can look from the outside into the skull and see what's there in your head.

The specific parallel to be drawn is to Keats' notion of "negative capability," written out in a letter to his brother. He was considering Shakespeare's character and asking what kind of quality went to form a man of achievement, especially in literature. "Negative capability," he wrote, "is when a man is capable of being in uncertainties, mysteries, doubts, without any irritable reaching out after fact and reason." This means the ability to hold contrary or even polar opposite ideas or conceptions in the mind without freaking out—to experience contradiction or conflict or chaos in the mind without any irritable grasping after facts.

The really interesting word here is "irritable," which in Buddhism we take to be the aggressive insistence on eliminating one concept as against another, so that you have to take a meat-ax to your opponent or yourself to resolve the contradictions—as the Marxists took a meat-ax to their own skulls at one point, and as the neo-conservatives at this point may take a meat-ax to their own inefficient skulls. A current example might be the maniacal insistence that the Sandinistas* are the force of evil and that our C.I.A. terrorists are patriots like George Washington. That's a completely

---

* Sandinistas—Nicaraguan revolutionary socialist government under President Daniel Ortega forced into Soviet communist sphere by U.S. Latin American policies.

polarized notion of the universe—the notion that everything is black and white.

A basic Buddhist idea from 150 A.D. is that "Form is no different from Emptiness, Emptiness no different from Form." That formulation is one that Keats and all subtle poets might appreciate. The American poets Philip Whalen, Gary Snyder, Kerouac and Burroughs in their work do appreciate this "highest perfect wisdom," both in their own intuition and from their study of *Prajnaparamita* texts.

As part of "purification" or "de-conditioning" we have the need for clear seeing or direct perception—perception of a young tree without an intervening veil of preconceived ideas; the surprise glimpse, let us say, or insight, or sudden Gestalt, or I suppose you could say *satori*, occasionally glimpsed as esthetic experience.

In our century Ezra Pound and William Carlos Williams constantly insist on direct perception of the materials of poetry, of the language itself that you're working with. The slogan here—and henceforth I'll use a series of slogans derived from various poets and yogis—is one out of Pound: "Direct treatment of the thing." How do you interpret that phrase? Don't treat the object indirectly or symbolically, but look directly at it and choose spontaneously that aspect of it which is most immediately striking—the striking flash in consciousness or awareness, the most vivid, what sticks out in your mind—and notate that.

"Direct treatment of the 'thing' whether subjective or objective," is a famous axiom or principle that Pound pronounced around 1912. He derived that American application of twentieth-century insight from his study of Chinese Confucian, Taoist and Japanese Buddhist poetry. There was a Buddhist infusion into Western culture at the end of the nineteenth century, both in painting and in poetry. Pound put in order the papers of "the late professor Ernest Fenollosa," the celebrated essay on "The Chinese Written Character as a Medium for Poetry." Fenollosa/Pound pointed out that in Chinese you were able to have a "direct treatment" of the object because the object was pictorially there via hieroglyph. Pound recommended the adaptation of the same idea: the Chinese poetic method as a corrective to the conceptual vagueness and sentimental abstraction of Western poetry. In a way he was asking for the inter-cession of the *bodhisattvas* of Buddhist poetry into Western poetics because he was calling for direct perception, direct contact without intervening conceptualization, a clear seeing attentiveness, which, as you may remember, echoing in your brain, is supposed to be one of the marks of Zen masters, as in their practice of gardening, tea ceremony, flower arranging or archery.

That idea was relatively rare in late-nineteenth-century aca-demic Western poetry, though Pound also drew from advanced Western models—old Dante to the French modernist poets Jules Laforgue, Tristan Corbière and Rimbaud. The tradition was ini-tiated by Baudelaire, who had updated the poetic consciousness of the nineteenth century to include the city, real estate, houses, carriages, traffic, machinery. As Walt Whitman said, "Bring the muse into the kitchen, Drag the muse into the kitchen? She's there, installed amidst the kitchenware."

Another slogan that evolved around the same time as Pound's and with the same motif was William Carlos Williams' famous "No ideas but in things." He repeats it in his epic *Paterson*, a little more clearly for those who haven't understood: "No ideas but in facts." Just the facts, ma'am. Don't give us your editorial; no general ideas. Just "give me a for instance"—correlate the conception with a real process or a particular action or a concrete thing, localized, imme-diate, palpable, practicable, involving direct sense contact.

In one of the immortal bard's lyrics, divine Shakespeare gives you nothing but things:

> When icicles hang by the wall
> And Dick the shepherd blows his nail
> And Tom bears logs into the hall,
> And milk comes frozen home in pail . . .
> And Marian's nose looks red and raw . . .

That was Shakespeare's vivid presentation of unmistakable winter. You don't need to make the generalization if you give the particular instances. A poet is like a Sherlock Holmes, assembling the phalanx of data from which to draw his editorial conclusion. William James' notion was of "the solidity of specificity." Kerouac's phrase for it was, "Details are the life of prose." To have it you've got to have "direct treatment of the thing." And that requires direct perception—mind capable of awareness, uncluttered by abstraction, the veil of conceptions parted to reveal significant details of the world's stage.

Williams has another way of saying it—homely advice to young poets and American art practitioners: "Write about things that are close to the nose." There's a poem of his, much quoted by Buddhist poets, called "Thursday." It goes like this:

> *I have had my dream—like others —*
> *and it has come to nothing, so that*
> *I remain now carelessly*
> *with feet planted on the ground*
> *and look up at the sky—*
> *feeling my clothes about me,*
> *the weight of my body in my shoes,*
> *the rim of my hat, air passing in and out*
> *at my nose—and decide to dream no more.*

Just try! Actually that one single poem is the intersection between the mind of meditation—the discipline of meditation, letting go of thoughts—and the Yankee practice of poetry after William James, where the poet is standing there, feeling the weight of his body in his shoes, aware of the air passing in and out of his nose. And since the title of this series of talks is "Spiritual Quests" we might make a little footnote here that "spirit" comes from the Latin *spiritus*, which means "breathing," and that the spiritual practices of the East are primarily involved with meditation, and that meditation practices usually begin with trying to increase one's awareness of the space around you, beginning with the fact that you're breathing. So generally you follow your breath, in Zen or in Tibetan style. It's a question of following the breath out from the tip of the nose to the end of the breath and then following it back into the stomach, perhaps, or the lower abdomen. So it's sort of charming that Williams arrived at this concept of his own: "air passing in and out at my nose—and decide to dream no more."

Another Pound phrase that leads the mind toward direct treatment of the thing, or clear seeing, is: "The natural object is always the adequate symbol." You don't have to go chasing after far-fetched symbols because direct perception will propose efficient language to you. And that relates to another very interesting statement, by the Tibetan lama poet Chögyam Trungpa: "Things are symbols of themselves." Pound means that the natural object is identical with what it is you're trying to symbolize in any case. Trungpa is saying that if you directly perceive a thing it's completely there, completely itself, completely revelatory of the eternal universe that it's in, or of your mind as it is.

In Kerouac's set of thirty slogans called "Belief and Technique for Modern Prose" there are a few mind-arrows, or mind-pointers, which are instruction on how to focus in, how to direct your mind to see things, whether it's "an old teacup in memory," or whether you're looking out a window, sketching verbally. Kerouac advised writers: "Don't think of words when you stop but to see picture better." William Blake's similar slogan is: "Labor will the Minute Particulars, attend to the Little-ones." It's very pretty actually; take care of the little baby facts. Blake continues:

He who would do good to another, must do it in Minute Particulars
General good is the plea of the scoundrel hypocrite and flatterer:
For Art and Science cannot exist but in minutely organized Particulars

A classic example of William Carlos Williams in America seeing minute particulars clearly, precisely, thoroughly, is in the famous and most obvious of Imagist poems, "The Red Wheelbarrow." Because the thing was seen so completely the poem seems to have penetrated throughout the culture, so that people who are not interested in poetry—high school kids or thick-headed businessmen—know this as the totem modern poem.

so much depends
upon

a red wheel
barrow

glazed with rain
water

beside the white
chickens.

That's considered the acme Imagist poem of direct perception. I think it was written in the twenties. It's not much, actually. Williams didn't think it was so much; he said, "An inconsequential poem—written in 2 minutes—as was (for instance) The Red Wheelbarrow and most other short poems." But it became a sort of sacred object.

Why did he focus on that one image in his garden? Well, he probably didn't focus on it—it was just there and he saw it. And he remembered it. Vividness is self-selecting. In other words, he didn't prepare to see it, except that he had had a life's preparation in practicing awareness "close to the nose," trying to stay in his body and observe the space around him. That kind of spontaneous awareness has a Buddhist term for it: "the Unborn." For where does a thought come from? You can't trace it back to a womb, a thought is "unborn." Perception is unborn, in the sense that it spontaneously arises. Because even if you tried to trace your perceptions back to the source, you couldn't.

To catch the red wheelbarrow, however, you have to be practiced in poetics as well as practiced in ordinary mind. Flaubert was the prose initiator of that narrowing down of perception and the concretization of it with his phrase "The ordinary is the extraordinary." There's a very interesting formulation of that attitude of mind in writing poetry by the late Charles Olson, in his essay "Projective Verse." This is kind of caviar, but William Carlos Williams reprinted this famous essay for the transmission of his own ideas to another generation. It contains several slogans commonly used by most modern poets that relate to the idea of direct seeing or direct awareness of open mind and open form in poetry. Here's what Olson says:

> This is the problem which any poet who departs from closed form is especially confronted by. And it evolves a whole series of new recognitions. From the moment he ventures into FIELD COMPOSITION [Olson means the field of the mind] . . . he can go by no track other than the one that the poem under hand declares for itself. Thus he has to behave, and be, instant by instant, aware of some several forces just now beginning to be examined. . . .

The principle, the law which presides conspicuously over such composition and when obeyed is the reason why a projective poem can come into being. It is this: FORM IS NEVER MORE THAN AN EXTENSION OF CONTENT. (Or so it got phrased by one Robert Creeley, and it makes absolute sense to me, with this possible corollary, that right form, in any given poem is the only and exclusively possible extension of the content under hand.) There it is, brothers, sitting there for USE.

By "content" I think Olson means the sequence of perceptions. So the form—the form of a poem, the plot of a poem, the argument of a poem, the narrative of a poem—would correspond to the sequence of perceptions. If that seems opaque to you, the next paragraph from Olson's "Projective Verse" essay might explain more. He says this:

> Now the *process* of the thing, how the principle can be made so to shape the energies that the form is accomplished. And I think it could be boiled down to one statement (first pounded into my head by Edward Dahlberg): ONE PERCEPTION MUST IMMEDIATELY AND DIRECTLY LEAD TO A FURTHER PERCEPTION. It means exactly what it says, is a matter of, at *all* points . . . get on with it, keep moving, keep in, speed the nerves, their speed, the perceptions, theirs, the acts, the split-second acts [the decisions you make while scribbling], the whole business, keep it moving as fast as you can, citizen. And if you set up as a poet, USE, USE, USE the process at all points. In any given poem always, always one perception must, must, must [as with the mind] MOVE INSTANTER ON ANOTHER! . . . So there we are, fast there's the dogma. And its excuse, its usableness, in practice. Which gets us . . . inside the machinery, now, 1950, of how projective verse is made.

I interpret that set of words—"one perception must move instanter on another"—as similar to the dharmic practice of letting go of thoughts and allowing fresh thoughts to arise and be registered, rather than hanging onto one exclusive image and forcing Reason to branch it out and extend it into a hung-up metaphor. That was the difference between the metaphysically inspired poetry of the thirties to the fifties in America after T.S. Eliot and the Open Form, practiced simultaneously by Ezra Pound and William Carlos Williams and later by Charles Olson and Robert Creeley. They let the mind loose. Actually, that's a phrase by one of the founders of our country: "The mind must be loose." That's John Adams, as reported by Robert Duncan in relation to poetics. Try that on the religious right. Leave the mind loose. One perception leads to another. So don't cling to perceptions, or fixate on impressions, or on visions of William Blake. As the young surrealist poet Philip Lamantia said when he was asked in 1958 to define "hip" as distinguishable from "square": Hip is "Don't get hung up."

So we have, as a ground of purification, letting go—the confidence to let your mind loose and observe your own perceptions and their discontinuities. You can't go back and change the sequence of the thoughts you had; you can't revise the process of thinking or deny what was thought, but thought obliterates itself anyway. You don't have to worry about that, you can go on to the next thought.

Robert Duncan once got up and walked across the room and then said, "I can't revise my steps once I've taken them." He was using that as an example to explain why he was interested in Gertrude Stein's writing, which was writing in the present moment, present time, present consciousness: what was going on in the grammar of her head during the time of composition without recourse to past memory or future planning.

Meditators have formulated a slogan that says, "Renunciation is a way to avoid conditioned mind." That means that meditation is practiced by constantly renouncing your mind, or "renouncing" your thoughts, or "letting go" of your thoughts. It doesn't mean letting go of your whole awareness—only that small part of your mind that's dependent on linear, logical thinking. It doesn't mean renouncing intellect, which has its proper place in Buddhism, as it does in Blake. It doesn't mean idiot wildness. It means expanding the area of awareness, so that your awareness surrounds your thoughts, rather than that you enter into thoughts like a dream. Thus the life of meditation and the life of art are both based on a similar conception of spontaneous mind. They both share renunciation as a way of avoiding a conditioned art work, or trite art, or repetition of other people's ideas.

Poets can avoid repetition of their obsessions. What it requires is confidence in the magic of chance. Chögyam Trungpa phrased this notion, "Magic is the total delight in chance." That also brings magic to poetry: chance thought, or the unborn thought, or the spontaneous thought, or the "first thought," or the thought spoken spontaneously with its conception—thought and word identical on the spot. It requires a certain amount of unselfconsciousness, like singing in the bathtub. It means not embarrassed, not jealous, not involved in one-upmanship, not mimicking, not imitating, above all not self-conscious. And that requires a certain amount of jumping out of yourself—courage and humor and openness and perspective and carelessness, in the sense of burning your mental bridges behind you, outreaching yourself; purification, so to speak, giving yourself permission to utter what you think, either simultaneously, or immediately thereafter, or ten years later.

That brings a kind of freshness and cleanness to both thought and utterance. William Carlos Williams has an interesting phrase about what's wrong when you don't allow that to happen: "There cannot be any kind of facile deception about it . . . prose with a dirty wash of a stale poem over it." Dirty wash of a stale poem over your own natural thought?

When I met Chögyam Trungpa in San Francisco in 1972 we were comparing our travels and our poetry. He had a heavy schedule and a long itinerary, and I said I was getting fatigued with mine. He said, "That's probably because you don't like your poetry."

So I said, "What do you know about poetry? How do you know I don't like my poetry?"

He said, "Why do you need a piece of paper? Don't you trust your own mind? Why don't you do like the classic poets? Milarepa made up his poems on the spot and other people copied them down."

That's actually the classical Buddhist practice among Zen masters and Tibetan lamas, like the author of "The Hundred Thousand Songs of Milarepa." These songs are the most exquisite and hermetic as well as vulgar and folk-art-like works in all of Tibetan culture—classic folk poetry, known by every Tibetan. But Milarepa never could write. The method, again, was spontaneous mind, on-the-spot improvisation on the basis of meditative discipline.

What Trungpa said reminded me of a similar exchange that I had with Kerouac, who also urged me to be more spontaneous, less worried about my poetic practice. I was always worried about my poetry. Was it any good? Were the household dishes right, was the bed made? I remember Kerouac falling down drunk on the kitchen floor of 170 East Second Street in 1960, laughing up at me and saying, "Ginsberg, you're a hairy loss." That's something that he made up on the spot, a phrase that just came out of his mouth, and I was offended. A hairy loss! If you allow the active phrase to come to your mind, allow that out, you speak from a ground that can relate your inner perception to external phenomena, and thus join Heaven and Earth.

Winter 1987

Statement [On Censorship]

My poetry has been broadcast uncensored for thirty years, particularly the poems *Howl, Sunflower Sutra, America, Kaddish, Kral Majales*, and *Birdbrain*. In the last two decades all these poems have been recorded on disk by Atlantic, Fantasy and Island Records, issued commercially and been broadcast by university, public educational and listener supported stations, such as the Pacifica stations.

Most of these poems have been republished in standard anthologies used for college and high school English courses throughout America. *Howl* alone has been translated into 24 languages, even recently published in hitherto forbidden Iron Curtain countries from Poland to China.

Translations and publications into Polish, Hungarian, Czechoslovakian, Chinese, Macedonian, Serbo-Croatian, Lithuanian and Romanian have been part and parcel of the *glasnost* or freedom of speech and literature accumulated in the last half-decade in those countries. In a recent article by Bill Holm on teaching literature (including D.H. Lawrence) to students in China titled, "In China, Loving Lady Chatterley" (*New York Times Book Review*, February 18, 1990, pages 1, 30-31), we read: "Orwell's description of Big Brother's attempts to destroy and pervert sexual life is exactly and literally true. Change the names and it describes any institution like China, name your own preferred church or government." Fundamentalists, mass media hucksters, Senator Jesse Helms, and the Heritage Foundation are attempting to enforce in U.S.A. this Orwellian doublethink in destroying and perverting representation of sexual life in our art and literature.

What is their motive? Professor Holm states it precisely: "My Chinese students existed in a state of sexual suspended animation and yet underneath this mad repression, I sensed that many Chinese are hopeless romantics, doors waiting to be opened. Real sexual energy is a genuine threat to political authority. The moral Stalinists are not wrong."

I remember the insistent language of Moscow Writers Union bureaucrat Mr. Sagatelian at a Soviet American literary conference November 1985 in Vilnius just before the announcement of *glasnost*. I complained of political and erotic censorship; he replied "Henry Miller will never be published in the Soviet Union."

Broadcast censorship of my poetry and the work of my peers is a direct violation of our freedom of expression. I am a citizen. I pay my taxes and I want the opinions, the political and social ideas and emotions of my art to be free from government censorship. I petition for my right to exercise liberty of speech guaranteed me by the Constitution. I reject the insolence of self-righteous moralistic fundraising politicians or politically ambitious priests in using my poetry as a political football for their quasi-religious agendas. I have my own agenda for emotional and intellectual and political liberty in U.S.A. and behind the Iron Curtain. This is expressed in my poetry.

The poems named above were part of a large-scale domestic cultural and political liberalization that began with ending print and broadcast censorship of literary works 1957-1962. A series of legal trials, beginning with my poem *Howl*, liberated celebrated works including books by Henry Miller, Jean Genet, D.H. Lawrence, William Burroughs, and other classic writings.

Much of my poetry is specifically aimed to rouse the sense of liberty of thought and political social expression of that thought in young adolescents. This is the very age group which the Heritage Foundation and Senator [Jesse] Helms' legislation and FCC regulations have attempted to prohibit me from reaching with vocal communication of my texts over the air. It is in the body, speech and mind of these young people that the state of our nation rests and I believe I am conducting spiritual war for liberation of their souls from the mass homogenization of greedy materialistic commerce and emotional desensitization. Since Walt Whitman, who foresaw this situation, many generations have suffered alienation of feeling and sympathy with their own bodies and hearts and with the bodies and hearts of all those in America and other continents that do not fit into a commercially or politically stereotyped convention of color, sex, religion, political allegiance, or personal sense of self.

Pseudo-religious legal interference with my speech amounts to setting up a state religion much in the mode of intolerant Ayatollah or a Stalinoid bureaucratic party line.

In this situation neo-conservative and religious ideologues have taken the weapons of their old communist enemies: party line, censorship, Catch-22 evasion of authority of their own solidified thought police religious and ethical systems. How dare I compare these so-called patriotic citizens to communist bureaucrats? In the words of William Blake: "They became what they beheld."

These censors would abridge my rights of artistic and political freedom of speech just as communist countries did in censoring my work in 1957-1985.

Here an aesthetic consideration enters the argument. A major characteristic of my poetry, at least for its wide circulation, has been its quality of American speech, idiomatic and vernacular, a diction drawn from living language and clarity of vocalization. My ideal is a poetry of majestic and dignified proclamation. I've tried to practice unobstructed vocalizations of sometimes inspired verse, the human voice sounded with its various rhythms and emotional tones, a poetry spoken from head, throat and heart centers; as reading out loud has been my study and my art. This practice has affected many poets in many countries and is part of a long American tradition from the day of Walt Whitman through William Carlos Williams to the lyricist Bob Dylan. Proposed FCC regulation could forbid broadcast of *Howl* (a critique of nuclear hypertechnology), *King of May* (a denunciation of both "communist and capitalist assholes"), *Sunflower Sutra* (panegyric to individual self-empowerment), *America* (a parody of cold-war stereotypes), *Birdbrain* (a satire on Eastern and Western ecological stupidities), and *Kaddish* (a pouring forth of real grief and love for my mother). How can this speech be censored from broadcast without violating our U.S. Constitution?

Censors may fulminate all they wish over the word "indecency," which is never precisely defined, but those who want to extend the Helms amendment to ban this mystific "indecency" on the air 24 hours a day cannot deny they are trying to censor art and socially relevant speech. In the case of the texts specified above, the position of neo-conservatives is quite parallel to that of Nazi book burners of "degenerate works," Chinese dictators who launch attacks on "spiritual pollution," and old Stalinists forbidding erotic texts. The purpose of such censorship is to concentrate all emotional authority in the State, and eliminate all ideological and emotional competition. Conservatives proclaim their ideology to be "get the government off our backs." I petition these so-called "neo-conservative" authoritarians to get off my back.

Walt Whitman called specifically for candor of poets and orators to follow him. Despite the unconstitutional bans that have been put on my poetry, I repeat that call and affirm that I have fulfilled the Good Gray Poet's prescription for a patriotic, candid, totally American art.

Feb. 19, 1990

PART FOUR

Journals

Allen Ginsberg, Jack Kerouac, William S. Burroughs,
John Clellon Holmes, and other Beat Generation writ-
ers were endlessly fascinated by the existential lives
of the overlooked, downtrodden, or overlooked in
society—the Times Square hustlers, drug addicts, jazz
musicians, hipsters, petty thieves, street people, and
others who relied on their wits to get from day to day—
people who, in the words of John Clellon Holmes, were
willing "to wager the sum of their resources on a single
number." Herbert Huncke was one of the first such char-
acters whom they knew personally, and he had a pro-
found effect on their thinking and writing.

Huncke also played a prominent role in one of the
critical events in Ginsberg's young adult life. Described
in "Howl" as one "who walked all night with their shoes
full of blood on the snowbank docks waiting for a door
in the East River to open to a room full of steamheat
and opium," Huncke appeared at Ginsberg's apart-
ment door, homeless and destitute and suicidally
depressed. The following journal entries, the opening
of a lengthy document supposedly written for an attor-
ney, describe Huncke and the results of his early fateful
stay with Ginsberg. Aside from the character portrayal,
these passages detail Ginsberg's 1948 "Blake Visions"
and the fragile state of the poet's mind at the time of
Huncke's arrival.

New York: ca. late-winter 1949

Portrait of Huncke

I

There was a knock at the door, surprising me because it was only eight o'clock in the morning, and it was snowing outside. I had been sitting on a couch, with no thought on my mind, staring at a huge map of the world. I saw a dim familiar figure in the hall, and I guessed immediately it was Herbert Huncke, though I hadn't seen him for over sixty days, which was the time he had been spending in jail. I had made up my mind about a month before this not to put him up anymore, but he looked so much like a ragged saint at my door, that I waved him into the living room, and followed him in silently.

"Did you get my letter on Riker's Island?"

"No," he said, "thank you for thinking of me, though." He began to take off his shoes, gingerly. They were wet, and the socks, for all their wetness smelled dank. His feet were bloody, covered with blisters and raw spots, and dirty. He hadn't slept for several days, the last time in the 50th Street Greyhound Bus Terminal. He hadn't eaten except for irregular doses of Benzedrine, coffee and donuts. He had no money. We discussed these things with some humor and I began to take pleasure in provisioning and rehabilitating his wardrobe.

I boiled up a pot full of hot water and helped wash his feet, his legs were stiff by this time. I was aware of how little love had been shown him in the last ten days of half hallucinated wandering. Yet I washed with averted eyes.

Then he went to sleep on the couch and slept for a day and a night.

II

The day and night's sleep dismayed me because I hadn't planned to leave him alone in the house without further talk with him, reassurance that he wouldn't run off with any of my valuables. The last time I'd been his host he'd done just that. Small radios were missing, cheap rugs, jackets, one at a time, with good reason—a matter of keeping him warm or getting him food. I would be petulant, I would even become secretly enraged. It didn't actually make too much difference to me, because I was too preoccupied with the charm of his company, and the misery of my own thoughts.

But the last time I'd put him up, it was a different matter. I was living in an apartment loaned from a friend, a mad "pad" in the middle of Harlem, six flights up in the sky with a view of 125th Street.

I would look out of the window, not at the street, but at the sky, staring out of my own emptiness at the light of heaven. My daily program was almost the same—I would go to school for an hour in the morning. The class I had was the last course I needed to get out of the school after six years of irregular study. After class I worked two hours in the small musty office of a nearly defunct learned journal of political economy. I worked at that office for two years.

On my way home, I would walk down the shopping street of Italian East Harlem, a crowded avenue where I purchased cheap meats and exotic vegetables. When I got home I would sleep for a few hours, then go out for another walk around Harlem.

I had no preoccupation, no plans, no purpose, no real interest. This was quite unlike me, actually as I had nourished myself in the seven years following my adolescence, on a contradictory but long thought out program of intellectual self improvement. This had meant to me going down in the gutter of Times Square and Harlem. Yet suddenly, after seven years of rocking myself back and forth in the cradle of intellect and youth-wildness, I suddenly lost my curiosity. I lost my motive, my reason. I wanted to lose the sense of my own character and emerge with a voice of rock, a grave, severe sense of love of the world, an asperity and directness of passion. I wanted to make people shudder when they looked into my eye, suddenly wakened from a vast dream of the will.

Needless to say—and I am not passing judgment on the attempt itself—it had not succeeded. I gave up, I shut down the machinery,

I stopped thinking, I stopped living. I never went out to see people anymore.

So there I stopped and thought no more about it, except on that level of renunciation, and lived for months in complete surprise and emptiness at the strange conclusion of my spiritual progress. What to do then, after that, I didn't know—nothing but to keep myself fed and comfortable and away from temptations to effort and ecstasy. So I stopped writing poetry, stopped using my weekly round of visits to friends, and stopped using drugs to excite my senses to eerie knowledge.

Nothing I had experienced in my life led me to expect what would happen to me in my loneliness. One day in the middle of the summer as I was walking down 125th Street, I suddenly stopped and stared around me in amazement. It was as if I had just awakened from a long dream that I'd walked around in all my life. I threw over all my preoccupations with ideas and felt so free that I didn't know who I was or where I was. The whole appearance of the world changed in a minute when I realized what had happened, and I began to look at people walking past me. They all had incredible sleepy, bestial expressions on their faces, yet no different from what they usually looked like. I suddenly understood everything vague and troubled in my mind that had been caused by the expression of people around me. Everybody I saw had something wrong with them. The apparition of an evil, sick, unconscious wild city rose before me in visible semblance, and about the dead buildings in the barren air, the bodies of the soul that built the wonderland shuffled and stalked and lurched in attitudes of immemorial nightmare all around.

When I saw people conversing around me, all their conversation, all their bodily movements, all their signs, the thoughts reflected on their faces were of fear of recognition and anguished fear that someone would take the initiative and discover their masks and lies. Therefore every tone of voice, movement of the hand, carried a negative overtone: this in the world is called coyness and shyness and politeness, or frigidity and hostility when the awareness becomes too overpowering. I felt that I would be crucified if I alluded with any insistence to the divine nature of ourselves and the physical universe. Therefore I did not speak but only stared in dumb silence.

This so overpowering draught of knowledge lasted until I began

to move again, and think, and I was once more baffled by the inscru-
table appearance of things. I was staring out the window when I saw
a vast gleam of light cover the sky, the bowl of heaven was suffused
with an eerie glow, as if the world about my eyes was a vast sea
creature and this was the interior of leviathan. When I recognized
that something extraordinary was happening to me, I realized that
what I was seeing had been there all the time—indeed excited in
me a recognition of that aspect of the imagination which is referred
to as the eternal—longer than my own life, extending beyond my
life and my former consciousness. I was staring at no human objects
except the tops of buildings and at nature. Of the human objects,
I remember that I understood in this one glance, their utility and
significance. I can say that I saw not the objects but the idea behind
them. The most absorbing aspect of the spectacle was the actual
placement of the intelligence, for I perceived that the guiding intel-
ligence was in the objects themselves, not in some far corner of the
universe, and that the world as we see it is complete: there is noth-
ing outside of it. It seemed also to open itself up to disclose itself to
me for the moment, allowing its secret to be understood.

When I returned to my apartment my first impulse was to con-
sult an old author, William Blake, whom I remembered from earlier
days, for the then baffling beauty and directness of his observations
on the divine nature of the soul. I remembered particularly, apro-
pos of my own astonishing moment in the street, a famous poem in
which the poet wandered on the byways of London several hundred
years ago,

> *"and mark in every face I meet*
> *marks of weakness, marks of woe."*

I read this poem again, but found that it did not shed any further
light on what I was after, and turned idly over the pages till my eye
was caught by the lines

> *"seeking after that sweet golden clime*
> *where the travelers journey is done."*

I felt at that moment a wave of such great sadness pass over me
that I knew that my vision of the early afternoon had returned, and

this time in such intensity that I stared stupefied with knowledge of the words written on the page, as if there had been a magical formulation of my own awakening comprehension of joy. I looked out the window at the sky above Harlem, beyond the bare, stained, brick wall of the next building, through the massive distances of the cloudless and immobile atmosphere toward the unseen stars, and felt the gigantic weight of Time.

I then found the poem "The Sick Rose" and when I came to

> *"the invisible worm*
> *that flies in the night*
> *in the howling storm"*

and read on to

> *"his dark secret love*
> *does thy life destroy"*

I realized once more that the last and most terrible veil had been torn from my eyes, a final shuddering glimpse through death. Then I moved across the room with the gnawing pulse of animality engulfing my body with slow carnal undulations of my frame, and shrieked and collapsed in silent agony, moaning on the floor, my hands grasping and hollowed in my thighs.

I spent a week after this living on the edge of a cliff in eternity. It wasn't so easy after that. I would get glimmerings, hints of possibility, secret amazements at myself, at the world, at "the nature of reality," at some of the wisdom other people seemed to reflect, at poets of the past, even at Shelley. I reread Dante and wormed through some of Shakespeare, Plotinus, St. Augustine, Plato, anything that caught my fancy.

It was in this frenzied preoccupation that I received Herbert at the door that summer. I didn't even notice him, except to ask him what sensations he had while walking cold and hungry down the street in his own days. So I waited for the descent of the dove while Herbert hungered around the apartment. He went out, days and nights at a time, and returned with gossip of the underworld, which I listened to with an ear for the bizarre, the fantastic, eventually the cosmic. A new social center had been established on Times

Square—a huge room lit in brilliant fashion by neon glare and filled with slot machines, open day and night. There all the apocalyptic hipsters in New York eventually stopped, fascinated by the timeless room.

I was absorbed in my alchemical studies, leading nowhere, but promising the key to that light which I'd experienced. Every author I looked at had his own light, his own method, his own renunciations. I became confused by my own theories and those of others. Meanwhile Herbert came and went, and one day disappeared entirely.

By then I had begun to notice that the bookshelves were barer than before, that my radio, typewriter, winter clothes, and an oriental statuette were not there anymore. Suddenly I realized that Herbert had been robbing me to feed a heroin habit. I had seen him shooting it in the veins, but I had supposed that he at least had had the courtesy to provide his own dope, since I was already providing everything else for him. The worst of it was that they weren't my books, but belonged to a theological student friend.

I spent part of that fall lurking around Times Square with [Russell] Durgin, the theologist, looking for Herbert. I didn't hear from him for another year, until I had settled in my own apartment, was working at night in a cafeteria as a dishwasher, had made partial repayment to the theologist for his books which were worth at least $150. It was from an old acquaintance on Times Square that I heard Herbert was in jail again on charges of possession of marijuana. I wrote him a letter and didn't hear from him again till the knock on my door.

III

Herbert had finally wakened when I came home the next day from work. He looked at me and laughed, nodding his head with a conciliatory upward lift. The ironic mask remained, as did my fixed and frozen inquiring smile. I had thought of him all day and night, with alternating rage and gentleness, and had made plans. I was waiting for an opening.

He sighed. "You didn't by any chance think of bringing home a tube of Benzedrine?" He looked at me as if he knew I hadn't with an ill humored, petty reproachfulness.

"No, I don't have enough money."

"Well money, money. God knows there's enough money for an inhaler to get me up at least out of your couch and out into the snow. If you can't think for yourself you might at least think of some small way of making it a little easier for me to get into operation again."

"There's no rush. I'm not going to send you out into the snow—yet."

"You might just as well, for all the good I feel at the moment. I don't think I'll ever get up." He turned to me, a touch of humor in his voice, and yet with narrow eyes. "I think I'm going to die."

I nodded without comment. He spoke as if he were telling me something that he had been aware of for days.

"Why? Do you want to kill yourself?"

"No," he said. "I had thought of it and started going through with some routine or other on that issue a week ago." He shrugged his shoulders, as if annoyed that he had not. "I'll kill myself slowly, like this, if I do it at all, unless I get more beat than I am now, and I doubt that I can get any lower."

His death and my vision seemed to hold equal finality for each of us in the scheme of things.

"Then what makes you think that you are going to die?"

"It's not dying, exactly, it's like an animal—extinction. I'm tired. I have nothing, and I don't think I want anything enough to put out the effort involved in getting it." He spoke with great delicacy, choosing his words halting and spitting them out wearily, as if the effort at conversation were futile, and any expression he could use was cliché. An impatient gesture of the wrist signified that this was his own fault, his own lack of drive, or lack of polish in speech. His gestures were apologetic. He spread his hands again, explaining what it was that was so unspeakable. "All happening to me is unnecessary. I have been feeling all morning that I am caught in a gigantic whirlpool. I was frighteningly dizzy. I hoped to lose consciousness again. But something assured me I would not. It is all very terrifying. It is making me very sick."

He began to talk about his body. For years, since a trip to North Africa on a merchant ship, his dark face had carried on it the lingering remains of a skin disease that appeared soon after he got back. It began with a rash, almost fungus-like, below his mouth, and spread till it covered his lips and began eating its way up the cheeks. It was not a mortal growth, it appeared to do no harm, other than to complete the destruction of the dark beauty on his face.

His teeth were gone, and his visage had changed from what I had understood to have been wiry, precocious, original charm, with large dark eyes, jet black hair combed in waves in each side backward to the base of his skull. The youthfulness of his charm had long disappeared; he was now 30 and an old man to me. He had spent his adolescence at the center of large groups of the city's underworld in Boston, Chicago, New Orleans, and New York. He had been used to being kept by men of curious tastes older than himself. Now that was out of the question; not only was he a monster in his body, but the same monstrousness had emerged in his mind. The former youthful curiosity and freedom had been replaced with an almost saintly obsession with homelessness; his taste for the strange and exotic in personal habits, in perceptions, in love, was transformed to a weary disillusion with his own body. His original curiosity about his own passions had died, and he was left listless, all energy directed to the extermination of his personality, in an endless nausea at his sense of self, his vanity, his wants.

And yet all this was displayed and sometimes admitted with the charm of an old, knowledgeable roué, or a woman looking backward nostalgically and with gaity, at the charm of her own youth; not merely forgiving her innocence, but with a lovely human surprise at the wickedness of her own conquests, and winking at the youth that inherited her frivolity among the fortunes of the world.

So, as Herbert spoke it was this bitter lament for time well spent and now unavoidably past; and with some regret for wasted opportunities—frail earlier ambitions—and with good humor, almost mature self contempt. As so often the case with people of any intrinsic interest, Herbert's face and its expressions were so much the hub of my experience that I find myself returning to his naked visage as the key to my memory.

In the masked smile I have spoken of so often there was yet fellow-creaturely questioning of an almost conspiratorial nature. He often smiled at me when appraising some effort of mine at teasing him and awakening his interest in himself or some project that I had in mind for him. It was, I guessed, an expression of recognition and coyness of his own, for I had often seen him converse, with this sane look on his face, with powerful and violent hoodlums on

Times Square. Certainly, it was also the look of a mother with no illusions about her young.

> *Once he had recovered, Huncke essentially took over Ginsberg's place and, after connecting with two small-time thieves, used the apartment to store their stolen goods. Ginsberg eventually ordered them to remove the purloined items, which they were in the process of doing when they crashed their car and the stolen property was discovered. All were arrested, Ginsberg as an accessory to the crimes. As the result of a plea bargain, Ginsberg was spared prison time, but was ordered to seek in-patient treatment at a psychiatric institute. While staying at the hospital, he met Carl Solomon, a fellow patient who would become a major figure in "Howl," and to whom the landmark poem would be dedicated.*

Ginsberg's early poems were almost exclusively limited to rhymed imitations of his father's lyric verse and the works of the masters he studied at Columbia. A few of the better efforts would be published in the Columbia student journal, but Ginsberg realized that, for all of his hard work, the poems did not say what he intended them to say. Others, such as Columbia professors Lionel Trilling and Mark Van Doren, agreed. William Carlos Williams, who lived in nearby Rutherford, New Jersey, to whom Ginsberg had shown his early work, was blunt in his assessment of Ginsberg imitations: "In this mode, perfection is basic," he told Ginsberg.

Then, in early 1952, in an attempt to please the local celebrity poet and mentor, Ginsberg looked through his old journals, selected what he felt were some of the more interesting entries, and broke down their lines into what appeared to be structured poetry. Ginsberg had little confidence in these new poems, which he likened to "a bunch of short crappy scraps I picked out of my journals and fixed up like poems, the like of which I would write 10 a day to order."

Williams's response to the poems was stunning. "How many of such poems do you own?" he asked. "You must have a book. I shall see that you get it. . . These are it."

Ginsberg immediately went to work at assembling a book-length collection of this type of poem. The following journal entry, notes for a preface to the book (which he was calling Empty Mirror*), very briefly describes this breakthrough in his writing—a breakthrough he would honor for the rest of his life.*

New York: May 20, 1952

For Preface—Apology, etc.

Poems, some of them in *Empty Mirror* have a wholeness and style of their own, a form which includes completeness and pleasing rhythm, others are just statements of fact. Whatever I have to say had best be left as is, as said, distortion removes original spring from the sentences, the purity of the thought, and the exactness of expression. What I really think is what I am after. There may be a way of getting nearer by more work, which I find oppressive and impossible. There may be a way of refinement to symmetry but this would take out what is important, the nakedness which is truth. Perhaps art is not truth, but otherwise art seems empty. Art may be greater truth than that which I offer, this may be appraised but not criticized.

Our thoughts where they meet reality are intense and poetical; this is the underlying idea. I have not written this book to prove it, but I have collected these fragments because they seemed interesting to others, and archetypical to myself, in my own life.

The only things we "know" are what we think in the moments we give ourselves away, "tip our mitt." I prefer those rare moments in authors when they are not trying to formulate an official policy for themselves or the real world.

Throughout his life, Allen Ginsberg kept an exten-
sive, descriptive record of his dreams, many of which
included his friends and family, and involved alternate
realities that Ginsberg found fascinating and revealing.
The unfettered meanderings of the inner mind, uninhib-
ited by the factors that controlled conscious thinking,
was an obsession shared by Kerouac and Burroughs,
whose selected dreams wound up in published volumes.
"White Shroud," one of Ginsberg's major later works,
was an example of how he worked a dream into poetry.

In this journal entry, Ginsberg writes about a dream
involving Joan Vollmer, a close friend from his Colum-
bia University days and the live-in companion of Bur-
roughs. The two had moved to Mexico, their lives largely
dictated by overindulgence in drugs and alcohol. One
night, after a day of heavy drinking, Burroughs had
been goaded into playing a game of Willian Tell, in
which he was to shoot a glass placed on Vollmer's head.
Burroughs missed his target, and Vollmer was killed.
Vollmer's death haunted Ginsberg for many years, and
he would occasionally write about her in his journals.
The prose in this dream entry was eventually translated
into the poem, "Dream Record: June 8, 1955."

San Francisco: June 8, 1955

I dreamed this during a drunken night in my house when I brought home John R. and we lay peacefully at a late hour in each other's arms asleep. I was visiting [St. Louis, a new city] big city, and there saw Joan Burroughs who has been dead now five years—she sat in a chair in a garden with the smile on her face: restored to its former beauty, the sweetness of intelligence which I eternalized in my imagination, that had been lost thru years of Tequila in Mexico City, for Tequila had ruined her face & beauty before the bullet in her brow. And we spoke of her old lover boy John Kingsland, and Burroughs lately in Africa, her children I have not seen with grand-parents scattered, in Syracuse, of Kerouac writing sunk in woe & loneliness from Rocky Mount, myself in San Francisco living a different life with new loves, and Joe Army whose mute smile and guarded eyes in photo look down on me as I write this at my desk in the sunny afternoon. Then I realized that this was a dream: and said, "Joan," as she smiled and talked again as would a traveler resting on return, waiting to hear what life he's missed at home—"Do the dead have memory, still love their mortal acquaintances, & do they still remember us," but she faded before there was a reply and in the place where her ghost was I saw her small rain-stained tombstone, scarred, engraved with a Mexican epitaph in an unknown cemetery under a gnarled branch in the unkempt grass garden—a foreign cemetery unvisited.

Following this I realized that since I had leisure in the city I was visiting I should go seek out & pay visit to her grave—and another mission?

*The following journal entry was written after Gins-
berg took* ayahuasca *(also known as* yage) *for the third
time. Under the drug's influence, he discovered, he had
the extraordinary ability to experience (as opposed to
observing) the nether regions of his consciousness while
remaining aware of the present. This was both exhila-
rating and terrifying: was this truth or was it madness?
Ginsberg's mother, Naomi, had been institutionalized
for much of her adult life, diagnosed as paranoid schizo-
phrenic and ultimately lobotomized. After his Blake
visions, Ginsberg's father, Louis, worried that his son
was following his mother's path. Allen had always been
obsessed with huge questions—death, eternity, one's
place in the universe, the existence of God, infinity, etc.—
and* ayahuasca *seemed to bring him into direct contact
with all this and more. Ginsberg feared for his sanity
and was horrified by much of what he experienced under
the influence of* yage, *yet he felt obliged to continue. Was
his mind being destroyed by madness, like so many of
those he immortalized in "Howl," or was he reaching a
redemptive self-awareness? His journal entries were
therapeutic. He filled many journal pages with his puz-
zlings and flights of imagination, giving readers today a
remarkable glimpse of his inner struggles.*

Ayahuasca III in Pucallpa: June 11, 1960

All day worried, fearing the spectral Calvary of the last
drunkenness—came later in darkness and mud walking 4 km.
from Yarininicocha and then bus, missed meet with Ramon—
arriving shining flashlight by sizeable group—10 people waiting—I
drank second in the little sidehut, went outside sat on wood plat-
form bordering the house, then Ramon carried bench out in the
moonlight—sat there awhile and then went and lay down, afraid
to close my eyes on the stars over my head thru the trees—but
subtly felt the marreea or intoxication—stealing over senses—slight
motion—something strange coming over me—I put an Aludrox in
my mouth to try avoid bad stomach—the instant it touched my
mouth I was nauseated and still desperately chewing the superficial
Aludrox rushed aside to the shrubbery and began vomiting—flash
of yellow fire devils like the serpents last time—same beasties—tho
much swifter in passage, just an instant of perception like the flash
glow of each retch, the Savage Cat Fanged Serpent self vomiting
up Death, vomiting out its extinction—not ready for death. Then
lay down on bench still perturbed worried what was to come—and
sense of failure already, my body and soul having so (after one-half
hour) rejected the potion of Death—a physical cowardice from rec-
ollection that made me early nauseous—so felt culpable of avoiding
the cavalry to come, postponing again then slowly the ayahuasca
did take some stronger effect and I found myself back in the same
Universe as before, a self condemned to worry about its Life—
and God is Death—thus I who wanted to see God entire balk at
the actual moment of realization of the Identity of the Mystery—
because realization destroys consciousness & destroys life itself—O
Icarus—and Death is no imaginable thing, nor God, tho there are

an infinite number of possible visions of the Final Identity because the Final Identity has no Final Identity but is—as the swoop cry of some nameless Frogbird whoopsing it up under a dark leaf in the jungle with a whistle like a comet that curves from Nothingness for a half minute to its own extinction—As each soul does with seemingly longer duration—as perhaps God or many Gods does— Yet always the same cry, always same Snell-Nosed familiar whoops of illusion manifesting its presence, reborn a myriad million myriad times in each being—and the Great-to-Us void of Nothingness where it all emerges from & goes back to—and at the same time as the isolate whoops in Infinity, the concurrent whistle of a thousand locusts within earshot, radiating outward wherever locusts are to the limits of invisible sound, and the croak of life frogs, the racket of tomtoms in huts by the oil tanks, aggrieved dogbarks and goofy jug-jug grunts from huge toads in the rainmud, the curandero hum- ming na na na in tender tune to all—punctuated by a celestial rifle shot to signal the race of infinity from some civilized bar keep— and my consciousness lying on the beach outside the hut revolving the mirror of its existence on itself and getting no answer—"I see everything except my Eye" said Ramon.

Except the presence of the Snell-Void, that is a thing, a Noth- ing, Distant, near enough to Feel however with a seemingly Mock- human Presence in my consciousness, a presence *felt*, like, and like I feel the presence of Father, Brother, dead Mother, Family—my immediate family of Being combined in one presence—and so began a long funny conversation.

Naomi-Madness—different real universes—the madman changes from One to the other each real, very confusing to the consciousness of Being—and a flash comes each time the universes shift (schizophrenia)—a flash of—Nothing—or a flash reflected in the Mirror of whatever Being is conscious at the moment—reflected in the way the form of the mirror is built—so that each Incarnation (of Nothing, Zero) is different—even for the same person, each vision of mine is different & contradictory to the previous—except they all involve the indescribable *personal familiar* plastic-sentient (Snell-nosed)—thus how the Hindus make a god with 4 differ- ent faces in 4 different directions—many incarnations out of one Discarnate—dog-faced gods, snell-nosed.

As to the Universe—it is out there, here, where I Allen am—I opened my eyes & saw the beautiful familiar stars of my present existence, all I ever knew—all I will ever know—glad to still live and share in this Existence that I am so used to—but that later I must depart—Must I?

Well if you don't want to. . . But I will grow old, hairless, dying.

That's the way this existence is—do you *want* to live forever?

No! No! except maybe forever like I am now young with beard—

Became I conscious then that to live forever in this state of torture too, because always faced with missing out on the great One entrance to the Final—thus always Allen the poet tortured by a goal incapable of reaching—knowledge of truth which is in Death—but afraid of that Truth too—so stuck in this half life—and still with all the old human problems, boys, fear of women, no babies—

I should leave poetry & learn. Mechanics & help out this human existence illusion—it's a permanent illusion—

To be or not to be—Hamlet I thought for the first time what that meant, really, it's God's question, too, of Himself—he's created us out here, like toys, sent us forth from himself in the only way possible, built a whole universe toy apart from his inside Black other self—and made us completely free of him—made us completely—unconscious and inconscient of the Nescience of Death which we are the Free opposite, Independent entity, of—I.e. he's given us the only form possible outside of his own, he's actually invented a new form independent of him—probably has invented a billion forms independent—the great creature has sent forth whole worlds of universes—pure creation—just to bear life—but they all (perhaps)—all the separate God entities—all come back to the one same beginning—end in Death—or do they?—If he's set them free to develop, all these baby—why the poor universe is just a baby, beginning to talk—perhaps the Universe will grow up to be a God one day & create its own baby universes—will even turn around and attack God—but by that time, the consciousness necessary to attack God & reach him will still be the same consciousness that God has—and all perhaps a universe can do is to commit suicide— like Buddha—but another Whoops somewhere else will emerge illusionly in Nothing—so the process will endlessly repeat itself— and

I Allen Ginsberg in this Universe home here and afraid of dissolution of Me—

But the Me is such a trap & figment—there's a million Me's—and it's all one Me—why worry about this universe's Allen's me.

And the Xray flash of the Death of me to come.

God doesn't say Me—he just reflects all the different Me's. "There is no mirror" 5th Patriarch.

Shakespeare was God's poet—and the Tempest, Illusion—"leave not a rack behind" the final statement—perturbed, him too for his Death—"This conscience does make cowards of us all."

And Carl Solomon? Them 50 shocks gave him a forced taste of the Void—knows too much to stay in this illusion—yet always still, is looking in mirror of Self—has to as we all—so in Void & this world—makes no difference where he is—had trouble thinking of Carl—he's another snell-nosed me—he is me, another me that I'm aware of as another me (all man's another me but I only get the conscious smell taste of me in some like Carl). And the sadness of that awareness that we are all the same creative living many different illusions the same creature dying a million deaths & coming back to itself with each one, only to lose that self too in despair knowing another Same-Self will be somewhere else born or dying and remember Me, too, at the last familiar snell-nosed minute of extinction.

Vomiting, all the drinkers vomiting Death—Death Vine is a taste of Great Death—which the body rejects by vomiting when it gets too near—and the Vomiter sees himself in a flash, a living illusion (like a self-serpent) vomiting out knowledge premature knowledge of the Truth, of its own extinction, vomiting away, getting rid of God.

God is to be got rid of to live, if not you die.

We are God's vomit, he vomited out consciousness out of himself into our Being in order to be conscious of himself. If we did not exist there would be no consciousness on this human level there would only be X-type consciousness which is not consciousness, God knows—perhaps he is aware of his Being thru us—that's the only way he could be aware, in this way of awareness.

Or perhaps he has a million other, infinite other modes of being he has created that he is conscious in.

To be or not to be? Does God want to continue the experiment?

Do you, Allen (asks God). It's all up to the creatures created, if they want to go on or not. They can always come back to me. (God)

Then I should go on & improve this universe?

"Yes, if you want to," says God.

But I want you!

Well you had me the other day & didn't like it. Besides in the long run you'll get Me alright. Do you want me now?

No! No! Yes! No! I want both, I want both life here & life in you, I want *All*.

Well I told you what all is you'll get it.

I want to feel you now.

Well lay back & feel a little & stop asking questions then.

So I lay back & felt a little, just a little, afraid to feel too far. Felt strange, happy, a funny conversation with God—as in a mirror—as with a part of my own mind. Sometimes both.

The whoop of the frogbirds, the dogbarks muffled near & far, the crooning of the Crooner Curandero,—my eyes open—the blue blue biblical sky & veil of holy clouds as in the ancient stagesets of the Prophets—the yellow stars—out there those Unknown presences of Futurity—good to still be alive—What mystery in *this* Creation— and behind it all a Mirror, and behind the Mirror a Great What?

A great What!?

Well you're always asking me human questions. Ask me something inhuman & you'll get inhuman. I'm you, says God.

Just me?

Right now.

But God being nothing has infinite aspects & he might be someone else next time I get high.

Disillusion of returning to life unchanged, with the same Death problem unsolved—no other way to solve it but die—words words words—"Death Problem," and Sexlove.

What should I do about women?

Make love to them.

If I drank another cup would I get the horrors? Would I throw up—I didn't try & accepted the mad game of as is for awhile— conscious of the skull afar, afraid to go in again.

The word God unsatisfactory as the Word Die. When dying, forget about the void because the experience is something new & strange—same with God who is Real, & the word is unreal.

Allen Ginsberg and Peter Orlovsky arrived in Bombay, India, on February 15, 1962. Ginsberg planned for an extended stay, not unlike his earlier journeys to Mexico, South America, and Europe. Eastern thought, religion, and culture, Ginsberg felt, had much to teach him. He would not return to the United States until July 1963.

As usual, Ginsberg immersed himself in the customs, beliefs, practices, and artistic culture of the places he visited. India was desperately crowded and impoverished, and Ginsberg, traveling with very little money, could only afford the cheapest of accomodations. He lived among the impoverished, malnourished, and, often, the dying. He ventured often to the burning ghats, where the dead were given public cremations in religious rituals. He spoke to many holy men, hoping for enlightenment in his quest to understand his visionary experiences, first, in his Harlem visions of 1948, and, later, what he had seen under the influence of different drugs.

His journal entries, like his writing whenever he was on the road, recorded the minute details of what he was seeing, often juxtaposed on the deep questions he asked whenever he experienced the lives and surroundings of his previously unexplored places. The following entry, recorded as his stay in India was drawing near its conclusion, finds Ginsberg applying what he had learned in more than a year in India to what he saw every day on the streets. His humanity toward the dying street figure is touching.

Benares, India: Shivaratri 1963 Feb 22—
11. A.M.—(Shiva's Birthday)

Early noon at the pavement above fires by the open steps into the pit yard

Passing with Peter thru Manikarnika, the old dark man I'd seen days earlier crouching in shadow curld up on Steps—fires &

Confusion!—Someone come waiting early to die—

Now as first time seen lying too near the fire—his hair white frizzy skull dry ashen high temples & yellow eyes open

Beckoning with kindling thin bony arms—the brown foot swollen & shiny—calling me—Down steps—he opened his eyes & said Panni! He? Panni—and a clay ashen cup at his head—

Legs now stretched out hollow no muscles long Buchenwald skeletal legs & no cheek but a bone, flat pelvis under the white thick loincloth in the grey ashes—

A burn-sore on the right ankle—flies festering on wound & near eyelid—

Eyes closed—flitting by eyebrow eared big in dry grey ash head—delicate large starved bony nose—

Inexpressible grey in the holes of transparent Who looks in, out of these eyeballs—rheumy

Mouth open the large grinning teeth of Skeleton—"Panny" with dry bright red living tongue—

I washed cup at lower step & brought large mouthful—he lifted his arm birdcrane hand with the red brickcolor tea-cup

—Peter standing above holding butter & milk can in Israeli net bag—

Pourd water into his deep mouth—"My sadhana was pouring
wine & being poured"
And then beckoned me nearer in Hindi To Ask—
What I could not garble from between his teeth & gentle tired
wave of his long arm—
I went & up Stps past tree, gound basket of yellow curry
potatos—left
Wrong hysterical leaf plate of potatos in the ash-step near his
head—a cow's brown nose
Waved aside by that rakehandle arm—He didn't eat.

Later bathing near the fires on steps surrounded by boats I pushed
& hung my head under the prow in deep water
Washed underwear on wet steps with red soap—my hair
scrubbed & cracks of feet & ears in red loincloth—
Climbed up to where the Naked Man I'd saluted earlier—by his
holiday fire with shriveled soft ashey cock lap—resting between
legs—hand held up in
Soft reassurance Shambu Bharti Baba sat—some wheaten pan-
cake & peas in ghee & potato leaf mouthfuls—a pipe passed with
the university employee
in white underwear—who greeted me on the mat "you have just
come from your bath?"—seated crosslegged with loincloth hanging
on iron pipe—
"That man I didn't understand his ashey Hindi idea, could we
ask why he was dying?"—
How long & what need I couldn't tell—except potatos—tho now
as we went down, a clay cup of milk
half emptied near his face—Leaning over seeing his weak knobs
& under his garment
the sharp shrunken flesh hung on hairy bonewracks—"To be
taken down—to the water—too hot up here"—
Flies buzzing on his forehead in the bright sunlight glaring over
his forehead's deep bridge—
over the burning ghats—carried under the sky my hand at his
inner knee & wooden backbone—head hanging carried by the arms
my companion
"Said he's wants to cold, hot, river down leave"—

Down to the river on a step, weak & foot hanging over step then pelvis slipping down next step near water—we lifted him up after

Inquiring of the Skullhead which fainted & woke at once looking up with

Its eyes at ours blandly—Been there 2 weeks I seen him before at night by high coals arm raised to protect his forehead eyes held weightless bar—

Some extreme Sadhu? Just come here to die—who was he?—We left him there

& went on to Scindia gate out of the high castle balcony—

Down the river in the clear blue air clean after last nite black rain—

We'd seen, walking before—by the crowded Sky Crow-vultures wheeling over the Mosqued Embankment—in the water the white decaying cow afloat, sat on by birds & plucked bobbing in the slow flood—drift & forget—$— vultures

flagging the sky now for that same Cow whose head twisted back tied to the shoulder thru mouth

Slung on two poles front & back & five loinclothed workmen in the midnite sludging down the steps bearing the felt-grey

Bloat-weight of the stomach pregnant with white mouths—

Untied & slumped forward to the water

on a shelf head hung back waiting for the sleeping boatman of cows—

Peeped from a tower next afternoon the waves of blackflap meatbirds—

Arrived at Bursar's mandir cow-shed—drawings in white & bright red powder Swastika on the

damp cow smell stone—a small peaked whitewashed altar under the cell

roof, huge stone bowls in the corner on blocks—a perch half-way up the wall by window into great chanting temple and closer a stone cluttered, walled, private two-yard nook—

playing with babe while cows ate straw-water, mush & old Brahmin chanted & flattered the cow-neck dewlap with mantric hand—

Inside the large temple, songs of Sakar—Sanskrit chorsus & answer-question word calls—

His daughter by the door, his tea we sat at stall porch over street—I back walking thinks past Manikarnika—

Greeted by Chandar the pole-man who'd given him—as he lay on humid puny ground four steps away from flower-ashy brown water—

"—" a tobacco—one Chandal rubbed it in his palm—& dropped the few grains between

The skeleton's teeth who smiled upside down I'd seen him close his cheooth & mum mouth the bitterness grains

Now he's here I am pointed he lies close-eyed stretched on the bottom step foot swollen I the shallow lapping purple dreep—

Head resting on top white step in its grey frizzy skull flies on the dead sore & eyelids mucus closed—silent—still—

The chandal pointed to heaven—"Haribol!"

Namaste at the figure—I sauntered to see chose his quiet thin body at rest—instant gone—Who now and where? . . .

In late-1964, Cuba's minister of culture invited Ginsberg to participate in a literary conference in Havana—an invitation he was especially happy to accept during the Cold War era, when American citizens were usually prohibited from traveling to Cuba. Ginsberg arrived in Havana in mid-January 1965, and he immediately drew government suspicion by speaking out on such forbidden subjects as freedom of speech, capital punishment, and homosexuality. He persisted in expounding on these topics, despite pleadings that he tone down his rhetoric. When government officials had heard enough, they expelled Ginsberg from the country—an action that made international news. The following journal entry is Ginsberg's account of his expulsion.

Havana, Cuba: Feb. 18-19, 1965

Woke with sudden knock on the door—Who?—I cried—"ICAP"—I got up and put on—"one minute"—Indian pajamas—I was naked . . .—supposed to be early visit to Sugar Central Factory today but I'd told Mario Gonzalez of ICAP w/his little nice mustache that I'd stay home this morn and work with Nicanor—

Opened the door—the ICAP face familiar but not one of the boys assigned to me—with three soldiers in olive green neat pressed uniforms beside him—"What's up"—they come in "If you please get dressed and come with us"—"Where?"—"Please pack all your belongings also"—"But what's happening"—"We will accompany you to the Immigration Department this morning"—"What for"— "The officer there wants to speak with you"—I realized the jig was up and got chill thru my back—adrenalin panic—more like a cold fear thrill—everything sharp and clear as in a dream but I was still too sleepy—"What time is it"—"8:25"—"Dios, it's too early for this, I went to bed at 5 in the morning"—"Please get your clothes on." They were looking around the room. What did I have on me— The $10 for pot—that's ok—I was moving around sort of blurrily looking for my underwear thinking—"My notebook! Libreta de Technicos black notebook on the bed table—yesterday's description of love scene with M.—Thank God I used his initials—but there's still enough in there for them to get me on something political or amoral?—Will they search?—Can they read my scribbled English?"—"Right now?"—I meant, Naked? "here."—I dropped my pajamas and sat in chair putting on undershorts—kind of funny fearful modesty—still worried about the little black notebook— What were they going to do?—Fear of jail, kidnapping—"Have you called the Casa de Las Americas" "No, it is not usual in this procedure." "I think you should call Haydee Santamaria and the Casa and check out if this procedure is regular"—"This is the regular procedure"—"Who wants to see me?"—"Capt. Varona"—"Who is that"—"Head of Immigration"—Well that sounded not bad, maybe technical, it's not Lacra Social or Dept. of Interior or G-police. Still total uneasiness in my body, and worry about Manola and Jose—have they been picked up again? –Find out later—I dressed, awkwardly, and went into bathroom brushed teeth—

"Electric toothbrush?" one of the soldiers in green cap.

"Si electricidad, muy utile & sano"—I said by this time regain some composure tho still cold-thrilled. I should have known it was serious and not been so loose with my talk—last night the Espins complained? Who finked?—But my notebook full of secrets and thrills!

I started emptying drawers wondering if I should protest—"I want to call the Casa"—"Not allowed to make calls"—So I sat knapsack on bed and put in pants and a few odd bed table books and odd empty notebooks, picked up the black full sexy one and put it under jeans in bottom of sack—then filled in—put Feezo's crazy coffeecup in a sock, and Santa Barbara statue that Manakosa'd given me 2 days ago—chango suncretistic substitute—in a sock—put on both beads and then took off the big one and put that in little carryall bag— emptied drawers and envelopes into big envelopes and put in sack— "To hurry the process"—a soldier had brought my sweater and torn skin jacket in from the closet, all still over hangers, on the bed— managed to get everything packed except big pile of books—soldiers sat around, I kept asking "Are you sure you know what you're doing and have the authority for this?"—Icap man sent for a fresh elevator to be waiting—I didn't know what to do with all the Cuban books and newspapers—they piled them all around on a hand cart and I was ready. Thru hall wanting to shout, as if being kidnapped by Nazis?—or just being bothered for a few questions—but they'd made me completely clean out my room of possessions—to disappear?— down elevator into the lobby—stept out and ah! Mr. Lundquist and his wife with eyeglasses—"Ah, Mr. Lundquist—Mira, yovoy—" I began in Spanish confused—and continued in English. "I seem to be arrested—" "Ah" said he jovially stupid almost: "That's alright, same thing happened to the Danish journalist I told you about, they'll hold you in jail till there's a plane and send you out of Cuba"—I was still worried about my notebook on the bottom of my knapsack on the hand truck—oddly they stopped—soldiers around me Icap guide—to let me converse—"Listen, tell Parra what happened,"—"It will be all right, they'll put you on a plane"—"I mean, call the Casa de Las Americas." His wife interrupted more urgently "Arthur, he's saying you should call"—"Yes call the Casa and tell them what's happening—fast"—He finally got the message and assured me he would, immediately.

I went out front hotel, saluted the cab boys, blue uniformed door keepers—everybody staring but with old kindly Kafkian smiles—scared and sympathetic or just dumbed?—got in car with the three green attendants and waited—nothing yet. They put my bag in the truck. I saw Mario Gonzales coming up the walk to work—As he came near the car and called him: "Oh Mario?"—He leaned in surprised and tentative—"What's happening?"—identifying himself as hotel Icap chief—They explained "Detenado por Immigration"—

He looked at me—"Did anything happen last nite?"—"No," I said, everything as usual, no special scene,—call the Casa—"Call Haydee or Marcia or Maria Rosa"—"I'll do that now," he said—keeping his diplomatic aplomb—tho surprised he accepted the scene without temper or question—"Adios Mario"—

We rode off—along Malecon to old Havana sidestreet white ancient edifice Immigration Service and they put me in huge hall-door, waiting. "The officer will come soon." Then I picked out my finger cymbals and began chanting very slowly and low so as not disturb much. After awhile they led me in to barred window locker room on one side—offered me chair, bed, went to buy me cigarettes—came back with Hoy—I sit and sang a little and glared nervously thru paper—"1,332,056 children vaccinated as of yesterday"—"Cuban Soviet business 440 Million"—"USSR Rockets with 100 Million tons of TNT"—"Mexico won't break Relations with Cuba"—"Employ Yankee and Gusano pilots in Uganda Bombings"—a photo of Vilma Espin inauguration some Plan Bureau—an Editorial on new Soviet declaration Isvestia says they're mistaken "those who think they can promote good relations with USSR and same time maintain aggressive line against other Socialist countries." Great sugar harvest. Statement by Chilean Communist Octopus. The world is a mountain of dogs. If they kick me out it's an unthinkable scene. That rigidity both sides a vision of war. Caught between lines.

A huge window with high bars looking out on the small street—suddenly an anonymous other soldier appeared sat on bed and said, "We've arranged your departure this morning at 10:30-plane to Prague London and N.Y.—You have your passport?"—"No, they took it when I came in at the airport"—"Oh, Icap has it, it'll be waiting at airport. We'll leave now."

"Fine but if I may ask, what's this all about, why, and have you not made a mistake? Have you consulted the Casa de Las Americas?"

"No, we will call them. I have an appointment with Haydee S. at noon."

"And your name?"

"Carlos Varona."

"Your position?"

"Chief of Immigration"—"For all Cuba"—"Yes."

We got in car and went off along Malecon—passing the ships in harbor—suddenly on prow of a cargo boat the name "MAN-TRIC"—I pulled out my cymbals and began singing very low OOOM OOM OOM SARAWA BUDA DAKINI VEH BENZA WANI YEH BENZA BERO TSA NI YEH HUM HUM HUM PHAT PHAT PHAT SO Hum. And then Hari Krishna Hari Hari Krishna Krishna Hari Hari Hari Rama Hari Rama Rama Rama Rama Hari Hari, singing easily and low for some time. It cleaned my senses a bit, very useful and felt good steadying influence as we drove out thru city. Varona reached for the car radio so I put my cymbals away.

"But exactly, can you tell me what is the purpose or reason? & why so suddenly?"

"We called for you last night but you weren't in."

"I was in Espin's house." Hoping that would surprise him—He didn't register.

"Well," I continued, "what about Czech visa—I want to stop over there and have business a book coming out work with translator have you arranged a visa."

"You can do it easily in Prague."

"Are you sure you're not making a mistake acting so rapidly without consulting the Casa?"

"We know what we're doing, as this is a Revolution we must do things quickly, we do lots of things rapidly." He smiled.

"Yes but on what exact basis are you kicking me out—it's an embarrassing situation for me *and* you—I admire your revolution and have sympathy basically and so am embarrassed to be"—He leaned back—"What's that?"

"I say I basically sympathize—basically—with your Revolution but a situation like this makes it difficult for both of us—In any case have you anything specific in my activities you are acting on, or what?"

"Respect for our Laws, compliance with our laws."

"But *what* laws?"

"Cuban Laws."

"No I mean which specific laws"—

"Oh just basic immigration policy . . . also a question of your private life . . . your personal attitudes"—

"What private life I haven't had much of that since I've been here." I laughed, so did he. "Too much public life."

I figured I still might talk him out of it by some inspired yak but—at this point they weren't going to look thru my papers apparently so—almost—glad excited to be going on—this too much nightmare here—and didn't want to beg, hypocritical—what truth to say?

"Especially are you sure you're not making a mistaken judgment on the basis of chismei (gossip)—I have heard much gossip exaggerated about myself."

"In that case it's not gossip because gossip is behind your back," he replied.

"I mean, Havana is a small town and full of exaggerated gossip"—

"Havana has more work to do than gossip. Havana is a serious place I'll have you understand. Do you understand?"

"Yes certainly but are you sure you're not mistaking rumor for real acts and kicking me out for nothing serious."

"We may be making a mistake."

"Well then why not take your time and discuss it with Haydee S."

"I called her—I am sure she will accept our decision. I have appointment with her at noon."

"What time plane leaves?"

"10:30."

I sat back. Relieved really, it was only the airport, for Prague, not a jail or interrogation about the boys or pot or gossip or Che Guevara's narcissism from Argentina.

Arrived at airport filed thru to a waiting room office on the side—several soldiers guarding, going in out office, I sat in chair and opened my knapsack to pick out Ferlinghetti letter with Czech addresses and my address book—hoping they wouldn't get new ideas when I pulled thru papers and books. But it was already 10:15—

Passport arrived, a guard examined it and filled out a form—

["Renodita?"]

"No—Poeta," I replied and he filled that in.

Outside waiting to go toward huge silver jetplane with CZECHOSLOVAKIA painted along it like the backbone of a fish—great gang of Czech visitors being greeted farewell—

Changed that pot 10 pesos for $ at air bank—saw cute eye-glass lawyer Icap fellow I'd given Whitman lecture to in [Veradero (?)] I waved goodbye—he was at entrance waiting for another delegation to arrive, the neurophysiologists?—coming next week?—"Looks like I'm being expulsado"—"Oh" he said?—"Goodbye"—"Ho!" I said back—

The milicanos standing waiting—to each other "I'm going to report you for this kidding," picking at an empty buttonhole on the uniform and then examining each other's relaxed uniforms for signs of sloppiness, an ill tied shoelace here, a loose belt buckle there—and my knapsack with interest—same color as their uniform—"Aluminum"—I said pointing the frame—"Too narrow" they criticized—"No good for a gordo or if you have wide hips"—I'd noticed that when I bought it.

Shook hands with them goodbye—walked out, silent and lone to the crowd of Czechoslovakians and got on plane—before entering turned around and waved at the Cuban soldiers waiting across the airfield. They waved back.

Ginsberg was at his Cherry Valley, New York, farm when he received a call informing him that Jack Kerouac had died. Ginsberg, Gregory Corso, and others were considering a response to Kerouac's controversial essay, "After Me, the Deluge" (Kerouac's last published writing during his lifetime) when they received the news, and Ginsberg, true to form, was more tolerant and forgiving of Kerouac's insults than others. His journal notes reacting to Kerouac's passing are revealing.

Cherry Valley, New York: October 22, 1969

Two watches ticking in the dark, fly buzz at the black window, telephone calls all day to Florida and Old Saybrook, Lucien, Creeley, Louis,—"drinking heavily" and "your letter made him feel bad" said Stella—

All last nite (as talking on farm w/Creeley day before) in bed brooding re Kerouac's "After Me, the Deluge" at middle of morning watch I woke realizing he was right, that the meat suffering in the middle of existence was a sensitive pain greater than any political anger or hope, as I also lay in bed dying

Walking with Gregory in bare treed October ash woods—winds blowing brown sere leafs at feet—talking of dead Jack—the sky an old familiar place with fragrant eyebrow clouds passing overhead in Fall Current—

He saw them stand on the moon too.

At dusk I went out to the pasture & saw thru Kerouac's eyes the sun set on the first dusk after his death.

Didn't live much longer than beloved Neal—another year & half—

Gregory woke at midnite to cry—he didn't really want to go so soon—from the attic—

His mind my mind many ways—"The days of my youth rise fresh in my mind"—

Our talk 25 years ago about saying farewell to the tender mortal steps of Union Theological Seminary 7th floor where I first met Lucien—

Tonite on phone Lucien said, having quit drinking in Penna. Several weeks ago, he'd had convulsions split his nose & broke out all his false front teeth, chewed his tongue almost in half— unconscious taken to hospital—

Jack had vomited blood this last weekend, would not take doctor care, hemorrhaged, & with many dozen transfusions lay in hospital a day before dying operated under knife in stomach—

PART FIVE

Interviews

Thomas Clark Interviews Allen Ginsberg
The Paris Review 6/10/65

Tom Clark: I think Diana Trilling, speaking about your reading at Columbia, remarked that your poetry, like all poetry in English when dealing with a serious subject, naturally takes on the iambic pentameter rhythm. Do you agree?

Allen Ginsberg: Well, it really isn't an accurate thing, I don't think. I've never actually sat down and made a technical analysis of the rhythms that I write. They're probably more near choriambic—Greek meters, dithyrambic meters—and tending toward de DA de de DA de de . . . what is that? Tending toward dactylic, probably. Williams once remarked that American speech tends toward dactylic. But it's more complicated than dactyl because dactyl is a three, three units, a foot consisting of three parts, whereas the actual rhythm is probably a rhythm which consists of five, six, or seven, like DA de de DA de de DA de de DA DA. Which is more toward the line of Greek dance rhythms—that's why they call them choriambic. So actually, probably it's not really technically correct, what she said. But—and that applies to certain poems, like certain passages of "Howl" and certain passages of "Kaddish"—there are definite rhythms which could be analyzed as corresponding to classical rhythms, though not necessarily English classical rhythms; they might correspond to Greek classical rhythms, or Sanskrit prosody. But probably most of the other poetry, like "Aether" or "Laughing Gas" or a lot of those poems, they simply don't fit into that. I think she felt very comfy, to think that that would be so. I really felt quite hurt about that, because it seemed to me that she ignored the main prosodic technical achievements that I had proffered forth to the academy, and they didn't even recognize it. I mean not that I want to stick her with being the academy.

TC: And in "Howl" and "Kaddish" you were working with a kind of classical unit? Is that an accurate description?

AG: Yeah, but it doesn't do very much good, because I wasn't really working with a classical unit, I was working with my own neural impulses and writing impulses. See, the difference is between someone sitting down to write a poem in a definite preconceived metrical pattern and filling in that pattern, and someone working with his physiological movements and arriving at a pattern, and perhaps even arriving at a pattern which might even have a name, or might even have a classical usage, but arriving at it organically rather than synthetically. Nobody's got any objection to even iambic pentameter if it comes from a source deeper than the mind— that is to say, if it comes from the breathing and the belly and the lungs.

TC: American poets have been able to break away from a kind of English specified rhythm earlier than English poets have been able to do. Do you think this has anything to do with a peculiarity in English spoken tradition?

AG: No, I don't really think so, because the English don't speak in iambic pentameter either; they don't speak in the recognizable pattern that they write in. The dimness of their speech and the lack of emotional variation is parallel to the kind of dim diction and literary usage in the poetry now. But you can hear all sorts of Liverpudlian or Gordian—that's Newcastle—you can hear all sorts of variants aside from an upper-tone accent, a high-class accent, that don't fit into the tone of poetry being written right now. It's not being used like in America—I think it's just that British poets are more cowardly.

TC: Do you find any exception to this?

AG: It's pretty general, even the supposedly avant-garde poets. They write, you know, in a very toned-down manner.

TC: How about a poet like Basil Bunting?

AG: Well, he was working with a whole bunch of wild men from an earlier era, who were all breaking through, I guess. And so he had that experience—also he knew Persian, he knew Persian prosody. He was better educated than most English poets.

TC: The kind of organization you use in "Howl," a recurrent kind of syntax—you don't think this is relevant any longer to what you want to do?

AG: No, but it was relevant to what I wanted to do then, it wasn't even a conscious decision.

TC: Was this related in any way to a kind of music or jazz that you were interested in at the time?

AG: Mmm . . . the myth of Lester Young as described by Kerouac, blowing eighty-nine choruses of "Lady Be Good," say, in one night, or my own hearing of Illinois Jacquet's *Jazz at the Philharmonic*, Volume 2; I think "Can't Get Started" was the title.

TC: And you've also mentioned poets like Christopher Smart, for instance, as providing an analogy—is this something you discovered later on?

AG: When I looked into it, yeah. Actually, I keep reading, or earlier I kept reading, that I was influenced by Kenneth Fearing and Carl Sandburg, whereas actually I was more conscious of Christopher Smart, and Blake's Prophetic Books, and Whitman and some aspects of Biblical rhetoric. And a lot of specific prose things, like Genet, Genet's *Our Lady of the Flowers* and the rhetoric in that, and Céline; Kerouac, most of all, was the biggest influence I think—Kerouac's prose.

TC: When did you come onto Burroughs's work?

AG: Let's see . . . Well, first thing of Burroughs's I ever read was 1946 . . . which was a skit later published and integrated in some other work of his, called *So Proudly We Hail*, describing the sinking of the *Titanic* and an orchestra playing, a spade orchestra playing "The Star Spangled Banner" while everybody rushed out to the lifeboats and the captain got up in woman's dress and rushed into the purser's office and shot the purser and stole all the money, and a spastic paretic jumped into a lifeboat with a machete and began chopping off people's fingers that were trying to climb into the boat,

saying, "Out of the way, you foolth . . . dirty thunthufbithes."
That was a thing he had written up at Harvard with a friend
named Kells Elvins. Which is really the whole key of all his
work, like the sinking of America, and everybody like fright-
ened rats trying to get out, or that was his vision of the time.

Then he and Kerouac later in 1945—forty-five or forty-
six—wrote a big detective book together, alternating chap-
ters. I don't know where that book is now—Kerouac has his
chapters and Burroughs's are somewhere in his papers. So I
think in a sense it was Kerouac that encouraged Burroughs
to write really, because Kerouac was so enthusiastic about
prose, about writing, about lyricism, about the honor of writ-
ing . . . the Thomas Wolfe-ian delights of it. So anyway he
turned Burroughs on in a sense, because Burroughs found
a companion who could write really interestingly, and Bur-
roughs admired Kerouac's perceptions. Kerouac could imitate
Dashiell Hammett as well as Bill, which was Bill's natural
style: dry, bony, factual. At that time Burroughs was reading
John O'Hara, simply for facts, not for any sublime stylistic
thing, just because he was a hard-nosed reporter.

Then in Mexico around 1951 he started writing *Junkie*.
I've forgotten what relation I had to that—I think I wound up
as the agent for it, taking it around New York trying to get it
published. I think he sent me portions of it at the time—I've
forgotten how it worked out now. This was around 1949 or
1950. He was going through a personal crisis, his wife had
died. It was in Mexico or South America . . . but it was a very
generous thing of him to do, to start writing all of a sudden.
Burroughs was always a very *tender* sort of person, but very
dignified and shy and withdrawn, and for him to commit
himself to a big autobiographical thing like that was . . . at
the time, struck me as like a piece of eternity is in love with
the . . . what is it, "Eternity is in love with the productions of
Time"? So he was making a production of Time then.

Then I started taking that around. I've forgotten who I
took that to but I think maybe to Louis Simpson who was
then working at Bobbs-Merrill. I'm not sure whether I took it
to him—I remember taking it to Jason Epstein who was then
working at Doubleday I think. Epstein at the time was not as

experienced as he is now. And his reaction to it, I remember when I went back to his office to pick it up, was, well this is all very interesting, but it isn't really interesting, on account of if it were an autobiography of a junkie written by Winston *Churchill* then it'd be interesting, but written by somebody he'd never heard of, well then it's *not* interesting. And anyway I said what about the *prose*, the prose is interesting, and he says, oh, a difference of opinion on that. Finally I wound up taking it to Carl Solomon who was then a reader for A. A. Wynn Company, which was his uncle; and they finally got it through there. But it was finally published as a cheap paperback. With a whole bunch of frightened footnotes; like Burroughs said that marijuana was nonhabit-forming, which is now accepted as a fact, there'd be a footnote by the editor, "Reliable, er, responsible medical opinion does not confirm this." Then they also had a little introduction . . . literally they were afraid of the book being censored or seized at the time, is what they said. I've forgotten what the terms of censorship or seizure were that they were worried about. This was about 1952. They said that they were afraid to publish it straight for fear there would be a Congressional investigation or something, I don't know what. I think there was some noise about narcotics at the time. Newspaper noise . . . I've forgotten exactly what the arguments were. But anyway they had to write a preface which hedged on the book a lot.

TC: Has there been a time when fear of censorship or similar trouble has made your own expression difficult?

AG: This is so complicated a matter. The beginning of the fear with me was, you know what would my father say to something that I would write. At the time, writing "Howl"—for instance, like I assumed when writing it that it was something that could not be published because I wouldn't want my daddy to see what was in there. About my sex life, being fucked in the ass, imagine your father reading a thing like that, was what I thought. Though that disappeared as soon as the thing was real, or as soon as I manifested my . . . you know, it didn't make that much importance finally. That was sort of a help for writing, because I assumed that it wouldn't be published, therefore I could say anything that I wanted.

So literally just for myself or anybody that I knew personally well, writers who would be willing to appreciate it with a breadth of tolerance—in a piece of work like "Howl"—who wouldn't be judging from a moralistic viewpoint but looking for evidences of humanity or secret thought or just actual truthfulness.

Then there's later the problem of publication—we had a lot. The English printer refused at first I think, we were afraid of customs; the first edition we had to print with asterisks on some of the dirty words, and then the *Evergreen Review* in reprinting it used asterisks, and various people reprinting it later always wanted to use the *Evergreen* version rather than the corrected legal City Lights version—like I think there's an anthology of Jewish writers, I forgot who edited that, but a couple of the high-class intellectuals from Columbia. I had written asking them specifically to use the later City Lights version, but they went ahead and printed an asterisked version. I forget what was the name of that—something like *New Generation of Jewish Writing*, Philip Roth, et cetera.

TC: Do you take difficulties like these as social problems, problems of communication simply, or do you feel they also block your own ability to express yourself for yourself?

AG: The problem is, where it gets to literature, is this. We all talk among ourselves and we have common understandings, and we say anything we want to say, and we talk about our assholes, and we talk about our cocks, and we talk about who we fucked last night, or who we're gonna fuck tomorrow, or what kind love affair we have, or when we got drunk, or when we stuck a broom in our ass in the Hotel Ambassador in Prague—anybody tells one's friends about that. So then— what happens if you make a distinction between what you tell your friends and what you tell your Muse? The problem is to break down that distinction: when you approach the Muse to talk as frankly as you would talk with yourself or with your friends. So I began finding, in conversations with Burroughs and Kerouac and Gregory Corso, in conversations with people whom I knew well, whose souls I respected, that the things we were telling each other for real were totally different from what was already in literature. And that was

Kerouac's great discovery in *On the Road*. The kinds of things that he and Neal Cassady were talking about, he finally discovered were the subject matter for what he wanted to write down. That meant, at that minute, a complete revision of what literature was supposed to be, in his mind, and actually in the minds of the people that first read the book. Certainly in the minds of the critics, who had at first attacked it as not being . . . proper structure, or something. In other words, a gang of friends running around in an automobile. Which obviously is like a great picaresque literary device, and a classical one. And was not recognized, at the time, as suitable literary subject matter.

TC: So it's not just a matter of themes—sex, or any other one—

AG: It's the ability to commit to writing, to write, the same way that you . . . are! Anyway! You have many writers who have preconceived ideas about what literature is supposed to be and their ideas seem to exclude that which makes them most charming in private conversation. Their faggishness, or their campiness, or their neurasthenia, or their solitude, or their goofiness, or their—even—masculinity, at times. Because they think that they're gonna write something that sounds like something else that they've read before, instead of sounds like them. Or comes from their own life. In other words, there's no distinction, there should be no distinction between what we write down, and what we really know, to begin with. As we know it every day, with each other. And the hypocrisy of literature has been—you know like there's supposed to be formal literature, which is supposed to be different from . . . in subject, in diction, and even in organization, from our quotidian inspired lives.

It's also like in Whitman, "I find no fat sweeter than that which sticks to my own bones"—that is to say the self-confidence of someone who knows that he's really alive, and that his existence is just as good as any other subject matter.

TC: Is physiology a part of this too—like the difference between your long breath line and William Carlos Williams's shorter unit?

AG: Analytically, ex post facto, it all begins with fucking around and intuition and without any idea of what you're doing, I think. Later, I have a tendency to explain it, "Well, I got a longer breath than Williams, or I'm Jewish, or I study yoga, or I sing long lines. . . ." But anyway, what it boils down to is this, it's my *movement*, my feeling is for a big long cranky statement—partly that's something that I share, or maybe that I even got from Kerouac's long prose line; which is really, like he once remarked, an extended poem. Like one long sentence page of his in *Doctor Sax* or *Railroad Earth* or occasionally *On the Road*—if you examine them phrase by phrase they usually have the density of poetry, and the beauty of poetry, but most of all the single elastic rhythm running from beginning to end of the line and ending "mop!"

TC: Have you ever wanted to extend this rhythmic feeling as far as, say, Artaud or now Michael Arthur McClure have taken it—to a line that is actually animal noise?

AG: The rhythm of the long line is also an animal cry.

TC: So you're following that feeling and not a thought or a visual image?

AG: It's simultaneous. The poetry generally is like a rhythmic articulation of feeling. The feeling is like an impulse that rises within—just like sexual impulses, say; it's almost as definite as that. It's a feeling that begins somewhere in the pit of the stomach and rises up forward in the breast and then comes out through the mouth and ears, and comes forth a croon or a groan or a sigh. Which, if you put words to it by looking around and seeing and trying to describe what's making you sigh—and sigh in words—you simply articulate what you're feeling. As simple as that. Or actually what happens is, at best what happens, is there's a definite body rhythm that has no definite words, or may have one or two words attached to it, one or two key words attached to it. And then, in writing it down, it's simply by a process of association that I find what the rest of the statement is—what can be collected around that word, what that word is connected to. Partly by simple association, the first thing that comes to my mind like "Moloch is" or "Moloch who," and then whatever comes out. But that also goes along with a definite rhythmic impulse, like DA de de DA de de DA de de DA DA. "Moloch whose eyes are a thousand blind windows." And before I wrote "Moloch whose eyes are a thousand blind windows," I had the word, "Moloch, Moloch, Moloch," and I also had the feeling DA de de DA de de DA de de DA DA. So it was just a question of looking up and seeing a lot of windows, and saying, Oh, windows, of course, but what kind of windows? But not even that—"Moloch whose eyes." "Moloch whose eyes"—which is beautiful in itself—but what about it, Moloch whose eyes are what? So Moloch whose eyes—then probably the next thing I thought was "thousands. " O. K., and then thousands what? "Thousands blind." And I had to finish it somehow. So I hadda say "windows." It looked good *afterward.*

Usually during the composition, step by step, word by word and adjective by adjective, if it's at all spontaneous, I don't know whether it even makes sense sometimes. Sometimes I do know it makes complete sense, and I start crying. Because I realize I'm hitting some area which is absolutely true. And in that sense applicable universally, or understandable universally. In that sense able to survive through time—in that sense to be read by somebody and wept to, maybe, centuries later. In that sense prophecy, because it touches a common key . . . what prophecy actually is is not that you actually know that the bomb will fall in 1942. It's that you know and feel something which somebody knows and feels in a hundred years. And maybe articulate it in a hint—concrete way that they can pick up on in a hundred years.

TC: You once mentioned something you had found in Cézanne—a remark about the reconstitution of the *petites sensations* of experience, in his own painting—and you compared this with the methods of your poetry.

AG: I got all hung up on Cézanne around 1949 in my last year at Columbia, studying with Meyer Schapiro. I don't know how it led into it—I think it was about the same time that I was having these Blake visions. So. The thing I understood from Blake was that it was possible to transmit a message through time which could reach the enlightened, that poetry had a definite effect, it wasn't just pretty, or just beautiful, as I had understood pretty beauty before—it was something basic to human existence, or it reached something, it reached the bottom of human existence. But anyway the impression I got was that it was like a kind of time machine through which he could transmit, Blake could transmit, his basic consciousness and communicate it to somebody else after he was dead—in other words, build a time machine.

Now just about that time I was looking at Cézanne and I suddenly got a strange shuddering impression looking at his canvases, partly the effect when someone pulls a Venetian blind, reverses the Venetian—there's a sudden shift, a flashing that you see in Cézanne canvases. Partly it's when the canvas opens up into three dimensions and looks like wooden objects, like solid-space objects, in three dimensions rather than flat. Partly it's the enormous spaces which open up in Cézanne's landscapes. And it's partly that mysterious quality around his figures, like of his wife or the cardplayers or the postman or whoever, the local Aix characters. They look like great huge 3-D wooden dolls, sometimes. Very uncanny thing, like a very mysterious thing—in other words, there's a strange sensation that one gets, looking at his canvases, which I began to associate with the extraordinary sensation—cosmic sensation, in fact—that I had experienced catalyzed by Blake's "Sun-flower" and "Sick Rose" and a few other poems. So I began studiously investigating Cézanne's intentions and method, and looking at all the canvases of his that I could find in New York, and all the reproductions I could find, and I was writing at the time a paper on him, for Schapiro at Columbia in the fine-arts course.

And the whole thing opened up, two ways: first, I read a book on Cézanne's composition by Earl Loran, who showed photographs, analyses and photographs of the original motifs, side by side with the actual canvases—and years later I actually went to Aix, with all the postcards, and stood in the spots, and tried to find the places where he painted Mont-Sainte-Victoire from, and got in his studio and saw some of the motifs he used, like his big black hat and his cloak. Well, first of all, I began to see that Cézanne had all sorts of literary symbolism in him, on and off. I was preoccupied with Plotinian terminology, of time and eternity, and I saw it in Cézanne paintings, an early painting of a clock on a shelf which I associated with time and eternity, and I began to think he was a big secret mystic. And I saw a photograph of his studio in Loran's book and it was like an alchemist's studio, because he had a skull, and he had a long black coat, and he had this big black hat. So I began thinking of him as, you know, like a magic character. Like the original version I had thought of him was like this austere dullard from Aix. So I began getting really interested in him as a hermetic type, and then I symbolically read into his canvases things that probably weren't there, like there's a painting of a winding road which turns off, and I saw that as the mystical path: it turns off into a village and the end of the path is hidden. Something he painted I guess when he went out painting with Bernard. Then there was an account of a very fantastic conversation that he had had. It's quoted in Loran's book: there's a long long long paragraph where he says, "By means of squares, cubes, triangles, I try to reconstitute the impression that I have from nature: the means that I use to reconstitute the impression of solidity that I think-feel-see when I am looking at a motif like Victoire is to reduce it to some kind of pictorial language, so I use these squares, cubes, and triangles, but I try to build them together so interknit [and here in the conversation he held his hands together with his fingers interknit] so that no light gets through." And I was mystified by that, but it seemed to make sense in terms of the grid of paint strokes that he had on his canvas, so that he produced a solid two-dimensional surface which when you looked into it, maybe from a slight distance with your eyes either unfocused or your eyelids lowered slightly, you could see a great three-dimensional opening, mysterious, stereoscopic, like going into a stereopticon. And I began discovering in "The Cardplayers" all sorts of sinister symbols, like there's one guy leaning against the wall with a stolid expression on his face, that he doesn't want to get involved; and then there's two guys who are peasants, who are looking as if they've just been dealt Death cards; and then the dealer you look at and he turns out to be a city slicker with a big blue cloak and almost rouge doll-like cheeks and a fat-faced Kafkian-agent impression about him, like he's a cardsharp, he's a cosmic cardsharp dealing out Fate to all these people. This looks like a great big hermetic Rembrandtian portrait in Aix! That's why it has that funny monumentality—aside from the quote plastic values unquote.

Then, I smoked a lot of marijuana and went to the basement of the Museum of Modern Art in New York and looked at his water colors and that's where I began really turning on to space in Cézanne and the way he built it up. Particularly there's one of rocks, I guess "Rocks at Garonne," and you look at them for a while, and after a while they seem like they're rocks, just the rock parts, you don't know where they are, whether they're on the ground or in the air or on top of a cliff, but then they seem to be floating in space like clouds, and then they seem to be also a bit like they're amorphous, like kneecaps or cockheads or faces without eyes. And it has a very mysterious impression. Well, that may have been the result of the pot. But it's a definite thing that I got from that. Then he did some very odd studies after classical statues, Renaissance statutes, and they're great gigantesque herculean figures with little tiny pinheads . . . so that apparently was his comment on them!

And then . . . the things were endless to find in Cézanne. Finally I was reading his letters and I discovered this phrase again, *mes petites sensations*—"I'm an old man and my passions are not, my senses are not coarsened by passions like some other old men I know, and I have worked for years trying to," I guess it was the phrase, "*reconstitute* the *petites sensations* that I get from nature, and I could stand on a hill and merely by moving my head half an inch the composition of the landscape was totally changed." So apparently he'd refined his optical perception to such a point where it's a real contemplation of optical phenomena in an almost yogic way, where he's standing there, from a specific point studying the optical field, the depth in the optical field, looking, actually looking at his own eyeballs in a sense. The attempting to reconstitute the sensation in his own eyeballs. And what does he say finally—in a very weird statement which one would not expect of the austere old workman—he said, "And this *petite sensation* is nothing other than *pater omnipotens aeterna deus.*"

So that was, I felt, the key to Cézanne's hermetic method
. . . everybody knows his workman-like, artisan-like,
pettified-like painting method which is so great, but the
really romanticistic motif behind it is absolutely marvelous,
so you realize that he's really a saint! Working on his form
of yoga, all that time, in obvious saintly circumstances of
retirement in a small village, leading a relatively nonsociable
life, going through the motions of going to church or not,
but really containing in his skull these supernatural phenom-
ena, and observations . . . you know, and it's very humble
actually, because he didn't know if he was crazy or not—that
is a flash of the physical, miracle dimensions of existence,
trying to reduce that to canvas in two dimensions, and then
trying to do it in such a way as it would look—if the observer
looked at it long enough—it would look like as much three
dimension as the actual world of optical phenomena when
one looks through one's eyes. Actually he's reconstituted the
whole fucking universe in his canvases—it's like a fantastic
thing!—or at least the appearance of the universe.

So. I used a lot of this material in the references in the last
part of the first section of "Howl": "sensation of Pater Omnip-
otens Aeterna Deus." The last part of "Howl" was really
an homage to art but also in specific terms an homage to
Cézanne's method, in a sense I adapted what I could to writ-
ing; but that's a very complicated matter to explain. Except,
putting it very simply, that just as Cézanne doesn't use per-
spective lines to create space but it's a juxtaposition of one
color against another color (that's one element of his space),
so, I had the idea, perhaps overrefined that by the unexplain-
able, unexplained nonperspective line, that is, juxtaposition
of one word against another, a gap between the two words—
like the space gap in the canvas—there'd be a gap between
the two words which the mind would fill in with the sen-
sation of existence. In other words when I say, oh . . . when
Shakespeare says, "In the dread vast and middle of the night,"
something happens between "dread vast" and "middle." That
creates like a whole space of, spaciness of black night. How
it gets that is very odd, those words put together. Or in the
haiku, you have two distinct images, set side by side without

drawing a connection, without drawing a logical connection between them the mind fills in this . . . this space. Like

> O *ant*
> *crawl up Mount Fujiyama,*
> *but slowly, slowly.*

Now you have the small ant and you have Mount Fujiyama and you have the slowly, slowly, and what happens is that you feel almost like . . . a cock in your mouth! You feel this enormous space-universe, it's almost a tactile thing. Well, anyway, it's a phenomenon-sensation, phenomenon hyphen sensation, that's created by this little haiku of Issa, for instance.

So, I was trying to do similar things with juxtapositions like "hydrogen jukebox." Or . . . "winter midnight smalltown streetlight rain." Instead of cubes and squares and triangles. Cézanne is reconstituting by means of triangles, cubes, and colors—I have to reconstitute by means of words, rhythms of course, and all that—but say it's words, phrasings. So. The problem is then to reach the different parts of the mind, which are existing simultaneously, choosing elements from both, like: jazz, jukebox, and all that, and we have the jukebox from that; politics, hydrogen bomb, and we have the hydrogen of that, you see "hydrogen jukebox. " And that actually compresses in one instant like a whole series of things. Or the end of "Sun-flower" with "cunts of wheelbarrows," whatever that all meant, or "rubber dollar bills"—"skin of machinery"; see, and actually in the moment of composition I don't necessarily know what it means, but it comes to mean something later, after a year or two, I realize that it meant something clear, unconsciously. Which takes on meaning in time, like a photograph developing slowly. Because we're not really always conscious of the entire depth of our minds—in other words, we just know a lot more than we're able to be aware of, normally—though at moments we're completely aware, I guess.

There's some other element of Cézanne that was interesting . . . oh, his patience, of course. In recording the optical phenomena. Has something to do with Blake: with not through the eye—"You're led to believe a lie when you see with not through the eye." He's seeing through his eye. One can see through his canvas to God, really, is the way it boils down. Or to Pater Omnipotens Aeterna Deus. I could imagine someone not prepared, in a peculiar chemical-physiological state, peculiar mental state, psychic state, someone not prepared who had no experience of eternal ecstasy, passing in front of a Cézanne canvas, distracted and without noticing it, his eye traveling in, to, through the canvas into the space and suddenly stopping with his hair standing on end, dead in his tracks, seeing a whole universe. And I think that's what Cézanne really does, to a lot of people.

Where were we now? Yeah, the idea that I had was that gaps in space and time through images juxtaposed, just as in the haiku you get two images which the mind connects in a flash, and so that *flash* is the *petite sensation;* or the *satori*, perhaps, that the Zen haikuists would speak of—if they speak of it like that. So, the poetic experience that Housman talks about, the hair-standing-on-end or the hackles-rising, whatever it is, visceral thing. The interesting thing would be to know if certain combinations of words and rhythms actually had an electrochemical reaction on the body, which could catalyze specific states of consciousness. I think that's what probably happened to me with Blake. I'm sure it's what happens on a perhaps lower level with Poe's "Bells" or "Raven," or even Vachel Lindsay's "Congo": that there is a hypnotic rhythm there, which when you introduce it into your nervous system, causes all sorts of electronic changes—permanently alters it. There's a statement by Artaud on that subject, that certain music when introduced into the nervous system changes the molecular composition of the nerve cells or something like that, it permanently alters the being that has experience of this. Well anyway, this is certainly true. In other words, any experience we have is recorded in the brain and goes through neural patterns and whatnot: so I suppose brain recordings are done by means of shifting around of little electrons—so there is actually an electrochemical effect caused by art.

So . . . the problem is what is the maximum electrochemical effect in the desired direction. That is what I was taking Blake as having done to me. And what I take as one of the optimal possibilities of art. But this is all putting it in a kind of bullshit abstract way. But it's an interesting—toy. To play with. That idea.

TC: In the last five or six months you've been in Cuba, Czechoslovakia, Russia, and Poland. Has this helped to clarify your sense of the current world situation?

AG: Yeah, I no longer feel—I didn't ever feel that there was any answer in dogmatic Leninism-Marxism—but I feel very definitely now that there's no answer to my desires there. Nor do most of the people in those countries—in Russia or Poland or Cuba—really feel that either. It's sort of like a religious theory imposed from above and usually used to beat people on the head with. Nobody takes it seriously because it doesn't mean anything, it means different things in different countries anyway. The general idea of revolution against American idiocy is good, it's still sympathetic, and I guess it's a good thing like in Cuba, and obviously Viet Nam. But what's gonna follow—the dogmatism that follows is a big drag. And everybody apologizes for the dogmatism by saying, well, it's an inevitable consequence of the struggle against American repression. And that may be true too.

But there's one thing I feel certain of, and that's that there's no human answer in communism or capitalism as it's practiced outside of the U. S. in any case. In other words, by hindsight, the interior of America is not bad, at least for me, though it might be bad for a spade, but not too bad, creepy, but it's not impossible. But traveling in countries like Cuba and Viet Nam I realize that the people that get the real evil side effects of America are there—in other words, it really is like imperialism, in that sense. People in the United States all got money, they got cars, and everybody else starves on account of American foreign policy. Or is being bombed out, torn apart, and bleeding on the street, they get all their teeth bashed in, tear gassed, or hot pokers up their ass, things that would be, you know, considered terrible in the United States. Except for Negroes.

So I don't know. I don't see any particular answer, and this month it seemed to me like actually an atomic war was inevitable on account of both sides were so dogmatic and frightened and had nowhere to go and didn't know what to do with themselves anymore except fight. Everybody too intransigent. Everybody too mean. I don't suppose it'll take place, but . . . Somebody has got to sit in the British Museum again like Marx and figure out a new system; a new blueprint. Another century has gone, technology has changed everything completely, so it's time for a new utopian system. Burroughs is almost working on it.

But one thing that's impressive is Blake's idea of Jerusalem, Jerusalemic Britain, which I think is now more and more valid. He, I guess, defined it. I'm still confused about Blake, I still haven't read him all through enough to understand what direction he was really pointing to. It seems to be the naked human form divine, seems to be Energy, it seems to be sexualization, or sexual liberation, which are the directions we all believe in. He also seems, however, to have some idea of imagination which I don't fully understand yet. That is, it's something outside of the body, with a rejection of the body, and I don't quite understand that. A life after death even. Which I still haven't comprehended. There's a letter in the Fitzwilliam Museum, written several months before he died. He says, "My body is in turmoil and stress and decaying, but my ideas, my power of ideas and my imagination, are stronger than ever." And I find it hard to conceive of that. I think if I were lying in bed dying, with my body pained, I would just give up. I mean, you know, because I don't think I could exist outside my body. But he apparently was able to. Williams didn't seem to be able to. In other words Williams's universe was tied up with his body. Blake's universe didn't seem to be tied up with his body. Real mysterious, like far other worlds and other seas, so to speak. Been puzzling over that today.

The Jerusalemic world of Blake seems to be Mercy-Pity-Peace. Which has human form. Mercy has a human face. So that's all clear.

TC: How about Blake's statement about the senses being the chief inlets of the soul in this age—I don't know what "this age" means; is there another one?

AG: What he says is interesting because there's the same thing in Hindu mythology, they speak of This Age as the Kali Yuga, the age of destruction, or an age so sunk in materialism. You'd find a similar formulation in Vico, like what is it, the Age of Gold running on to the Iron and then Stone, again. Well, the Hindus say that this is the Kali Age or Kali Yuga or Kali Cycle, and we are also so sunk in matter, the five senses are matter, sense, that they say there is absolutely no way out by intellect, by thought, by discipline, by practice, by sadhana, by jnanayoga, nor karma yoga—that is, doing good works—no way out through our own will or our own effort. The only way out that they generally now prescribe, generally in India at the moment, is through bhakti yoga, which is Faith-Hope-Adoration-Worship, or like probably the equivalent of the Christian Sacred Heart, which I find a very lovely doctrine—that is to say, pure delight, the only way you can be saved is to sing. In other words, the only way to drag up, from the depths of this depression, to drag up your soul to its proper bliss, and understanding, is to give yourself, completely, to your heart's desire. The image will be determined by the heart's compass, by the compass of what the heart moves toward and desires. And then you get on your knees or on your lap or on your head and you sing and chant prayers and mantras, till you reach a state of ecstasy and understanding, and the bliss overflows out of your body. They say intellect, like Saint Thomas Aquinas, will never do it, because it's just like me getting all hung up on whether I could remember what happened before I was born—I mean you could get lost there very easily, and it has no relevance anyway, to the existent flower. Blake says something similar, like Energy, and Excess . . . leads to the palace of wisdom. The Hindu bhakti is like excess of devotion; you just, you know, give yourself all out to devotion.

Very oddly a lady saint Shri Matakrishnaji in Brindaban, whom I consulted about my spiritual problems, told me to take Blake for my guru. There's all kinds of different gurus, there can be living and nonliving gurus—apparently whoever initiates you, and I apparently was initiated by Blake in terms of at least having an ecstatic experience from him. So that when I got here to Cambridge I had to rush over to the Fitzwilliam Museum to find his misspellings in *Songs of Innocence*.

TC: What was the Blake experience you speak of?

AG: About 1945 I got interested in Supreme Reality with a capital S and R, and I wrote big long poems about a last voyage looking for Supreme Reality. Which was like a Dostoevskian or Thomas Wolfeian idealization or like Rimbaud—what was Rimbaud's term, new vision, was that it? Or Kerouac was talking about a new vision, verbally, and intuitively out of longing, but also out of a funny kind of tolerance of this universe. In 1948 in East Harlem in the summer I was living— this is like the Ancient Mariner, I've said this so many times: "stoppeth one of three./'By thy long grey beard . . . '" Hang an albatross around your neck. . . . The one thing I felt at the time was that it would be a terrible horror, that in one or two decades I would be trying to explain to people that one day something like this happened to me! I even wrote a long poem saying, "I will grow old, a grey and groaning man,/ and with each hour the same thought, and with each thought the same denial./ Will I spend my life in praise of the idea of God?/ Time leaves no hope. We creep and wait. We wait and go alone." Psalm II—which I never published. So anyway— there I was in my bed in Harlem . . . jacking off. With my pants open, lying around on a bed by the window sill, looking out into the cornices of Harlem and the sky above. And I had just come. And had perhaps hardly even wiped the come off my thighs, my trousers, or whatever it was. As I often do, I had been jacking off while reading—I think it's probably a common phenomenon to be noticed among adolescents. Though I was a little older than an adolescent at the time. About twenty-two. There's a kind of interesting thing about, you know, distracting your attention while you jack off—that is, you know, reading a book or looking out of a window, or doing something else with the conscious mind which kind of makes it sexier.

So anyway, what I had been doing that week—I'd been in a very lonely solitary state, dark night of the soul sort of, reading Saint John of the Cross, maybe on account of that everybody'd gone away that I knew, Burroughs was in Mexico, Jack was out in Long Island and relatively isolated, we didn't see each other, and I had been very close with them for several years. Huncke I think was in jail, or something. Anyway, there was nobody I knew. Mainly the thing was that I'd been making it with N.C., and finally I think I got a letter from him saying it was all off, no more, we shouldn't consider ourselves lovers any more on account of it just wouldn't work out. But previously we'd had an understanding that we—Neal Cassady, I said "N.C." but I suppose you can use his name—we'd had a big tender lovers' understanding. But I guess it got too much for him, partly because he was three thousand miles away and he had six thousand girl friends on the other side of the continent, who were keeping him busy, and then here was my lone cry of despair from New York. So. I got a letter from him saying, Now, Allen, we gotta move on to new territory. So I felt this is like a great mortal blow to all of my tenderest hopes. And I figured I'd never find any sort of psychospiritual sexo-cock jewel fulfillment in my existence! So, I went into . . . like I felt cut off from what I'd idealized romantically. And I was also graduating from school and had nowhere to go and the difficulty of getting a job. So finally there was nothing for me to do except to eat vegetables and live in Harlem. In an apartment I'd rented from someone. Sublet.

So, in that state therefore, of hopelessness, or dead end, change of phase, you know—growing up—and in an equilibrium in any case, a psychic, a mental equilibrium of a kind, like of having no New Vision and no Supreme Reality and nothing but the world in front of me, and of not knowing what to do with that . . . there was a funny balance of tension, in every direction. And just after I came, on this occasion, with a Blake book on my lap—I wasn't even reading, my eye was idling over the page of "Ah, Sun-flower," and it suddenly appeared—the poem I'd read a lot of times before, overfamiliar to the point where it didn't make any particular meaning except some sweet thing about flowers—and suddenly I realized that the poem was talking about me. "Ah, sun-flower! weary of time, / Who countest the steps of the sun; / Seeking after that sweet golden clime, / Where the traveller's journey is done." Now, I began understanding it, the poem while looking at it, and suddenly, simultaneously with understanding it, heard a very deep earthen grave voice in the room, which I immediately assumed, I didn't think twice, was Blake's voice; it wasn't any voice that I knew, though I had previously had a conception of a voice of rock, in a poem, some image like that—or maybe that came after this experience.

And my eye on the page, simultaneously the auditory hallucination, or whatever terminology here used, the apparitional voice, in the room, woke me further deep in my understanding of the poem, because the voice was so completely tender and beautifully . . . ancient. Like the voice of the Ancient of Days. But the peculiar quality of the voice was something unforgettable because it was like God had a human voice, with all the infinite tenderness and anciency and mortal gravity of a living Creator speaking to his son. "Where the Youth pined away with desire, / And the pale Virgin shrouded in snow, / Arise from their graves, and aspire / Where my Sun-flower wishes to go." Meaning that there *was* a *place*, there was a sweet golden clime, and the *sweet golden*, what was that . . . and simultaneous to the voice there was also an emotion, risen in my soul in response to the voice, and a sudden *visual* realization of the same awesome phenomena. That is to say, looking out at the window, through the window at the sky, suddenly it seemed that I saw into the depths of the universe, by looking simply into the ancient sky. The sky suddenly seemed very *ancient*. And this was the very ancient place that he was talking about, the sweet golden clime, I suddenly realized that *this* existence was *it!* And, that I was born in order to experience up to this very moment that I was having this experience, to realize what this was all about—in other words that this was the moment that I was born for. This initiation. Or this vision or this consciousness, of being alive unto myself, alive myself unto the Creator. As the son of the Creator—who loved me, I realized, or who responded to my desire, say. It was the same desire both ways.

Anyway, my first thought was this was what I was born

for, and second thought, never forget—never forget, never renege, never deny. Never deny the voice—no, never *forget* it, don't get lost mentally wandering in other spirit worlds or American or job worlds or advertising worlds or war worlds or earth worlds. But the spirit of the universe was what I was born to realize. What I was speaking about visually was, immediately, that the cornices in the old tenement building in Harlem across the back-yard court had been carved very finely in 1890 or 1910. And were like the solidification of a great deal of intelligence and care and love also. So that I began noticing in every corner where I looked evidences of a living hand, even in the bricks, in the arrangement of each brick. Some hand placed them there—that some hand had placed the whole universe in front of me. That some hand had placed the sky. No, that's exaggerating—not that some hand had placed the sky but that the sky was the living blue hand itself. Or that God was in front of my eyes—existence itself was God. Well, the formulations are like that—I didn't formulate it in exactly those terms; what I was seeing was a visionary thing, it was a lightness in my body . . . my body suddenly felt light, and a sense of cosmic consciousness, vibrations, understanding, awe, and wonder and surprise. And it was a sudden awakening into a totally deeper real universe than I'd been existing in. So, I'm trying to avoid generalizations about that sudden deeper real universe and keep it strictly to observations of phenomenal data, or a voice with a certain sound, the appearance of cornices, the appearance of the sky, say, of the great blue hand, the living hand—to keep to images.

But anyway—the same . . . *petite sensation* recurred several minutes later, with the same voice, while reading the poem "The Sick Rose." This time it was a slightly different sense-depth-mystic impression. Because "The Sick Rose"—you know I can't interpret the poem now, but it had a meaning—I mean I can interpret it on a verbal level, the sick rose is my self, or self, or the living body, sick because the mind, which is the worm "That flies in the night, In the howling storm," or Urizen, reason; Blake's character might be the one that's entered the body and is destroying it, or let us say death, the worm as being death, the natural process of death, some kind of mystical being of its own trying to come in and devour the body, the rose. Blake's drawing for it is complicated, it's a big drooping rose, drooping because it's dying, and there's a worm in it, and the worm is wrapped around a little sprite that's trying to get out of the mouth of the rose.

But anyway, I experienced "The Sick Rose," with the voice of Blake reading it, as something that applied to the whole universe, like hearing the doom of the whole universe, and at the same time the inevitable beauty of doom. I can't remember now, except it was very beautiful and very awesome. But a little of it slightly scary, having to do with the knowledge of death—my death and also the death of being itself, and that was the great pain. So, like a prophecy, not only in human terms but a prophecy as if Blake had penetrated the very secret core of the entire universe and had come forth with some little magic formula statement in rhyme and rhythm that, if properly heard in the inner inner ear, would deliver you beyond the universe.

So then, the other poem that brought this on in the same day was "The Little Girl Lost," where there was a repeated refrain,

> 'Do father, mother, weep?
> Where can Lyca sleep?
>
> 'How can Lyca sleep
> If her mother weep?
>
> 'If her heart does ache
> Then let Lyca wake;
> If my mother sleep,
> Lyca shall not weep.'

It's that hypnotic thing—and I suddenly realized that Lyca was me, or Lyca was the self; father, mother seeking Lyca, was God seeking, Father, the Creator; and " 'If her heart does ache / Then let Lyca wake'"—wake to what? *Wake* meaning wake to the same awakeness I was just talking about—of existence in the entire universe. The total consciousness then, of the compete universe. Which is what Blake was talking about. In other words a breakthrough from ordinary habitual quotidian consciousness into consciousness that was really seeing all of heaven in a flower. Or what was it—eternity in a flower . . . heaven in a grain of sand? As I was seeing heaven in the cornice of the building. By heaven here I mean this imprint or concretization or living form, of an intelligent hand—the work of an intelligent hand, which still had the intelligence molded into it. The gargoyles on the Harlem cornices. What was interesting about the cornice was that there's cornices like that on every building, but I never noticed them before. And I never realized that they meant spiritual labor, to anyone—that somebody had labored to make a curve in a piece of tin—to make a cornucopia out of a piece of industrial tin. Not only that man, the workman, the artisan, but the architect had thought of it, the builder had paid for it, the smelter had smelt it, the miner had dug it up out of the earth, the earth had gone through aeons preparing it. So the little molecules had slumbered for . . . for Kalpas. So out of *all* of these Kalpas it all got together in a great succession of impulses, to be frozen finally in that one form of a cornucopia cornice on the building front. And God knows how many people made the moon. Or what spirits labored . . . to set fire to the sun. As Blake says, "When I look in the sun I don't see the rising sun, I see a band of angels singing holy, holy, holy." Well, his perception of the field of the sun is different from that of a man who just sees the sun sun, without any emotional relationship to it.

But then, there was a point later in the week when the intermittent flashes of the same . . . bliss—because the experience was quite blissful—came back. In a sense all this is described in "The Lion for Real" by anecdotes of different experiences—actually it was a very difficult time, which I won't go into here. Because suddenly I thought, also simultaneously, Ooh, I'm going *mad!* That's described in the line in "Howl," "who thought they were *only* mad when Baltimore gleamed in supernatural ecstasy"—"who thought they were *only* mad. . . ." If it were only that easy! In other words it'd be a lot easier if you just were crazy, instead of—then you could chalk it up, "Well, I'm nutty"—but on the other hand what if it's all true and you're *born* into this great cosmic universe in which you're a spirit angel—terrible fucking situation to be confronted with. It's like being woken up one morning by Joseph K's captors. Actually what I think I did was there was a couple of girls living next door and I crawled out on the fire escape and tapped on their window and said, "I've seen God!" and they *banged* the window shut. Oh, what tales I could have told them if they'd let me in! Because I was in a very exalted state of mind and the consciousness was still with me—I remember I immediately rushed to Plato and read some great image in the *Phaedrus* about horses flying through the sky, and rushed over to Saint John and started reading fragments of *con un no saber sabiendo . . . que me quede balbuciendo*, and rushed to the other part of the bookshelf and picked up Plotinus about The Alone—the Plotinus I found more difficult to interpret.

But I *immediately* doubled my thinking process, quadrupled, and I was able to read almost any text and see all sorts of divine significance in it. And I think that week or that month I had to take an examination in John Stuart Mill. And instead of writing about his ideas I got completely hung up on his experience of reading—was it Wordsworth? Apparently the thing that got him back was an experience of nature that he received keyed off by reading Wordsworth, on "sense sublime" or something. That's a very good description, that sense sublime of something far more deeply interfused, whose dwelling is the light of setting suns, and the round ocean, and the . . . the *living* air, did he say? The living air—see just that hand again—*and* in the heart of man. So I think this experience is characteristic of all high poetry. I mean that's the way I began seeing poetry as the communication of the particular experience—not just any experience but *this* experience.

TC: Have you had anything like this experience again?

AG: Yeah. I'm not finished with this period. Then, in my room, I didn't know what to do. But I wanted to bring it up so I began experimenting with it, without Blake. And I think it was one day in my kitchen—I had an old-fashioned kitchen with a sink with a tub in it with a board over the top—I started moving around and sort of shaking with my body and dancing up and down on the floor and saying, "Dance! dance! dance! dance! spirit! spirit! spirit! dance!" and suddenly I felt like Faust, calling up the devil. And then it started coming over me, this big . . . creepy feeling, cryptozoid or monozoidal, so I got all scared and quit.

Then I was walking around Columbia and I went in the Columbia bookstore and was reading Blake again, leafing over a book of Blake, I think it was "The Human Abstract": "Pity would be no more. . . ." And suddenly it came over me in the bookstore again, and I was in the eternal place *once more*, and I looked around at everybody's faces, and I saw all these wild animals! Because there was a bookstore clerk there who I hadn't paid much attention to, he was just a familiar fixture in the bookstore scene and everybody went in the bookstore every day like me, because downstairs there was a café and upstairs there were all these clerks that we were all familiar with—this guy had a very *long* face, you know some people look like giraffes. So he looked kind of giraffish. He had a kind of a long face with a long nose. I don't know what kind of sex life he had, but he must have had something. But anyway, I looked in his face and I suddenly saw like a great tormented soul—and he had just been somebody whom I'd regarded as perhaps a not particularly beautiful or sexy character, or lovely face, but you know someone familiar, and perhaps a pleading cousin in the universe. But all of a sudden I realized that *he* knew also, just like I knew. And that everybody in the bookstore knew, and that they were all hiding it! They all had the consciousness, it was like a great unconscious that was running between all of us that everybody *was* completely conscious, but that the fixed expressions that people have, the habitual expression, the manners, the mode of talk, are all masks hiding this consciousness. Because almost at that moment it seemed that it would be too terrible if we communicated to each other on a level of total consciousness and awareness each of the other—like it would be too terrible, it would be the end of the bookstore, it would be the end of civ—. . . not civilization, but in other words the position that everybody was in was *ridiculous*, everybody running around peddling books to each other. Here in the universe! Passing money over the counter, wrapping books in bags and guarding the door, you know, stealing books, and the people sitting up making accountings on the upper floor there, and people worrying about their exams walking through the bookstore, and all the millions of thoughts the people had—you know, that I'm worrying about—whether they're going to get laid or whether anybody loves them, about their mothers dying of cancer or, you know, the complete death awareness that everybody has continuously with them all the time—all of a sudden revealed to me at once in the faces of the people, and they all looked like horrible grotesque masks, grotesque because *hiding* the knowledge from each other. Having a habitual conduct and forms to prescribe, forms to fulfill. Roles to play. But the main insight I had at that time was that everybody knew. Everybody knew completely everything. Knew completely everything in the terms which I was talking about.

TC: Do you still think they know?

AG: I'm more sure of it now. Sure. All you have to do is try and make somebody. You realize that they knew all along you were trying to make them. But until that moment you never break through to communication on the subject.

TC: Why not?

AG: Well, fear of rejection. The twisted faces of all those people, the faces were twisted by rejection. And hatred of self, finally. The internalization of that rejection. And finally disbelief in that shining self. Disbelief in that infinite self. Partly because that particular . . . partly because the *awareness* that we all carry is too often painful, because the experience of rejection and lacklove and cold war—I mean the whole cold war is the imposition of a vast mental barrier on everybody, a vast antinatural psyche. A hardening, a shutting off of the perception of desire and tenderness which everybody *knows* and which is the very structure of . . . the atom! Structure of the human body and organism. That desire built in. Blocked. "Where the Youth pined away with desire, / And the pale Virgin shrouded in snow." Or as Blake says, "On every face I see, I meet / Marks of weakness, marks of woe." So what I was thinking in the bookstore was the marks of weakness, marks of woe. Which you can just look around and look at anybody's face right next to you now always—you can see it in the way the mouth is pursed, you can see it in the way the eyes blink, you can see it in the way the gaze is fixed down at the matches. It's the self-consciousness which is a substitute for communication with the outside. This consciousness pushed back into the self and thinking of how it will hold its face and eyes and hands in order to make a mask to hide the flow that is going on. Which it's aware of, which everybody is aware of really! So let's say, shyness. Fear. Fear of like total feeling, really, total being is what it is.

So the problem then was, having attained realization, how to safely manifest it and communicate it. Of course there was the old Zen thing, when the sixth patriarch handed down the little symbolic oddments and ornaments and books and bowls, stained bowls too . . . when the *fifth* patriarch handed them down to the sixth patriarch he told him to hide them and don't tell anybody you're patriarch because it's dangerous, they'll kill you. So there was that immediate danger. It's taken me all these years to manifest it and work it out in a way that's materially communicable to people. Without scaring them or me. Also movements of history and breaking down the civilization. To break down everybody's masks and roles sufficiently so that everybody has to face the universe *and* the possibility of the sick rose coming true and the atom bomb. So it was an immediate messianic thing. Which seems to be becoming more and more justified. And more and more reasonable in terms of the existence that we're living.

So. Next time it happened was about a week later walking along in the evening on a circular path around what's now I guess the garden or field in the middle of Columbia University, by the library. I started invoking the spirit, consciously trying to get another depth perception of cosmos. And suddenly it began occurring again, like a sort of breakthrough again, but this time—this was the last time in that period—it was the same depth of consciousness or the same cosmical awareness but suddenly it was not blissful at all but it was *frightening*. Some like real serpent-fear entering the sky. The sky was not a blue hand anymore but like a hand of death coming down on me—some really scary presence, it was almost as if I saw God again except God was the devil. The consciousness itself was so vast, much more vast than any idea of it I'd had or any experience I'd had, that it was not even human any more—and was in a sense a threat, because I was going to die into that inhuman ultimately. I don't know *what* the score was there—I was too cowardly to pursue it. To attend and experience completely the Gates of Wrath—there's a poem of Blake's that deals with that, "To find a Western Path / Right through the Gates of Wrath." But I didn't urge my way there, I shut it all off. And got scared, and thought, I've gone too far.

TC: Was your use of drugs an extension of this experience?

AG: Well, since I took a vow that this was the area of, that this was my existence that I was placed into, drugs were obviously a technique for experimenting with consciousness, to get different areas and different levels and different similarities and different reverberations of the same vision. Marijuana has some of it in it, that awe, the cosmic awe that you get sometimes on pot. There are certain moments under laughing gas and ether that the consciousness does intersect with something similar—for me—to my Blake visions. The gas drugs were apparently interesting too to the Lake Poets, because there were a lot of experiments done with Sir Humphrey Davy in his Pneumatic Institute. I think Coleridge and Southey and other people used to go, and De Quincy. But serious people. I think there hasn't been very much written about that period. *What went on* in the Humphrey Davy household on Saturday midnight when Coleridge arrived by foot, through the forest, by the lakes? Then, there are certain states you get into with opium, and heroin, of almost disembodied awareness, looking down back at the earth from a place after you're dead. Well, it's not the same, but it's an interesting state, and a useful one. It's a normal state also, I mean it's a holy state of some sort. At times. Then, mainly, of course, with the hallucinogens, you get some states of consciousness which subjectively seem to be cosmic-ecstatic, or cosmic-demonic. Our version of expanded consciousness is as much as *un*conscious information—awareness comes up to the surface. Lysergic acid, peyote, mescaline, psilocybin, Ayahuasca. But I can't stand them any more, because something happened to me with them very similar to the Blake visions. After about thirty times, thirty-five times, I began getting monster vibrations again. So I couldn't go any further. I may later on again, if I feel more reassurance.*

.However, I did get a lot out of them, mainly like emotional understanding, understanding the female principle in a way—women, more sense of the softness and more desire for women. Desire for children also.

TC: Anything interesting about the actual experience, say with hallucinogens?

AG: What I do get is, say if I was in an apartment high on mescaline, I felt as if the apartment and myself were not merely on East Fifth Street but were in the middle of all space time. If I close my eyes on hallucinogens, I get a vision of great scaly dragons in outer space, they're winding slowly and eating their own tails. Sometimes my skin and all the room

---

* Between occasion of interview with Thomas Clark June '65 and publication May '66 more reassurance came. I tried small doses of LSD twice in secluded tree and ocean cliff haven at Big Sur. No monster vibration, no snake universe hallucinations. Many tiny jeweled violet flowers along the path of a living brook that looked like Blake's illustration for a canal in grassy Eden: huge Pacific watery shore, Orlovsky dancing naked like Shiva long-haired before giant green waves, titanic cliffs that Wordsworth mentioned in his own Sublime, great yellow sun veiled with mist hanging over the plant's oceanic horizon. No harm. President Johnson that day went into the Valley of Shadow operating room because of his gall bladder & Berkeley's Vietnam Day Committee was preparing anxious manifestoes for our march toward Oakland police and Hell's Angels. Realizing that more vile words from me would send out physical vibrations into the atmosphere that might curse poor Johnson's flesh and further unbalance his soul, I knelt on the sand surrounded by masses of green bulb-headed Kelp vegetable-snake undersea beings washed up by last night's tempest, and prayed for the President's tranquil health. Since there has been so much legislative miscomprehension of the LSD boon I regret that my unedited ambivalence in Thomas Clark's tape transcript interview was published wanting this footnote.

Your obedient servant
Allen Ginsberg, *aetat* 40
June 2, 1966

seem sparkling with scales, and it's all made out of serpent stuff. And as if the whole illusion of life were made of reptile dream.

Mandala also. I use the mandala in an LSD poem. The associations I've had during times that I was high are usually referred to or built in some image or other to one of the other poems written on drugs. Or after drugs—like in "Magic Psalm" on lysergic acid. Or mescaline. There's a long passage about a mandala in the LSD poem. There is a good situation since I was high and I was looking at a mandala—before I got high I asked the doctor that was giving it to me at Stanford to prepare me a set of mandalas to look at, to borrow some from Professor Spiegelberg who was an expert. So we had some Sikkimese elephant mandalas there. I simply describe those in the poem—what they look like while I was high.

So—summing up then—drugs were useful for exploring perception, sense perception, and exploring different possibilities and modes of consciousness, and exploring the different versions of *petites sensations*, and useful then for composing, sometimes, while under the influence. Part II of "Howl" was written under the influence of peyote, composed during peyote vision. In San Francisco—"Moloch." "Kaddish" was written with amphetamine injections. An injection of amphetamine plus a little bit of morphine, plus some Dexedrine later on to keep me going, because it was all in one long sitting. From a Saturday morn to a Sunday night. The amphetamine gives a peculiar metaphysical tinge to things, also. Space-outs. It doesn't interfere too much there because I wasn't habituated to it, I was just taking it that one weekend. It didn't interfere too much with the emotional charge that comes through.

TC: Was there any relation to this in your trip to Asia?

AG: Well, the Asian experience kind of got me out of the corner I painted myself in with drugs. That corner being an inhuman corner in the sense that I figured I was expanding my consciousness and I had to go through with it but at the same time I was confronting this serpent monster, so I was getting in a real terrible situation. It finally would get so if I'd take the drugs I'd start vomiting. But I felt that I was duly bound and obliged for the sake of consciousness expansion, and this insight, and breaking down my identity, and seeking more direct contact with primate sensation, nature, to continue. So when I went to India, all the way through India, I was babbling about that to all the holy men I could find. I wanted to find out if they had any suggestions. And they all did, and they were all good ones. First one I saw was Martin Buber, who was interested. In Jerusalem, Peter and I went in to see him—we called him up and made a date and had a long conversation. He had a beautiful white beard and was friendly; his nature was slightly austere but benevolent. Peter asked him what kind of visions he'd had and he described some he'd had in bed when he was younger. But he said he was not any longer interested in visions like that. The kind of visions he came up with were more like spiritualistic table rappings. Ghosts coming into the room through his window, rather than big beautiful seraphic Blake angels hitting him on the head. I was thinking like loss of identity and confrontation with nonhuman universe as the main problem, and in a sense whether or not man had to evolve and change, and perhaps become nonhuman too. Melt into the universe, let us say—to put it awkwardly and inaccurately. Buber said that he was interested in man-to-man relationships, human-to-human—that he thought it was a human universe that we were destined to inhabit. And so therefore human relationships rather than relations between the human and the nonhuman. Which was what I was thinking that I had to go into. And he said, "Mark my word, young man, in two years you will realize that I was right." He was right—in two years I marked his words. Two years is sixty-three—I saw him in sixty-one. I don't know if he said two years—but he said "in years to come." This was like a real terrific classical wise man's "Mark my words, young man, in several years you will realize that what I said was true!" Exclamation point.

Then there was Swami Shivananda, in Rishikish in India. He said, "Your own heart is your guru." Which I thought was very sweet, and very reassuring. That is the sweetness of it I felt—in my heart. And suddenly realized it was the heart that I was seeking. In other words it wasn't consciousness, it wasn't *petites sensations*, sensation defined as expansion of mental consciousness to include more data—as I was pursuing that line of thought, pursuing Burroughs's cutup thing—the area that I was seeking was heart rather than mind. In other words, in mind, through mind or imagination—this is where I get confused with Blake now—in mind one can construct all sorts of universes, one can construct model universes in dream and imagination, and with the speed of light; and with nitrous oxide you can experience several million universes in rapid succession. You can experience a whole gamut of possibilities of universes, including the final possibility that there is none. And then you go unconscious—which is exactly what happens with gas when you go unconscious. You see that the universe is going to disappear with your consciousness, that it was all dependent on your consciousness.

Anyway, a whole series of India holy men pointed back to the body—getting *in* the body rather than getting out of the human form. But living in and inhabiting the human form. Which then goes back to Blake again, the human form divine. Is this clear? In other words, the psychic problem that I had found myself in was that for various reasons it had seemed to me at one time or another that the best thing to do was to drop dead. Or not be afraid of death but go into death. Go into the nonhuman, go into the cosmic, so to speak; that God was death, and if I wanted to attain God I had to die. Which *may* still be true. So I thought that what I was put up to was to therefore break out of my body, if I wanted to attain complete consciousness.

So now the next step was that the gurus one after another said, Live in the body: this is the form that you're born for. That's too long a narration to go into. Too many holy men and too many different conversations and they all have a little *key* thing going. But it all winds up in the train in Japan, then a year later, the poem "The Change," where all of a sudden I renounce drugs, I don't renounce drugs but I suddenly didn't want to be *dominated* by that nonhuman any more, or even be dominated by the moral obligation to enlarge my consciousness any more. Or do anything any more except *be* my heart—which just desired to be and be alive now. I had a very strange ecstatic experience then and there, once I had sort of gotten that burden off my back, because I was suddenly free to love myself again, and therefore love the people around me, in the form that they already were. And love myself in my own form as I am. And look around at the other people and so it was *again* the same thing like in the bookstore. Except this time I was completely in my body and had no more mysterious obligations. And nothing more to fulfill, except to be willing to die when I am dying, whenever that be. And be willing to live as a human in this form now. So I started weeping, it was such a happy moment. Fortunately I was able to write then, too, "So that I do live I will die"—rather than be cosmic consciousness, immortality, Ancient of Days, perpetual consciousness existing forever.

Then when I got to Vancouver, Olson was saying "I am one with my skin." It *seemed* to me at the time when I got back to Vancouver that everybody had been precipitated back into their bodies at the same time. It seemed that's what Creeley had *been* talking about all along. The *place*—the terminology he used, the *place* we are. Meaning this place, here. And trying to like be real in the real place . . . to be aware of the place where he is. Because I'd always thought that that meant that he was cutting off from divine imagination. But what that meant for him was that this place would be everything that one would refer to as divine, if one were really here. So that Vancouver seems a very odd moment, at least for me—because I came back in a sense completely bankrupt. My energies of the last . . . oh, 1948 to 1963, all completely washed up. On the train in Kyoto having renounced Blake, renounced visions—renounced *Blake!*—too. There was a cycle that began with the Blake vision which ended on the train in Kyoto when I realized that to attain the depth of consciousness that I was seeking when I was talking about the Blake vision, that in order to attain it I had to cut myself off from the Blake vision and renounce it. Otherwise I'd be hung up on a memory of an experience. Which is not the actual awareness of now, now. In order to get back to now, in order to get back to the total awareness of now and contact, sense perception contact with what was going on around me, or direct vision of the moment, now I'd have to give up this continual churning thought process of yearning back to a visionary state. It's all very complicated. And idiotic.

TC: I think you said earlier that "Howl" being a lyric poem, and "Kaddish" basically a narrative, that you now have a sense of wanting to do an epic. Do you have a plan like this?

AG: Yeah, but it's just . . . ideas, that I've been carrying around for a long time. One thing which I'd like to do sooner or later is write a long poem which is a narrative and description of all the visions I've ever had, sort of like the *Vita Nuova*. And travels, now. And another idea I had was to write a big long poem about everybody I ever fucked or slept with. Like sex . . . a love poem. A long love poem, involving all the innumerable lays of a lifetime. The epic is not that, though. The epic would be a poem including history, as it's defined. So that would be one about present-day politics, using the methods of the Blake *French Revolution*. I got a lot written. Narrative was "Kaddish." Epic—there has to be totally different organization, it might be simple free association on political themes—in fact I think an epic poem including history, at this stage. I've got a lot of it written, but it would have to be Burroughs' sort of epic—in other words, it would have to be dissociated thought stream which includes politics and history. I don't think you could do it in narrative form, I mean what would you be narrating, the history of the Korean War or something?

TC: Something like Pound's epic?

AG: No, because Pound seems to me to be over a course of years fabricating out of his reading and out of the museum of literature; whereas the thing would be to take all of contemporary history, newspaper headlines and all the pop art of Stalinism and Hitler and Johnson and Kennedy and Viet Nam and Congo and Lumumba and the South and Sacco and Vanzetti—whatever floated into one's personal field of consciousness and contact. And then to compose like a basket—like weave a basket, basket-weaving out of those materials. Since obviously nobody has any idea where it's all going or how it's going to end unless you have some vision to deal with. It would have to be done by a process of association, I guess.

TC: What's happening in poetry now?

AG: I don't know yet. Despite all confusion to the contrary, now that time's passed, I think the best poet in the United States is Kerouac still. Given twenty years to settle through. The main reason is that he's the most free and the most spontaneous. Has the greatest range of association and imagery in his poetry. Also in "Mexico City Blues" the sublime as subject matter. And, in other words the greatest facility at what might be called projective verse, if you want to give it a name. I think that he's stupidly underrated by almost everybody except for a few people who are aware how beautiful his composition is—like Snyder or Creeley or people who have a taste for his tongue, for his line. But it takes one to know one.

TC: You don't mean Kerouac's prose?

AG: No, I'm talking about just a pure poet. The verse poetry, the "Mexico City Blues" and a lot of other manuscripts I've seen. In addition he has the one sign of being a great poet, which is he's the only one in United States who knows how to write haikus. The only one who's written any good haikus. And everybody's been writing haikus. There are all these *dreary* haikus written by people who think for weeks trying to write a haiku, and finally come up with some dull little thing or something. Whereas Kerouac thinks in haikus, every time he writes anything—talks that way and thinks that way. So it's just natural for him. It's something Snyder noticed. Snyder has to labor for years in a Zen monastery to produce one haiku about shifting off a log! And actually does get one or two good ones. Snyder was always astounded by Kerouac's facility . . . at noticing winter flies dying of old age in his medicine chest. Medicine cabinet. "In my medicine cabinet / the winter flies / died of old age." He's never published them actually—he's published them on a record, with Zoot Sims and Al Cohn, it's a very beautiful collection of them. Those are, as far as I can see, the only real American haikus.

So the haiku is the most difficult test. He's the only *master* of the haiku. Aside from a longer style. Of course, the distinctions between prose and poetry are broken down anyway. So much that I was saying like a long page of oceanic Kerouac is sometimes as sublime as epic line. It's there that also

I think he went further into the existential thing of writ-
ing conceived of as an irreversible action or statement, that's
unrevisable and unchangeable once it's made. I remember I
was thinking, yesterday in fact, there was a time that I was
absolutely astounded because Kerouac told me that in the
future literature would consist of what people actually wrote
rather than what they tried to deceive other people into
thinking they wrote, when they revised it later on. And I saw
opening up this whole universe where people wouldn't be
able to lie any more! They wouldn't be able to *correct* them-
selves any longer. They wouldn't be able to hide what they
said. And he was willing to go all the way into that, the first
pilgrim into that new-found land.

TC: What about other poets?

AG: I think Corso has a great imaginative genius. And also
amongst the greatest *shrewdness*—like Keats or something. I
like Lamantia's nervous wildness. Almost anything he writes
I find interesting—for one thing he's always registering the
forward march of the soul, in exploration; spiritual explora-
tion is always there. And also chronologically following his
work is always exciting. Whalen and Snyder are both very
wise and very reliable. Whalen I don't *understand* so well.
I did, though, earlier—but I have to sit down and study his
work, again. Sometimes he seems sloppy—but then later on
it always seems right.

   McClure has tremendous energy, and seems like some sort
of a . . . seraph is not the word . . . not herald either but a . . .
not demon either. Seraph I guess it is. He's always moving—
see when I came around to, say, getting in my skin, there I
found McClure sitting around talking about being a mammal!
So I suddenly realized he was way ahead of me. And Wieners
. . . I always *weep* with him. Luminous, luminous. They're all
old poets, everybody knows about those poets. Burroughs is a
poet too, really. In the sense that a page of his prose is as *dense*
with imagery as anything in St.-John Perse or Rimbaud, now.
And it has also great repeated rhythms. Recurrent, recurrent
rhythms, even rhyme occasionally! What else . . . Creeley's
very stable, solid. I get more and more to like certain poems
of his that I didn't understand at first. Like "The Door," which

completely baffled me because I didn't understand that he was talking about the same heterosexual problem that I was worried about. Olson since he said, "I feel one with my skin." First thing of Olson's that I liked was "The Death of Europe" and then some of his later Maximus material is nice. And Dorn has a kind of long, *real* spare, manly, political thing— but his great quality inside also is tenderness—"Oh the graves not yet cut." I also like that whole line of what's happening with Ashbery and O'Hara and Koch, the area that they're going for, too. Ashbery—I was listening to him read "The Skaters," and it sounded as inventive and exquisite, in all its parts, as "The Rape of the Lock."

TC: Do you feel you're in command when you're writing?

AG: Sometimes I feel in command when I'm writing. When I'm in the heat of some truthful tears, yes. Then, complete command. Other times—most of the time not. Just diddling away, woodcarving, getting a pretty shape; like most of my poetry. There's only a few times when I reach a state of complete command. Probably a piece of "Howl," a piece of "Kaddish," and a piece of "The Change." And one or two moments of other poems.

TC: By command do you mean a sense of the whole poem as it's going, rather than parts?

AG: No—a sense of being self-prophetic master of the universe.

The Craft Interview

Mary Jane Fortunato, Lucille Medwick, and Susan Rowe interviewed Allen Ginsberg on December 17, 1970. The interview, sometimes referred to as "the Craft Interview," was published in the New York Quarterly *and included in the book* The Craft of Poetry.

NYQ: You have talked about this before, but would you begin this interview by describing the early influences on your work, or the influences on your early work?

Allen Ginsberg: Emily Dickinson. Poe's "Bells"—"Hear the sledges with the bells—Silver bells! . . ." Milton's long line breath in *Paradise Lost*—

> *Him the almighty power*
> *Hurled headlong flaming from the ethereal sky*
> *With hideous ruin and combustion down*
> *To bottomless perdition, there to dwell*
> *In adamantine chains and penal fire,*
> *Who durst defy the omnipotent to arms.*

Shelley's "Epipsychidion"—"one life, one death,/ One Heaven one Hell, one immortality,/ And one annihilation. Woe is me!" The end of Shelley's "Adonais"; and "Ode to the West Wind" exhibits continuous breath leading to ecstatic climax.

Wordsworth's "Intimations of Immortality"—

> *Our birth is but a sleep and a forgetting:*
> *The soul that rises with us, our life's Star,*
> *Hath had elsewhere its setting,*

Also Wordsworth's "Tintern Abbey" exhortation, or what-
ever you call it:

> *a sense sublime*
> *of something far more deeply interfused,*
> *Whose dwelling is the light of setting suns,*
> *And the round ocean and the living air,*
> *And the blue sky, and in the mind of man;*

That kind of poetry influenced me: a long breath poetry that
has a sort of ecstatic climax.

NYQ: What about Whitman?

AG: No, I replied very specifically. You asked me about my *first*
poetry. Whitman and Blake, yes, but in terms of the *early*
poems I replied specifically. When I began writing I was
writing rhymed verse, stanzaic forms that I derived from my
father's practice. As I progressed into that I got more involved
with Andrew Marvell.

NYQ: Did you used to go to the Poetry Society of America
meetings?

AG: Yes, I used to go with my father. It was a horrifying experi-
ence, mostly old ladies and second-rate poets.

NYQ: Would you elaborate?

AG: That's the PSA I'm talking about. At the time it was mainly
people who were enemies of, and denounced, William Carlos
Williams and Ezra Pound and T. S. Eliot.

NYQ: How long did it take you to realize they were enemies?

AG: Oh, I knew right away. I meant enemies of poetry, very spe-
cifically. Or enemies of that poetry which now by hindsight is
considered sincere poetry of the time. *Their* highwater mark
was, I guess, Edwin Arlington Robinson, "Eros Turannos" was
considered, I guess, the great highwater mark of twentieth-
century poetry.

NYQ: Where did you first hear long lines in momentum?

AG: The texts I was citing were things my father taught me
when I was prepubescent.

NYQ: Did he teach them to you as beautiful words or as the
craft of poetry?

AG: I don't think people used that word "craft" in those days. It's sort of like a word that has only come into use in the last few decades. There were texts of great poetry around the house, and he would recite from memory. He never sat down and said now I am going to teach you: Capital C-R-A-F-T. Actually I don't like the use of the word craft applied to poetry, because generally along with it comes a defense of stressed iambic prosody, which I find uncraftsmanly and pedantical in its use. There are very few people in whose mouths that word makes any sense. I think Marianne Moore may have used it a few times. Pound has used it a couple of times in very specific circumstances—more often as a verb than as a general noun. "This or that poet has crafted a sestina."

NYQ: Would you talk about later influences on your work? William Blake? Walt Whitman?

AG: Later on for open verse I was interested in Kerouac's poetry. I think that turned me on more than anyone else, I think he is a very great poet and much underrated. He hadn't been read yet by poets.

NYQ: Most people associate Kerouac with prose, with *On the Road*, and not so much with *Mexico City Blues*. Or maybe they differentiate too strictly between prose and poetry.

AG: I think it's because people are so preoccupied with the use of the word craft and its meaning that they can't see poetry in front of them on the page. Kerouac's poetry looks like the most "uncrafted stuff" in the world. He's got a different idea of craft from most people who use the word craft. I would say Kerouac's poetry is the craftiest of all. And as far as having the most craft of anyone, though those who talk about craft have not yet discovered it, his craft is spontaneity; his craft is having the instantaneous recall of the unconscious; his craft is the perfect executive conjunction of archetypal memorial images articulating present observation of detail and childhood epiphany fact.

NYQ: In *Howl*, at the end of Section One, you came close to a definition of poetry, when you wrote:

Who dreamt and made incarnate gaps in Time & Space through
images juxtaposed, and trapped the archangel of the soul between
2 visual images and joined the elemental verbs and set the noun
and dash of consciousness together jumping with sensation of
Omnipotens Aeterna Deus.

AG: I reparaphrased that when I was talking about Kerouac. If you heard the structure of the sentence I was composing, it was about putting present observed detail into epiphany, or catching the archangel of the soul between two visual images. I was thinking then about what Kerouac and I thought about haiku—two visual images, opposite poles, which are connected by a lightning in the mind. In other words "Today's been a good day; let another fly come on the rice." Two disparate images, unconnected, which the mind connects.

NYQ: Chinese poets do that. Is this what you are talking about?

AG: This is characteristic of Chinese poetry as Ezra Pound pointed out in his essay "The Chinese Written Character as a Medium for Poetry" nearly fifty years ago. Do you know that work? Well, 'way back when, Ezra Pound proposed Chinese hieroglyphic language as more fit for poetry, considering that it was primarily visual, than generalized language-abstraction English, with visionless words like Truth, Beauty, Craft, etc. Pound then translated some Chinese poetry and translated (from Professor Fenollosa's papers) this philosophic essay pointing to Chinese language as pictorial. There is no concrete picture in English, and poets could learn from Chinese to present image detail: and out of that Pound hieroglyph rose the whole practice of imagism, the school which is referred to as "Imagism." So what you are referring to is an *old* history in twentieth-century poetry. My own thing about two visual images is just from that tradition, actually drawing from Pound's discovery and interpretation of Chinese as later practiced by Williams and everybody who studied with Pound or who understood Pound. What I'm trying to point out is that this tradition in American poetry in the twentieth century is not something *just* discovered. It was done by Pound and Williams, precisely the people that are anathema to the PSA mediocrities who were attacking Pound and Williams for not having "craft."

NYQ: In that same section of *Howl*, in the next line, you wrote:

> *to recreate the syntax and measure of poor human prose and stand before you speechless and intelligent and shaking with shame, rejected yet confessing out the soul to conform to the rhythm of thought in his naked and endless head.*

AG: Description of aesthetic method. Key phrases that I picked up around that time and was using when I wrote the book. I meant again that if you place two visual images side by side and let the mind connect them, the gap between the two images, the lightning in the mind illuminates. It is the *Sunyata* (Buddhist term for blissful empty void) which can only be known by living creatures. So, the emptiness to which the Zen finger classically points—the ellipse—is the unspoken hair-raising awareness in between two mental visual images. I should try to make the answers a little more succinct.

NYQ: Despite your feeling about craft, poets have developed an attitude towards your work, they have discovered certain principles of breath division in your lines—

AG: Primary fact of my writing is that I don't have any craft and don't know what I'm doing. There is absolutely no art involved, in the context of the general use of the words art and craft. Such craft or art as there is, is in illuminating mental formations, and trying to observe the naked activity of my own mind. Then transcribing that activity down on paper. So the craft is being shrewd at flashlighting mental activity. Trapping the archangel of the soul, by accident, so to speak. The subject matter is the action of my mind. To put it on the most vulgar level, like on the psychoanalyst's couch is supposed to be. Now if you are thinking of "form" or even the "well made poem" or a sonnet when you're lying on the couch, you'll never say what you have on your mind. You'd be babbling about corset styles or something *else* all the time instead of saying, "I want to fuck my mother," or whatever it is you want. So my problem is to get down the fact that I want to fuck my mother or whatever. I'm taking the most hideous image possible, so there will be no misunderstanding about what area of mind you are dealing with: What is socially unspoken, what is prophetic from the unconscious, what is universal to all men, what's the main subject of poetry, what's underneath, *inside* the mind. So, how do you get that out on the page? You observe your own mind during the time of composition and write down whatever goes through the ticker tape of mentality, or whatever you hear in the echo of your inner ear, or what flashes in picture on the eyeball while you're writing. So the subject is constantly interrupting because the mind is constantly going on vagaries—so whenever it changes I have a dash. The dashes are a function of this method of transcription of unconscious data. Now you can't write down everything that you've got going on—half conscious data. You can't write down *everything*, you can only write down what the hand can carry. Your hand can't carry more than a twentieth of what the mind flashes, and the very fact of writing interrupts the mind's flashes and redirects attention to writing. So that the observation (for writing) impedes the function of the mind. You might say "Observation impedes Function." I get down as much as I can of genuine material, interrupting the flow of material as I get it down and when I look I turn to the center of my brain to see the next thought, but it's probably about thirty thoughts later. So I make a dash to indicate a break, sometimes a dash plus dots. Am I making sense?—

Saying "I want to fuck my mother"—that's too heavy. It waves a red flag in front of understanding, so we don't have to use that as the archetypal thought. Like "I want to go heaven" may be the archetypal thought, instead of "I want to fuck my mother." I just wanted to get it down to some place that everybody knows where it is. If I say "I want to go to heaven" you might think it's a philosophic conception.

NYQ: How much do you revise your work?

AG: As little revision as possible. The craft, the art consists in paying attention on the actual movie of the mind. Writing it down is like a by-product of that. If you can actually keep track of your own head movie, then the writing it down is just like a secretarial job, and who gets crafty about that? Use dashes instead of semicolons. Knowing the difference between a dash—and a hyphen -. Long lines are useful at certain times, and short lines at other times. But a big note-book with lines is a helpful thing, and three pens—you have to be shrewd about that. The actual materials are import-ant. A book at the nightstand is important—a light you can get at—or a flashlight, as Kerouac had a brakeman's lantern. That's the craft. Having the brakeman's lantern and knowing where to use the ampersand "&" for swiftness in writing. If your attention is focused all the time—as my attention was in writing "Sunflower Sutra," "TV Baby" poem later, ("Wich-ita Vortex Sutra" later, in a book called *Planet News*)—when attention is focused, there is no likelihood there will be much need for blue penciling revision because there'll be a sen-suous continuum in the composition. So when I look over something that I've written down, I find that if my atten-tion has lapsed from the subject, I begin to talk about myself writing about the subject or talking about my irrelevant left foot itch instead of about the giant smog factory I'm observ-ing in Linden, New Jersey. Then I'll have to do some blue penciling, excising whatever is irrelevant: whatever I inserted self-consciously, instead of conscious of the Subject. Where self-consciousness intervenes on attention, blue pencil exci-sion means getting rid of the dross of self-consciousness. Since the subject matter is really the operation of the mind, as in Gertrude Stein, anything that the mind passes through is proper and shouldn't be revised out, almost anything that passes through mind, anything with the exception of self-consciousness. Anything that occurs to the mind is the proper subject. So if you are making a graph of the movements of the mind, there is no point in revising it. Because then you would obliterate the actual markings of the graph. So if you're inter-ested in writing as a form of meditation or introspective yoga, which I am, then there's no revision possible.

NYQ: Your poem about the sunflower shows remarkable powers of concentration.

AG: "Sunflower Sutra," the original manuscript in pencil's some-where at Columbia University Library. In examining it you will see published poem deviates maybe five or ten words from the original penciled text, written in twenty minutes, Kerouac at the door, waiting for me to go off to a party, and

I said, "Wait a minute, I got to write myself a note." I had the Idea Vision and I wanted to write it down before I went off to the party, so I wouldn't forget.

NYQ: Did it dictate the sense, or did you just do it for yourself?

AG: Observing the flashings on the mind. As somebody said, the craft is observing the mind. Formerly the "craft" used to be an idea of rearranging your package, rearranging. Using the sonnet is like a crystal ball to pull out more and more things from the subconscious (to pack into the sonnet like you pack an ice cream box). Fresher method of getting at that material is to watch mind flow instantaneously, to realize that all that is, is there in the storehouse of the mind within the instant any moment: that's the Proust of eternal recall, remember, the entire *Remembrance of Things Past* came to him just as he was dunking that little bit of madeleine cake into his tea. You know, the whole content of that one instant: that epiphanous instant, working with that instant—the mind then and there. That method I learned from Kerouac and I am interested in. That method is related to other "classical" methods of art composition and meditation like Zen Buddhist calligraphic painting, haiku composition also a spontaneous art, *supposed* to be spontaneous. People don't sit around revising haikus. They are supposed to be sitting around drinking saki, near a little hibachi (charcoal stove) with fireflies and fans and half moons through the window. And in the summertime you are supposed to say, "Ah, the firefly has just disappeared into the moon . . ." Make it up then and there. It's got to come from the perception of the moment. You can't go home the next day and send your friend the haiku and say "I thought of a funny one: the firefly just . . ." That wouldn't be real.

NYQ: Do you see time used as a unit of structure, as well as a point of view?

AG: Time of composition is the structure of the poem. That is the subject. What is going on in the mind during that moment is the subject. "Time is of the essence," said Kerouac in a very great little essay on writing poetry, one-page set of advice, *Essentials of Spontaneous Prose**, in back of Don Allen's *The*

---

* *Evergreen Review* no. 5, Summer 1958. Grove Press, NY, 1958.

New American Poetry: 1945-1960, the section is devoted to composition theory. I learned my theory from Kerouac. The preoccupations I have are Hindu, Buddhist, Hassidic—I spend every morning one hour sitting cross legged, eyes closed, back straight, observing my consciousness and quieting my consciousness, watching processions of mental imagery. Someone who isn't into that kind of meditation might find it an unknown territory to go into, chaos, and see it as much too chaotic to get involved with.

NYQ: You once wrote, I won't write my poem until I'm in my right mind.

AG: Yes. Of course, *that* poem is like a series of one-line jokes, so to speak. At the expense of the body politic, at the expense of the mass media Hallucination of Being entertained by the middle class.

NYQ: Does this refer to an attitude of yours about state of mind?

AG: I'm referring to a nervously comical attitude toward America. It ends "I'm putting my queer shoulder to the wheel." What I'm saying is, my poetry—this particular poem—my poetry in general—shows as such drivel because the United States is in such a state of apocalyptic drivelhood, that we're destroying the world, actually, and we're really destroying ourselves, and so I won't write my poems until I'm in my right mind. Until America gets out of its silly mood.

NYQ: Would you discuss travel, when you're in different places do you find yourself affected by the prosody of the place?

AG: I try to learn what I can. I got involved with mantra chanting when I was in India and brought it back to America. I do a lot of mantra chanting here. Just because I was interested in it and it had something to do with poetics, I thought. It also had to do with vocalization in that it did relate to preoccupations that I was familiar with in Pound's dictum "Pay attention to the tone leading of vowels." Sanskrit prosody has great ancient rules involving vowels and a great consciousness of vowels or a consciousness of quantitative versification. Like Pound is conscious of that too, tried to bring that to the awareness of poets in the twentieth century, tried to make people more conscious of the tone leading of vowels and renounce hyper attention to accentual rhythm. Pound said that he thought the future America prosody would be "an approximation of classical quantity," he thought that would be a formal substitute for iambic count, stress count. The whole poetic movement of the century climaxed in what was known as Beat of San Francisco or Hippie or whatever Renaissance movement was finally a realization of a new form of prosody, a new basis for the prosody. Actually I've written a great deal about the subject. I don't know if you're familiar with much of it, but some poetics is covered in a *Paris Review* interview. The relationship between Poetics and Mantra is gossiped on in a *Playboy* interview. A closer analysis of stress prosody, that kind of craft, sits in a preface to my father's book*—where I referred—(in answer to an earlier question) to one of the books that influenced me when I was young called *American Poetry*, edited with Introduction, Notes, Questions, and Biographical Sketches by A. B. De Mille, Simmons College, Boston, Secretary of the New England Association of Teachers of English, Boston, Allyn and Bacon, 1923, Academy Classic Series. It was, like the high school anthology, for most older high school teachers who teach now, their education. It was the standard anthology of the early twenties and used around the schools. So, they say in this book . . . I read Dickinson and Poe and Archibald Rutledge and Whittier and Longfellow and Thoreau and Emerson and John Hay Whitney, all the bearded poets of the nineteenth century in that book. This book described accentual prosody as "particularly well adapted to the needs of English poetry . . . definite rules, which have been carefully observed by all great poets from Homer to Tennyson and Longfellow." They gave as an example of accentual prosody in this book for teachers and students:

Thou tóo/sail ón,/O Shíp/of Státe./

Remember that line? They had it marked: as above. As you notice they had an unaccented mark for "O" and then an

* *Morning in Spring*, Louis Ginsberg, New York, William Morrow & Co., Inc., 1970.

accented mark for "Ship." When you read it you will realize that O is an exclamation, and, by definition, you *can't* have an unaccented mark for that and an accented mark for "Ship." Which means that by the time 1923 had come about teachers of English prosody had so perverted their own ears and everybody else's ears that they could actually write down "O" as unaccented. See, it was done like that. Well, what it means is that nobody could pronounce the line right. They were teaching people to mispronounce things. It would have to be: Thou too/sail on,/O Ship of State, many long vowels. But when you got up on the elementary or high school lecture platform, they used to say: "Thou tóo/ sail ón,/ O Shíp/ of Státe." Hear? Another example they had in there was:

Whose héart/ -strings are/ a lúte

when it quite obviously is : Whose héart-stríngs are a lúte. So, in other words, that's where "craft" degenerated. That's why I'm talking about how do we get out from under that. Because that was the Poetry Society of America's standard of poetics. And that's what Pound was fighting against. And replacing with a much more clear ear. And of course that's what Williams was working on, and that's what Creeley, Olson and Kerouac have always been compensating for. That's why I'm so mean about the use of the word "craft." Because I really wanted to make it clear that whatever people think craft is supposed to be, that what they've been taught at school, it's *not* that at all. One had better burn the word than abuse it as it has been abused, to confuse everybody.

NYQ: You have been giving readings with your father.

AG: We've done about four a year since 1965. We started at the PSA. But we don't do it often. It would get to be too much of an act or something. Generally we do it when there's some sentimental or aesthetically interesting occasion. Like at the PSA, that was interesting aesthetically. At the Y the other night, that was interesting because it is the traditional place for "distinguished poets" to read. I do it because, partly, to live with my father, because he's not going to be here forever. Nor am I. As a poet I'm interested in living in the same universe with him, and working in the same universe with him. We both learn something from it, get a little bit into each other's souls, the world soul. A father can learn a son's soul and a son can learn a father's soul, it's pretty much knowing God's soul, finally. It's like a confrontation with my own soul which is sometimes difficult. But it usually winds up pleasurable. Sometimes I have to see things in myself or face things in my father that are quite hideous. Confront them. So far this has turned out to reconcile us more and more.

NYQ: You read the "Wales Visitation" poem on the Buckley TV interview?

AG: Yes—"Wales Visitation."

NYQ: Is this your favorite poem?

AG: Of my most recent poems, this is, like an imitation of a perfect nature poem, and also it's a poem written on LSD which makes it exemplary for that particular modality of consciousness. It's probably useful to people as a guidance, mental guideline for people having bum trips because if they'll check through the poem they'll see an area which is a good trip. An ecologically attuned pantheistic nature trip. Also it's an example of the fact that art work can be done with the much maligned celebrated psychedelic substances.

NYQ: Didn't T. S. Eliot say that he didn't believe in that?

AG: Yeah, but Eliot was not a very experienced writer, he didn't write very much, he didn't write very much poetry. Anyhow there's a tremendous amount of evidence that good work can be done in all states of consciousness including drugs. Not that drugs are necessary. It's just that it's part of the *police* mythology that nothing can be done, that LSD leads only to confusion and chaos. That's nonsense.

NYQ: In nondrug states, do you ever work half asleep?

AG: Yes, as I said I keep a notebook at my bedside for half-conscious, preconscious, quasi-sleep notations. And I have a book out now called *Indian Journals* which has such writing in it, including poems emerged out of dreams and remembered in half waking, long prose-poetry paragraphs, using double talk from a half sleep state.

NYQ: That seems a very relaxed and vulnerable kind of writing, as opposed to what you spoke of before, where you tried to get everything into the mind.

AG: They're both related to consciousness study. Take it as part of a tradition going back to Gertrude Stein who was a student of William James at Harvard, whose subjects were varieties of religious experience and alterations of consciousness. That was James' big subject—the pragmatic study of consciousness, the modalities of consciousness. She applied her Jamesian studies and her medical studies to the practice of composition and saw composition as an extension of her investigations into consciousness. That's the tradition that I would like to classify myself within, and I think that's a main legit tradition of poetics, the articulation of different modalities of consciousness, almost, you can't say *scientific*, but the *artful* investigation or articulation of extraordinary states of consciousness. All that rises out of my own preoccupation with higher states of consciousness on account of, as I said over and over, when I was young, twenty-four or so, some poems of Blake like "The Sunflower," "The Sick Rose" and "The Little Girl Lost" catalyzed in me an extraordinary state of mystical consciousness as well as auditory hallucinations of Blake's voice. I heard Blake's voice and also saw epiphanous illuminative visions of the rooftops of New York. While hearing Blake's voice. While reading the text of "The Sunflower," "The Sick Rose" and "The Little Girl Lost." This was described at great lengths in other occasions. But I want to go back to that just to reiterate that I see the function of poetry as a catalyst to visionary states of being and I use the word visionary only in these times of base materialistic media consciousness when we are so totally cut off from our own nature and nature around us that anything that teaches nature seems visionary.

NYQ: You once said you were a worry wart. Yet you have such a sense of joy and freedom, in reading, and in writing, too.

AG: Ideally, the ambition, my childhood desire, is to write during a prophetic illuminative seizure. That's the idea: to be in a state of such complete blissful consciousness that any language emanating from that state will strike a responsive chord of blissful consciousness from any other body into which the words enter and vibrate. So I try to write during those "naked moments" of epiphany the illumination that comes every day a little bit. Some moment every day, in the bathroom, in bed, in the middle of sex, in the middle of walking down the street, in my head, or not at all. So if it doesn't come at all, then that's the illumination. So then I try to write in that too. So that's like a rabbinical Jewish Hassidic trick that way. So I try to *pay attention all the time.* The writing itself, the sacred act of writing, when you do anything of this nature, is like prayer. The act of writing being done sacramentally, if pursued over a few minutes, becomes like a meditation exercise which brings on a recall of detailed consciousness that is an approximation of high consciousness. High epiphanous mind. So, in other words, writing is a yoga that invokes Lord mind. And if you get into a writing thing that will take you all day, you get deeper and deeper into your own central consciousness.

NYQ: And does this lead you to a greater reality?

AG: A greater attention. Not attention, more feeling emerging out of that. So you walk down the city streets in New York for a few blocks, you get this gargantuan feeling of buildings. You walk all day you'll be at the verge of tears. More detail, more attention to the significance of all that robotic detail that impinges on the mind and you realize through your own body's fears that you are surrounded by a giant robot machine which is crushing and separating people, removing them from nature and removing them from living and dying. But it takes walking around all day to get into that state. What I mean is if you write all day you will get into it, into your body, into your feelings, into your consciousness. I don't write enough, actually, in that way. *Howl, Kaddish* and other things were written in that way: all-day-long attention.

PART SIX

Letters

Allen Ginsberg [New York, NY] to Neal Cassady [San Francisco, CA] *ca.* April 21, 1949

Dear Neal:

Are you too occupied to write, or don't you want to for some reason concerning your relationship with us in N.Y.? No reason occurs to me that seems important, despite the usual fantasies of hassle.

The golden day has arrived for Jack [Kerouac] and he has sold his book [*The Town and the City*]. He has a % promise, on sales, 85% on movie rights (which I believe will materialize as a matter of course after considering the nature of his work; but this has been my opinion for a long time; it now seems to be more generally accepted, and so may be true) and most important for the actual money, $1,000.00 (a thousand) cash advance, which has been in his possession for several weeks. He is not mad at you; as matter of fact 5 out of the 15 sandwiches he denied you in Frisco went bad before he could eat them.

Bill Burroughs has been arrested and faces a jail term in Louisiana for possession of narcotics and guns, *etc.* There is now no telling what will happen but he may get out of it without jail. Joan [Burroughs] wrote, and he wrote the next day having got out on bail quickly. If he is to be jailed I expect to invite Joan [to] NY to stay with me with children at my apartment. If he gets out, he will have to leave Texas and Louisiana as it is hot there for him; perhaps to Chicago, or Yucatan; doubtful of N.Y. as his family objects to this city, and much will depend on them financially, I think.

Claude [Lucien Carr] is writing stories and being psychoanalyzed. These are radical developments which I, at least, have hoped for and I believe it is the beginning of his regeneration and the assumption of an ideal power and humanity for him. He broke with Barbara this month. As long as I have thought of us as artists, it has been Claude who I thought of as central to any active inter-inspiring school or community of creation, and him to whom I have looked for the strength to assume responsibility for the truest aesthetic knowledge and generosity; it appears, somehow, that the unseen magnet has begun to draw him at last. And so a kind of potential millennium, that I dreamed of years ago with juvenile and romantic prophetic power, is being actualized in its truest forms, and in the only necessary and inevitable way. I talked with him all last night, heard him outline the method, plot, and technique (to give his ideas categories) and it sounded, what he had to say, essential, accurate, and so unexpected as to be inspired to my mind; and yet proceeding logically from his whole past position; but surpassing it. Anyway, another myth come true. His concern is with action and facts and things happening; but he seems (I say but because though that is the concern of all writers, ostentatiously, except crackbrained alchemists like myself) he seems successfully concerned with facts and their harmony and relationships, and all suggestion of what I would look for as the metaphysical or divine seem to rise from his stories as they do from life, and more so, because of the objectivity and sympathy and seemingly self enclosed structure of his tales; so that there is nothing extraneous or purposeless in his work; he says everything he says because he intends to. This self evident principle I discovered for my own poetry (everything must have a point and not be rhetoric) last summer consciously; but I have not been able to perfect many poems to clear realization because of my own abstract and vaporous tendencies; but I see it successfully applied in Claude potentially more than Jack. When Claude's imagination becomes freed of fear he will be a great man. I dwell so much on this because now Claude is again in the fold, the great RAM of the fold much improved from before; once again we are involved in the same work of truth and art all together. Maybe I am making too much of a good thing, however so let it pass.

I am again in a doldrums, a weak link in a chain, only surpassed in weakness by yourself perhaps. Herbert has been with me draining my money and vitality for months; now Vicki and a man named Little Jack have joined us, and are operating out various schemes successfully. Money is beginning to come in; I am to sublet my apartment to join Joan and Bill [Burroughs]: they will pay my way (Little Jack, *etc.*) in return for apartment for summer and now. But Bill's arrest casts a shade on that and I do not know what I will do. I would like to leave the city for the summer (June, July, August) if possible to stay with Joan and Bill. I am not writing much or well, but I have always been dissatisfied with what and how I have written; now however my artistic impotence now seems more real and radical and I will have to act someday, not only writing more, but on large scale, commercially usable (poetic dramas for television as I dream) *etc.* However my theoretical and visionary preoccupations – fixation, based on experience which was gifted, as it seemed, from a higher intelligence of conscious Being of the universe, or hallucination, as the doctor dismissed it when I went to arrange for therapy beginning September, has left me confused and impotent in action and thought and a prey to all suggestions, winds of abstract thought, and lassitude's and sense of unworthiness and inferiority that rise continually before my now dulling eyes, and a prey to all suspicions, my own and others, that come forth. The household set up which I both hate and desire, that I have, is an example of my uncertainty of path and dividedness. It seems that the road to heaven or back to sanity require me to deal in realities of time and circumstance which I have never done, and to learn new things, which I'm unused to. But I seem to have, like Joan, passed some point in my brain which I cannot go back from, and for the moment forward either except by some violent effort I have been incapable of since I can remember. But perhaps therapy will help me. Anyway, I am making preparations to teach in Cooper Union College this fall, and so have some financial security more than now at A.P. Then I will be by myself and try to think unless something unexpected happens from the outside to change me or my relations with others. Next year this all amounts to saying, I will try again; now I am caught up in weariness and defeat and sterility and circumstances which have no end or meaning. Perhaps by leaving town I will activate and escape this inertia. Perhaps if you thought well of it I will come to California. At the moment however, I am not in any active suffering, and my mind is active and comparatively clear. It is long inaction and too much introspection and lack of practical ambition that weighs me down. However my pad is hot, and I expect a visit from the narcotics people since they seized several of my letters to Bill in the course of his fall. If I were able to keep clean that would be OK, but with Vicki and others pursuing their busy rounds there is always something for the law to object to. I can't seem to put my foot down, or make up my mind to, mostly because that is why they are using my pad in the first place, to operate out of, and my end is to get enough to travel off their work. Perhaps I shall find that I have been self destructively greedy on this score. But when I see the treasures rolling in I find it a powerful argument against any cautionary impulses, of mine. And maybe nothing will happen. That about summarizes what goes on on York Ave. General intimidation. Herbert was beat, and now just begins to prosper, so I can't well put a stop to it all. Or not easily anyway. I guess this sounds cowardly; or maybe it's only a balloon I blow. Claude and Jack don't seem to approve, and that is why I am concerned at all. Or what brings the concern to my mind, anyway.

What are you doing? When will your heart weary of its own indignity and despotism and lack of creation? Why are you not in N.Y.? Can you do anything away from us? Can you feel anybody as you can feel us, even though in N.Y. you did your worst to surround yourself with a sensate fog of blind activity? Or are you learning something new wherever you are now? If you wonder the motive for these questions don't undercut it with suspicion of sexual motives of mine; I have none now and was not dominated by them when you were last in N.Y. [. . .]

Love,
Allen

Allen Ginsberg [Paterson, NJ] to John Clellon Holmes [Provincetown, MA] June 16, 1949

Dear John:

Thank you for investigating *Partisan*. The copy of the poem I sent you ["Stanzas: Written at Night in Radio City"] is dog eared, so I enclose another copy. I hope I can get some poems published soon; I have spent the last two weeks working steadily on the manuscripts you saw, and have revised them where they needed it (except for some things that are so tangled I haven't the character to untangle them) threw out a lot. There are about 50 poems left, on clean new paper (the same as this) and I am ready to go into business. I will give the book first to as many people who will read it and suggest improvements. I feel (this a most urgent specter in my poetic process) that the book is value-less, without positive content, and cannot escape that final conclusion despite the fact that I continue to work on it.

I am in Paterson; and have been since I saw you. I had intended to settle here and get a job and learn to love my family anew, and this resolution, coupled with concomitant perception of the fact that I have been harboring an enormous weight of irrational wrath, gave me a few peaceful hopeful days, but when my wrath was tried in circumstances which demanded absolute humility to my father I could not swallow my pride, without raging up again, and had to close up the wound by withdrawing from "engagement" among the family – failure of wholeheartedness without which there is no understanding – as exemplified in all the best novels. Anyway, independent of this, my lawyer, and the official analyst I saw, who dealt with the D.A. made a deal, that if I were to be given psychiatric care, charges would be dropped. I am in a few days going as an in-patient to the Columbia Psychiatric Clinic, on 168 Street N.Y. This is an experimental mental hospital, where as my analyst says (his name is Dr. Fagan), I will be given "the works," psychoanalytically. I do not know if I will be allowed out; I am to have a room, stay in the hospital, *etc*. Meanwhile I understand that the others have been indicted – the other day. I know nothing of what goes on since my lawyer has assumed all the burdens of activity – I had a sheltered life here. He is also following a program (in which I am grateful) of keeping from me what's going on, except the few essentials like going to the hospital I will find out about the rest later; for the moment I am at ease. At any rate, the legal weight is off.

I have been reading, too – Blake, Mona Wilson's commentaries, Dostoyevsky Diaries – his wife's comments, *The Possessed*, Yeats' autobiographies, essays, a book on E.A. Robinson by Van Doren, Racine's *Phedre*, Greek plays, Thos. Hardy's poems, Yeats' plays (Wheels and Butterflies); Pound's *Cantos*, Keats and a new book of Dr. Doolittle's adventures by Hugh Lofting. I have nothing else to do, except see movies, 3 or 4 a week, and see old friends from high school. I think a great deal – about the nature of tragedy, and the meaning or significance of light. But all such conclusions are only intellectual constructions of things which to a disciplined mind should be not obvious but *palpable*.

Jack and I have corresponded fitfully – I do most of the writing. In his first letter he says that he has rented a house @75$ month near Denver: "My house is near the mountains. This is the wrath of sources – The Divide where Rain and Rivers are decided . . . I am Rubens . . . this place is full of God and yellow butterflies." His second encloses a poem about a God with a Golden Nose, named Ling, one of the Giggling Lings.

> "*. . .And the Chinamen of the Night*
> *from Old Green Jails did creep,*
> *bearing the Rose that's Really White*
> *to the Lamb that's really Gold. . ."*

He is running around with Justin Brierley, an old Denver Gidean. A schoolteacher and lawyer of whom you may have heard. He is also

(Jack, that is) partly running around miserably wondering, *etc*. His family is there. He rode in a rodeo bareback. He docsn't believe in society. "It's all wrong and I denounce it and it can all go to Hell." "So roll your own bones, I say." He reads Racine and Malherbe and Blake.

Do you remember the jingle: "I love the lord on high / I wish He'd pull my daisy?" Jack contributed another fragment to it: "Pull my daisy, / Tip my cup, / All my doors are open." This has grown into a great monster paean. His stanza begins (my hand at that) "This token mug I tup / Runneth over broken, / Pull my daisy," *etc*. Other stanzas added since: one he based on a recent poem of mine that has a refrain, "Take them, said the skeleton, / But leave my bones alone." And on the navy captain of another myth: "The time I went to China / To lead the boyscout troops, / They sand my ocean line, / And all I said was oops."

So: "Tip my cup, / Roll my bones, / All my oops are doopsing."

Also there are fragments that go: "In the east they live in huts, / But they love where I am lolling; / Cut my thoughts / For coconuts, / All my figs are falling." And another begins: "I'm a pot and God's a potter / And my head's a piece of putty . . ." When it is all complete, we will have a great archetypical jingle, "Pull my daisy / Tip my cup, / cut my thoughts / For coconuts; / Tip my cup, / Roll my bones, / All I said was oops." And will sell it to Charlie Chaplin for his next picture or Groucho Marx. I can see it making a million dollars. Also associated, "I ask the Lady's what's a Rose, / She kicked me outa bed; / I ask a man, and so it goes, / He hit me on the head. / Nobody knows, / Nobody knows, / At least, nobody's said." Well, enough of this. Is [Ed] Stringham there? What does he do, and see? Are there artists there? I hope sometime this summer to be able to get out to visit Provincetown for I have never been there, and it would be wonderful to see you all there in that atmosphere. Marion [Holmes]? Boo! When you next write [Alan] Ansen, give him my regards and tell him what I am doing.

Now as to your request, I am glad to be able to give you any information that I have. You may not take seriously the values that I ascribe to certain experiences but since essentially I am actually involved with what I am talking of I will not bother to enervate the substance of what I say by pacifying irony.

I have attempted to put into language what I mean, events and interpretations, in letters to several people, in notebooks and miscellaneous writings, in conversation, and poems. I have not made a unified coherent or cohering statement because I am not yet ready; I do not object to a system or systematization, because that can be helpful, if properly understood; but approach through a strict rational process is not the most communicative way of transferring thoughts, or attaining rapport. Furthermore, my own use for systematization is limited because it is not system I seek (I have that, almost complete, in skeleton) but depth, value. Approach through reason, however, is one of the many ways; for some people, since it is their tool (as images are mine) it is the necessary way. We each have our own road to perfection. Also, as to your doubts in asking me, it is difficult to supply them satisfactorily (a whole history) because that is a whole mass of detailed explanations of hundreds of significant events, reasonings concerned with them, *etc.* There are perhaps certain "magic" formulae – recipes, religious apothegms, *etc.* – but what you are asking for is not so much the say abstract summary of relations between things, but elaborations of the ones I have already affirmed, explanations and details which would perhaps bridge the seemingly ungraspable theoretical abyss between theory and reality; quantity and quality, *etc.*, all the logical polarities. Remember that I write under the paradoxical burdens, now, of not being on the other side of the trick wall, and that what I say is the result of theory made in time about the experience – which has for me been momentary – of eternity. I have been out of time, but I am now back into its illusory world; so that anything I write has no absolute value, but is just abstract imagery based on recollection of what an absolute value is like; and the modifications of what I say can go on infinitely without true timeless value, unless at some point the Paradox of Infinity is understood by an altogether different mode of consciousness. The problem of communication, here, is related and similar to the problem of accurately stating exactly the difference of thought and sensation, between the world of dreams, and the world of day. Fortunately, we have all dreamed, we all have idealistic leanings, a sensation of the supernatural, aesthetic or religious, if vague, emotions, a sense of value – deficiency, fear that is overpowering, *etc.* These are the experiences of the world of day, the so called real world, which I would use to suggest the underlying motif of all our lives; that these feelings are all disguised forms of another unconscious world of reality. This as you see is actually the same as the new psychological formulation, and I think that in proper hands (perhaps only Freud himself was deep enuf) it is a sufficient key; that is why I trust analysis for myself, where as most do not, really. (Jack, Ansen, *etc.*)

Now, to your questions. I will overlook, temporarily, the clinical details which my above paragraph might suggest, and return to a more literary, or aesthetic, or visionary vocabulary. I may say, in confession, that I do so because my experience of analysis before visions was not what I now take the possibilities of analysis to be; and I believe that most psychoanalysis is an intellectual game empty of emotional value, and is interminable, not absolute, has not understood the practice, Infinite Paradox, and is conducted on a single leveled self-enclosed world. But here, I almost end my letter, and any theoretical difference that has existed between us, by saying that my experience of analysis will change with the new analysis in the hospital and render invalid or unnecessary all the confusing mystical vocabulary that I have used. So be it, I hope so; in that case I can only say that 1. other people almost without exception never have had an inkling of what a world there is possible, or 2. I have never had an inkling of what a world other people have always been living in. In moments of actual vision, I see clearly that other people <u>don't</u> know; in moments at the edge of vision, where I am faced with problems of understanding people (as I described on page one) I feel that the deficiency in value is my own; that I am the madman in an illusory world, trying to make my abstract mechanical notions and systems stick. And I say it would be quite a miraculous and wonderful surprise if one day as the result of analysis I should have my eyes open and see that I am what is troubling me in the world at large, and in other people's conduct, ideas, *etc.* That, like Oedipus, I am the criminal that has been bringing on all the plague; and this is actually the experience I have had in analysis, I wake up and see that it is all my own spiteful doing. But that would not account for the psychological and sociological problems of others, which, I understand are at this point in the outside world so deep as to involve practically everyone, in extremities of wrath and physical destruction. It would, however, account for my own wrath and discomfiture of being. So there it is all wrapped up and sufficient in a system, and an accepted one at that. In fact as I write,

I think it is undoubtedly true. The reason it has taken me so long to see this is because I had been so much out of contact with the world of flesh, and wrapped in my wrath and pride of intellect, that I could not comprehend, after those outbursts of the reality principle, that all along my usual unquestioned neurotic illusion world, was really a bad dream of my own, even though most others shared it in their own way, and all that I was seeing was the natural world of the organized and free senses. It was so removed from what I had known that it amounted to a miraculous change, altogether different sensations, values, even process of thought. So, seeing a light, I thought it was God. The point is, too, that that is, what everybody who had known about it before the 19th century, called god-era, had to give it a name. And those who never broke through but were still superstitious because their bound minds couldn't explain the source of being, and its irrational nature, paid homage to an idol which they invested all their reality principles in. Magic is just a subconscious expression of the sense of the real world which is in its true appearance, compared to the untrue sense of it that we have, full of vaster emotions even than the puny shadow that is summoned up by the myths of magic.

It is this very enormity, this incomprehensible difference, between the neurotic world of time and the free world of eternity, that makes me use visionary language; and it may be that I am one of a few people that has had contact with a real world, and so my language is not superfluous; if it should be the other way around I should be much chagrined, to the point of feeling it, in my pride, to be the very gate of wrath that I was always speaking about. And I feel that that is one of the keys to a final understanding of the Visionary. He only wants to be like everybody else, in the flesh, but he is afraid of love, so he makes a system which makes him prophet, confuses everybody (they all have their own systems) and forces his misdirected will into making them think the same abstractions as he.

Now I had had this construction, this system of analysis, with anthropological and sociological areas, all worked out before the visions, and I used Yeats' Unity of Being to express the psychological perfection of personality that I reasoned was possible; and I figured out rationally, schemed, even, to imitate the theoretical attitudes and activities of the happy warrior. This is, I suppose (I almost hope) what everybody does; the basis of all masks that people wear after figuring out their ideas; look to take a homely example, at Jack, with his imitation of the happy god with the golden nose; or you, with your search for a system of responsibilities, or a value in life (I am not making a joke; essentially we are looking for a value, all.) Or the New Yorker, with its concern for what it thinks is an attitude that has value; how it imitates its theoretical ideal, even to the point of absurdly forcing certain emotions and responses (mostly defensive and negative) on itself. What in all our phases we are searching for in ideas, is actually what cannot be found in a world of ideas; and that is the health of a unity of being. I and analysis (basically) and religionists and mystics, say that that health is a possible thing, and will solve all problems (or that once healthy, we will be free to solve problems that are insoluble now because we are afraid to see, act, be, clearly) I had never, before the "Vision," realized what I was saying; when I had a few momentary experiences of it (so take them to be; my doctor thinks they were hallucinations) I was so overwhelmed by the absolute wonder of the possibilities of what life was like, I suddenly realized that my thoughts, as it were, had meant much more than I thought they meant. I was quite surprised; and I felt at first that I had been wrong all along, because this attained, "ideal" was so different from what, in my frenzied dream of life, I had bargained on; I had unleashed a dragon of a reality. So in the sense that I have outlined, all I had done before, had been to make up out of my unconscious systems and images which, when they finally became substantial, at once proved them "theoretically," for all along this was what I had dreamed of – but disproved them for what they were, a reshuffled pack of cards, mere thoughts with no reality. So I abandoned making up systems and set about attempting to seek into myself for the springs of that energy, or life force, or reality, or supernaturality, that had been momentarily released – and this was no more a matter of making beautifully appealing verses, or rearranging thoughts like the furniture in a room.

Now to speak directly of the visions themselves. I told you all I could: that I saw nothing new in form, no angels, no smoke. I was in the bookstore and the bookstore was the same as ever, but with the addition of a new sense of reality, or supernatural existence,

indwelling in all the forms. The sense of prescience, fullness, abso-
lutions, and total significance of detail were all that they are in
the most other-worldly of night dreams, and all that I previously
might ascribe to the mystical or religious sense of the presence of
the Holy Ghost. Wherever I moved I seemed to see so deeply into
things that they appeared under the aspect of eternity which had
been talked about for centuries, and see so deeply that I saw all
there is to see, and was satisfied and peaceful. It is you might say,
and I affirm, a subjective matter. "Cleanse the doors of perception,"
etc. Blake's phrase about eternity in a grain of sand is a literal truth.
We are living in eternity. And one of the most astounding things
that I saw was the *souls* of the men and women in the room, on
their faces, in their attitudes and gestures; and what their souls
were doing was *hiding themselves from admitting their awareness of
the all inclusive peaceful prescience*, and restraining themselves from
acting in accordance with the *glad total community of mind and being*
which existed. They were all perfectly aware, as I was; their souls
were opened; but they were locked in some mechanical, [coil?],
withdrawal, they did not step into eternity, they refused. Inani-
mate objects, very substance, all partook of the prescience. The
religious phrase is "God is Love." This means that substance, all,
is love. And love is the stuff of substance. That I also saw, but am
unable to explain, except to say that a consciousness, or awareness,
or intelligence, seemed to be drifting through all things, the same
in lack thing, almost animal in nature, or, as well, living. The world
seemed to be alive, as a tree might be alive in a dream.

The sensation of other experiences at other times was quite sim-
ilar essentially, at one time I also sensed, further, that the great
beast of the universe was sick or sickening, slowly being self con-
sumed. (See Blake's sick rose) and that human evil was part of that
sickness. As if God were mad. The horror! The unspeakable horror!
As if Being itself were, like the sick human mind, being destroyed.
I look at your letter, the "Flesh will be the language *etc.*" Perhaps is
clear – substance is spirit. The body and mind are separated in men
(theory, as in me, from meaning and reality.)

My Reichian analyst? Theoretically he ought to know the
answers. In Reichian analysis, my "breakthroughs" were similar in
sensation. But he says my visions are hallucination. I trust them.

My father? I have been wounding him. Perhaps he has been

wounding me. Both are unconscious, but purposeful. I do not accept him as a real entity. I must then perhaps vice-versa.

The police? The same as everybody else, including my father. To enter a world of reality, its existence must be accepted. The acceptance of the existence of another thing involves love (substance is love). Not "Love me, Lord," but "I love you, Lord." To the universe. It requires a freeing of a bloc of feeling and perception and releasing energy which is itself love. The worry about releasing evil energies is a bogey man of the nightmares of a society founded on the repression of energy and love, which might possibly be changed or abandoned in its ways when love rules. Antisocial emotions are feared because "Society" is, I believe, hostile to emotion in the first place. I feared the police because I felt guilty about the reality of my negative activity which I should have known concerned others as well of myself. I was wrong and "tried" to accept that guilt, despite my inclination of contempt, horror, ego, *etc.* as far as the cruel police were concerned.

Now most important is that point where I believe we have a channel of understanding. "Did the symbolisms in my poetry become, after the visions, less symbological and more actual to you? In other words, did the symbol cease to be a denotive arrow referring to something below the surface, and become, in terms of your poetry, and your thinking, an object?" This is what I mean by the word value, and my previous attempt to explain the difference between theoretical and actual reality, which share forms, but not emotion. I am greatly interested in this question because it is the key to all problems of art. I must admit I am surprised that you should be able to formulate the key question so clearly. But perhaps, as I say, I am the one who has no sense of reality, and the outside world is there all the time. Of course there is no knowing what you mean by the question. But not only in the poems, but in sensation is this process of transformation to absolute value operant. It is the same process in art as in experience, a shifting, from one level of flat valuelessness, mere symbolism, to absolute, "eternal" concreteness and substantial fullness. This has been the burden of all my poems, an attempt to use language which is pure fact, not airy poetry, to suggest to the mind of the reader that substantial actuality of Being or reality or fact, *etc.* that he dreams of, and to affirm it, though it may seem like madness to him (for truly our world considers it madness; and people are afraid of reality.) The difference between what I was writing a year ago and what I now attempt to write (as yet not successfully) was that before I was mouthing dreams, and now I am more aware of the meaning of the words; or better, aware that the words have meaning, and therefore, a possible effect on the reader. If I can find the true meaning, the value, the effect on the reader will be absolute. So it is in certain of Blake's poems, and they are capable of summoning up in me, the sensation of eternity. There is only one person that I know really that understands. I spoke of him, Richard Weitzner, and he is far more advanced than me. He says my poetry has little content – however he has pointed to certain specific phrases in it which are total – these are few and far between –

> O *pass this passage in delight.*
> *Blind spectacle*
> *All through our land of wrath*
> *Dead eyes see, and dead eyes weep*
> *Shadow changes into bone*
> *The mind's forgotten meadow*
> *Sometime I lay down my wrath*

Etc. To him it is a matter of *voice*, deep voice, prophetic voice; that's his sensual approach. The phrase "Shadow changes into bone" sums up the whole business. My poetry is not yet literal because I am not yet literal in thought, and the more literal the mind, language become, the more prophetic or true it will be. I was surprised when I realized that Blake, Wordsworth, Coleridge, Dante, *etc.* were in greater or leaser senses literal. Who takes them literally? Who takes the core of the Bible literally? Who even takes Freud literally? Who takes the world literally?

Now as to people. I love Neal, Huncke, *etc. etc. etc.*, in varying degrees. They returned love, even physically. I was posed by them originally with the problem of expressing love, and what was love, *etc.* So they are basically instrumental in freeing me, and leading me in life. It's not presumptive to ask but I have a fear of detailed letters since my accident and so I leave that to conversation; particularly as there is too much detail, events, *etc.* and *etc.* Essentially our relations change as we grow, "L'affaire Auto," as you call it, will change things, too, welcomely. Neal, I haven't been in touch with, nor Huncke; nor Lucien, except in a few conversations by phone; Bill Burroughs I haven't written, either.

Knock and the door opens.

As ever,
Allen

Allen Ginsberg [Paterson, NJ] to
Jack Kerouac and Neal Cassady
[San Francisco, CA], *ca.* Feb. 1952

Dear Jack: and Neal:

O I'm so full of delirium today! Your letter arrived, and last night I opened a strange letter from the Hotel Weston in New York, I couldn't figger out who it was from. But I wrote W.C. Williams a crazy jazz letter (mentioning you) last week and sending him weird poems. And his letter (I repeat it entire for the sweetness of it) sed:

"Dear Allen:
Wonderful! really you shall be the center of my new poem – of which I shall tell you: the extension of *Paterson*. (I shall be proud to bring you the *Paterson IV*.)

For it I shall use your "Metaphysics" as the head (as some shit uses a quotation from some helpless Greek in Greek – to precede his poem)

How many of such poems as these do you own? You must have a book. I shall see that you get it. Don't throw anything away. These are it.

I am in N.Y.C. for a winter vacation. Home Sunday. The next week-end we'll do something. I'll get in touch with your father.

yours,
devotedly,
Bill"

I opened it and said aloud "God!" The poems he is referring to (he is also referring to an earlier request to me to take him down to River Street Paterson for an addition to his poem, after my father wrote him inviting him here, and he replied yes and sent me a message that he wanted to dig my Shrouded Street area) a bunch of short crappy scraps I picked out of my journals and fixed up like poems, the like of which I could write ten a day to order: like:

Metaphysics (which he refers to above)

> *This is the one and only*
> *firmament; therefore*
> *it is the absolute world;*
> *there is no other world.*
> *I am living in Eternity:*
> *The ways of this world*
> *are the ways of Heaven.*

and

Long Live The Spiderweb

> *Seven years' words wasted*
> *waiting on the spiderweb,*
>   *seven years'*
> *thoughts hearkening the host,*
>   *seven years' lost*
> *sentience naming images,*
> *narrowing down the name*
> *to nothing,*
>   *seven years'*
> *fears in a web of ancient measure,*
> *the words dead*
> *flies, a crop*
> *of ghosts.*
> *The spider is dead.*

and [7 other poems].

Now you realizes you old bonepoles, the two of you, whuzzat means? I can get a book out if I want! New Directions (I guess). Whaw? An you realize further, Williams is also nutty as a fruitcake. It also means we can <u>all</u> get books out (just you and me and Neal) (don't tell Lamantia, he's too polite) all we got to do: I have a new method of Poetry. All you got to do is look over your notebooks (that's where I got those poems) or lay down on a couch, and think of anything that comes into your head, especially the miseries, the mis'ries, or night thoughts when you can't sleep an hour before sleeping, only get up and write it down. Then arrange it lines of 2, 3 or 4 words each, don't bother about sentences, in sections of 2, 3 or 4 lines each. We'll have a huge collected anthology of American Kicks and Mental Musseries. The American Spiritual Museum. A gorgeous gallery of Hip American Devises. Like:

> *Today I am 32.*
> *What! So soon?*
> *Wha' hoppen to my wife?*
> *I kilt her.*
> *Wha hoppen to my hop?*
> *I smokt it.*
> *Wha hoppen to my kids?*
> *I et em for dinner*
> *lass week.*
> *Wha hoppen to my car?*
> *Smasht it agin a telephant pole.*
> *Wha hoppen to mine career?*
> *Down the drain, down the drain.*

So much for that.

I canna make tail of your letter? Who signed what? Who calleth me sweetheart? Don't you guys got names no more?

Stamp money I, impoverished, will send you. What happened when my poetry was read aloud? Anybody cry? Send me Peotl. Tell Lamantia I need Peotl for my methaphysical moo. Good! you wrote Bill. I will give Ginger one big abstraction. I still never seen John H. But he will appear.

BUSINESS:!!!!!

See? Carl [Solomon] sent contract. Lousy contract (what no million?) but its O.K.* Look it over. Also, finish book soon, so you don't have to wait alla way to 1954 to collect more moolah. Gene [Eugene Brooks] sent you legal letter. See boy? Alan Ansen they will publish, but don't really want to give him advance. Carl also asking French major friend of mine to translate Genet's *Journal du Voleur*. Also Carl pushing Bill's book for a Wyn paperbound. That's OK it means money, and posterity will have it, same as if it was New Directions. But I will work on New Directions.

Yes Jack *On the Road* will be the First American Novel. By gum we going places. Prose in letter was great. California and Neal are great for you. But what amante shall we find for Neal to make him keep writing? If I came out there would he do it? No, I'm afraid I'd only annoy the pants offa you, boy. But rillly, I'm feeling so fine — and there's a huge Eastern snowfall on my doorstep in Paterson.

Yes yess, add, add addup. Finish the novel soon. We'll all be on kicks. Speaking winkwise, I believe you its the first modern novel.

Oh Lucien he's just newly married, that's all that's wrong with him aside from a slight case of being a congenital sourpuss. Love Lucien, anyway.

But what can be done with Hal [Chase]? Nobody even knows his address? How can I reach him? Tell me in detail – or have [Al] Hinkle write me details etc. I will compose a huge insane letter and send him it; he won't know what to think, so maybe he'll answer. He's not sick, he's just showing off. First thing Kind King Mind must do is dye his golden hair green.

Really this letter is silly.

Pretty poems on Melville and Whitman. I sent Van Doren our mutually typed Melville notes. Haven't talked to him since.

Young friend named Gregory Corso left for coast, didn't see him before he left, but you may run into him. Two years ago he used to watch Dusty [Moreland] undress through window from furnished room across the street. I introduced him. He was in love with her. He too's a poet. But Dusty won't marry me, I asked her? What can I do? But I'll present your petition too. Maybe she'll marry all three of us? Think of the great wedding night ball.

---

* Carl Solomon, working for his uncle, A.A. Wyn at Ace Books, gave Kerouac a contract for *On the Road* offering him a $1,000 advance, but Kerouac never signed it.

You must meet Williams, he digs us, I'm giving him your books and will show him your letters. He's old, and not hip in our way, but he's innocence itself and picks up himself just like that.

Your abstraction is shore superior. Save the pastels. I incidentally knew it was yours minute I laid eyes in it. Like a signature.

I have been sleeping with all the girls [Elise Cowen] around Columbia, from Barnard, I mean. I'm entering a huge transformation to passivity now. I don't know when it happened, I don't make love no more, I just lay back and let people blow me. (It don't work on Dusty though – never lay her no more). Send on your whale of a bitch and I'll see that it gets in print, or send it to Carl and he'll do the leg work, I'm getting too hincty to do that free anymore (except for total recalcitrants like Neal who don't know what they're missing by not farting in public.)

The only man alive who really writes like us at all is Faulkner. *Soldier's Pay*. 25¢ pocket book.

I didn't read about Moby Dick, send clipping. I have huge candid photos from Lucien's wedding [Jan. 1952]. No, I'm shipping NMU [National Maritime Union] soon as I see Williams, as dishwasher on passenger ship, then after month being yeoman. Then come back and get ANALYZED. Yahh! Make Neal write me via wire recorder, you transcribe.

Whazzis 12 Adler? Whooz Ed. Roberts?

gone,
Allen

Allen Ginsberg [Berkeley, CA] to Louis Ginsberg [Paterson, NJ]. No date, *ca.* late-March 1956

Dear Louis:

Not written for long since I've been running around and busy. I'm working full time in Greyhound in the city, but haven't made decent living arrangements, so I only get back to Berkeley a few times a week where all papers and letters are on desk in a big mess. I stay over in city on various couches on weekdays, since I've been back I haven't had time to really sit down in leisure and figure out what to do about living arrangements. I almost moved back into SF tho I have to give up this cottage, and was in fact supposed to this weekend but too many things came up and I can't find time. I am really all up in the air.

Mainly I'm waiting for a ship or some equivalent moneymaking project since I do want to leave here and take off for Europe sometime this year. Meanwhile the Greyhound job brings in 50 a week, Seattle debts are being cleared off this month. I'm also surprisingly enough teaching one class a week at S. F. State College—State is the school that's been promoting poetry workshops, readings, etc. and I am now the local poet-hero so was invited to occupy the chair of guest gorilla at their writing class. I work with another regular teacher who handles all the details, registration, mimeographing of poems to be handed out and discusses etc, and I act as pro in conducting discussions. The class is about 20, half old ladies and half hip young kids who have been attracted by all the recent activity. My teaching technique could shock you undoubtedly and certainly get me kicked out of anywhere else or not be counterenanced, I bring in bums from North Beach and talk about Marijuana and Whitman, precipitate great emotional outbreaks and howls of protest over irrational spontaneous behavior—but it does actually succeed in communicating some of the electricity & fire of poetry and cuts through the miasmic quibbling about form vs. content etc. and does this phrase "work" and is that line "successful" and are all those "p & f" sounds too intense, etc. The woman who runs this program is a Prof. Ruth Witt-Diamant who has dug my work—there appears to be, according to Rexroth, a semimajor renaissance around the West Coast due to Jack and my presence— and Rexroth's wife said he'd been waiting all his life hoping for a situation like this to develop. The thing I do in class is get them personally involved in what they're writing and lambaste anything which sounds at all like they're writing "literature" and try to get them to actually express secret life in whatever form it comes out. I practically take off my clothes in class myself to do it. The students all dig it and understand and the class is now grown weekly to where it's too big to handle, starting with 8 and ending with 25.

W. C. Williams read "Howl" and liked it and wrote an introduction for the book; and meanwhile there is the possibility of expanding and making it a whole book of poems. We put on another reading in a theater here in Berkeley, I read some other poems, "Whitman," "The Sunflower," and a new poem called "America"—a sort of surrealist anarchist tract—all of which came off very well, so the publisher is now interested in a bookful of representative work not just the one poem. The reading was pretty great, we had traveling photographers, who appeared on the scene from Vancouver to photograph it, a couple of amateur electronics experts who appeared with tape machines to record, request from State college for a complete recording for the night, requests for copies of the recordings, even finally organizations of bop musicians who want to write music and give big west coast traveling tours of "Howl" as a sort of Jazz Mass, recorded for a company called Fantasy Records that issues a lot of national bop, etc. No kidding. You have no idea what a storm of lunatic fringe activity I have stirred up. On top of that the local poets, good and bad, have caught up and there are now three groups of people putting on readings every other week, there's one every weekend, all sorts of people—this week

Eberhart (Richard) arrived in town for readings at State, there is a party for him tonight, I was invited to give a private reading, refused (sheer temperament), and so the recordings will be played. Tomorrow night Rexroth invited me over to meet a group of Jazz musicians and discuss the possibility of making some form of jazz-poetry combo. There is also another group of musicians the leader of which used to arrange for Stan Kenton who wants to record with me. Finally I was asked to write an article which I haven't gotten around to for *Black Mountain Review*, & also contribute to 2 literary magazines starting here. Bob LaVigne, a painter whose work I've been buying and digging, has been putting up wild line drawings to plaster the walls of the readings and painting fantastic 7 foot posters a la Lautrec. Really a charming scene. My big problem now is not having enough time to do all I could, working at Greyhound and not having moved out of Berkeley, so I get little time for actual writing anymore—it will be a relief to get out from under and away on a ship or up to Alaska possibly on a fishing industry job.

Rexroth's house—Friday evenings, open house, 2 weeks ago Malcolm Cowley. I got drunk and made a big inflammatory speech denouncing him for publishing Donald Hall as a commercial shot and neglecting & delaying Kerouac, a funny scene, no blood spilled, last weekend Eberhart there, a long non drunken recollection of a party we'd met at in NY 5 years ago, he remembered the conversation in detail, I'd just got out of hospital and was hungup on the religious experience in the Groundhog poem.

English publishers won't handle *Howl*, that is English Printers (Villiers) and so there is now difficulty in getting it through unexpurgated. I revised it and it is now worse than it ever was, too. We're now investigating Mexico, if necessary will spend extra cost and have it done here tho. Civil Liberties Union here was consulted and said they'd defend it if it gets into trouble, which I almost hope it does. I am almost ready to tackle the U. S. Govt out of sheer self delight. There is really a great stupid conspiracy of unconscious negative inertia to keep people from "expressing" themselves. I was reading Henry Miller's banned book *Tropic of Cancer*, which actually is a great classic—I never heard of it at Columbia with anything but deprecatory dismissal comments—he and Genet are such frank hip writers that the open expression of their perceptions and real beliefs are a threat to society. The wonder is that literature does have such power.

How is Gene's new house? I think I'll begin shipping stuff home—where is there room?—for a box & trunk full of excess clothes & pictures & papers.

Allen

Allen Ginsberg [San Francisco, CA] to Richard Eberhart [New York, NY] May 18, 1956

Dear Mr. Eberhart:

Kenneth Rexroth tells me you are writing an article on S.F. poetry and asked for a copy of my manuscript. I'll send it.

It occurred to me with alarm how really horrible generalizations might be if they are off-the-point as in newspapers.

I sat listening sans objection in the car while you told me what you'd said in Berkeley. I was flattered and egotistically hypnotized by the idea of recognition but really didn't agree with your evaluation of my own poetry. Before you say anything in the *Times* let me have my say.

1) The general "problem" is positive and negative "values." "You don't tell me how to live," "you deal with the negative or horrible well but have no positive program" *etc.*

This is as absurd as it sounds.

It would be impossible to write a powerful emotional poem without a firm grasp on "value" not as an intellectual ideal but as an emotional reality.

You heard or saw *Howl* as a negative howl of protest.

The title notwithstanding, the poem itself is an act of sympathy, not rejection. In it I am leaping *out* of a preconceived notion of social "values," following my own heart's instincts – *allowing* myself to follow my own heart's instincts, overturning any notion of propriety, moral "value," superficial "maturity," Trilling-esque sense of "civilization," and exposing my true feelings – of sympathy and identification with the rejected, mystical, individual even "mad."

I am saying that what seems "mad" in America is our expression of natural ecstasy (as in Crane, Whitman) which suppressed, finds no social form organization background frame of reference or rapport or validation from the outside and so the "patient" gets confused thinks he is mad and really goes off rocker. I am paying homage to mystical mysteries in the forms in which they actually occur here in the U.S. in our environment.

I have taken a leap of detachment from the artificial preoccupations and preconceptions of what is acceptable and normal and given my yea to the specific type of madness listed in the Who section.

The leap in the imagination – it is safe to do in a poem.

A leap to actual living sanctity is not impossible, but requires more time for me.

I used to think I was mad to want to be a saint, but now what have I got to fear? People's opinions? Loss of a teaching job? I am living outside this context. I make my own sanctity. How else? Suffering and humility are forced on my otherwise wild ego by lugging baggage in Greyhound.

I started as a fair-haired boy in academic Columbia.

I have discovered a great deal of my own true nature and that individuality which is a value, the only social value that there can be in the Blake-worlds. I see it as a "social value."

I have told you how to live if I have wakened any emotion of compassion and realization of the beauty of souls in America, thru the poem.

What other value could a poem have – now, historically maybe?

I have released and confessed and communicated clearly my true feelings tho it might involve at first a painful leap of exhibition and fear that I would be rejected.

This is a value, an actual fact, not a mental formulation of some second-rate sociological-moral ideal which is meaningless and academic in the poetry of H——, *etc.*

Howl is the first discovery as far as *communication* of feeling and truth, that I made. It begins with a catalogue sympathetically and *humanely* describing excesses of feeling and idealization.

Moloch is the vision of the mechanical feelingless inhuman world we live in and accept – and the key line finally is "Moloch whom I abandon."

It ends with a litany of active acceptance of the suffering of soul of C. Solomon, saying in effect I am *still* your amigo tho you are in trouble and think yourself in a void, and the final strophe states the terms of the communication

"oh starry spangled shock of *Mercy*"

and mercy is a real thing and if that is not a value I don't know what is.

How mercy gets to exist where it comes from perhaps can be seen from the inner evidence and images of the poem – an act of self-realization, self-acceptance and the consequent and inevitable relaxation of protective anxiety and self hood and the ability to see and love others in themselves as angels without stupid mental self deceiving moral categories selecting *who* it is safe to sympathize with and who is not safe.

See Dostoyevsky and Whitman.

This process is carried to a crystal form in the *Sunflower Sutra* which is a "dramatic" context for these thoughts.

> *"Unholy battered old thing O sunflower O my soul*
> *I LOVED you then."*

The effect is to release self and audience from a false and self-denying self-deprecating image of ourselves which makes us feel like smelly shits and not the angels which we most deeply are.

The vision we have of people and things outside us is obviously (see Freud) a reflection of our relation to our self.

It is perhaps possible to forgive another and love another only after you forgive and love yourself.

This is why Whitman is crucial in development of American psyche. He accepted himself and from that flowed acceptance of all things.

The *Sunflower Sutra* is an emotional release and exposition of this process.

Thus I fail to see why you characterize my work as destructive or negative. Only if you are thinking an outmoded dualistic puritanical academic theory ridden world of values can you fail to see I am talking about *realization* of love. LOVE.

The poems are religious and I meant them to be and the effect on audience is (surprising to me at first) a validation of this. It is like "I give the primeval sign" of acceptance, as in Whitman.

The second point is technical. This point would be called in question only if you have not Faith. I mean it is beside the true point and irrelevant because the communication, the *sign* of communication if successfully made should begin and end by achieving the perfection of a mystical experience which you know all about.

I am also saying have faith that I am finally referring to the Real Thing and that I am trying to communicate it.

Why must you deny your senses?

But as to technique – [Ruth] Witt-Diamant said you were surprised I exhibited any interest in the "Line" *etc.*

What seems formless tho effective is really effective thru discovery or realization of rules and meanings of forms and experiments in them.

The "form" of the poem is an experiment. Experiment with uses of the catalogue, the ellipse, the long line, the litany, repetition, *etc.*

The latter parts of the first section set forth a "formal" esthetic derived in part incidentally from my master who is Cézanne.

The poem is really built like a brick shithouse.

This is the general ground plan – all an accident, organic, but quite symmetrical surprisingly. It grew (part III) out of a desire to build up rhythm using a fixed base to respond to and elongating the response still however containing it within the elastic of one breath or one big streak of thought.

As in all things a reliance on nature and spontaneity (as well as much experience writing and practicing to arrive at spontaneity which IS A CRAFT not a jerk-off mode, a craft in which near-perfection is basic too) has produced organic proportion in this case somewhat symmetrical (*i.e.* rationally apprehensible) proportion.

This is, however, vague generalization.

The Long Line I use came after 7 yrs. work with fixed iambic rhyme, and 4 yrs. work with Williams' short line free form – which as you must know has its own mad rules – indefinable tho they be at present –

The long line, the prose poem, the spontaneous sketch are XX century French forms which Academic versifiers despite their continental interests (in XIX century French "formal" forms, Baudelaire) have completely ignored. Why?

This form of writing is very popular in S.A. and is after all the most interesting thing happening in France.

Whitman
Apollinaire
Lorca

Are these people credited with no technical sense by fools who by repeating the iambic mouthings of their betters or the quasi-iambic of Eliot or the completely irrational (tho beautiful) myth of "clear lucid form" in Pound – who works basically by ear anyway and there isn't any clear mentally formulizable form in him anyway, no regular countable measure* [an error here, as Pound attempted to approximate classical quantitative measure. Allen Ginsberg, 1975] – I'm straying – people who by repeating *etc.*, are exhibiting no technical sensitivity at all but merely adeptness at using already formulated ideas – and *this* is historically no time for that – or even if it were who cares, I don't. I am interested in discovering what I do *not* know, in myself and in the ways of writing – an old point.

The long line – you need a good ear and an emotional ground-swell and technical and syntactical ease facility and a freedom "esprit" to deal with it and make of it anything significant. And you need something to say, *i.e.* clear realized feelings. Same as any free verse.

The lines are the result of long thought and experiment as to what unit constitutes *one speech-breath-thought.*

I have observed my mind
I have observed my speech   1) Drunk
                             2) Drugged
                             3) Sober
                             4) Sexy *etc.*

And have exercised it so I can speak *freely, i.e.* without self-conscious inhibited stoppings and censorships which latter factors are what destroy speech and thought rhythm.

We think and speak rhythmically all the time, each phrasing, piece of speech, metrically equivalent to what we have to say emotionally.

Given a mental release which is not mentally blocked, the breath of verbal intercourse will come with excellent rhythm, a rhythm which is perhaps unimprovable.

[Unimprovable as experiment in any case.
Each poem is an experiment
Revised as little as possible.

So (experiments) are many modern canvasses as you know. The sketch is a fine "Form."]

W.C. Williams has been observing speech rhythms for years trying to find a regular "measure"-

he's mistaken I think.

There is no measure which will make one speech the exact length of another, one line the exact length of another.

He has therefore seized on the phrase "relative measure" in his old age.

He is right but has not realized the implications of this in the long line.

Since each wave of speech-thought needs to be measured (we speak and perhaps think in waves) – or what I speak and think I have at any rate in *Howl* reduced to waves of relatively equally heavy weight – and set next to one another they are in a balance O.K.

The technique of writing both prose and poetry, the technical problem of the present day, is the problem of transcription of the natural flow of the mind, the transcription of the melody of actual thought or speech.

I have leaned more toward capturing the inside-mind-thought rather than the verbalized speech. This distinction I make because most poets see the problem via Wordsworth as getting nearer to actual *speech*, verbal speech.

I have noticed that the unspoken visual-verbal flow inside the mind has great rhythm and have approached the problem of strophe, line and stanza and measure by listening and transcribing (to a great extent) the coherent mental flow. Taking *that* for the model for form as Cézanne took Nature.

This is not surrealism – they made up an artificial literary imitation.

I transcribe from my ordinary thoughts – waiting for extra exciting or mystical moments or near mystical moments to transcribe.

This brings up problems of image, and transcription of mental flow gives helpful knowledge because we think in sort of surrealist (juxtaposed images) or haiku-like form.

A haiku as the 1910-20's imagists did *not* know, consists of 2 visual (or otherwise) images stripped down and juxtaposed – the charge of electricity created by these 2 poles being greater when there is a greater distance between them – as in Yeats' phrase "murderous innocence of the sea" – 2 opposite poles reconciled in a flash of recognition.

The mind in its flow creates such fantastic ellipses thus the key phrase of method in *Howl* is "Hydrogen Jukebox" which tho quite senseless makes in context clear sense.

Throughout the poem you will see traces of transcription, at its best see the last line of *Sunflower Sutra*, "mad locomotive riverbank sunset Frisco hilly tincan evening sitdown vision."

This is a curious but really quite logical development of Pound-Fenollosa-Chinese Written Character-imagist W.C. Williams' practice.

I don't see the metrics or metaphors as revolution, rather as logical development, given my own interests, experiences, *etc.* and time.

This (explanation) is all too literary as essentially my purpose has been to say what I actually feel, (not what I want to feel or think I should feel or fit my feelings into a fake "Tradition" which is a *process* really not a fixed set of values and practices anyway – so anybody who wants to hang on to traditional metrics and values will wind up stultified and self-deceived anyway despite all the sincerity in the world). Everybody thinks they should learn academically from "experience" and have their souls put down and destroyed and this has been raised to the status of "value" but to me it seems just the usual old fake death, much under Professor T—, whom I love, but who is a poor mental fanatic after all and not a free soul – I'm straying.

2) *The poetry situation in S.F.*

The last wave was led by Robert Duncan, highly over-literary but basic recognition of the spontaneous free-form experiment. He left for Mallorca and contacted Robert Creeley, editor of *Black Mountain Review*, they became friends and Duncan who dug Williams, Stein, *etc.* especially the Black Mountain influence of Charles Olson who is the head peer of the East Coast bohemian hipster-authors post Pound. Olson's *Death of Europe* in *Origin* last year (about a suicide German boy)- "oh that the Earth / had to be given / to you / this way." is the first of his poems I've been able to read but it is a great breakthrough of feeling and a great modern poem I think.

Creeley his boy came here [San Francisco] last month and made contact with us – and next issue of *Black Mountain Review* will carry me, Whalen and:

1) William S. Burroughs, a novelist friend of mine in Tangier. Great Man.
2) Gary Snyder, a Zen Buddhist poet and Chinese scholar 25 years old who leaves next week for further poetry study in a Zen monastery in Kyoto.
3) Jack Kerouac, who is out here and is the Colossus unknown of U.S. Prose who taught me to write and has written more and better than anybody of my generation that I've ever heard of. Kerouac you may have heard of but any review of the situation here would be ultimately historically meaningless without him since he is *the* unmistakable fertile prolific Shakespearean *genius* – lives in a shack in Mill Valley with Gary Snyder. Cowley (Malcolm) is trying to peddle him in N.Y.C. now [Cowley as editor at Viking was having difficulty persuading the management to publish *On the Road*. Allen Ginsberg, 1975] and can give you info. Kerouac invented and initiated my practice of speech-flow prosody.

I recount the above since anything you write will be irrelevant if you don't dig especially Kerouac – no shit, get info from Kenneth [Rexroth] or Louise Bogan who met him if you don't take my word.

The W.S. Burroughs above mentioned was Kerouac's and my mentor 1943-1950.

I have written this in the Greyhound between loading busses and will send it on uncensored.

I've said nothing about the extraordinary influence of Bop music on rhythm and drugs on the observation of rhythm and mental processes – not enough time and out of paper.

Yours,
Allen Ginsberg

Summary

I. Values

1) *Howl* is an "affirmation" of individual experience of God, sex, drugs, absurdity, *etc.* Part I deals sympathetically with individual cases. Part II describes and rejects the Moloch of society which confounds and suppresses individual experience and forces the individual to consider himself mad if he does not reject his own deepest senses. Part III is an expression of sympathy and identification with C.S. [Carl Solomon] who is in the madhouse – saying that his madness basically is rebellion against Moloch and I am with him, and extending my hand in union. This is an affirmative act of mercy and compassion, which are the basic emotions of the poem. The criticism of society is that "Society" is merciless. The alternative is private, individual acts of mercy. The poem is one such. It is therefore clearly and consciously built on a *liberation* of basic human virtues.

To call it work of nihilistic rebellion would be to mistake it completely. Its force comes from positive "religious" belief and experience. It offers no "constructive" program in sociological terms – no poem could. It does offer a constructive human value – basically the *experience* – of the enlightenment of mystical experience – without which no society can long exist.

2) *Supermarket in California* deals with Walt Whitman, Why?

He was the first great American poet to take action in recognizing his individuality, forgiving and accepting *Him Self*, and automatically extending that recognition and acceptance to all - and defining his Democracy as that. He was unique and lonely in his glory – the truth of his feelings – without which no society can long exist. Without this truth there is only the impersonal Moloch and self-hatred of others.

Without self-acceptance there can be no acceptance of other souls.

3) *Sunflower Sutra* is crystallized "dramatic" moment of self-acceptance in modern terms.

"Unholy battered old thing, O sunflower O my soul, I *loved* you then!"

The realization of holy self-love is a rare "affirmative" value and cannot fail to have constructive influence in "Telling *you* (R.E.) [Richard Eberhart] how to live."

4) *America* is an unsystematic and rather gay exposition of my own private feelings contrary to the official dogmas, but really rather universal as far as private opinions about what I mention. It says – "I am thus and so I have a right to do so, and I'm saying it out loud for all to hear."

II. Technique
   A. These long lines or Strophes as I call them came spontaneously as a result of the kind of feelings I was trying to put down, and came as a surprise solution to a metrical problem that preoccupied me for a decade.

I have considerable experience writing both rhymed iambics and short line post-WCW [William Carlos Williams] free verse.

Howl's 3 parts consist of 3 different approaches to the use of the long line (longer than Whitman's, more French).
   1. Repetition of the fixed base "Who" for a catalogue.
       A. building up consecutive rhythm from strophe to strophe.
       B. abandoning of fixed base "who" in certain lines but carrying weight and rhythm of strophic form continuously forward.
   2. Break up of strophe into pieces within the strophe, thus having the strophe become a new usable form of stanza – Repetition of fixed base "Moloch" to provide cement for continuity. *Supermarket* uses strophe stanza and abandons need for fixed base. I was experimenting with the form.

3. Use of a fixed base, "I'm with you in Rockland," with a reply in which the strophe becomes a longer and longer streak of speech, in order to build up a *relatively* equal nonetheless free and variable structure. Each reply strophe is longer than the previous I have measured by ear and speech-breath, there being no other measure for such a thing. Each strophe consists of a set of phrases that can be spoken in one breath and each carries relatively equal rhetorical weight. Penultimate strophe is an exception and was meant to be – a series of cries – "O skinny legions run outside O starry spangled shock of mercy O victory *etc.*" You will not fail to observe that the cries are all in definite rhythm.

The technical problem raised and partially solved is the break-through begun by Whitman but never carried forward, from both iambic stultification and literary automatism, and unrhythmical short-line verse, which does not yet offer any kind of *base* cyclical flow for the build up of a powerful rhythm. The long line seems for the moment to free speech for emotional expression and give it a measure to work with. I hope to experiment with short-line free verse with what I have learned from exercise in long.

B. Imagery – is a result of the *kind* of line and the kind of emotions and the kind of speech –and-interior flow-of-the-mind transcription I am doing – the imagery often consists of 1920s W.C.W. [Williams] imagistically observed detail collapsed together by interior associative logic – *i.e.*, "hydrogen jukebox," Apollinaire, Whitman, Lorca. But *not* automatic surrealism. Knowledge of Haiku and ellipse is crucial.

Allen Ginsberg [Tangier, Morocco] to Lawrence Ferlinghetti [San Francisco, CA] April 3, 1957

Dear Larry:

Received your letter of March 27 and was surprised by news of Customs seizure. [. . .] Offhand I don't know what to say about MacPhee.* I don't know what the laws are and what rights I got. Is it possible to get them in at New York P.O. and have them shipped on to you under other label or address? Transshipped from NY that is? Is it also possible to have any copies sent to me here from England? I suppose the publicity will be good I suppose – I have been here with Jack, Peter and Bill Burroughs all hung-up on private life and Bill's mad personality and writings and on digging the Arab quarter and taking majoun (hashish candy) and opium and drinking hot sweet delicious mint tea in Rembrandt dark cafes and long walks in lucid Mediterranean coast green grassy brilliant light North Africa that I haven't written any letters (this is the second in 2 weeks) or thought much about anything. I'll write to Grove to Don Allen and let him know, and he'll tell the lady from Time-Life. If you can mimeograph a letter and get some kind of statement from W.C. Williams, [Louise] Bogan, [Richard] Eberhart and send it around to magazines might get some publicity that way. Also let Harvey Breit at *NY Times* know for sure definitely – he'd probably run a story maybe. My brother is a lawyer and has recently done some research on the subject, I'll write him to get in touch with you and provide any legal aid – if any is useful from him in New York. I guess this

---

* Chester MacPhee. San Francisco Collector of Customs.

puts you up shits creek financially. I didn't think it would really happen. I didn't know it was costing you 200$ for reprint, I thought it was $80.00 each extra thousand. Sorry I am not there, we might talk and figure up some way for a U.S. edition, I guess that would be expensive tho. Be sure let the *Life* people in SF know about situation, they might include it in story. The woman in NY is Rosalind Constable c/o Time-Life, Rockefeller Center. She is very simpatico and would immediately call it to attention of Peter Bunzell who is (I heard) writing up the story for *Life* in NY. Send story too to *Village Voice*, they've been digging the scene. By the way I heard there was a lukewarm review in *Partisan Review*, could you send it to me? Might let them know, too, as they took a poem of mine for later. I guess the best way publicity wise is prepare some sort of outraged and idiotic but dignified statement, quoting the Customs man, and Eberhart's article and Williams, and *Nation* review, mimeograph it up and send it out as a sort of manifesto publishable by magazines and/or news release. Send one to Lu Carr at United Press, too. If this is worthwhile. Also write, maybe, [Randall] Jarrell, at Library of Congress and see if you can get his official intercession. I imagine these Customs people have to obey orders of their superiors; and that superiors in Washington, D.C., might be informed and requested to intercede by some official in Library of Congress. Maybe I'll write my congressmen – is there a friendly congressman in SF? This might be more rapid than a lawsuit. Copyright it under City Lights name – only thing is, if you ever make your money back and make some profit from all your trouble, and we go into a 4th or 17th edition, we divvy the loot. I don't think Grove book will knock out sales. They'll probably carry note about the full book. Send me clippings of reviews – I haven't got anything besides the *Nation*, if anything comes through; also any further news of the Cellar* *etc.* sounds charming. Everybody must be having a ball. How's Duncan. Regards to DuPeru, *etc. Ark* III out yet? Send one? I must say am more depressed than pleased, disgusted than pleased, about Customs shot, amusing as it is – the world is such a bottomless hole of boredom and poverty and paranoiac politics and diseased rags here *Howl* seems like a drop in the bucket-void and literary furor illusory

---

* The Cellar. Ferlinghetti and Rexroth did a series of poetry readings to jazz at this North Beach nightclub.

– seems like its happening in otherland – outside me, nothing to do with me or anything. Jack has a room I move into next week, full of light on a hill a few blocks above the beach from whence I'm writing now, can look over the veranda redstone tile, huge patio, over the harbor, over the bay, across the very sunlit straights and see the blue coast of Spain and ancient parapets of Europe I haven't been to yet, Gibraltar small and faraway but there in brilliant blue water, and a huge clear solid cloudless blue sky – I never saw such serene light as this, big classical Mediterranean beauty-light over a small world. I'll write Senor MacPhee myself, ask him to let my copies go, big serious poignant sad letter.

Write me and I'll answer, let me know how things go, if there's anything you want me to do let me know and send along any clippings if you can. These aerogrammes are only 10¢ postage if there are no enclosures.

Thank Kenneth [Rexroth] for efforts and say I hope he enjoys the scene – it is pretty funny, almost a set-up, I imagine they can't bug us forever, and will have to give in. Let me know what the law is.

Rock and Roll on all the jukeboxes here, just had a rock and roll riot at the moviehouse here a few weeks ago, and in fact before I left NY me and Peter picked up on the historic stageshow at the Paramount. I brought a few Little Richard and Fats Domino records here in fact.

Only interesting person here besides Burroughs is Jane Bowles whom I have only met with once.

As ever,
Allen Grebsnig

Nov. 15: Olympia rejected Bill's book but will still try change their mind and might. *Partisan* sent me $12 for a poem and I sent them three Corsos. We could get free ads and advertise to get $ to publish Bill ourselves or by subscription if worst comes.

Allen Ginsberg [Pucallpa, Peru] to William S. Burroughs [Tangier, Morocco] June 10, 1960

Dear Bill,

I'm still in Pucallpa, ran into a little plump fellow, Ramon P- who'd been friend to Robert Frank (photographer of our movie) in '46 or so here. Ramon took me to his Curandero, in whom he has a lot of faith and about whose supernatural curing powers he talks a lot, too much, about. The Maestro, as he's called, being a very mild and simple seeming cat of 38 or so, who prepared a drink for 3 of us the other night; and then last night I attended a regular Curandero all night drinking session with about 30 other men and women in a hut in jungly outskirts of Pucallpa behind the gaswork field.

The first time, much stronger than the drink I had in Lima, Ayahuasca can be bottled and transported and stay strong, as long as it does not ferment, needs well-closed bottle. Drank a cup, slightly old stuff, several days old and slightly fermented also, lay back and after an hour (in bamboo hut outside his shack, where he cooks), began seeing or feeling what I thought was the Great Being, or some sense of it, approaching my mind like a big wet vagina, lay back in that for a while. Only image I can come up with is of a big black hole of God-Nose thru which I peered into a mystery, and the black hole surrounded by all creation, particularly colored snakes, all real.

I felt somewhat like what this image represents, the sense of it so real.

The eye is imaginary image, to give life to the picture. Also a great feeling of pleasantness in my body, no nausea. Lasted in different phases about 2 hours, the effects wore off after 3, the fantasy itself lasted from 3/4 of hour after I drank to 2 1/2 hours later more or less.

Went back and talked to The Maestro, gave him 35 soles ($1.50) for services and talked with him about peyote and LSD, he'd heard of peyote. He's a mestizo who studied in San Martin (upper Huall-aga territory). He gave me samples of his mix, uses young cultivated Ayahuasca plant in his back yard, and mixes that about half and half with a catalyst known as the 'Mescla' which is another leaf known in Chama Indian language as Cahua (pronounced Coura) and locally by him in Pucallpa is called Chacruna. Said he'd get me more samples to bring back to Lima Natural History Museum to identify. Cooks the mixes together all day and strains the broth, gives the drained leaves a second cook too. Anyway the preparation is not excessively secret. I think Schultes [Peruvian botanist] saw and knows the preparation. Can add other leaves of other plants, too, I don't know these combinations to try out. He seems generally interested in drugs, serious, and not mercenary at all, good type, has quite a following here, does physical cures, his specialty.

Anyway to make long story short, went back to formal group session in huts last night, this time the brew was prepared fresh and presented with full ceremony, he crooning (and blowing cigarette or pipe smoke) tenderly over the cupmouth for several minutes before (enamel cup, I remember your plastic cup) then I light cigarette, blow a puff of smoke over cup, and drain. Saw a shooting star, Aer-olith, before going in, and full moon, and he served me up first, then lay down expecting God knows what other pleasant vision and then I began to get high, and then the whole fucking Cosmos broke loose around me, I think the strongest and worst I've ever had it nearly. (I still reserve the Harlem experiences, being natural, in abeyance. The LSD was perfection but didn't get me so deep in nor so horribly in). First I began to realize my worry about the mos-quitoes or vomiting was silly as there was the great stake of life and death. I felt faced by death, my skull in my beard on pallet on porch rolling back and forth and settling finally as if in reproduction of the last physical move I make before settling into real death, got nau-seous, rushed out and began vomiting, all covered with snakes, like a snake seraph, colored serpents in aureole all around my body. I felt like a snake vomiting out the universe, or a Jivaro in head-dress with fangs vomiting up in realization of the murder of the universe, my death to come, everyone's death to come, all unready, I unready, all around me in the trees the noise of these spectral animals the other drinkers vomiting (normal part of the cure sessions) in the night in their awful solitude in the universe, vomiting up their will to live, be preserved in this body, almost. Went back and lay down. Ramon came over quite tender and nurse-like (he hadn't drunk, he's sort of an aide to help the sufferers) asked me if I was OK and 'Bien Mareado' (Good and drunk?). I said 'Bastante' and went back to listen to the specter that was approaching my mind. The whole hut seemed rayed with spectral presences all suffering transfiguration with contact with a single mysterious thing that was our fate and was sooner or later going to kill us, the Curandero crooning, keeping up a very tender, repeated and then changing simple tune, comfort sort of, God knows what signified, seemed to signify some point of reference I was unable to contact yet. I was frightened and simply lay there with wave after wave of death-fear, fright, rolling over me till I could hardly stand it, didn't want to take refuge in rejecting it as illusion, for it was too real and too familiar, especially as if in rehearsal of last minute death my head rolling back and forth on the blanket and finally settling in last position of stillness and hopeless resignation to God knows what fate, for my being, felt completely lost strayed soul, outside of contact with some thing that seemed present. Finally had a sense that I might face the question there and then, and choose to die and understand, and leave my body to be found in the morning. I guess grieving everybody, couldn't bear to leave Peter and my father so alone. Afraid to die yet then and so never took the chance, (if there was a chance, perhaps somehow there was), also as if everybody in session in central radio-telepathic contact with the same problem, the great being within ourselves. Coming back from vomit saw a man knees to chest I thought I saw an X ray his skull I realized he was crouched there as in shroud (with towel mosquito protection wrapped round his face) suffering the same trial and separation. Thought of people, saw their images clearly, you, mysterious apparently know more than I do now and why don't you communicate, or can't you, or have I ignored it? Simon seemingly an angel in his annihilation of vanity and giving forth new life in children. If any interplanetary news comes through he said 'I'll be the first to be relaying it over the wires in a way that won't get it fucked up'. Francine his wife, sort of a seraph of woman, all women (as all men) the same, spectral creatures put here mysteriously to live, be the living gods, and suffer crucifixion of death like Christ, but either get lost and die in soul or get in contact and give new birth to continue the process of being (tho' they themselves die, or do they?) and I lost and poor Peter who depends on me for some heaven I haven't got, lost, and I keep rejecting women, who come to minister to me, decided to have children somehow, a revolution in the hallucination, but the suffering was about as much as I could bear and the thought of more suffering even deeper to come made me despair, felt, still feel, like lost soul, surrounded by ministering angels (Ramon, the Maestro, yourself, the whole common world of diers), and my poor mother died in God knows what state of suffering. I can't stand it, vomited again (Ramon had come over and told me to vomit off the porch where I was lying, if I had to later, very careful kind situation) I mean, is this a good group. I remember your saying watch out whose vision you get, but God knows I don't know who to turn to finally when the chips are down spiritually and I have to depend on my own serpent-self's memory of merry visions of Blake, or depend on nothing and enter anew, but enter what? Death? and at that moment, vomiting still feeling like a great lost serpent seraph vomiting in consciousness of the transfiguration to come, with the radio telepathy sense of a being whose presence I had not yet fully sensed, too horrible for me, still, to accept the fact of total communication with say everyone an eternal seraph male and female at once, and me a lost soul seeking help. Well slowly the intensity began to fade, I being incapable of moving in that direction spiritually, not knowing who to look to or what to look for. Not quite trusting to ask the Maestro, tho' in the vision of the scene it was he who was the local logical ministering spirit to trust, if anyone. Went over and sat by him (as Ramon gently suggested) to be 'blown', that is he croons a song to you to cure your soul and blows smoke at you, rather a comforting presence, tho' by now the steep fear had passed. That being over got up and took my piece of cloth I brought against mosquitoes and went home in moonlight with plump Ramon, who said the more you saturated yourself with Ayahuasca the deeper you go, visit the moon, see the dead, see God, see tree spirits, *etc.*

I hardly have the nerve to go back, afraid of some real madness, a changed universe permanently changed, tho' I guess change it must for me someday, much less as planned before, go up the river six hours to drink with an Indian tribe. I suppose I will. Meanwhile will wait here another week in Pucallpa and drink a few more times with same group. I wish I knew who, if anyone, there is to work with that knows, if anyone knows, who I am or what I am. I wish I could hear from you. I think I'll be here long enough for a letter to reach me, write.

Allen Ginsberg

Allen Ginsberg [Bombay, India] to
Jack Kerouac [n.p.] [May 11, 1962]

American Express
Calcutta India
12:AM – 5:PM

Bombay May 11, 1962

Dear Jack:

Well, we got a big cheap room on an ocean liner sometime last year
March? *United States*, [sic: S.S. America] and ate and took showers
all day and finally passed an Irish harbor and then arrived in Paris.
Eugene and Louis and sad crowd Carl and Janine and Elise and
LeRoi and others had come to see us off like we were going to
another planet, and we were, as far as Elise, since she jumped off
her parents' roof apartment house on Manhattan Heights last
month – so Irving wrote me – and is dead. And when we got to
Paris, Burroughs wasn't there at 9 Git Le Coeur but had left as his
agent Brion Gysin who immediately whispered to me Burroughs
went away because he didn't want to see me and anyway was an
assassin responsible for various deaths Kammerer Joan Cannastra
Phil White – so I tried to be nice to Gysin and find out what all this
was about, felt sad about Bill, why he no wait and leave message say
where meet him. He didn't even say where he was going and left
London as last address, except several days later Gysin showed me
letter from Tangier. So then we were almost broke and Alan Eager
and Bob Thompson were in town, and also the cast of *The Connec-*
tion Carl Lee in white pants and Shirley Clarke being lovers, she
directed movie of it. On top of that the first day Peter and I rushed
out to St. Germain and met and embraced Gregory around the
corner from the great cafes, he'd arrived from Greece the same day
expecting us next week. So in all this confusion we settled down

for a month on Rue Git Le Coeur – and then Stan Persky arrived and a couple of dulls from San Fran, moving next door, and John Hohnsbean in a big 16th century lesbian penthouse on the corner overlooking the Seine, he gave a cocktail party one afternoon. Peter and I met Michaux on a street corner too and had an hours coffee and talked about what people did *after*, with their lives, not in the visions. So we all got high and visited stained glass windows and French poets some other evenings and Paris felt nostalgic, Gregory had a huge swanky party at Girodias' Olympia Press St. Severin Cave velvet restaurant, his book *American Express* out, and I gave dreary conferences to ARTS newspaper with negro Algerian poets, also it was springtime, just about that time Hemingway was getting sick somewhere else. We all drove out to Celine's house but he was also sick and not at home so we stared at his lawn full of rusty bedsprings – meanwhile messages from Tangier, Bill finally writes he be glad to see us. Gysin shows us his flicker machine which is a homemade stroboscope which makes you see inside-mind colored mandalas with eyes closed (black cylinder set on 78 rpm phono, 10 equidistant holes, electric light hung on wire down in cylinder, turn on machine, turn on light, close eyes, and let the light flicker on yr eyeballs 13 times per second or 780 blinks per minute, causes electronic feedback to alpha brain rhythm, causes optical fireworks, very interesting, costs 20 cents for a black piece of flexible art paper you cut holes with a razor and scotch tape it into cylinder and balance it on turntable as directed above. Try.) And I read proofs of Bill's *Soft Machine* and proudly write dust jacket blurb for it that they used – great poetry book, his cut ups I resented but nathless he makes up exquisitest poetry from moon and star worlds and science fictional visions recombined out of it, he cuts up and revises. Then we all got into train – Peter Gregory Alan Eager an actor from Living Theater with big salami mustache, all carrying pockets full of heroin, I went into train bathroom with Eager and we fixed up with needles and bloods and electric train clackets and slomped back to compartment where everybody else was sniffing and nodding all night, to Marseilles and then to Cannes for the Film Festival. *The Connection* movie had a little house there outside of Cannes and so offered us the basement to inhabit free and as we were broke and without prospects we decided to hide out there and see free movies – so for a month, packets of H arriving from Paris by mail, the scene in the villa same as on movie screen, Gregory high and irritated with girlfriend he brought along, and Peter making it with tall Jewish English girl with leather jacket, and we get free tickets to movies and all Hollywood soap operas on display, lousy movies – except we went to Polish movie cocktail party and met Polish film critics with sympathetic grey hair. Gregory gambling at the Casino. One day we get car and drive 50 miles down coast to St. Tropez and who we meet but Jacques Stern, French millionaire friend of last Paris trip and ex-junky – so he invites us to stay with him, we have nowhere to go after Cannes, so we wind up 2 weeks in St. Tropez with French movie stars and spies living in an enormous mansion on midst of ancient vast French farm sniffing ether and junk and Gregory quarrelling with Stern ("you stinky cripple" – "you stupid loudmouth poet") until that's unbearable – going swimming with chauffeurs to beach club, nights in huge house or hotel, lobsters, ten dollar meals all on Stern – who likes us but with Gregory drinking its impossible to maintain amiable calm. Finally he gives us boat fare from Marseilles to Tangier and says he'll maybe join us later – he almost goes with us on a yacht there – but the yacht disappeared when he got divorced. So we train to Marseilles and find more junk from Arabs, and take second class on boat, not like you in hold – except that arriving in Tangier Bill is nowhere to be seen with spy-glasses on dock, he's sitting at home oblivious of our arrival tho we'd sent him telegrams and letters – and Gregory is stopped by police his passport's expired. He weeps on dock and screams at American consul who won't help, they kick him downstairs to the hold under police guard and the ship pulls off for Casablanca, so I jump on to keep him company and we arrive in Casablanca 30 hours later, Gregory under arrest, the man without a country – Peter stayed behind in Tangier to take care of luggage and wire us some money to Casa – where I get off and go to Embassy and they rush down and rescue Gregory with new passport, very kind and friendly not like the mean asst. consul from Tangier who didn't lift finger, Gregory was justifiably hysterical – and had spent night on bed of straw in hold talking to negro cooks who fed him when he refused to eat, coffee over long wood table. So we arrived by bus back in Tangier and there was Bill, I must say rather indifferent to all our dreary hegira. Any way that began a month, and a half months of (looking back on it) incomprehensible petty jealousies and horrors, actually a great weird scene, I think I wrote you? Bill now working on advanced electrical cut ups, said poetry and words were finished, didn't even read Kaddish, he was doing a thousand interesting things but difficult to have rapport with since he had a new acolyte, an angelic looking narcissistic young English lord who sat and simpered with Bill at us for months and never left us alone with him and meanwhile Bill was putting down Peter and Peter was getting hoarse voiced and angry, Gregory rushing back and forth thinking it was all velvet serious magic he didn't believe in, I was worried Bill was so changed and Peter so pained, and I was so pained also so I wound up quarrelling with Peter trying to cool him to watch and wait, - the whole basis of all this panic, being, Bill had declared independence from all passions, affections, mayas, thoughts and language and was sitting around listening to the messages of static on transistor radios and staring at stroboscopes and taking photographs of photographs of his own and making super collages (all developing from you) remember the brown collages of old photos of Vienna and Tangier he had on wall last time in Tangier? Well photos of photos of that trying to get the message and essence of all that reduced to a blur and he'd sit and stare at that and point out interesting blobs and ghosts and phantoms, plus new photos of collages of newspapers and *Time*, Khrushchev's mouth in Kennedy's forehead, - all the time trying by means of language cut ups and mind consciousness cut-ups to track down the original master agents of the cosmos who were using us humans as TV screens to project their schemes – he declaring the universe an Allah-like blank into which these forces had invaded. Actually all pure classical advaita (nondualist) Indic philosophy with really great means for breaking up conceptions. Except he so inhuman it scared me, also he had his own conceptions and likes and dislikes and wasn't really a benevolent blank, playing favorites with his acolytes and persecuting Peter. Whole scene a drag like some dreary Alistair Crowley decadent Blavatsky black magic – trapped me in it because I wouldn't let Bill be, and kill him as my Guru and be indifferent to his great new phases myself – and he did put the finger on my ATTACHMENT to Peter and to himself and my dependence on the Olde Camaraderie brotherhood and the sentimentality and grasping nature of that. So it all did me some good because by the time I was able to resign myself to lose Peter and Bill and poetry and myself at the end I was a sadder wiser man and about ready for any new life. So he was assassin there and did good lovely job, like guru shd. Finally Leary arrived with mushrooms preaching against language too; same day Peter took off alone to escape the madness (FIRST time in my life I ever been taken in by black magic, it really shook my self confidence and that's a good thing too because why cling to self confidence) (shook my trust and faith, etc.). I haven't explained all this, I mean the structure or idea-lan of the conflicts there; except let us say, it consisted in Bill's not accepting any verbal or phenomenal appearance as reality, and cutting them all up, including our old amity. And while theoretically I thought that was correct from Zen void mystic point of view, and while practically it produced with him weird beautiful poetry (Wind Hand caught in the door) I still resented him operating on what I thought was sacred like old friendships. But actually why not? He really is was dedicated to escaping the wheel – really a great guru. Except certain personal foibles of his own made the scene a little more confused than necessary. On hindsight Bill the only classical void preaching guru in the west who's carrying it out. From that point of view Lucien's aristocratic anger in vain. Probably Bill avoided you Lucien etc me etc to avoid as like demons grasping with material hands to drag him back into the created universe, we're all maya, with ambitions. Shit, I wish you'd met him, I would have liked to see that, you're both masters of disillusion, it would have been some kind of bleak magic. But tho he was always laughing he wasn't funny, nor any more little blue boy tenderness I'd always seen in him. Well, it took me time in Tangier to adjust to that, especially with his little English boys (he had two, one a lord and one a more likeable thin mathematics-physics genius from Cambridge who was planning to build huge electronic cut up machines for him) scampering and skipping behind his elbows like demons, simpering at us all. Gregory took it better than I, being able to go along with the game and not believing in anything anyway, except himself as poet. But when Bill began nullifying poetry and making magic against that phantom even Gregory got shook a little. What a hero. What a grim Prospero!

So I went off a week to the heats of Marrakech with Bowles and got friendly with him as a relief and left poor Peter, sick and dysinteric and later to come down with hepatitis, in that hell. Gregory and Peter quarrelling too. By the time I came back Peter thought Gregory, Bill, and I were all conspiring against him, and so we split our money and Peter took off to be alone in Near East – a good move, first time he on his own traveling – and I stayed behind to see the dissolution of that Tangier season. Leary and Bill and boys off to London, then Bill and Leary to Harvard where Bill said he would get machines and experiment to locate the different brain areas controlling different hallucinatory universes and realities. He was respectful and friendly to Leary. But later when they got to Harvard Bill got suspicious and thought he was being used to sell mushrooms to beatniks and didn't find any machinery and anyway was bugged by mushrooms (which seems inconsistent since as you say they do cut up your Who) and cut out, calling Leary an evil horses ass financed by Luce and sinister forces. Which I think is crude of Bill. And so Bill went back and is in London and I wrote him the other day, describing India, neutral letters. Gad I don't know what's happening anymore. And Gregory the last night in Tangier gamboled away the last 200 dollars in casino and went to England broke and is in NY now preparing to fly here he says (Come with Him!) (It'll be weird scene) and Peter, alone went by boat to Greece a week, and then with knapsack all thru Istanbul and buses into Turkey to Beirut and Damascus markets and Aleppo and boat to Port Said and Cairo and climbed the pyramid and looked on Sphinx alone and back to Beirut and Jordan and Old Arab Jerusalem and entered Israel where we had a silent rendezvous again. And I went later to Greece and stayed there and walked around alone, like hit on the head, and stopped writing and sat by myself, and made it with Greek boys and read Homer *Iliad* and *Odyssey* thru, and shipped to Crete and Mycenae and the plains of Argos and climbed Mt. Parnassus and saw shepherds with pipes and tinkle music of sheep flocks far below in valleys of Delphi and met Greek poets and cafe tables in Athens. Two and half months, getting high and sitting on Acropolis watching cockroaches on the white marble – "color of my sneakers" as Gregory writ – listening to Greek Bazookey music, I sent Lucien some records maybe you heard. Greek boys dance to it alone like prayers, and old men watch them happy – the youths sleep with any man for a dollar too, it's respectable and traditional, really like in symposium it made me cry it was so unlike hardhearted America.

Then I took ship to Israel and landed in Haifa which is like a ratty looking Bronx, amazingly full of Jewish people who all think they're Jewish, under a Jewish sky with Jewish streetcars and Jewish airplanes and armies and Jewish speeches and dances and theaters and Jewish newspapers, so after awhile I felt like an Arab. Except like being surrounded with millions of relatives from Newark, so I felt kind of lost and lonely, and the poets all dreary like Howard Moss – and Tel Aviv, met an old artist friend of Henry Miller – met Peter on a street corner looking for me, so we were together again still amazed by what happened in Tangier and still not comprehending. He with long hair and torn red sneakers babbling about young kids in Port Said who taught him a lot of Arabic words finally and he climbed pyramids and written poems in Turkey. Same Peter, and me same too. I had meanwhile walked near Galilee and sunk my foot in that water, couldn't sustain me, and saw Mount of the sermon and went to Nazareth and wrote poem about the smell of urine down near Mary's Well and near Nazareth to ancient Hassidic Rabbi town in Mts where they wrote the Kabala, then we went to Jerusalem finally for a week and saw Martin Buber the great bearded sage and asked him about mushrooms (he said visions were not important) and Kabala scholars and old synagogues with mantric shouting and rocking by Hasidic choirs making the room electric on Sabbath night, we walked in one and were hit by the religious orgones streaming from their beards, young kids and old men rocking and shrieking Hebrew names of Jaweh till everybody <u>felt</u> the shekinah light. That's the greatest thing in Israel. Also a bus trip thru desert where Moses wandered, down to the Red Sea where I went skin diving with mask and snorkel for first time and saw silent coral cities with purple green fish in the wavy blue invisible heaven-waters. We couldn't find a ship to get out of Israel, I went from office to office a month, till we were broke almost – and they didn't treat me like international Jewish poet hero either. I was anyway not reading aloud and mostly anonymous and lost. Finally I wrote *Playboy* Spectorsky and he wired me $500 on promise of article on India and we got $23 ship to Mombassa Kenya, and stayed there a month waiting for boat to India third deck class – bus rides to Nairobi and around Kilimanjaro hid in mist, we lived in Indian flophouse hotels and saw Kenyatta orating in stadium filled with 30,000 negroes, we the only whites, and went to Tom Mboya's wedding dance and got kicked out for not wearing jackets and ties, and bus ride into Tanganyika and some small towns and I shipped a huge skin drum to Paterson for 5 dollars. Kenya a big bore like Israel, everybody thinks they're negro, this was independence year, and the whites we met were unbearably like Debora Kerr. Lots of Ganja, right on the street bench across from our hotel a couple shoeshine boys. Finally we got boat and 13 day trip for 50 dollars across Arabian ocean to – ah yes we'd stopped before in Djibuti and Massawa near end of Red Sea Rimbaud territory near Harrar and walked where we landed 3 months ago today practically, Feb. 15, 1962. Nice boat ride, cheap tickets good food, and we had bunks in the hold with 600 vomiting Indian families fleeing E. Africa because it's going to be independent, but portholes and huge door in the side of ship made big wind against our bunks so we lay all day and read Vedas and modern Indian novels and E.M. Forster and *Kim* and Hinduism primers.

Bombay, we landed with exactly one dollar left, except money waiting from Ferlinghetti year-end royalties since January at American Express huge gingerbread building in the middle of big crowded Victorian looking city, we took taxi there with knapsacks and drums and typewriters expecting note from Gary who'd landed in Ceylon Jan. 1 and was waiting for us to catch up with him, but no note, so we stayed in Bombay only 2 days and walked around streets and changed money on black market (rupee is about 7 to one dollar and you can get a great meal for 2 rupees or go to the big swanky downtown international beef restaurants and buy lobster thermador for 3 ½ rupees; the biggest hotel in town Taj Mahal costs 50 rupees a day huge room and vast meals in air-cooled ships' dining room; but we live on about 20 rupees a day between us if necessary and stay in cheap Indian flophouses or free ashrams or pilgrim hostels and eat 1 rupee vegetarian trays of food) (2 ½ rupees across town in taxi). So for several dollars each we got 3rd class train tickets for all day all night ride to Delhi, for 2 rupees you get a huge sleeping bunk-rack, bring your own blanket and sheet, and can sleep in comfort, no crazy crowding. In fact Indian 3rd class trains the best anywhere in the world for long distance traveling, cheap, comfortable, funny, India flowing past the window with huge plains and palm trees and cows and people shitting in the grasses and washing with loincloths in muddy rivers and water buffalos and the Ghats mts. in the heat haze way off – and can go to train diner and have vast meal 5 courses western style for 3 ½ rupees or for 87 nyapaesa (87 hundredths of a rupee or 10 cents) a big vegetarian Indian style tin tray of food. And sit there hours and drink soda or coffee. Third class is horrible if you don't reserve a place a day in advance, then you have to push and shove and stand for hours and sweat and old ladies with naked babies pee on your feet; but for long trips its great – in a few days we have sleeper bunks for 2000 mile 52 hour train trip across India to Calcutta where it's middle of heat season – I'll see what that's like.

So we arrived in Delhi way back in February and no Gary at American Express, he's somewhere in Nepal, we wait a week and stay at a Jain Dharamshala. All over India everywhere there's free or cheap places to stay. Dharamshalas are big YMCA's established in all cities and towns near every temple for free lodging and cheap food or free for anybody who's traveling on business or pilgrimage. Ashrams are like holy farms with free lodging and food, everywhere in India where a holy man once lived or a great temple or swami resides. You can stop over for a night or stay there all your life, nobody cares and they feed you rice and turnips in banyan leafs on the floor and free yoga lessons every day if you want, and if there's a holy man around you can have darshan (his presence) or talk with him, some of them don't talk. Or, if you want English style, the British left behind a huge network of airy, fann'd, white clean bungalows called Rest Houses and Inspection and Dak bungalows everywhere in India, hundreds of thousands of them at every rail junction, which you can rent for a few nites at 2 or 3 rupees a head, with servant. Or if you're too lazy to leave the RR station, every sizeable city and even small whistle-stop RR stations have "Retiring Rooms" attached, which is like a great huge motel-room you can stay at for 3 rupees. All these are especially open to US tourists. I never saw a place more convenient for wandering and traveling. We've been drinking the water everywhere and better bowels than Maroc: the Indian food no matter how beat like alleys on Mexico is always cheap and vegetarian healthy and filling, tho boring, so we eat in Chinese restaurants in big cities or at RR station restaurants cheap western meals or like here in Bombay or Delhi endless lovely diner-like eateries serving English style food, chicken gravy fish mutton French fries – only no beef, nobody kills cows, cows are

friends – in fact it's strange, almost all Hindus, that's the majority
population, doesn't eat meat, they're a really holy people – India is
Holy and lovely place to be, someplace to be. They don't eat meat
because it's traditional to leave the animals alone. But they don't get
mad at meat eaters either. So Peter and I and Gary when we met
went around eating vegetables for months and didn't notice the dif-
ference, much, (except their cooking is dull.). So in Delhi we stayed
at Jain Dharamshala. Jains are a weird sect founded by Mahavira a
contemporary of Buddha – they finally quarreled and split – who
said that the Universe was an infinite repetitious cycle of Kalpas,
repeating exactly the same each time practically, and NOBODY
EVER gets out – except 24 Tirthankars or pure ones each Kalpa
who rise to the top of the universe and float free because they're so
light and pure on account of not eating onions and many prayers
and some even starve themselves to death suicide. They're sup-
posed to be naked, and chaste and most of them are in the jewelry
business – Mr. Jain (they're mostly all named Mr. Jain too) who
showed us the Dharamshala and stayed next door to us, a jeweler
from Jaipur, on a business trip to Delhi, took us all around old
Delhi alleys to friends who got us some opium and we met all the
alleyway jewelers of Delhi – and he explained he was a brahmach-
ari (no more sex) becuz "You see, you must not give away your jew-
els, you must retain your jew-els." Everybody in India is religious,
it's weird, everybody's on to some saddhana (method), and has
family guru or brahmin priest and knows all about how the uni-
verse is a big illusion; it's totally unlike the West – it really is another
dimension of time-history here – in fact every middle class house-
holder is expected at age 45 or 50 after he's founded family and
business to retire from world, take brahmachari vows and orange
robe and wander on the road in India with no possessions living free
in Ashrams (that's why there are Ashrams all over and Dharam-
shalas) and singing hymns and meditating on Shiva or Vishnu or
whoever he chooses to represent the void, its assumed that all gods
are unreal so one should respect all gods as purely subjective forms
of meditation to fix the mind on one image and still it down and be
peaceful – the gods are all interchangeably friendly – Saraswati for
people hung on music and learning; Lakshmi for people hung on
movie stars beauties and loot; Rhada for young lover devotees;
Krishna for cocksmen-cayote types; Ganesha the elephant-headed

god of prosperity and slyness for the Jerry Newmans and Peter Orlovsky (Peter has become a Ganesha devotee)'s of the universe, Buddhas for the Jacks, Kalis and Durgas for Bill and Ilk, anything you want – a huge cartoon religion with Disney gods with 3 heads and six arms killing buffalo demons – everybody so gentle about it all it's unbelievable – except the Moslems swept down in the 12th century with their one Allah like a bunch of hysterical Jews and smashed all the pretty Walt Disney statues before they calmed down and got happy like the Hindus. Weird thing is we met hundreds of retired householders (sunyassis) all over, they really do retire from the world. Imagine my father wandering around New Jersey in orange robes with his serious expression. It's like that here – so we were sitting in the middle of all this in Delhi with India dawning on us when Gary and Joanne his wife hit town after long months in trains and Benares and Calcuttas and Bubanishwars and sex temples and Ceylons and Madrases and Nepalses and we all meet, and hang around Delhi sightseeing a week, literary tea with Kushwant Singh a Sikh continental style author with a big silly turban ("How does it *feel* to be a Sikh," I ask? and he says "Great, because Sikhs are famous warriors and I'm a coward, but people think I'm a famous warrior so nobody hits me"). Then we take another all nite train to the holy town of Rishikesh, at the foot of Himalays, where the Ganges enters the Gangetic plain – we stay at famous old Swami Shivananda (Shiva-lovebliss) his Ashram, an old wrestler looking bald man stretched out in a couch sick and dying and murmuring <u>om</u> every time some American lady comes up with big questions about dualism – actually a big famous holy man but now weak and can't operate much tho he once founded hospitals and wrote 386 books ("I write with electric speed") charlatan of mass-production international nirvana racket – but actually quite a calm holy old man – he gave us all envelopes with 5 rupees each present and a little book to me on "Raja Yoga for Americans" – How many of you are there? "4" I say as he passes supported by attendants – "4 that's an auspicious number" he winks and goes away, I rather like him. Next day I asked, where can I get a Guru? And he smiles and touches his heart and says the only Guru is your own heart dearie or words to that effect and adds – you'll know your Guru when you see him because you'll love him, otherwise don't bother. Well not quite that funny but that was the message. Which made me feel quite good after all that Tangier austerity and paranoia and loveless gurus. So we moved across the Ganges river for a week to another Ashram – they give big empty rooms, you sleep on a mat on yr sleep bag or we have light air mattresses and white sheet – no other furniture, make yourself at home with big woodsy foothills and windows on the Ganges at this especially holy spot for bathing – big friendly fish crowd the banks, holy fish nobody eats or fishes for – in fact they feed the fish – breadcrumbs and rice – tomatoes – and we took walks and climbed up a few thousand feet to a peak and saw the panorama of inner Himalayas snows – 200 miles of white crags including Holy Mt. Kailash the abode of Shiva and all sorts of mythological Gangotris and Kedcernaths and Badernaths where there are temples near snow and many Yogas and holy men scattered in caves – walking along path near house, three half naked men sitting with fixed eyes and beards cross-legged all afternoon in trance under tree – one with a pet cow with a monstrous deformed jaw his friend – and tin beg cups on the deerskin mat they sit on – fixed bloodshot eyes on one, and Shiva tridents, like little Neptune tridents, stuck in the ground beside them – immobile hours all of them – then we climbed hill and talked to beautiful Jerry Heiserman clear skinned long-hair-like-girl shining-eyes youth who just came down from Himalayas for the spring, in long orange bramacharia robes, he invites us to astral lunch. Lives alone with another Yoga kid who's washing himself naked in the garden. We tell him about the sitting bloodshots down below on the path – he says "Ah, they're just advertisement posters for the real yogas whom you can't see way back in the mountains."

Look on a map you see Rishikesh straight north of Delhi where the Himalayas begin. And a few miles away is Hardwar – just at the time we were there, Hardwar another bigger town on Ganges, next town down the line, was beginning annual 12 year festival – congregation from all over mountains and plains of India of all holy men – lasts all month. 2 million pilgrims crowd this small town – the saddhus (different classes of holy lone wander monks) all come to bathe in Ganges (and purify it of all the shit that the rest of the people of India have washed away into it with their sins the last 12 years). So we went there on opening day of Kumbh Mela (full nectar pitcher) – and saw processions of hundreds of stark naked ash-smeared saddhus – (naked ones are called nagas or snakes) some beautiful kids with long matted hair and other old Breughel bellies and brown Indian balls and hair all over ass and some one legged naked yogis – one little guy sitting on wall had thin infantile paralysis spider legs criss-crosses in Padmasam position – with tin cup and smile – some riding elephants and horses and all the lady and gentlemen merchants and householders showering their path with flowers – one naked naga under a tree who lives permanently in Hardwar under that tree got up when the parade passed to the river and blew his conch horn triumphant to see his brothers pass in review – followed by bands of weeping singing homeless women walking along holding on to each other, with no hair and bald like holy humble Gertrude Stein suffering phantoms, actually they made me cry, all dressed in orange robes and singing Bajans (Sanskrit hymns to Nirvana) – and great parades of sunyassis in orange robes who've retired from the world too except wear clothes – all the different classes of Saints gathered together to purify the Ganges. So we watched them crowd down the steps to the river and bathe an old fat bearded naked leader saddhu first and then all go in and wash the ashes off themselves, and then go back up to the streets and to a temple where they rang bells and smeared themselves with white ashes all over again, and scattered all over India, later in the month when the Kumbh Mela was over. We should have stayed there all month talking to the holy men but we got train back to Delhi and then went next to Almora, deeper into Himalayas to see more snow and Nanda Devi peaks, and lived in Dak Bungalow on the edge of an Abyss valley confronting 300 mile wall of inner Himalaya panorama, and then we went on other huge train ride to Punjab to Pathankot to see *more* Himalayas from different view and this time climbed at night up to the snows 9000 feet, and a Dak Bungalow overnight there, next morning Gary in climbing shoes went on up alone to higher snows, we all exhausted. Gary meanwhile, older, still twinkling eyed and beard but gaunter, gentler now and a husband always arguing with his wife so they have big ball matching wits and arguments with each other but he boss because inside now he's really Walt Disney too, and she thinks its serious. He knows how to chant sutras in Japanese Sanskrit with big Tibetan-noh play sepulchral voice reechoing in caves and syncopating jijimuje syllables. Also strikes me as sweeter than imagined before, almost feminine in his tolerance and sense of play, no more knife fights in barrooms seaman boots. He described Zen practice in clearer way than I'd ever got from book Suzuki. Apparently the Zen series consists of 2 parts. First you sit and learn to empty mind meditate zazen, etc. Then your teacher inserts Koan in your mind, and you use the zazen-sitting to break the Koan. The meditation seems to consist in so concentrating that you literally have inner hallucination experience of *being* a rain storm in a teacup, etc. When you've mastered that hallucination exercise and had subjective experience of being dog etc., the master assigns you another from a fixed series of 2005 koans which cover specific areas in every direction, of specific subjective states and worlds etc. Gary says he's now passed thru 30 Koans or so, of the 2000. When you're done you can go to other Zen masters and test their experience of these states and compare notes and learn details from them too. Sounds like a simple, persevering, rigid, and well worked out scheme, apparently lots of time consuming work, doing mental exercises. So we came down from Himalayas to the town of Dharamshala where the Tibetan refugees are camped and visited the Dalai Lama of Tibet and talked with him an hour, Gary discussing techniques of sitting, and me babbling about mushrooms. Everything went fine and we'll put Leary in touch with the Dalai Lama. Then we got on train and went to Jaipur way down in the middle of India which was a big boring red walled city full of Maharaja palaces that Kennedy's wife visited the week before, then we went on further trains to further serious touring taking weeks and weeks, to Sanchi, a big Buddhist stupa with carvings, then the Caves of Ajanta and then the great rock cut cave temples of Ellora where the Great GLORY of Indian art really is makes Michelangelo's renaissance low Western little, I mean they got great dancing shivas balanced with ten arms doing cosmic dances of creation 20 feet tall, and fantastic skully Kali's invoking nightmare murders in another yuga, thousands of statues dancing all over huge temple built like Mt. Kailash the Himalayan abode of Shiva. And Ganesha with fat belly and elephant head and snakedhead belt and trunk in a bowlful of sweets riding on his vehicle a mouse – How can Da Vinci beat an elephant on a mouse? Anyway, all that statuary's endless and there are 30 caves full of it at Ellora alone. Stayed there and nearby city Aurangabad a few days, and then train to Bombay where after 2 months travel we all collapsed in great huge mat-floored cool electric fan

369

room in rich Indian lady's house on Malabar Hill in Bombay, with big trees outside and Bhima the barefoot servant brings us a tray full of tea thrice daily – friends of Dorothy Norman. Now Gary's sailed away to Japan and me and Peter stayed on here almost a month stretching hospitality, I answering all piled up mail, your letter the last and longest I have to finish – sorry so long a silence. Meanwhile here in Bombay we eat good and it's cheap living, we wear Indian pajamas clothes all over of Gandhi Khadi cloth and our hair is long below the neck so I look Bengali and in sandals Peter's looks golden, out on streets in like flowing pajama robes, cool – the hot season is in full swing but it's great, I sweat but it's like NY summer at worst – everything frightful about India been exaggerated – it's easier than Mexico everybody even speaks English. Peter had his hepatitis in Maroc, here he's barelegged and healthy. And the opium dens! Real chinamen in slums in bamboo shacks, we go in, lie down on hip with head on a tin can or brick and he prepares us 12 pipefuls a piece and I go home hours later happy – smoked opium infinitely best way superior to all m's and swallowed black C's and H needles. It is smoother and higher quality high feeling and deeper and longer. Half way to hallucinogen but feeling good all the way. And Bhang mixed with milk is drunk by pious business families before temple services in some temples, respectable. Charas (cannabis like bhang) all over, little bamboo clubs in suburbs where bank employees relax at dusk smoking special charas pipes. Also no alcohol. Prohibition in India – except tourists like us can get free liquor permits and have ration. But I haven't bothered yet. Also legendary Meher Babas and Gurus almost every city you can go and visit. The one respected superconscious holy man of XX century India everybody from all religions and sects says was a genuine genius Maha Rishi was a man from south called Ramana Maharshi – preached a non dualist (advaita) introspection – said the world was unreal and the self movie screen should be dug not the movie – by means of constant probing Who am I, but he disapproved of all disciplines, rituals, yogas, Zens, Saddhanas, as being hung up when the immediate path was open. All the yogins and sects nonetheless agree he's right and he's laid the bane of all formalism. Says no guru can help since it's all unreal, there's nothing to do, no mental activity useful, no attempt and search useful since any move you make is a move in maya (like Bill says), so nothing left but let go and do nothing. So he Ramana Maharshi sat in bed all day silent and only answered questions when someone asked him a question and wrote only one poem maybe and was superconscious or everyone says all the time. So here is what Maharshi wrote:

XXIII
(from 30 verses or the Quintessence of Wisdom)
Since there is no separate knowledge
to know Being, the Real,
Being cannot be known.
That is a hard saying
because delusion is ancient and fixed
and we seek to know the Lord
in the Kingdoms of Division.
But there is no separate self
separate Knower and Knowledge.
How can the real be twain?
We are the real ourselves.

XXVII
When Being realized
and the Knower is Awareness itself
Vision is no more separate,
but the endless ecstasy of Being
in all forms,
all embraces of experience.
Life is the deathless honey
of consciousness.

XXX (last verse)
And this is the true Penance
and culmination of YOGA
to live and move in the silence
utterly free of the illusory 'I'
the root of mind in serfdom.
So spake Ramana
who moves not apart from the Lord.

Meanwhile he described the phenomenal and mental world as strictly illusory, a la classical oriental thought, but said that consciousness without an I or an I's *body*, was complete and final end, - and apparently spoke from continuous absorption in that, rather than fitful experiences of same. Some of his disciples also are alive, he died ten years ago. Of course there are thousands of such arbitrary saints and yogins and swamis here but he seems to me so far of all legends and person the straightest and most classical and genuine and the subjective result on me of India has thus been to start dropping all spiritual activity initiated since Blake voice days and all mental activities I can discard, and stop straining at heaven's door and all that mysticism and drugs and cut ups and gurus and fears of hells and desire for god and as such, as result, in sum, I feel better and more relaxed and don't give a shit and sometimes sit in cafe downtown Bombay being interviewed *India Illustrated Weekly* (which treats us like visiting saints) (and will publish my picture of the vomiter and Peter's self sketches and conversations with us) and my brain does get empty and filled with big thrilling cosmic indic Persian gulf sunset XX Century. Meanwhile as I'm finishing all this Peter's all drest in flowing silken shirt and headed downtown to Mahim to the Chinaman humming Bach. The Indians are all friendly and dig him as some sort of American saddhu, so he's expansive and talks a lot and now I shut up and get mad at him occasionally but then I realize who cares? and go about my sunset. So all's well here. On top of that, the music, all the celestial twanging we've heard, I met a great Tabla (drum) player Chatur Lall, who told me what musicians to listen to, and so every week we go to one or two concerts – the classical music live is greater than the records – two guys Chatur Lall and Ravi Shankar or Ali Akbar Kahn the greatest musician in India, sit on a stage or in a room and the string man begins tweedling meditatively on his raga (notes) and pretty soon tabla begins like on records and they then play not for 15 minutes like on records but 50 60 70 choruses *every time* hours on end sometimes, chasing each other a la purest improvised jazz with all the spontaneous comedy of that until they are in telepathic trance and leading each other back and forth across the floors of flowers of non-music, and they go *on*, they don't end after ten choruses or 20 or 30. So that a concert of 2 or three ragas can start at 9 in the evening and they'll play till midnite and if they feel good with full dress concert audience they go on till dawn – tho the latest I've seen was 3AM. And Indian singing is something else, a guy sits down

surrounded – they all play sitting down barefoot anyway in paja-
mas – everybody, workers, walk around in the streets in underwear
regular striped Hollywood nightmare shorts with open flies like
Americans have nightmares being caught in the streets in – so the
singer sits down and begins groaning and stretches his hand out to
catch the groan and whirls it above his head, any noise that comes
into his throat like a butterfly, and throws it away with his left hand
and catches another hypnotic gesture note with his right hand and
whirls it around, his voice follows weirdly way up into high icky
giggle gargle sounds and brings it down like Jerry Collonna and stirs
it around with his forefinger like it's all Jell-O and throws it away
with a piercing little falsetto into the curtain and does this over and
over working himself up until he's shaking like an epileptic fit and
his fingers are flying all over trying to catch the myriad little sounds
coming in his ear like butterflies, I said that, like, I mean flies, well
mosquitoes, little eees and zoops and eyerolling wheeps! Very much
like my ipskiddy yikkle song on your tape but infinitely further out
delicately lasting for hours and ending back on the original groaning
eternity OOM, low blues. So we hear all that music at concerts and
costs 14 cents or 80 cents for front seat depending how rich you
are, also great dancing that makes Barrault seem amateur, it took
a thousand years to prepare a wink, cosmic dances of creation and
Kali dances and hands fluttering in front of male-female god faces
and a weird form of super tap-dancing barefoot where I saw a man
flying across the stage with his body rigid straight up and his feet
fluttering flat on the ground like pogo sticks a dozen times a second,
improving this to frantic tabla tattoos – Kathak dancing they call
that – Fred Astaire be amazed in his grey age – so would you you
old bore – and the churly jargot dancing girls in stone at Sanchi are
the only world chicks I would think of fucking, once I saw them
statues from their behinds. Jack I'm telling you this place is weird.
Anyway I'm having a good time. Don't drink so much, Gregory said
you drank and you said you drank and got mean to Lucien upsetting
his chair, well, come to India where it's prohibition and cast off
yr clothes and we'll go naked or walking in white pajamas unbe-
knowable up and down the foothills of Sikkim and talk to refugee
tibetal lamas about balloons. I do wish you were here, only calm
and peaceful and not yelling at me much, and we could take long
3rd class comfy train trips to the Himalayas and read Mahabharatas

and spend a few months goofing in the Inde, and listen to music concerts. Even the journalists are gentle and would accept you as a saint-saddhu not a mean beatnik – people even come up and kiss yr hand and stroke your hair – you'll see how much gentleness you're missing in Machineryland – but it don't make difference since travel is all Maya – except this particular Indian red dust is good kicks compared to the dust of any other nation I've visited so far. India a great NATION – a holy Nation. Anyway I feel good and hope you do too and if you can, get on a plane and come visit mythical east for a nonce, it's really here and mythic as any Maya. Now, as to existence is suffering, the original word is *Dukka* or some such spelling. Which means *not* suffering, but unsatisfactoryness. Suffering's too categorical and also inaccurate. So I heard this stockbroker in Pajamas who shows us around temples, he said, repeating thrice with impatient sad and angry voice, "dukka, dukka, dukka" like saying trouble trouble trouble annoyed at the light bill, or money money money, always asking me for money. dukka dukka dukka. So meanwhile now I'm writing an Ode to Kali, superimposing ten armed durga on the Statue of Liberty, 22 verses imitated from Sanskrit Kali Hymn I read translation of. And a gang of young hip Marathi poets has already translated (before we met them) Scripture of Golden Eternity and Old Angel Midnight into Marathi. They were interested in the sounds, and they all know Burroughs, a lovely characteristic group of 5 poor poets who took us to meet the Chinamen, so Peter and I hang around with them and bring them to uptown Bombay literary teacup parties, where hung-up critics ask us about Robert Graves. Imagine translating Angel Midnight into Marathi – that's the language of Bombay. We leave for Calcutta Monday 14 May. Write there.

Love,
Allen

P.S. Come to India! It's summer beginning, we're going to Calcutta where it's hot, and from there a train up to cool hill station of Darjeeling and from there bus into Himalayan Sikkim, medieval Gangtok Tibetan Buddhist town like. We can take long non-strenuous walks around Himalayan hills and even see Everest. After that when the rains start, I'm going to come down to the Ganges to Benares and the Deer Park and Nalanda University and side trip to Bodh Gaya and maybe Lumbini in Nepal border – maybe Katmandu Nepal too – and a month in Benares listening to Sanskrit chanting and music and see dancing and I have friends scholars there and can stay there cheap or free in Gandhi or Krishnamurti ashram and meet a famous lady saint named Anandamayee and other saints and watch bodies burning on funeral pyres and we can follow Peter around because he follows cows ambling down the street all the time. Then as fall comes we are going south to Konarah sex temples, and further south to Madras and more dancing and music and scholars on the subject of Ganesha and then to Ceylon and maybe Bowles be there in December and slowly back up the West coast back here to Bombay and next year sometime sail off to Japan or somewhere else. Anyway come here for a few weeks if you feel like and we'll be your guide and protect you from amoebas and alcohols. Or stay on and we relax and wander and maybe settle down in Madras or Ceylon for a few months and have household and you write novels about coconut trees. Also bigger whore streets in Bombay than Mexcity and costs 2 or 3 rupees pretty girls – down the block they have houses full of hermaphrodites and further down the block a bunch of cots on the pavement where middle aged transvestites sit and put on rouge with bald spots on their head and comb their long black hair down to their waist and cop on corner sits in his cop box and guards everybody from harm. Tibetan tankas and statues are flooding the art market. Send me 100 dollars and I'll buy you a great Walt Disney classical Tibetan tanka. Gary and I bought and are sending you a small yabyum shakta-shakti statue as of old. He'll mail it from Japan. In ten years all these Tibetan arts will be impossible to find again forever and worth much more than now. Also great collections of Persian paintings here, in museums and antique stores, mogul miniatures for 20 or 30 dollars, cheap, like little naturalistic Klees.

Another weird thing is the Bhakti cults – Faith and devotion cults. For instance this stockbroker and his wife worship Krishna, the bluebodied avatar of Vishnu who was brought up as a human being and fucked 16,000 gopi girls (cow girls) (Peter calls them the goopey girls) and plays flute and – so they worship him as a baby, and have statue of him crawling on floor, and dress up the doll statue, and play tops with it and push it on miniature swing and put it to bed in a silver bed with silk cover at night – this big important stockbroker playing dolls on the floor two hours a day happily every morn before work – as his saddhana (means of devotion or path of self perfection). He tells me that every Hindu middleclass form of worship – two-times her husband with Krishna officially and considers herself K's secret cunt; and every husband also considers himself a woman lover of Krishna as well as a man husband of his wife; i.e. in relation to Krishna, all men assume feminine lover role and go to temples and stock market and tell each other about the latest thrills. Everybody here is so inexpressibly hip! The stockbroker gave me bhang. He also read *On the Road* and *Dharma Bums*. Peter says hello from the cows, and he'll write you a letter too.

Allen Ginsberg [Portland, OR] to Nicanor Parra [Santiago, Chile] August 20, 1965

Dear Nicanor dear:

I got your letter from Santiago July 9 and am now up in Northwest with Gary Snyder an old friend poet who's been living in Japan studying Zen Jap tongue and Chinese for last 8 years. We're camping with sleeping bags in forests and beaches and preparing to climb snowy glacier mountains for a month. Then back to San Francisco and October 15-16 I take part in anti-Vietnam war demonstration and maybe end up in jail or maybe not for a month or so. Well I'll see. Happy to hear from you, I had some very mad adventures since I left Cuba, I even spent a few evenings till 4 AM with Alessandro Jodorowsky in Cupola Cafe in Paris. But anyway to begin where we left off.

8:30 AM after the party at the Havana-Riviera where I last saw you in your pajamas giggling I woke up with knock on my door and 3 *miliciano* entered and scared me. I thought they were going to steal my notebooks, they woke me up in the middle of hangover sleep I'd only been in bed 2 hours. Told me pack my bags the immigration chief wanted to talk to me, and wouldn't let me make phone call, took me down to office in old Havana to a Mr. Verona head of immigration who told me they were putting me on first plane out. I asked him if he'd notified Casa* or Haydee and he said no, they had appointment with Haydee that afternoon and she would agree after

---

* Casa De Las Americas. Ginsberg had been invited to Cuba as their guest, by the director, Haydee Santamaria.

she heard their reasons. What reasons? "Breaking the laws of Cuba." "But which laws?" "You'll have to ask yourself that," he answered. As we drove to airport I explained I was simpatico with revolution and embarrassed both for self and for them and also explained that my month was up, the rest of, most of, the delegates were leaving that weekend anyway, wouldn't it be more diplomatic and save everyone entanglement if they left me to leave normally with the rest for Prague, and why act hastily without notifying Casa? "We have to do things fast in a revolution."

When I landed in Prague, I wrote Maria-Rosa long letter and mailed it at airport explaining what happened and asked for advice and said I won't talk to reporters *etc.* and would keep quiet so's not to embarrass her or Casa or Cuba but thought ultimately I'd have to tell friends. It would get out and look silly of Cuban bureaucracy, so perhaps best ask Haydee to invite me back, at least formally to erase the comic [expulsion] and so have been in contact with her and Ballagas ever since. Saw [friends] in Prague and later in London and they opined the police were using me to get at the Casa. Meanwhile I hear there's been increased wipe-out of fairies in university and finally this month Manuel Ballagas wrote that Castro at university had spoken badly of *El Puente* and now *El Puente* is dissolved and he's depressed. I certainly didn't know what I was getting into consciously but I seem to have been reacting with antennae to a shit situation that everyone was being discreet about. I doubt if things would not have come to a head without my bungling, I mean it would probably have ended the same way if I weren't there, the hostility and conniving was in the works all along, that was what I was sensing and yelling about.

Well anyway in Prague I found I had royalties for a new book, and back money due me for foreign Lit. mag and 2 years back royalties for stage performances of my poesy in Viola poetry cafe, enough to live well for a month and pay for 3 days intourist and train fare return to Moscow via Warsaw. Met a lot of young kids, heard all the gossip conducted myself discreetly, sang mantras all over the streets and literary offices, gave a poetry reading and answered questions for audience of 500 students at Charles University. They let me loose, I talked freely, the walls of the State didn't fall, everybody was happy, sex relations with anyone male or female is legal over age of 18 (in Poland all [sex] over age 15 is legal) and I left for Moscow. See, when I came I explained to Writers Union friends what had happened in Cuba to forewarn them so they wouldn't get into trouble over me, I also tried to be as little abrasive as possible and confined my criticism to ideological double-talk instead of saying directly what I thought in my own terms. So that worked out fine and I went off in a train to Moscow. Spent the first few days with Rominova and Luria and little girl interpreter and got 2 weeks invitation, saw Akaionov and Yevtushenko night after night and briefly one day with Voznesensky and visited Achmedulina in country and his Buba and Aliguer who remembered and asked after you. I had hotel transferred to Bucharest below Moskovskya bridge and passed thru Red Square every morning and evening and wrote poems in snow by the wall and stood there at midnight watching the guards and yelling Slavic lovers in GUM [largest department store in the world] doorway, fast 4 days train to Leningrad Hermitage, saw my old cousins in Moscow ("It wasn't Stalin's fault, it was Beria, Stalin didn't see, and Beria was in the pay of Scotland Yard" explained my uncle – and K. Simonov commented "Yr uncle is a very naive man"). Yevtushenko was godly reciting drunk one nite in composer's house after midnight profiled golden against wall his neck cords straining with power-speech, but at first meeting very funny, "Allen I have your books you *gran poeta nosotros respectamos mucho, consego hay mucho escandalo sobre su nombre, marihuaniste, pederaste, perro yo conosco no es verdad.*" "Well, er – *pero is verdad pero yo voy explicar*" so I spent 15 min. trying to elucidate scientifically the difference between effects of alcohol marijuana heroin ether laughing gas lysergic acid mescaline yage *etc.* His gaze wandered, he had a headache, popped a codeine pill in his mouth, and finally said, "Allen I respect you very much as poet but this conversation demeans you. It is your personal affair. Please, there are two subjects do not discuss with me: homosexuality and narcotics." Despite all this comedy I saw a lot of him while I was there and he was very open and simpatico with me and took me out a lot evenings and his wife and I were all drunk in the Georgian restaurant and he came to train to see me off the last day with Aksionov – another weird scene, as that very last day I'd succeeded in contacting [Alexander] Yessenin-Volpin and spent all day with him at his house talking philosophy of law, relations of individual and state. He's working on big project to define socialist legality inasmuch as they put him in bughouse for complaining about police treatment. His sanity certification depended on him signing statement that police had not abused him at one point. He has fine sentimental sense of humor and human mind – in fact because of his position as sort of writers-union-rejectee he has more recognizably real sense of social humor and reality than anyone else – at least by my heart's standards – very reassuring to see a completely natural mind working on basic emotional reactions rather than thru the medium of what's socially acceptable for the season. So there was Yessenin-Volpin the comic pariah at night by the train door and up rushes fur-collared heroes Yevtushenko and tipsy manly Aksionov and they stumble on each other and meet socially for the first time as I waved goodbye from iron door as the train pulled out for Warsaw. I'd not had a chance to meet much younger people or even give a reading there, toward the end they let me meet a group of Univ. Satiric Club theater youths, and there were a few formal conferences with select professors and editors at Writer's Union and Dangulov's staff at Foreign Literature Institute and Foreign Literary Club but no opening for big poesy reading like kindly Prague. So I sang mantras to anyone who'd listen and Romanova listened and all the girls at Writer's Union, in taxicabs.

Quiet month in Warsaw, I stayed alone mostly or drank with Irridensky a young rimbaud-ish marlon brando writer at Writer's Union and long afternoons with editor of *Jazz* magazine who'd printed my poems, a Jewish good man who'd been in Warsaw Ghetto, escaped, and covered rest of war as journalist with Russian Army and stood across river from Warsaw at end and saw the city destroyed by Germans and nationalist underground killed off; apparently Stalin didn't want to move his army across river to help them because he didn't want competition in postwar control of Poland. Then a week in Krakow which hath a beauteous cathedral with giant polychrome altarpiece by medieval woodcarver genius Wit Stoltz, and car ride to Auschwitz with some boy scout leaders who were trying to pick up schoolboys hanging around the barbed wire gazing at tourists.

Then by train thru Poland to Prague again April 30, and called up friends to walk with on next day May Day parade. Students heard I was back, and this year on May 1 afternoon they were allowed to hold Majales (Student May Festival) for the first time in

20 years – last few years students had battled cops with dogs and fire hoses, so this year Novotny President had stepped forth and reinstated the old medieval students fiesta. They have parade to park and elect a May Queen and May King, and the Polytechnic School asked me if I'd be their candidate for May King – each school proposes one – so I asked around if it was nonpolitical and safe and writer friends said it was OK so I waited in my hotel after marching in morning May Day parade past the bandstand on Wenceslas Street with the Chairman of the Ideological Committee and the Minister of Education and economics and shoes all waving down on the crowd – and a gang of polytechnical students dressed in 1890s costumes and girls in ancient hoopskirts came up to hotel near RR station to get me with a gold cardboard crown and scepter and sat me up on creaky throne on a truck and took me off with wine to the Polytechnic school where there were hundreds of students and a jazz band crowded in the courtyard and I was requested to make speech – which was short "I want to be the first naked King" – and we set out in procession thru the backstreets of Prague to the main avenues downtown. By the time we'd gone half-a-mile we had a crowd of several thousand trailing behind us singing and shouting long live Majales; stopping every ten minutes for traffic and more wine and so I had my cymbals and sang every time they put the bullhorn loudspeaker to my mouth for a speech – mostly sang a mantra Om Sri Maitreya – Hail Mr. Future Buddha – a mixed hindu-buddhist formula for saluting the beauty that is to be. By this time there were more and more people and by the time we moved into the old square in old town Staremeskaya Nameske where Kafka used to live there were floods of people crowding the huge plaza maybe 15,000 souls and I had to make another speech "I dedicate the glory of my crown to the beautiful bureaucrat Franz Kafka who was born in the building around the corner here." (Kafka was published finally in Prague in '61) and the procession moved on past the House of the Golden Carp where he wrote *The Trial*, which I pointed out to the crowd and got drunker on beer and sang more and louder, finally we crossed the bridge over the Vltava River people lining the bridge and the huge dragon-masses of city-folk following before and after our trucks and Dixieland jazz playing ahead and citizens sitting on the cliff ahead watching it all with their children – everybody in Prague who could walk came out

spontaneously. When we got to the park of Culture and Rest there were over 100,000 people and half a dozen rock-and-roll bands and everybody happy and amazed. They'd only expected 10 or 15 thousand out that afternoon. So finally at 3 PM the medical school candidate wrapped in bandages got up and made his speech in Latin and the law school candidate in kings robes got up and made a long sexy speech about fornication as his campaign speech, I got up and sang Om Sri Maitreya for 4 minutes and sat down, and finally was elected May King by the strange masses. So realized it was a politically touchy day and behaved myself, wandered around soberer than any one else with a gang of Polytechnic students. Meanwhile in this Garden of Culture and Eden the Chairman of the Ideological Committee and Minister of Education were wandering around complaining. I had slipped off to be alone a few hours and listen to music, I later learned they were looking for me; that night we all reassembled on the podium to elect a May Queen, I was sitting in my throne looking out at the crowds and floodlights and opened my notebook and wrote a poem and dwelled in my Self for a yogic fifteen minutes. Meanwhile the bureaucrats had given an order to the Student Festival committee to depose me, I didn't know that, suddenly 10 brown shirted Student Police lined up in front of me and the master of ceremonies spoke a few sentences into loudspeaker saying I was deposed to be instead Prime Minister and a Czech student would be put in King's place, and the police lifted me up off my chair and put me on the side with the May Queen judge and a drunken Czech student who didn't know what was happening was put on the throne where he sat for an hour confused and embarrassed. But the crowd thought it was just another student prank and didn't hear or know the difference everybody so drunk anyway the gesture was too late and small to be understood and May Queen was elected but I didn't get a chance to marry and sleep with her as was tradition for the night. In fact I was supposed to have the run of Prague and do anything I wanted and fuck anybody and get drunk everywhere as King, but instead I went to the Polytechnic dormitories with 50 students and we sat up all night singing and talking – along with a couple of business-suited middle-aged fellows who brought some Scotch and a tape recorder. Said they were trading officials but I supposed they were agents, perhaps I'm paranoid. But anyway we made them welcome. Meanwhile I figured I'd better leave in a few days so at Writer's Union next day made inquiries bout whether I had money in Hungary, next stop maybe, and waited for telegram answer, and wandered around Prague making movies with filmmakers and singing Hari Krishna and making tape recorded interview on consciousness evolution and sex logic and space age feelings for student magazines and had some secret nighttime orgies here and there and went to rock and roll concerts and wrote poems – and suddenly lost my notebook, or suddenly it disappeared from my pocket. But anyway there wasn't much in it, it was sketchy and vague, names of people disguised, a number of dreams and six poems including the one I'd wrote under klieg lights and some political gossip ("All the capitalist lies about communism are true and vice versa") and descriptions of orgy scenes with a few students and an account of masturbating in my room at the Hotel Ambassador kneeling on the bathroom floor with a broomstick up my ass – things I wouldn't necessarily want anyone to read and for that reason have never published my journals so as to keep them raw and subjectively real – but nothing illegal and nothing I wouldn't be happy to have read in Heaven, or by Man – embarrassing to a police ear or a politician's – fortunately not detailed like in Cuba or Russia as I was enjoying myself too much to write anything but concentrated Poesy. That nite I went to Viola and met the two business suits who gave me vodka till I was drunk and went out at midnight singing Hari Om Namo Shiva on Narodni Street. Police car picked me up asking for identification – which I didn't have since the hotel had my passport for registration. I explained at station I was May King Tourist Poet and they let me go I really wasn't so drunk just happy. Next nite however, since I saw I was followed around all day by bald plainclothesmen, I stayed sober visiting the Viola, and left with a young couple to go to all night post office to mail postcards to you or someone and as we turned midnight corner on lonely street a man came up from around corner, hesitated, saw me and suddenly rushed forward screaming *bouzerant* (*maricon* [fairy]) and knocked me down, hit me on the mouth, my glasses fell off, I scrambled up and grabbed them and started running down the street, the couple I was with tried to hold him, he chased me and had me down on the ground again in front of the post office and a police car full of captains pulled up immediately and I found myself on the ground with 4 police rubber clubs lifted over my head, so I said OM and stayed quiet, they pulled me into police car and we spent all nite in police station telling the story, the couple I was with said what happened accurately, the kafkian stranger said we'd been exposing ourselves on the street and when he passed we attacked him. Finally I asked to call lawyer or U.S. consulate and they let me go and said it was all over, nothing more would be heard of it, I was free. Well I reported all that in to Writer's Union and Foreign Literature mag. friends and decided I'd better leave town, tarrying foolishly for Hungarian telegrams, still, and next day I was followed again and in evening in remote cafe with student friends on outskirts of town was picked up by plainclothesmen: "We've found your notebook, if you'll come to lost and found with us and identify it we'll return it to you and you'll be back here in half an hour." So I went to Convictskaya Street Police and identified and signed paper for it and soon as I signed the detective's face froze and he spoke, "On sketchy examination we suspect that this book contains illegal writings so we are holding it for the public prosecutor." Next morning at breakfast downtown I was picked up with student friend I knew slightly who volunteered to stay with me that day make sure I didn't have troubles and taken to Convictskaya Street again, same plainclothesmen, brought upstairs to office with 5 pudgy-faced eyeglassed bureaucrats around polished table: "Mr. Ginsberg we immigration chiefs have received many complaints from parents scientists and educators about your sexual theories having a bad effect on our youth, corrupting the young, so we are terminating your visa." They said the notebook would be returned by mail, maybe. I explained that I was waiting for Hungarian telegram, and if that didn't work out had plane ticket to London so could leave on my own the next day, and it would be more diplomatic and spare them the embarrassment of exiling the May King if they left it to me to go voluntarily. I certainly didn't want to get kicked out of ANOTHER socialist country. And it might be difficult to explain to the students *etc.* Deaf ears, incompetent bureaucracy again. So was taken out to hotel and sat in my room with detective all afternoon and not allowed phone call to Writer's Union or U.S. Embassy or friends and put secretly on plane for London that afternoon and pretty girl I knew who was receiving LSD thereby at state mental hospital met me at hotel door wanted to speak with me but cop stepped in between us. At airport the eyeglass bureaucrat said humorously "Is there any last message you want to deliver to the young lady who met you at the door of your hotel?" Also the last I saw of my student guard from breakfast, he was being pushed around a little and asked for identity papers by the police on Convictskaya Street as I was being led upstairs in elevator. So I flew off to England on plane, and kept my mouth shut again. I didn't want to make a stink or get anybody I knew connected with me in scandal there, so was discreet from May 7 on when I flew in air to England and also wrote a nice poem *Kral Majales*, I'll send you in a month when printed – big paranoid hymn about being May King sleeping with laughing teenagers – and landed in England and found Bob Dylan (folk singer, you remember, I had his record in Havana?) was there spent days with him watching him besieged by a generation of longhaired English ban-the-bomb girls and boys in sheepskin coats with knapsacks – and in his Savoy hotel spent a drunken night talking about pot and William Blake with the Beatles, gave a few small readings in London Liverpool Newcastle Cambridge and met my NY girlfriend there, made more film and had a birthday party after reading at Institute Contemporary Arts, took off all my clothes at 39th birthday party drunk singing and dancing naked, the Beatles came at midnight and got scared and ran away laughing over their reputations, then Voznesensky came to town and we met again – we'd seen each other another night in Warsaw – and Corso and Ferlinghetti came over from Paris so we hired Albert Hall and filled it with 6,000 hairy youths and bald middle-aged men of letters, Indira Gandhi and Voznesensky sitting at my side holding hands, 17 poets English German Dutch all read, Voznesensky shy to read because *Daily Worker* wrote it up as anticapitalist antiwar demonstration and perhaps too political for his visit, Neruda said he'd come read but didn't, went to some official university scheduled for him alas instead, big funny night all the poets filled with wine, a lot of bad poetry and some good, but everybody happy and England waked poetically a little. A few nights later Ferlinghetti, Corso and I read at Architectural Assn. together and Fernandez and Voznesensky and another Georgian poet came, I read from *Kaddish* and Gregory read *Bomb* poem and last Voznesensky got up and read like a lion from his chest, poem dedicated to all artists of all countries who gave life and blood for poesy, poem imitating sound of Moscow bells in Kremlin towers, he read better than anyone and was happy and came up and kissed me after and stuck his tongue in my mouth like a Russian should in Dostoyevsky, we said goodbye, then I flew to Paris but had no money left I'd taken no money for Albert Hall or other readings so had to walk street all night with Corso first night and finally slept a week upstairs in Librarie Mistral bookstore room with customers sitting on bed reading Mao Tze Tung at 10 AM when I woke, and flew back to NY on still-valid Cuban ticket, arrived in NY and as I entered customs was stopped by U.S. guards and taken into room and searched, they collected the lint from my pockets looking for marijuana. I was scared, I'd stayed with Tom Maschler a few weeks in London and he'd given me his old clothes and I didn't know what he'd ever had in his pockets, but they found nothing tho they stripped me down to my underwear. I saw their letter of orders they negligently left on the desk face upwards "Allen Ginsberg (reactivated) and Peter Orlovsky (continued) – These persons are reported to be engaged in smuggling narcotics. . ." and meanwhile back in England on May 18 I heard rumors and got phone calls from journalists and found that the Czech Youth Newspaper had big article attacking me as dope fiend homosexual monster who'd abused Prague hospitality, so they didn't have enough sense to shut up about their own idiocy. They didn't report any accusations I hadn't already said myself publicly in my own way, I never made a secret of the fact that I smoke pot and fuck any youth that'll stand still for it, orgies *etc.*, that's exactly the reason they elected me May King in the first place – aside from Mantras and Poesy – the journalese rhetoric like in an old creaky movie – and they published a drawing and a few selected pieces of dirty writing from my notebook – properly censored so as not to be too offensive – suppressed the fact that I'd been elected May King while they were at it. Anyway the police there still have my notebook and some poems I didn't copy out – fortunately they can't destroy it or they destroy their own evidence so it's safe – probably in fact copies of it are being passed around and read by amused littérateurs in the Party, it'll find its way down to the students in time even and back to me in 1972 in Outer Mongolia from the hands of a lamaist monk who practices ancient tantric sex yoga or Neruda will find it in his Ambassador hotel room drawer next time he visits Prague.

So back in NY after I got thru Kafkian customs search I came home, dope-fiends had visited and robbed Peter Orlovsky's Indian harmonium and my last typewriter and then we came out to San Francisco to a Berkeley University poesy conference with Creeley and Olson and Gary Snyder and more raving barefoot apocalyptic teenagers. This country slowly revealing its total madness also, I wound up with the Berkeley student sit-in demonstrators singing mantras thru microphone to them in front of courthouse where they were going to be tried by judges. I'm supposed to take part October 16 in more teach-in protests, meanwhile with Guggenheim money award I bought Volkswagen transistorized camper miniature bus-trailer that rides 65 mph and lasts 10 years or more with bed and icebox and writing desk and radio and tiny closets inside and now riding thru redwood forests and reading maps and visiting Snyder's northwest youth country to climb maybe Mt. Olympus before he goes back to Zen monastic studies this fall. We get up in morning with his girlfriend and read a chapter of the 100,000 Songs of Mila-Repa (Tibetan 12th Century saint poet all about illusion and dream stuff of universe) (and flying thru the air) – stopped over in friend's household with children and cats and typewriter, everybody now asleep but me it's midnight past, so I shut up with *abrazos* and *saludos* and *dosvedanyas* and *laegitos, feliz* and *fatiguado, adios por uns momentito* Shri Shivati Comrade Comanchero Sir Zeus Nicanor, *Senor.*

Love
Allen

Allen Ginsberg [New York, NY] to Robert Creeley [Buffalo, NY] November 28, 1967

Dear Bob:

Came back to Lower East Side 2 weeks ago, cleaned house up and foot thick pile of letters war resistance brochures books telegrams off desk answered finally, Peter back from driving Irving Rosenthal cross-country to settle near [Dave] Haselwood in S.F., Julius living with Barbara Rubin and girlfriends up on 3rd Ave and talking and socializing a little at last; so I finally started picking thru last 7 years poetry for City Lights book, house clean quiet and phone off.

The bulk of the scribblings difficult to range together because except for 'historic' paeans like *The Change* or *May King* or *Who Be Kind To*, the mass of other occasional journal-writing has "too many words" (said Bunting); what I got is a lot of spontaneous music and natural language gaiety but I can put my finger thru holes in every other line. So I'm revising a little mostly blue-pencil to condense words already there, put them closer together and cut syntactic fat. Only fear is the stiffness that comes from revision, unnatural compression. I'd like a surface you can read clearly like clear talk and not have to "study." So now about a third thru the poems, maybe done in couple weeks; then put together another book re U.S. Vietnam-States-Volkswagen tape machine *Wichita Vortex*, that's about 100 pages I hope.

I'm scheduled to read in Buffalo March 5, not seen correspondence (handled by agent) – is that a poetry festival? Will you be there then? I heard rumor you were going back to New Mexico, and then opposite gossip. John W. [Wieners] with long peroxide blond hair?

Got busted by local cops in Spoleto over *Who Be Kind To* text (came for me in coffeehouse half hour after reading, out of blue, unexpected, in fact surprising, I didn't do nothing, in fact I thought when they said 'come with us' it must have something to do with dope which fortunately I didn't have any on me). Menotti said he'd take care of legalities (according to Italian law anything formally "art" is exempt from obscenity bust so everything is ultimately safe.) Trouble is that Italian legal structure (prosecutors and upper courts) is still operating on fascist premises, *i.e.* laws and personnel the same, unchanged, as in Mussolini's day. Opposite U.S. where best chance is elders of Supreme Court, the last appeal Constitutional Court in Italy is all old men who were respectable judges during fascist days and so all Vatican and old order oriented; and the laws were patchwork thru 30s uncancelled by postwar constitution – requiring definite legislative revision or Constitutional Court decision to liberalize in line with theoretically liberal constitution. So to this day all public gatherings over 5 people require formal authorization by police as "manifestation" – except for political gatherings which don't require license. That's fine except it excludes anybody unorganized as a political party *i.e.* you can't have be-ins. So everything in Italy's ossified, as far as polis goes; so for years police vans have been swooping down on Duomo Sq. Milan or Spanish Steps Rome arresting "Capelloni" – longhairs – so naturally by good fortune when I went with family to Italy *en famille* staying at Hotel Engleterre 2 blocks from Keats' death room over Spanish Steps, and sat down on steps one dusk to converse furtively with local ragazzi I did by god get busted again for 3 hours. I tried to get out of it by sneaking across street when vans rumored arriving but got nabbed just after I thought I was safe.

Anyway that was later: went to England from Spoleto and stayed in style with Panna Grady and ran around a lot, finished proofs small book now published Cape-Goliard, yakked on TV and sang Hari Krishna in Hyde Park pot picnic, spent evening with Paul McCartney (He says "We are all one" *i.e.* all the same mystic-real being), spent a lot of evenings with Mick Jagger singing mantras and talking economics and law-politics during his court crisis – found him very delicate and friendly, reading Poe and Alistair Crowley – on thick carpets with incense and wearing ruffled lace at home – later spent nite in recording studio with Jagger, Lennon and McCartney composing and fixing voices on pretty song "Dandelion Fly Away" everybody exhilarated with hashish – all of them drest in paisley and velvet and earnestly absorbed in heightening the harmonic sounds inch by inch on tape, turning to piano to figure out sweeter variations and returning to microphone to try it out – lovely scene thru control booth window, I got so happy I began conducting like a madman thru the plate glass.

Waited in London for my father and stepmother, they stayed a week at Panna's in garden studio, we gave a reading together at Institute Contemporary Arts and he came on so vibrant (first time in Europe after 71 years) one of the smaller publishers offered him a book, which he needs and hasn't been able to get since his last, 30 years ago, so that was a capital event; then we went on to Paris and sat on Pont des Arts and looked at the summer trees along the Seine and sat in cafes and sightsaw, I got hotels and taxis and carried luggage and had the pleasure of him realizing how much I knew of the outer world, and him experiencing that dimension, outside of images of movies and newspaper books – his big dream always was to stroll by wooden bookstalls on left bank, and so we did just that and bought views of wooden bookstalls etchings. Then a week in Rome where my arrest livened things up (he came down to the *questura* to try and get me out and saw the scene and so in reality and person was on my side in what otherwise would've been for him a faraway dubious newspaper scandal hallucination) (Tho I was already out of jail, nonetheless he said he enjoyed striding into police station resolved to get an explanation from the culprit authority.) And saw Vatican and a lot of statues, family began getting tired, a couple days in Venice refreshing, then they left for U.S., he wept – old nostalgia – going thru ticket taker to plane ramp.

So I stayed in Milan with Nanda Pivano a month, worked on translations with her – rewrote poems into Italian word by word for next book – amphetamine babble syntax difficult but I think we did something novel in the tongue. FINALLY, got reply from Olga Rudge and went to Rapallo to spend afternoon with Pound, he wouldn't talk except "Would you like to wash your hands, she asks?" before lunch; and during lunch said *"Ouvert à la Nuit"* when

Olga R and I asked him name of book by Paul Morand 30 years ago – drove to Portofino with him for hour's silent sit in cafe, he nodded negative when I asked if he's ever tried hashish. Sang Prajnaparamita and Hari Krishna. I babbled a bit, but basically he's stubborn as Julius was, I figured probably for similar reasons (Julius thought good was battling evil in universe and all the evil was coming from him so figured it was best to not do or say anything.)

Then went back to Milan and worked some more and wrote asked Rudge for date again in Venice, she wrote yes so I went alone to Venice and stayed in pension round corner from her tiny house. First day came to lunch as invited and brought gift *Sgt Pepper's Lonely Hearts Club Band* and *Blonde on Blonde* and more Beatles and Dylan and Donovan, drank some wine and smoked a stick of pot at table over coffee (without calling attention) looked Pound in eye and said, "Well old man, how old <u>are</u> you?" so he finally spoke "82 in several days." Then turned on Beatles and Dylan, recited lyrics so he could distinguish "Sad Eyed Lowland Lady" words, he wouldn't say nothing but sat thru 3/4 hour of loud rock smiling, then I sang for an hour and went away and got drunk in Harry's Bar.

Then for the next 2 1/2 weeks I hung around, saw him on street, we went to concert Vivaldi in church one night, ate occasionally together in pension on days when Rudge didn't cook, Italian TV was there making birthday documentary (he was 82 October 30). After a day or so I began asking specific questions textual. "Where are the soap-smooth stone posts at San Vio, I went and looked and there they're all rough" and he began answering. I kept record of everything he said, so, in sum stringing it all together exact words but sans context over 2 weeks: "No! No! (to Rudge's demand he have more Zucchini) . . . Yes, when the font was filled, now they've changed it, it used to be like that (to my question about "in the font to the right as you enter / are all the gold domes of San Marco" in *Pisan Cantos*) . . . Don Carlos the *pretender* (what's this "house that used to be of Don Carlos"?) . . . Yes but my own work does not make sense . . . Too late (when I asked if he'd like to read in Buffalo) . . . Bunting told me there was too little presentation and too much reference . . . A mess . . . my writing, stupidity and ignorance all the way through . . . the intention was bad, anything I've done has been an accident, in spite of my spoiled intentions, the preoccupation with stupid and irrelevant matters . . . I do (give me, Allen, his blessing, after I demanded it) . . . but my worst mistake was the stupid suburban anti-Semitic prejudice, all along that spoiled everything . . . I found after seventy years that I was not a lunatic but a moron . . . I should have been able to do better . . . No (smiling) he never said that to me (when I reported W.C. Williams told me Pound had a mystical ear) . . . (*Cantos*) it's all doubletalk . . . it's hard for me to write anything . . . I didn't read enough poetry . . . (*Cantos*) it's all tags and patches . . . a mess . . . my depression is mental not physical . . . it would be ingenious work to see any influence (his on younger poets as I described it including quoting from memory some of your poems, Robert) . . . Williams was in touch with human feelings . . . You know a great deal about the subject (replying after I'd explained LSD pot scene asking if I was making sense to him) . . . Worse, and alive . . ." That's weeks boiled down.

So, I hung around till I thought my presence was getting heavy and left for States – having delivered many concise accurate pep-talks – nicest evening was his birthday, Olga R. invited me in to sing for him by fireplace late in evening, alone, sang Prajnaparamita "No Nirvana no path no wisdom and no attainment because no attainment" he sat quietly, sad, ate some birthday cake, sipped some champagne, said no he hadn't read Crane's *Atlantis* (which I thereat recited 20 lines from memory), signed 110 Canto pamphlet for "Alan Guinzberg dall'autore." (Had said he hadn't read any of my poetry, knew yours or recognized your name quickly knew who you were – also responded very fast yes head nod he'd received *Briggflats* [by Basil Bunting]).

Olga Rudge says that oddly nobody has invited him to the U.S. lately, the last invitations situation wasn't sure and Laughlin I think'd interfered, or someone had. I asked if it would be alright to make discrete inquires at Buffalo or Berkeley. I think if it were handled gently, without too much fuss, he could be invited to Buffalo (Rudge knows about your and poesy activity there, as a center) especially for a festival. She said there is an invite for Opera Villon from Buffalo. But if situation is OK there, is it possible to invite him to appear like for a short poetry reading, – which he can and does still do – (as he still does write) ? I think they would come. It would be glorious if it worked. They're worried about a fuss (political and otherwise) being made – need a smooth journey and comfort/privacy/attention for an old man – would presumably have quiet dinners with few people, maybe attend a concert or reading, and give a reading. He has spry physical strength. Don't know how much money they'd need. But we could all get together and contribute. Mainly I said I'd inquire (said to Rudge) if inquiries could be made without large gossip. Meant to write you earlier. I told Rudge the great scene also would be for him to visit SF read perhaps at Berkeley or SF State. If something can be done at Buffalo, and Rudge and Pound are willing, maybe contact Parkinson. I don't think they'd be able to do more in public than that, if that. Rudge sort of takes care of him, food, letters, visitors, travel arrangements, *etc.* Can write her, she said not to circulate address, otherwise.

OK – Bravo! Cheers! love to Bobbie, and where's Olson? Tell John Wieners *salve*. Peter says "Tell him a lotta good things."

As ever
Allen

Tone of this letter strange to me. I waited so long to write, the letter got to be long, and I couldn't figure out where to begin about Pound so kept describing other things. Also saw Pasolini, Antonioni, Quasimodo, Montale, Ungaretti and all the Feltrinellis, Mondadoris and Balistrinis and Nonos in sight.

Allen Ginsberg [Cherry Valley, NY] to Gary Snyder [Kyoto, Japan] July 8, 1968

Dear Gary:

Kept putting off writing because I had so much to say, so I'll be brief. I bought (or am buying) a farm upstate NY, isolated 2000 feet up near Cooperstown, surrounded by State Forest – 70 acres and old 8 room house $9,000.00, spending a few thousand more to fix up for the winter. Peter and Julius been up there several months, Gregory Corso and his girl, Barbara Rubin pining for me (ugh!) (ouch I mean) and a young competent film-maker farm couple. We have 3 goats (I now milk goats) 1 cow 1 horse (chestnut mare for pleasure) 15 chickens 3 ducks 2 geese 2 fantail pigeons, small barn right size, nearby a friendly hermit been up there sans electric since 1939 teaching us how to manage and what to repair. More Kibbutz than commune, very loose, but the place is getting organized, Julius has work to do and speaks, Peter's mostly off meth and calm. No electric, now hand pump, we're digging well up in our woods so as to have gravity fed running water. 15 acres of woods one side, the other sides all state woods permanent – pine oak and maple *etc*. Got lotsa books on flowers. Table is meatless, we eat fish tho. So that's started. Will also build simpler place sooner or later in California land. Visited Tassajara finally one nite.

Local (U.S.A.) sociopolitics confusing. This yippie hippie be-in shot in Chicago has been a big drag since undercurrents of violence everywhere (state and street Black Mask *etc*.) make peaceful gestures seem silly. Yippie organization's in wrong hands sort of.

Would like to get out or redirect it to some kind of prepositional new nation confabulation, but I don't have time.

Finished proofs of *Planet News Poems 61-67* for Ferlinghetti, and *Indian Journals* for Auerhahn Haselwood. Next, collected poesy volume and collected interview/essay/manifesto volume to compile – all work's done except editing that.

Skandas Snyder??? Sounds Norwegian (Poor l'il Skandas). Well lets see, a name – lets see the body of bliss first. Other gossip – I'd spent ¾ hour w/ Robert Kennedy discussing pot, ecology, acid, cities, *etc.* a month before he started running for Prexy and died. Peter/ meth big Karmaic problem. Gave up (drifted off) sex with him to take off pressure if that was it. Lightens our relations a lot.

I'm driving to Mexico w/ brother and 5 nephews and sister in law, 2 weeks and thence to SF again meet my father and show him around 2 weeks – then likely back to the farm – maybe trip out to convention Chicago and back, hole in for several months.

Wrote one fantastical poem about being screwed in ass with repeated refrain "please master" which really got me a little embarrassed, but read it at last SF Poesy Renaissance big reading and it turned out to be, as usual, universal, one hole or another, one sex or another. Really amazing year after year I stumble on to areas of same or fear and their catharsis of community awareness takes off the red-cheeked bane.

How's fatherhood? Babyhood? I wrote Kapleau and he sent me his prajnaparamita translation – he chants it English monosyllables one of the Tassajara Senseis or Roshis is a Sanskrit expert, we can check out w/ him on your next trip here. Any plans? OK.

> Love, as ever
> Allen

I keep straying on mental anger warpaths, and then come back to milking the goats.

Allen Ginsberg [Boulder, CO] to Diana Trilling [New York, NY] January 15, 1979

Dear Diana:

Peter showed me your note to him of a month ago, I'd hoped to answer before I left NY but was due here to teach Blake (mostly Vala The Four Zoas) and am only now catching up on mail.

What I finger-traced in dust on Livingston Hall dorm window to attract attention and cause window-cleaning by Irish lady whom I sophomorically contemned as inattentive to her duty to a window thick enough with dust to write on was as follows:

BUTLER HAS NO BALLS

[2 drawings]

FUCK THE JEWS

The first slogan was paraphrased from a local "Barnard" song "No balls at all / No balls at all / She married a man who had no balls at all." The second slogan, jejune as it was, was also in the mode of college humor aimed at the cleaning lady who I thought was, being Irish, anti-Semitic, and therefore maybe not cleaning up my room. The drawing was a cock and balls and also (unless my memory's mistaken on this final detail only) a death's head.

I wouldn't have thought the matter of serious importance but the cleaning lady, who did apparently have some edge of querulousness, reported these dusty terrors to the authorities instead of cleaning the window and obliterating any evidence of my evident depravity.

As it happened that very weekend Jack Kerouac who'd been banned from setting foot on the campus as an "unwholesome influence" on his friends among students (Dean McKnight's phrase) came to see me after a long talk with Burroughs who'd warned him solemnly that if he continued to cling to his mother's apron strings he'd find his destiny to be closed in narrower and narrower circles around her figure – an uncannily factual prophecy that astounded Jack! So he appeared in my dorm room on Friday midnight, just as I was finishing my most immense piece of juvenilia, *The Last Voyage* a poem modeled on both *Bateau Ivre* of Rimbaud and *Le Voyage* of Baudelaire done in iambic quatrains imitative of my father's poetries, saying young farewell to "Society."

We talked of life and art long into the night, and as it was too late for him to return to Ozone Park he bedded down with me, chastely as it happens, since I was a complete virgin, much too shy to acknowledge loves that dare not speak names, as far as I understood, on that campus, in that time and of that place.

Morning came and with it a Dean of Student-Faculty Relations coach to athletic department and football team that Kerouac had quit to study poesy (thus losing his football scholarship) – was it Mr. Furman? [sic: Furey] who rapped loudly on the suite entrance, then burst in the unlocked door, we were still snoozing innocent in bed. Kerouac opened an eye, saw the enemy coach loose in the dorm-suite jumped out of bed in his skivvies, rushed into the entrance room and jumped into the bed there – (my roommate William Wort Lancaster Jr. son of Chairman of National City Bank, head of Amer-Soviet Friendship Society, whose mother as member of Karen Horney Society'd paid for years of adolescent analysis for him as he had an awful tic round eye and mouth, had risen early and gone to class) – as I writ, Kerouac jumped into bed and pulled the covers over his head and went to sleep leaving me alone trembling bare legged in my underwear to face the fury of the Assistant Dean who pointed angrily at the window and demanded: "Who is responsible, who did this?" "Me," I admitted my guilt and he insisted, "Wipe that off immediately." I grabbed a towel and dirtied it clearing the window of what charwoman and assistant dean considered speakably objectionable. "The Dean will want to see you later," and he departed. When I went downstairs an hour later, I found a $2.75 dorm bill for an overnight guest and a note informing me I was wanted at the Dean's Office in an hour. Entering Dean

McKnight's office he greeted me, "Mr. Ginsberg, I hope you realize the enormity of what you've done."

Actually I hadn't done much of anything, and on Burroughs' advice I'd been reading C.F. Céline's *Journey to the End of the Night* wherein the second chapter the hero finds himself in the middle of a World War I battlefield and recognizing that everyone about him is completely mad, crazily shooting and being shot at near a ravaged woods, decides to flee the scene immediately.

"Oh yes I do, Sir, I do, whatever can I do to explain or make amends." This seemed to be the best tactic. "Mr. Ginsberg, I hope you realize the enormity of what you've done."

Diana, by the time the story got to you and Lionel I have no idea what it sounded like but I assume the only devil that remained imprinted in faculty memory was "Fuck the Jews" as if in some awful psychological self-mutilation this poor sensitive madmother'd student was internalizing the torments of rejection he might have supposed were being laid on him by an authoritative society or class beyond his innocent comprehension *etc*. I'm not sure what psychological system was devised to "understand" this case. However, no evidence of the situation remained after dust and whispered gossip (I hope) had vanish'd to oblivion, other than the single "shocking" or "old" slogan "Fuck the Jews" which seemed to be the only thing remembered of the entire comedy when, a decade and half later, you recollected "The Other Night at Columbia."

So, around that time, after your essay, I wrote you, or Lionel, or both, a long letter on mailgram stationary, from San Francisco I think, explaining in detail, as I have again just now, the entire contents of the vanished windowpane, and the context, pleading for some common sense and humor, as well as accuracy, also hoping to disburden you and he of whatever weight of anxiety you might have felt about my poor relation to my "Self" or heritage.

I was somewhat disappointed to get a 1959 reply from Lionel that you had both read my letter, and understood it, but that I was making a mountain out of a molehill, that it was not so serious a matter that it made any difference what I particularly wrote on the window. I was disappointed because I thought that much had been made by you of the phrase "Fuck the Jews" out of context of "Butler has no balls" *etc.*; yet it made me seem foolish to take it seriously enough to correct and write you about it. Did you feel it was important but he didn't feel so? Did I feel it was important but you didn't? I never could figure it out. But in any case I'd written the matter up in detail, sent you the account, and done my best to be reasonable. Still, decade after decade, Columbia wits who read your essay do ask me, is it true you wrote "Fuck the Jews" and did get kicked out of Columbia? "Oh yes" I reply, "but you see it was like this *etc. . . .*" And as a matter of fact I've laid out in scholarly print one place and another public and private the Full Compleat and Unexpurgated Tale of the Rape of the Windowpane . . . but especially to you and Lionel back around 1959 as above described, and so if you have access to old letters from me you may locate it, and Lionel's reply is sitting available at 801 Butler in Special Collections, where he so kindly helped me place my papers for archive.

So it was a little jolting to see your note to Peter saying "because he had written in the dust on a window in one of the halls 'Nicholas Murray Butler has no balls!' But this is not at all what Allen wrote. Surely he must remember that he wrote: 'Fuck the Jews.'"

Now I have gone through all these three pages to give you precise detailed accounting, as I went through two pages same a decade or more ago, yea two decades, about an event 3 ½ decades mellowed in the cask. I hope it relieves you of the fear that all these decades I have been nursing some terrible neurosis of Jewish Self, a shameful secret more awful to recollect than the openly joyful recollection of most "terrible" family tragedies in the poem *Kaddish*. See? Don't worry, I've been alright all along.

Meanwhile, as the precise Text on the Vanish'd Windowpane has been established for scholars (actually I was dismayed your scholarly husband didn't seem to recognize that I was doing that, formally, in 1959 letter, as this as well) I've taken the liberty recently, when the matter rose among scholars, to emphasize the phrase "Butler Has no Balls" as co-equal to and, in fact, on one rare occasion, pre-eminent above "Fuck the Jews."

I reasoned that since half of my impertinent remarks in the dust were so exclusively emphasized in the past, I might take at least one time, in graybeard maturity, the liberty of making emphatic notice of the other half of this entirely trivial text which has, much through your efforts, appear'd to've gained temporary immortality. Doubtless, patient scholars future will see thru this recent college humor.

It is not your information or opinions I am contesting, correcting or challenging here: what I'm aiming at is decades old, an attitudinal vanity masked as moral responsibility, and inability to get basic facts straight disguised as superior sinceritas.

"Don't strike at the heart" say Buddhist slogans. True. Goodnight. I've written you a long long letter, I don't believe in eternal damnation, you probably do, poor girl . . . it's not important to be right.

As ever
Allen Ginsberg

PART SEVEN

Photographs

"Portrait snapshot by W. S. Burroughs, Kodak Retina 1953, my apartment roof
E. 7ᵗʰ St., we edited *Yage Letters*."*

* Note: All captions are by Allen Ginsberg.

"Jack Kerouac, railroad Brakeman's rule book in pocket, couch pillows airing on the fire escape south view overlooking back-yard clotheslines three flights up, my apartment 206 East 7th St. between Avenues B and C. Lower East Side Manhattan. He'd completed *On the Road*, *Visions of Cody*, *Dr. Sax* & had begun *Book of Dreams* and *Pic*, was in midst of *Subterraneans* affair with 'Mardou Fox', that novel completed same year along with his romance *Maggie Cassady*. Burroughs then in residence edited *Yage Letters* and *Queer* mss., Gregory Corso visited that season, probably September 1953."

"We went uptown to look at Mayan Codices at Museum of Natural History & Metropolitan Museum of Art to view Carlo Crivelli's green-hued Christ-face with crown of thorns stuck symmetric in his skull—here Egyptian wing William Burroughs with a brother Sphinx, Fall 1953 Manhattan."

"Kerouac at Staten Island Ferry dock, New York Fall 1953, we used to wander thru truck parking lots at dockside & under Brooklyn Bridge singing rawbone blues & shouting Hart Crane's *Atlantis* to the traffic above. Time of *Dr. Sax* & *The Subterraneans*."

"Neal Cassady and his love of that year, Natalie Jackson conscious of their roles in eternity, Market Street San Francisco. Cassady had been prototype for Kerouac's late '40's *On The Road* saga hero Dean Moriarty, as in later 1960's he'd take the wheel of Ken Kesey's psychedelic era crosscountry bus 'Further'. His illuminated American automobile mania and erotic energy had already written his name in bright in signs of our literary imagination before movies were made imitating his Charm. That's why we stopped under the marquee to fix the passing hand on the watch, 1955."

"1010 Montgomery Street San Francisco. My front room in Eternity 1955. Wherein I wrote *Howl* Part I. Robert LaVigne's watercolors, Bach and clock. Checkered blanket hung over alley window."

"Gregory Corso Poet eating grapes in Paris attic 9 Rue Git-Le-Coeur 1957."

"Peter Orlovsky legs crossed handsome mysterious haired, Wm. Burroughs thoughtful with hat to shade Mediterranean sun and camera, Allen Ginsberg white pants earnest, Alan Ansen resolute visiting from Venice to help type Post-*Naked Lunch* apocalyptic cut-ups, Gregory Corso sunglassed and Minox'd, Ian Sommerville assisting sound collage electronics & stroboscope Alpha rhythm Dream Machine experiments with Bill B. and Brion Gysin then in town, Paul Bowles squinting in bright midday light seated on ground, all assembled outside Bill's single room, my Kodak Retina in Michael Portman's hands, old garden Villa Muneria, Tanger Maroc 1961 July."

"From roof of Brahmin's house wherein we'd rented room down on third floor six months December to May 1963, could see past temple mandir tops to other shore across Ganges River. Our balconies hung over vegetable-meat market one side, other side overlooked sacred paved way down to Dasasumedh Ghat bathing steps peopled by beggars pilgrims sodhus & wand'ring cows; monkeys visited and snatched our bananas, Peter Orlovsky held my Retina, Benares India Spring '63."

"Timothy Leary psychedelic research pioneer and Neal Cassady first
meeting at Millbrook N.Y. in Ken Kesey-Merry Pranksters' 'Further'
bus which Neal'd driven crosscountry S.F. to N.Y. via Texas before
Fall 1964 presidentiad, with 'A vote for Goldwater is a Vote for Fun'
logo painted large across bus side, L.S.D. cool-aid pitcher in icebox.
Neal scratching amphetamine itch in his driver's palm."

"Lawrence Ferlinghetti in his office with Pooch, Whitman photo, files, coat racks, book bags, posters, at City Lights up on balcony, B'way and Columbus Avenues, San Francisco, October 1984."

"Anne Waldman, orator poet directress of Naropa Institute Poetics School at Jane Faigaos's table, August 15, 1985. Robert Frank's *The Americans* under her wrist."

"Peter Orlovsky born 1933 visiting his family—Lafcadio age 47 who'd lived with us San Francisco-N.Y 1955-61 & later intermittent years; Katherine Orlovsky age 78 totally deaf after botched mastoid/nerve operation Eye Ear Hospital N.Y. circa 1930's; Laff's twin sister Marie who'd lived in our Lower East Side apartment 1959 for Baby Nurse School in Jersey but quit jobs soon after, angry hearing voices filthy gossip. Second floor flat on lonely road Long Island, they need taxi to supermarket shop faraway with Social Service Indemnity checks, July 26, 1987."

"William Seward Burroughs relaxing on old brokendown foam-rubber couch in side-yard of his house, looking up through tree tops into the sky, Lawrence, Kansas, May 28, 1991."

"Old-timer & survivor Herbert E. Huncke, Beat Literary pioneer, in earlier decades thief, who introduced Wm. Burroughs Kerouac & me to floating population hustling & drug scene Times Square 1945. From '48 on he penned remarkable musings collected auto-biographic vignettes, anecdotes & storyteller's tales in the classic *The Evening Sun Turned Crimson* (Cherry Valley, 1970) and later *Guilty of Everything* (Paragon House, 1990). Here age 78 in basement apartment backyard near Avenue D on East 7th Street, Lower East Side, New York, May 18, 1993."

"Self portrait on my seventieth birthday Borsalino hat and cashmere silk scarf from Milan & Dublin thornproof tweed suit, Oleg Cassini tie from Goodwill shirt same source, kitchen window midday, I stayed home and worked on *Selected Poems 1947-95* proofs after returning from Walker Art Center reading-Beat exhibition weekend. Monday, June 3, 1996, N.Y."

ACKNOWLEDGMENTS

Many people assisted Allen Ginsberg in the publication of his books. All deserve gratitude for their efforts; a few should be given special mention, for this book would not have been possible without them.

Lawrence Ferlinghetti, Ginsberg's friend, fellow poet, editor, and publisher, issued Ginsberg's first book, *Howl and Other Poems*, as part of his City Lights Books "Pocket Poets" series, beginning a partnership that lasted for many years and books, and helped change the face of modern poetry.

Gordon Ball, filmmaker, educator, and manager of Ginsberg's East Hill Farm, edited two volumes of Ginsberg's journals (*Journals Early Fifties Early Sixties* and *Journals Mid Fifties*), as well as a collection of his lectures (*Allen Verbatim*).

David Carter, author of the definitive book-length account of the Stonewall riots, scaled a mountain of Ginsberg's published and unpublished interviews before editing *Spontaneous Mind*, a book that proves that the interview in skilled hands can be an artform of its own.

Juanita Lieberman-Plimpton not only worked as an office assistant, helping control the general mayhem of Ginsberg's day-to-day professional obligations; she also took on the delicate task of co-editing *The Book of Martyrdom and Artifice*, a volume of Ginsberg's youthful journals that offers scholars an unflinching starting point for the poet's personal and artistic development.

David Stanford co-edited *Jack Kerouac and Allen Ginsberg: The Letters*, continuing the work of the late Jason Shinder, whose devotion to the project was unflagging, even when the going was tough.

Steven Taylor, musician companion on many of Ginsberg's reading tours, was influential in Ginsberg's development as a songwriter. Much of their collaboration is featured on such recordings as *First Blues* and *Holy Soul Jelly Roll*. Barry Miles, Ginsberg biographer and Beat Generation scholar, visited Ginsberg's Cherry Valley farm and nudged along Ginsberg's initial songwriting adventures by recording his early attempts at writing music to accompany the works of William Blake.

Raymond Foye examined thousands of Ginsberg photographs, many of which had to be printed from old, undeveloped rolls of film. Foye undertook the yeoman's chore of creating contact sheets, going over the photos with Ginsberg, selecting the very best of the images, and seeing that they were professionally printed into gallery size for the many showings in museums in galleries around the world.

Terry Karten and the staff at HarperCollins have been working on Ginsberg projects since the publication of *Collected Poems 1947–1980*. Andrew Wylie has been Ginsberg's literary agent for more than three decades, and the Wylie Agency continues to oversee the publication of his books, long after the poet's death. In recent years, Jeff Posternak, along with his assistant, Jessica Henderson, have handled the bulk of the duties, including the expanded *Collected Poems 1947–1997*. Luke Ingram and Davara Bennett in the Wylie Agency's London office were invaluable in the foreign publication of Ginberg's work.

Bill Morgan, Ginsberg's friend, biographer, archivist, and bibliographer has edited three volumes of Ginsberg's letters (*The Letters of Allen Ginsberg, The Selected Letters of Allen Ginsberg and Gary Snyder*, and *Jack Kerouac and Allen Ginsberg: The Letters*); he coedited one volume of his journals (*The Book of Martyrdom and Artifice*) and a book of poems (*Death & Fame*). As a consultant, Morgan has been invaluable in advancing and assisting other works by and about Allen Ginsberg.

Bob Rosenthal, poet and teacher, while working as Ginsberg's office manager for more than 30 years, witnessed the entire Allen Ginsberg spectrum, from mundane to extraordinary, memorable to forgettable, maddening to exhilarating—and did so with admirable patience and cheer. Co-editor of *Death & Fame*, Rosenthal acted as an assistant, mediator, and advocate for many other Ginsberg projects.

Peter Hale, co-editor of *Death & Fame*, is the willing and able custodian of the Allen Ginsberg Trust and of Allen Ginsberg's online web presence (allenginsberg.org), keeping the flame burning for a new generation of readers ready to explore the work of this twentieth-century artist.

My deep gratitude to all.

Michael Schumacher
May 1, 2014

ABOUT THE EDITOR

MICHAEL SCHUMACHER has written extensively about the Beat Generation writers and their work, his articles, reviews, profiles, and interviews appearing in newspapers and magazines throughout the United States. He is the author of *Dharma Lion*, a biography of Allen Ginsberg, and editor of *Family Business*, the selected correspondence between Allen Ginsberg and his father, Louis Ginsberg. He lives in Wisconsin.

WORKS BY ALLEN GINSBERG

WHITE SHROUD
Poems 1980-1985
Available in Paperback

COSMOPOLITAN GREETINGS
Poems 1986-1992
Available in Paperback

JOURNALS MID-FIFTIES
1954-1958
Available in Paperback

DELIBERATE PROSE
Selected Essays 1952-1995
Available in Paperback

DEATH & FAME
Last Poems 1993-1997
Available in Paperback

SELECTED POEMS 1947 - 1995
Available in Paperback

SPONTANEOUS MIND
Selected Interviews 1958-1996
Available in Paperback

COLLECTED POEMS 1947 - 1997
Available in Paperback and eBook

HOWL
Original Draft Facsimile, Transcript, and Variant Versions, Fully Annotated
by Author, with Contemporaneous Correspondence, Account of First
Public Reading, Legal Skirmishes, Presursor Texts, and Bibliography
Available in Paperback

HOWL: A GRAPHIC NOVEL
Available in Paperback

Available wherever books are sold.